Education
and
Society

Education and Society

Joseph A. Scimecca *George Mason University*

HOLT, RINEHART AND WINSTON   New York   Chicago   San Francisco   Dallas   Montreal
Toronto   London   Sydney

For my first teachers—my parents, Frank and Frances Scimecca

Library of Congress Cataloging in Publication Data

Scimecca, Joseph.
   Education and society.

   1. Educational sociology.   I. Title.
LC189.S42   370.19′3   79-17991
ISBN 0-03-038466-4

Acknowledgments

The author wishes to express his thanks for the following material: From *Schooling in Capitalist America: Educational Reform and the Contradictions of Economic Life,* by Samuel Bowles and Herbert Gintis, © 1976 by Basic Books, Inc., Publishers, New York and Routledge & Kegan Paul Ltd., London. Sarene S. Boocock, *An Introduction to the Sociology of Learning.* Copyright © 1972 by Houghton Mifflin Company. Used by permission. Ray C. Rist, "Student Social Class and Teacher Expectations: The Self-Fulfilling Prophecy in Ghetto Education," *Harvard Educational Review, 40* (1970), pp. 416–451. Copyright © 1970 by President and Fellows of Harvard College. From page 8 in *The Civil Rights of Teachers* by Louis Fischer and David Schimmel. Copyright © 1973 by Louis Fischer and David Schimmel. Reprinted by permission of Harper & Row, Publishers, Inc. *Status of the American Public School Teacher, 1970–1971* and *Status of the American Public School Teacher, 1975–1976.* Reprinted with permission. © National Education Association. Reprinted by permission of the publisher, from Raymond E. Callahan, "The American Board of Education, 1789–1960" in *Understanding School Boards: Problems and Prospects,* edited by Peter J. Cistone (Lexington, Mass.: Lexington Books, D.C. Heath and Company, copyright © 1975, D.C. Heath and Company). John Pfeiffer, *New Look at Education.* Copyright © 1968 by The Bobbs-Merrill Company. Reprinted by permission. From *The Politics of Communication: A Study in the Political Sociology of Language, Socialization, and Legitimation* by Claus Mueller. Copyright © 1973 by Oxford University Press, Inc. Reprinted by permission. From *Governing American Schools: Political Action in Local School Districts* by L. Harmon Zeigler and M. Kent Jennings. © 1974 by Wadsworth, Inc., Belmont, Ca. 94002. Reprinted by permission of the publisher, Duxbury Press. Richard Carlson, *School Superintendents: Careers and Performance.* Copyright © 1972 by Charles E. Merrill Publishing Co. Reprinted by permission. Marshall O. Donley, *Power to the Teacher*. Copyright © 1975 by Indiana University Press. Reprinted by permission. From *Ghetto School: Class Warfare in an Elementary School* by Gerald Levy, copyright © 1970 by Western Publishing Co., Inc., reprinted by permission of The Bobbs-Merrill Company, Inc. *Making Inequality: The Hidden Curriculum of High School Tracking* by James Rosenbaum. Copyright © 1976 by John Wiley & Sons, Inc. Reprinted by permission of John Wiley & Sons, Inc. Meyer Weinberg, *A Chance To Learn*. Copyright © 1977 by Cambridge University Press. Reprinted by permission. Adapted from Robert J. Havighurst and Bernice L. Neugarten, *Society and Education*, Fourth Edition. Copyright © 1975 by Allyn and Bacon, Inc. Reprinted with permission. Data from *Economic of the President* (1973, pages 155–159). Excerpted from *The Academic Revolution* by Christopher Jencks and David Riesman. Copyright © 1968 by Christopher Jencks and David Riesman. Reprinted by permission of Doubleday & Company, Inc. From L. L. Medsker and J. W. Trent, "The Influence of Different Types of Public Higher Institutions on College Attendance from Varying Socioeconomic and Ability Levels," Berkeley: Center for the Study of Higher Education, University of California, 1965. Reprinted by permission. Alexander W. Astin, Robert J. Panos, and John Creager, *National Norms for Entering College Freshmen—Fall 1966* (Washington, D.C.: American Council on Education, 1967), p. 22. Reprinted by permission. Jerome Karabel, "Community Colleges and Social Stratification: Submerged Class Conflict in American Higher Education," *Harvard Educational Review,* 42 (1972), p. 528. Copyright © 1972 by President and Fellows of Harvard College. Charles S. Benson, Paul M. Goldfinger, E. Gareth Hoachlander, and Jessica S. Pers, *Planning for Educational Reform: Financial and Social Alternatives*. Copyright © 1974 by Dodd, Mead and Company. Reprinted by permission of Harper & Row, Publishers.

Preface

This book takes a decidedly different approach than other works in the sociology of education. It offers a historically based conflict analysis of education and schooling in American society. The conflict perspective takes as given that human beings are conflict-prone. They pursue their own interests in institutional settings (for the purposes of this work, the educational institution), and their behavior cannot be understood without focusing upon the concept of power. Power relationships, the relative ability to induce others to do one's bidding whether they desire to or not, are treated as the most important behavior-shaping experiences. Educational inequality, for example, is seen as resulting from the efforts of one group to maintain its advantage in a conflict-prone framework. This dominance of one group over another may or may not be a reflection of economic interests, depending upon the historical context in which the original struggle for power took place. The conflict approach offered in the following pages, though as critical as the Marxist perspective has been of American education, is much broader than one which relies solely on economic and class distinctions. Religious and racial conflicts and quarrels over the amount and extent of autonomy in a bureaucracy are as much a part of our educational history as are class struggles.

Another reason that *Education and Society* differs from other works in the field is that it is based on my own educational experiences. Although trained as a sociologist, for seven years I taught in a graduate school of education. My immediate impression was that books written for education students by education professors only superficially offered a sociological perspective. On the other hand, works by sociologists did not cover the topics that those who worked or hoped to work in the schools were interested in. In this book I have tried to bridge this gap, by offering a strong sociological approach and by dealing with educational topics not generally covered by sociologists: the role of the principal and school superintendent, clashes between school boards and superintendents, collective bargaining, the implications of Title IX, and school finance, to name just a few. *Education and Society,* therefore, can be used not only in sociology of education courses, but in foundations of education and educational administration courses—indeed, in any course that takes the social context of education into consideration.

This book also represents something very special to me. It is the culmination of a seven-year period (1970–1977) during which I was associated with a very special group of people, the Foundations of Education Department at the State University of New York at Albany. The Foundations Department consisted of a nucleus of approximately ten faculty and ten doctoral students in any given year. The faculty were trained in traditional disciplines such as sociology, history, and philosophy, and most of the students came with master's degrees in these areas. We shared both an interest in education and a desire to change it. So intense were we that we immodestly referred to ourselves as the "conscience" of the School of Education. Unfortunately, consciences become expendable in lean times, and the Foundations Department was one of the first casualties of the financial crunch that characterized the New York State System of Higher Education in 1976. Some of us left; others became submerged in a larger unit. We hope that the spirit of reform we began remains.

For me, the years at Albany represented much more of a learning experience than a teaching one. Although I was a faculty member, the distinction between faculty and student was a moot one; we all, to borrow from Chaucer, gladly taught and gladly learned in a collective effort. This is why, for the first time, I am writing in the third person; I finally understand how a single author can use "we." This book is very much a joint effort (although many will not agree with everything I write, some, perhaps, with nothing) of the following members of the Foundations Department: Arnold Anderson-Sherman, Mark Berger, Sam Bodanza, Gertrude Buchner, Jill Bystzdzienski, Stan Calhoun, Fred Childs, Kevin Connelly, Tim Costello, Gorden Dellahunt, George Eaton, Ed Ehrlbacher, Larry Epstein, Frank Femminella, Mike Foster, Charles Fox, Richard Genest, Peter Hopke, Hy Kuritz, Dick Livoroni, Janice Lieberman, Roger Longo, Larry Mannion, Joe Meda, Jim McClellan, Tim McLean, Dick Naylor, Chris Nelsen-Healy, Linda Nicholson, John Pennachio, Sandra Peterson-Hardt, Peter Pollak, Shari Popen, Gerry Postiglione, Bob Pring, Dennis Reichard, Ed Sarjeant, Shirley Sartori, Dan Schultz, Barbara

Sjostrom, Peter Stoll, Dick Syphax, Wallace Taylor, Don Van Cleve, Dennis Van Essendelft, Liliana Vogt, Paul Vogt, Jennifer Whittle, and Russ Wise. My apologies to anyone I have inadvertently omitted.

Other colleagues who read and commented on various parts and drafts of this work and who must be thanked for their help are: David Ermann, Jeanne Kohl Jenkins, J. Steven Picuo, Richard Robbins, and Arthur Vidich.

Special thanks to editors Jim Bergin, who helped at the beginning, and Robin Gross, who edited the final draft (and, I might add, without offending the author—a rare gift indeed).

My gratitide to those who helped type the manuscript at various stages: Lynn Lazenby Johnson, Kathleen Murphy, Cecile Ormsby, and the cheerful crew at the George Mason University Research Typing Service: Ann Baumann, Sue Cooper, and May Thompson.

Finally, I come to my wife Elsie, whose experience as a psychologist in the schools forced me to honestly confront the biases of the ivory tower and whose love and encouragement kept me going when I wanted to quit more times than I would like to admit; to our daughter, Kirsten, whose love of learning has instilled in us a vigilance to ensure that schooling does not destroy this love as it has done to so many children; and to the newest member of our family, our daughter Faith, who will someday make the journey through the educational institution.

Fairfax, Virginia   Joseph A. Scimecca
July 1979

Contents

II

Conflict in the Schools   *33*

IV

Changing the System   *235*

I

Introduction

1

The Sociological Study of Education

Human beings are social animals, and sociology is concerned with understanding human social interaction and patterned behavior. As a distinct discipline, sociology, in the words of Robert Bierstedt, "has a long past but only a short history."[1] By this he means that all inquiries were once a part of philosophy, and one by one the various disciplines cut the apron strings. Sociology's turn came in the nineteenth century, fashioned out of the writings of Auguste Comte.[2] It was Comte (1798–1857) who in 1839 first coined the word *sociology*. The term is a hybrid one taken from the Latin *socius,* meaning "society," and the Greek *logos,* the suffix of which *(logy)* can be translated as "study of." As legend would have it, Comte wanted to call this new study of society *social physics,* but Adolphe Quetelet, a contemporary of Comte, and a man of whom Comte thought very little, had already begun to undertake statistical studies of society and had labeled his inquiries social physics.

What, then, is this discipline which seeks to understand how individuals behave in society? Basically, it is a way of perceiving the world. Just as, say a

3

Freudian psychologist focuses on sexual drives, death wishes, and oedipal complexes, or an economist looks to the production and distribution of goods and services to explain human behavior, so the sociologist looks to the social structure—the society—and how it affects the personality of an individual.

The following example should more clearly illustrate what is meant by the term *sociological perspective*. One of the more obvious changes in the United States in recent years is the rising rate of divorce. The statistical chances are approximately two out of five that a couple marrying today will be divorced in their lifetime. And if this couple resides in California where the divorce rate is over 50 percent, the odds are greater that they will divorce than they will remain married. While a non-Californian might humorously attribute this high California divorce rate to the effects of staying out too long in the hot sun, the sociologist looks to changes in the society for an explanation. It is obvious that divorces are easier to obtain than ever before. The church, the family, and peer groups no longer have as great a control on individuals as they once did; women are questioning their traditional familial role more than ever, and so on. The explanation for the rising divorce rate therefore lies outside of the individual, and is to be found in what the sociologist calls the social structural level, rather than in individual unhappiness, alienation, or discontent.

C. Wright Mills pinpointed what is meant by the sociological perspective when he differentiated between "private troubles" and "public issues."[3] To continue our illustration, when two people marry and then find that they are experiencing marital difficulties which eventually lead them to a divorce court, they experience very "private troubles," personal and idiosyncratic agonies. However, when we look at the divorce statistics in America, we see that a public issue is involved here; something in the social structure is making couples seek divorces. The root of the problem is social. Individuals interact, choose, and engage in a give-and-take relationship with the world, and the context in which these choices occur is defined by external and social factors.

An example related to education should further clarify the distinction. Educators are fond of the words "disadvantaged" and its equivalent, "socially deprived." The label is thought to account for the child's failure to learn in school. The stress is upon "the child's failure." Very rarely, if ever, is the problem located outside the individual—in the school, for example. Given the obvious fact that lower-class education in the United States is an abysmal failure and that lower-class children are on the average two or three years below grade level in such basic skills as reading and math (the late Paul Goodman sarcastically commented that "poor children become dumber the longer they stay in school"), why so much focus on the child and so little on the structure of the lower-class school? The answer to this is an obvious one: the field of education has been dominated by an individualistic perspective at the expense of a sociological one. Educators have concentrated their efforts too often and too long on the individual. They have sought to change the individual through "compensatory" programs of one kind or another without trying to alter the social conditions that produce "public issues" which in turn shape "private troubles."

It should be stressed at this point that the individualistic perspective is not to be condemned out of hand, nor should all compensatory education programs be scrapped. Reading specialists, for example, whose job it is to teach reading to those who have not learned to read or who are experiencing difficulty in learning, should obviously keep trying to do their job. However, those who are in positions to effect change in American education must be made to realize that compensatory programs which focus on the individual inadequacies of the student are extremely slow and time-consuming and at best will achieve very limited results. If any real changes in the educational status quo are to be made, these changes must be made at the structural level. The individualistic perspective, while not to be abandoned completely, should, however, be seen as only one view, not the *only* view, as has so often been the case among educators. The individualistic approach must be subordinated to the sociological approach.

THE SOCIOLOGICAL PERSPECTIVE[4]

As we said, the sociological perspective, as opposed to the individualistic perspective, locates the source of human conduct outside of the individual and in the various social institutions and structures. It enables the sociologist to concentrate on roles and how playing roles affects one's image of one's self. Expectations are attached to roles, and these expectations are embedded in the social context. To the sociologist, there are few, if any, inborn character traits. For example, it is not human nature to be competitive. One is competitive because one has been socialized to be competitive. American society, dominated by a capitalistic economy, stresses competition and individual achievement; individuals who embody these traits are produced. The family, the schools, and other aspects of life stress competition, and the individual is socialized to manifest this trait. A simple diagram illustrates this process:

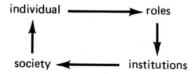

Through socialization, individuals learn their society's priorities. People come to play roles that are valued by institutions, which are in turn shaped by the total society. Human beings are social actors and must be analyzed in terms of their social actions; they must be understood in terms of motives which are defined by a social context rather than in terms of stimulus and response. The individual's psychological functions are shaped by specific configurations of roles which he or she has incorporated from his or her society. The most important aspect of personality is, of course, the individual's concept of self, the idea of what kind of person one is. The image of self one holds is formulated through an interpersonal context by taking into account what other people think of him or her. "Their attitudes of approval and disapproval guide us in learning to play the roles we are assigned or which we assume. By internalizing these attitudes of others toward us and our conduct, we not only gain new roles, but in time an image of ourselves."[5]

Institutions form persons. An individual's personality is shaped by the various roles he or she enacts in an institutional framework. Institutional frameworks, in turn, make up a society. The roles one plays and the image one holds of one's self are thus entrenched in a social context. For example, school superintendents, as will be shown in Chapter 7, are conservative, both politically and morally, because it is a role which the community expects and demands them to play.

What follows is an analysis of the educational institution in the United States using the sociological perspective. One method of analysis—that of conflict theory—will underlie our attempt to show the relationship of the growth and development of the public schools to the basic transformation of American society. A conflict approach is chosen because we believe it to be the most sophisticated model of analysis at the sociologist's disposal. This does not mean that all data correlate completely to the conflict perspective, or any other perspective, for that matter. Conflict is simply used throughout as a fisherman might use a net, to enable one to pull in as much as possible.[6] Before laying out our net, though, something must be said about other sociological perspectives. In particular, structural-functionalism, which has dominated the field of sociology and by extension the sociology of education for so long, will be paid special attention, along with a recent challenger to its dominance, Marxist theory.

STRUCTURAL-FUNCTIONALISM

Structural-functionalism, or functionalism, developed out of the works of classical sociologists such as Herbert Spencer and Emile Durkheim, and the anthropologists Bronislaw Malinowski and A. R. Radcliffe-Brown. A common thread throughout their works was the perception of societies as self-regulating, self-maintaining systems. These organizations had basic needs which had to be met to ensure and preserve their stability. Society envisioned as a macrosystem was conceptualized as having interrelated and interdependent parts, as does the human body. In short, society is an entity which needs to perform certain functions in order to maintain its equilibrium.

Modern functionalists continue to see social systems in terms of prerequisite needs for survival, advocating a basic correlation between the needs of the social system and needs of the individuals within it.[7] What is good for one is good for the other. Basically, most functionalists tend to view society as a social system with various needs of its own which must be met if the needs and desires of its members are to be fulfilled. By assuming that needs are associated with the system itself, functionalists unfortunately beg the question of the origin of the needs.[8]

The question of change, too, offers a problem for the functionalists. Here functionalism's answer is linked with the concept social evolution; the end toward which a system moves is to establish equilibrium. Social structures exist in environments and the relationship between the system and the environment is determined by the functioning of the parts of the system itself. Change occurs because systems get out of balance—they are in a state of disequilibrium—and they eventually must move back to the state of equilibrium. Based on an organistic analogy, changes in the social system result from attempts to cope with changes in the environment. This is the first principle of evolutionary thinking; change is a response to the environment. But if one does not accept the basic assumption that society is functionally equivalent to the body, the functionalist view of change becomes highly problematic.

Another telling criticism of functionalism is that it is based on a metaphysical premise. The social system is seemingly some sort of supernatural entity, that it not only has an existence of its own but a mind or will of its own as well. Along these same lines, functionalists also make teleological assumptions. That is, the system is thought of as being goal-directed, creating these goals by itself.

Perhaps the most important criticism of all is that functionalists exaggerate the stability, unity, and harmony of social systems and, therefore, tend to regard existing social institutions as necessary and indispensable. This in turn produces a conservative bias in the analysis of the functionalist.[9] Such conservatism can readily be seen when we turn to applications of the theory to education. The late Talcott Parsons' views on the school classroom can be used to substantiate this idea.

Functionalism and the Sociology of Education: The Influence of Talcott Parsons

Talcott Parsons, the most famous advocate of functionalism in sociology, has also been one of the most important influences upon the sociology of education. Parsons' now famous article, "The School Class as a Social System: Some of Its Functions in American Society," can be taken as representative of the functionalist argument concerning the role of the school and its components in the United States. Here Parsons argues that the classroom must be seen primarily as an agent of socialization and allocation. It is a place where the values of society are learned, as well as being an important agency of manpower allocation. Regarding the latter, Parsons states that "in American society there is a very high, and probably increasing, correlation between one's status level in the society and one's level of educational attainment."[10] Social status and educational level are related to occupational status. Therefore, success in occupational attainment is linked to educational achievement, which means completion of a high school education at a minimum, and usually graduation from college. Parsons is interested in the dynamics of the elementary school class, because the process of sorting out future college students from the rest begins here. The eventual dividing line is usually enrollment in a college preparatory course of study in high school, a determination made in the ninth grade. Parsons argues that selection is based upon the student's record of school performance in elementary school. Although he discusses social class briefly, his whole argument is that the selection process is genuinely fair. Parsons is willing to admit that a father's occupation is correlated with his children's college attendance, but explains it away as a consequence of ascriptive factors which have some influence on achievement factors. Even though his own data (based on a sample of 3,348 Boston high school boys and collected by himself, Samuel Stouffer, and Florence Kluckhorn) shows that within the top quartile in ability only 29 percent of laborers' sons intend to go to college as compared to 89 percent of the sons of white-collar workers in the same quartile, Parsons nevertheless concludes "that the main process of differentiation (which from another point of view is selection) that occurs during elementary school takes place on the single main axis of achievement."[11] The fact that 71 percent of high ability laborers' sons and only 11 percent of white-collar children of high ability do not intend to go on to college and are therefore, to use Parsons' own argument, denied access to occupational success, does not lead him to conclude that the educational system is perpetuating inequality. The fact that the "better-off families" have an advantage in sending their children to college does not bother him. What makes everything fair is that both the advantaged and the disadvantaged are subject to a uniform criterion of selection: achievement. That elementary schools are different, that in most lower-class elementary schools little learning (if any) takes place, and that the possibility that students are labelled and placed in roles which ensure failure[12] are never mentioned by Parsons. Instead, Parsons argues "that the most important single predispositional factor with which a child enters the school is his level of independence."[13] To Parsons, social class distinctions are negligible.

The problem with Parsons' argument in particular, and functionalism in general, is their reliance upon a model that assumes the world we live in is the best of all possible ones—that everyone and everything acts in the best interests of the society. One final example in Parsons' analysis brings this point home. Parsons concludes, after a description of the "typical" elementary school, that the classroom situation "is structured so that opportunity for particularistic treatment is severely limited. Because there are so many more children in a school class than in a family and they are concentrated in a much narrower age range, the teacher has much less chance than does a parent to grant particularistic favors."[14] The only weakness in Parsons' description here is that it mentions something that rarely, if ever, exists. Teachers favor some students and discriminate against others, usually lower-class ones. The evidence for the existence of discrimination (which ranges from the scholarly studies of Robert Rosenthal,[15] Ray Rist,[16] and Gerald Levy,[17] to the more popular descriptions of individuals who have taught in the public schools such as Jonathan Kozol,[18] Herbert Kohl,[19] and James Herndon[20]) is so overwhelming that the Parsonian argument for universality in the schools is unrealistic, to say the least.[21] In particular, Kozol's description of an incident involving Stephen, an eight-year-old black student of his, and a Boston art teacher is so vivid, so well written, and so perceptive that it warrants reproduction:

If Stephen began to fiddle around during a lesson, the Art Teacher generally would not notice him at first. When she did, both he and I and the children around him would prepare for trouble. For she would go at his desk with something truly like a vengeance and would shriek at him in a way that carried terror. "Give me that! Your paints are all muddy! You've made it a mess. Look at what he's done! He's mixed up the colors! I don't know why we waste good paper on this child!" Then: "Garbage! Junk! He gives me garbage and junk! And garbage is one thing I will not have." Now I thought that this garbage and junk was very nearly the only real artwork in the class. I do not know very much about painting, but I know enough to know that the Art Teacher did not know much about it either and that, furthermore, she did not know or care anything at all about the way in which you can destroy a human being. Stephen, in many ways already dying, died a second and third and fourth and final death before her anger.[22]

Because functionalists focus upon systems operations in abstract terms, rather than upon behavioral patterns of individuals or groups, such important aspects of political life as power and domination are ignored, thereby giving tacit sanctioning to the status quo. Marxists, in particular, have mounted this criticism of functionalism and it is to this perspective we now turn.

MARXISM[23]

Karl Marx (1818—1883), from whose name the theory of Marxism derives, was a materialist philosopher who believed that reality lay only in physical things. Society consisted of the organization of activities which helped to provide for material needs and wants. The economic factor, according to Marx, is the fundamental determinant of the shape and development of society. Politics, religion, education, and so on, are all shaped by the economic sphere and must be analyzed in terms of class interests.

Marx saw two basic classes or strata in society, those who owned the means of economic production (the *bourgeoisie*) and those who worked for the owners (the *proletariat*). Eventually, although the bourgeoisie or ruling class was firmly in charge of the society, the antagonism between the two groups would become so intense that a revolution would occur, resulting in the overthrow of the owning class by the working class. A classless society would be the result, a socialist society where private property was abolished and exploitation was eliminated.

Although there are differing interpretations of Marx, nearly all Marxist interpretors of education see the schools as providing a legitimatizing function for the capitalist system. Far and away, the most influential and sophisticated Marxist analysis of American education is contained in a recent work, *Schooling in Capitalist America,* by two radical economists, Samuel Bowles and Herbert Gintis.

Their book can therefore be taken as the best of what Marxist analyis has to offer to educational analysis.

Bowles and Gintis' Critique of Schools

Bowles and Gintis' position is that schools produce workers, who will take their place in the capitalist system, by imparting differential technical and social skills. The prevailing degree of economic inequality and personality development are shaped for the individual by property and power relationships which define the capitalist system. The educational system is best understood, in their view, as an institution whose primary purpose is to perpetuate the social relations of economic life. Bowles and Gintis are also quick to point out that the educational system does not operate this way through any conspiracy of educators, but instead through the correspondence between the relationship of authority in the schools and the hierarchical division of labor in the economy. Lastly, unlike so many other critics, they see that the process is never absolute, that some political consciousness does arise in the educational institution.[24]

Schools accomplish this by depoliticizing class antagonism, indoctrinating students to accept the belief that the economic and social position they attain is the best they can achieve. Success or failure in school is considered an individual responsibility. If the student does not do well, it is his or her fault. The individualistic perspective, according to the Marxist view, is used as a primary legitimatizing device for the acceptance of the capitalist system. Nowhere is this more evident than in the debate over IQ and standardized achievement tests. The data clearly states that children whose parents are highly educated do better in school (receive more years of schooling) than do children whose parents have less education. These figures indicate the class bias in our society, for as Bowles and Gintis write:

> Even among children with identical IQ scores at ages six and eight, those with rich, well educated, high status parents could expect a much higher level of schooling than those with less-favored origins. Indeed . . . an individual in the ninetieth percentile in social class background is likely to receive five more years of education than an individual in the tenth percentile; . . . also he is likely to receive 4.25 more years schooling than an individual from the tenth percentile with the same IQ.[25]

If schooling is a significant factor in explaining individual income (and the evidence seems to overwhelmingly support this position),[26] then four more years of education translated to the difference between a high school graduate and a college graduate can roughly mean the difference of $230,000 in one's working lifetime.[27]

According to Bowles and Gintis, then, the class inequalities in our society are too evident to be denied. Defenders of the school system (including the overwhelming majority of professional educators) are therefore forced to assert that things are getting better. Although this is true to some extent, there is little evidence to support the contention that education is making any real change in the pervasive system of inequalty. Indeed, as Bowles and Gintis point out, "The statistical association (coefficient of correlation) between parents' social status and years of education attained by individuals who completed their schooling three or four decades ago is virtually identical to the same correlation for individuals who terminated their schooling in recent years."[28] Bowles and Gintis thus make a strong argument that repression, individual powerlessness, inequality of incomes, and inequality of opportunity are not being changed by the school system in the United States; indeed, if anything, the educational system perpetuates this disparity. We disagree with Bowles and Gintis in their locating the roots of repression and inequality solely in the capitalist economy. These barriers to success are not unique to capitalist societies. They have been found in other social systems. Furthermore, although Bowles and Gintis do not envision schooling as absolutely repressive, they do have trouble explaining the upward mobility that occurs because of educational attainment. Finally, Bowles and Gintis' argument that schooling reflects the needs of economic elites is an extremely limited view of American education. As Christopher Hurn argues, their position

> neglects how much of what schools teach is irrelevant either to the acquisition of personal qualities that produce a compliant and docile labor force or to the effective learning of cognitive skills. The contention that schools are responsive to elite demands and much less responsive to the demands of educators who would like different outcomes for schooling fails to recognize the important respects in which schools are refractory institutions, responsive to no one's demands.[29]

In the end, then, Bowles and Gintis present too narrow a view of the educational system. Public schooling is not completely dominated by economic elites. Other factors enter into the picture. For example, we will argue in this work that the bureaucratic and hierarchical structure of education has shaped it as much as have any economic elites. Nor have conflicts in education always been economic. Catholics, early on, rebelled against what they perceived to be the Protestantization of public schools. Teachers have struggled for autonomy and prestige, foregoing in many instances economic considerations. This is why a conflict approach, more broadly defined than the economically based Marxist one, which sees power and not economics as shaping society and education, will be used as an underlying theme throughout this work.

A CONFLICT APPROACH TO THE SOCIOLOGY OF EDUCATION

Conflict theory can be traced back to Machiavelli and Hobbes, both of whom explained human behavior in terms of self-interest and violence and the perpetuation of the social order by the organized coercion of various groups over others. Human beings are seen as sociable but conflict-prone animals. Conflict occurs because violent coercion is always a potential resource; since being coerced is a universally unpleasant experience, any use of coercion, however small, results in an antagonism to being dominated.[30] Each individual, thus, pursues his or her own interests, and in many instances these interests are antagonistic to the interests of others. It is assumed that everyone uses whatever resources are available to them and that those in positions of power have more resources at their disposal; hence, they have more control over their own situations. To the conflict theorist, power is the most important variable for understanding human behavior and is defined as "the probability that one actor within a social relationship will be in a position to carry out his own will despite resistance, regardless of the basis on which the probability rests."[31] Power and its ramifications must be analyzed if we are to understand social behavior, for not only is conflict differentially derived from social power, but so is social order. Indeed, power can be said to lead to order and integration. Though society is composed of numerous groups with conflicting interests, social order is created and maintained by legitimizing factors. Socially created norms serve to mask the violent nature of life; their role is to induce the individual to abide by the laws of the land because these laws are seen as legitimate. This explanation of how power leads to order is based upon the insights of the great German social scientist, Max Weber, and should be an integral part of any conflict analysis. Whereas Karl Marx stressed that conflict is found everywhere, Weber devoted himself to the study of how conflict is resolved and order achieved in a given society. As James Duke, a conflict theorist, phrases it:

> A viable society . . . is characterized by order and integration rather than overt conflict. However, such order is achieved through the use of power (usually legitimized) to suppress or redefine the underlying conflict. Conflict is always present, but an effective power system is able to suppress, sublimate, or redefine the underlying conflict so that there are few if any external signs of its existence. If one chooses to focus on the mechanisms by which such order is achieved and conflict suppressed, one must focus first on the power of some to make rules and sanction the behavior of others to enforce their conformity to these rules. The basis of social organization, therefore, must be sought in power and in the process of legitimacy.[32]

This emphasis upon power and legitimacy and how they lead to order are focal points for the conflict sociologist, given that social inequality and social differentiation are constants in every society—valuables are unequally distributed; some get many, others get fewer, and still others get almost none at all. If, indeed, it is a basic fact of life that coercive power, especially as represented in the state, can bring one economic goods and emotional gratification, while at the same time denying them to others,[33] how is it that society is characterized by order and not disruption? This is an extremely important question, and it will be argued that a large part of the answer lies in the role schooling plays in legitimizing an unequal society.

The conflict approach, too, can be extremely sensitive to the organizational basis of modern education. For example, Randall Collins, a leading conflict theorist, posits, "Organizations are areas of struggle, and bureaucratic rules and task divisions are one means by which superiors attempt to control . . . their subordinates."[34] Examples of this in an educational setting range from administrators' attempting to define work situations for teachers to teachers' establishing rules of conduct within the classroom. Conflict in any organization, for Collins, arises because individuals attempt to gain certain things for themselves, in the process using others as means. Any patterns that emerge are thus best seen as the result of a struggle among individuals whose very inequality gives them different aims.[35] Much of the tension between the various groups that comprise the educational system can be seen in just these terms.

In short, conflict theory holds that the basic aspect of all social life is that individuals living together have different interests which come into opposition. Some of these individuals and/or groups gain greater power than others, and subsequently use this power to pursue their own interests. Social power, rather than economic power (in particular, the control over sanctions), serves both to organize society and to institutionalize the basic clashes over priorities present in the society.[36]

What follows, then, represents an application of this framework to public education. As such, it will include a historical view of the evolution of power differentials within the schools and the subsequent strife which emerges from these structural inequalities. This book is organized to illustrate this basic thesis on a number of levels. It is divided into four parts. Chapter 2, along with this chapter, comprises Part I. In Chapter 2, we analyze the structure of American society and the position of education within this structure. Public education is seen as a historical mechanism of social control, with the growth of bureaucracy providing a means of combining this function with schooling.

Part II consists of Chapters 3 to 8, and focuses upon conflict in the schools. Chapters 3, 4, and 5 look at the roles of students, teachers, and principals. In Chapter 6 we analyze the friction between these groups and the role of legitimacy within the school. Chapter 7 focuses upon the historical and contemporary discord between superintendents and school boards. Chapter 8 concludes Part II by analyzing teacher power and the growth of teacher militancy.

Part III is concerned with unrest within the society. Chapter 9 is an introduction to the problem of inequality and education. In Chapter 10 we deal specifically with minority groups and discrimination in education. Chapter 11 looks at discrimination against women. Chapter 12 extends the analysis introduced in Chapters 9, 10, and 11 to higher education.

Part IV analyzes the possibilities for changing the educational system. In Chapter 13 we look at the so-called revolution in school finances, the movement to divorce the quality of education from the wealth of particular school districts. Chapter 14, the last chapter, discusses some of the other major strategies for change, dividing them into liberal and radical. We end by presenting the strategy of decentralization—community control, which we see as the most viable approach for changing the public education system in the United States.

NOTES

1. Robert Bierstedt, *The Social Order,* 3d ed. New York: McGraw-Hill, 1970, p. 3.
2. See especially Harriet Martineau (translator and condenser), *The Positive Philosophy of Auguste Comte.* London: J. Chapman, 1853.
3. See C. Wright Mills, *The Sociological Imagination.* New York:Oxford University Press, 1959.
4. For a more fully developed conception of the sociological perspective offered here, see Hans H. Gerth and C. Wright Mills, *Character and Social Structure.* New York: Harcourt, 1953/Harbinger Books, 1964. Subsequent citations are from the 1964 edition.
5. Ibid., p. 22.
6. I am indebted to Paul Meadows for the use of this metaphor.
7. See in particular Robert K. Merton, *Social Theory and Social Structure.* New York: Free Press, 1963; and Talcott Parsons, *The Social System.* New York: Free Press, 1951.
8. An important exception to this is anthropologist Bronislaw Malinowski, who derived a functional theory of culture from an analysis of what he called "human nature." See in particular his work, *A Scientific Theory of Culture.* New York: Oxford University Press, 1960.
9. For a sophisticated critical analysis of structural-functionalism, see Irving M. Zeitlin, *Rethinking Sociology: A Critique of Contemporary Theory.* Englewood Cliffs, N.J.: Prentice-Hall, 1973, pp. 3—50.
10. Talcott Parsons, "The School Class as a Social System: Some of Its Functions in American Society," *Harvard Educational Review, 29* (Fall, 1959), pp. 279—318.
11. Ibid., p. 301.
12. See especially Gerald Levy, *Ghetto School.* New York: Pegasus Press, 1970; and Paul Lauter and Florence Howe, "How The School System Is Rigged for Failure," in Robert Lejeune (ed.), *Class and Conflict in American Society.* Chicago: Markham, 1972, pp. 197—216.
13. Parsons, "School Class," p. 300.
14. Ibid., p. 303.
15. Robert Rosenthal and Lenore Jacobsen, *Pygmalion in the Classroom: Teacher Expectations and Pupils' Intellectual Development.* New York: Holt, Rinehart and Winston, 1968.
16. Ray C. Rist, "Student Social Class and Teacher Expectations: The Self-fulfilling Prophecy in Ghetto Education," *Harvard Educational Review, 40* (1970), pp. 416—451.
17. Levy, *Ghetto School.*
18. Jonathan Kozol, *Death at an Early Age: The Destruction of the Hearts and Minds of Negro Children in the Boston Public Schools.* New York: Bantam Books, 1968.
19. Herbert Kohl, *36 Children.* New York: New American Library, 1967.
20. James Herndon, *The Way It Spozed to Be.* New York: Simon and Schuster, 1968.
21. In fairness to Parsons, the literature cited was written after he wrote his article. However, he never repudiated his views.
22. Kozol, *Death at an Early Age,* pp. 3—4.
23. For what is easily the best and most sophisticated introduction to the works of Karl Marx, see David McLellan, *Karl Marx: His Life and Thought.* New York: Harper Colophon Books, 1973.
24. Samuel Bowles and Herbert Gintis, *Schooling in Capitalist America.* New York: Basic Books, 1976, pp. 11—13.
25. Ibid., p. 32.
26. Although Christopher Jencks et al.'s study, *Inequality* (New York: Basic Books, 1972) is an important exception, Jencks' analysis omits a number of very important reasons for income, such as age, religion, number of weeks worked, and so on. Also, Jencks' conclusions are extremely tentative and the book is characterized throughout by such caveats and disclaimers as "it seems," and the like.
27. Computed from U.S. Bureau of the Census, Current Population Reports, Series P-60, No. 101,

"Money Income in 1974 of Families and Persons in the United States." Washington, D.C.: U.S. Government Printing Office, 1976, pp. 71–73.

28. Bowles and Gintis, *Schooling in Capitalist America*, p. 33. Their conclusions are based on Peter M. Blau and Otis D. Duncan, *The American Occupational Structure*. New York: Wiley, 1967.

29. Christopher J. Hurn, *The Limits and Possibilities of Schooling*. Boston: Allyn and Bacon, 1978, p. 81.

30. Randall Collins, *Conflict Sociology*. New York: Academic Press, 1975, p. 59.

31. Max Weber, *The Theory of Social and Economic Organization,* edited and translated by Talcott Parsons. New York: Free Press, 1964, p. 152.

32. James Duke, *Conflict and Power in Social Life*. Provo, Utah: Brigham Young University Press, 1976, p. 71.

33. Collins, *Conflict Sociology,* p. 59.

34. Ibid., p. 295.

35. Ibid., p. 315.

36. Duke, *Conflict and Power in Social Life,* p. 153.

2

American Society and Its Schools

THE STRUCTURE OF AMERICAN SOCIETY

The United States in the last quarter of the twentieth century is best characterized by the bureaucratic ethos. In the words of Bensman and Vidich, two perceptive analysts of this historically new type of society:

> One important aspect of the New Society is the everincreasing growth of the administrative structure of bureaucracy and of the scale of large organizations. Government, industry, education, trade unions, and churches carry out the internal and external operation of the bureaucratic mechanism.[1]

By far the most influential framework for analyzing the role that bureaucracy has played in industrialized society was developed by Max Weber in the early twentieth century. For Weber, the primary identifying characteristic of bureaucracy is its clearly specified areas of jurisdiction which are set by explicit rules.

17

These rules are enforced by those who occupy positions within the bureaucracy. Such persons possess authority through the roles they occupy in the bureaucratic hierarcy. This is the sole source of their authority—the fact that they occupy roles with specific duties and obligations in a bureaucracy. Their positions make their authority legitimate. Weber considered the following characteristics to be the most important in describing a bureaucracy:

> From the basic principle of fixed and official jurisdiction flow such vital practices and criteria as the regularization of channels of communication, authority, and appeal; the functional priority of the office to the person occupying it; the emphasis upon written and recorded orders in place of random, merely personal commands or wishes; the sharp separation of official from personal identity in the management of affairs and the superintending of finances; the identification of, and provision for, the training of "expertness" in a given office or function; the rigorous priority of official to merely personal business in the governing of an enterprise; and finally, the conversion of as many activities and functions as possible to clear and specifiable rules; rules that, by their nature, have both perceptive and authoritarian significance.[2]

The process of bureaucratization is for Weber the powerful manifestation of the principle of rationalization or efficiency. Weber was more concerned with describing the process of bureaucracy than with offering an explanation of why it had taken place, seeing two reasons for its growth. First, and most important, was that a tendency toward rationalization was simply part of the inevitable process of history. Secondly, Weber attributed the growth of bureaucracy to the fact that in the modern world organizations tended to be large and largeness leads to bureaucratization. Although Weber's description of the bureaucratization of modern industrial society is accurate, his explanation of the reasons for its growth is highly inadequate. First of all, there are numerous historical examples of the successful execution of large-scale efforts without the benefit of a bureaucratic structure. An obvious example is the building of the Egyptian pyramids. Secondly, Weber overlooks the possibility that it is not "large size" per se that disposes to bureaucracy, but that large size may only be important because it generates other forms which may in turn generate bureaucratic patterns.

It would seem, then, that more insight into the bureaucratic process is to be gained by linking the variable of power to bureaucratic structure—in other words, by asking, whose interests are best served by this phenomenon? Who ultimately benefits from the bureaucratization of society? How are the decisions to bureaucratize made? Who pays the price for bureaucratization once it is established, and who is responsible for perpetuating bureaucratic organization in the face of opposition?[3] Such questions, we feel, lead us directly to the relationship between bureaucracy and stratification or inequality. Thus, we will argue in this book that there is a fundamental relationship between bureaucracy and social inequality, that bureaucracy is not a historically inevitable, neutral trend, but represents the manifestation of the values of those in power as they seek to preserve their position of dominance. Bureaucracies do not necessarily represent "rational" organization, nor are they always the best, most efficient way of achieving an organization's goals. Indeed, it will be shown that in relation to education, the process of bureaucracy has in many instances done as much to restrict the stated goals of education as it has to perpetuate them.

Bureaucracy, in this view, though giving the appearance of being equitable and favorable to the poor, has in reality offered a differential advantage to the affluent and their children, in the process reinforcing the status quo.[4] The bureaucratic educational structure represents particular interests. For the most part, these priorities have been class-related ones. The middle class has, from the inception of public education, controlled the schools. To be sure, groups other than socioeconomic classes have been engaged in power struggles, and as we shall see, in many instances the result has been a great deal of strife. However, as we will emphasize throughout this work, it is the class system of education, in particular the struggles for control between the middle class and the lower class that has shaped the bureaucratic structure that public schooling in the United States has become.

The sociological approach focuses upon roles individuals play in a bureaucratically organized educational structure and the tensions produced as these roles are acted out. To this we would add that the educational system in the United States, if it is to be fully understood, must be analyzed in terms of power relationships and how these relationships lead to social order and integration. Education is a competitive struggle for social and economic rewards. It is essentially a fight to establish and maintain control over a limited resource, and as such is intrinsically related to the system of social inequality in the United States. In short, we must concentrate on the socioeconomic class—schooling relationship in this country.

STRATIFICATION: SOCIAL INEQUALITY AND EDUCATION IN AMERICAN SOCIETY

One definition of stratification which will be used in this work, is offered by Celia Heller, who sees stratification "as a system of structured inequality in the things that count in a given society, that is, both tangible and symbolic goods of that society."[5] The use of the word *structured* is important here because it indicates that inequality is patterned and legitimized by ideology. It is not a natural social condition. It is a purposeful human product held together by power relationships.

The study of stratification is the study of the ranking of people with respect to what is valued, and discovering in what respects these ranks differ and why.[6] Each rank or stratum in a society must be viewed as such because all of its members have similar opportunities to get those goods and experiences that are valued. Valuables can be anything from money to a professional occupation; experiences may run the gamut from having access to the "beautiful people" to being treated with respect. To be a member of a stratum is to share similar advantages with other members.

Four important dimensions of stratification—occupation, class, status, and power—provide a means for ranking individuals in accordance with the specific opportunity each has to obtain a given value. Taken together, these factors enable us to account for a wide range of different opportunities. Such characteristics are defined in the following manner:

> *Occupation:* a set of activities pursued more or less regularly as a major source of income.
> *Class* or *class situation:* the amount and source (property or work) of income as these affect the chances of people to obtain other available values.
> *Status:* the successful realization of claims to prestige; it refers to the distribution of deference in a society.
> *Power:* the realization of one's will, even if this involves the resistance of others.[7]

The above elements of stratification are to be understood as ways of focusing upon certain features of specific roles in the various institutional orders. These components are not neatly systematic, and they overlap at times. As Max Weber made clear, they are to be stated as probabilities on the basis of objectively defined situations.[8] By looking at the stratification system in the United States in terms of "life chances," we can begin to understand the similarities and differences among people. Although, of course, within any given stratum individuals will differ, we can still expect certain psychological traits to recur. The probability that people will have a similar outlook on life is increased the more homogeneous they are with respect to power, class, occupation, and prestige. Psychological factors are likely to be associated with strata. Individuals who are characterized by the intersection of the four dimensions should express a similar ideology. For our purposes, there should be a homogeneity in outlook concerning views toward education, which is directly related to the stratum one occupies.

THE CLASS STRUCTURE IN AMERICA[9]

The number of strata into which a society is divided varies, depending upon the theoretical justification for the division. For the most part, there is a general consensus among sociologists that the United States is a three-tiered strata system, comprised of an upper class, a middle class, and a lower class. These three are then usually divided into an upper and lower segment for each. It must be kept in mind that the six classes are simply heuristic devices, and as such have many exceptions. Nevertheless, even with this caveat, it can easily be shown that the class structure plays a dominant role in shaping American society and, by extension, its educational system. Since our major concern in this book is with education, the stratum's or class' attitude toward education will be highlighted in the descriptions that follow.

The Upper-upper Class

Although little is known about the details of the private lives of upper-class individuals, on the basis of what some sociologists have learned, we can offer some speculation and feel fairly confident regarding its accuracy.

The upper-upper class is composed of the older industrial aristocrats whose wealth was accumulated after the Civil War. Their fortunes were made in banking, chemicals, railroads, steel, shipping, oil, and automobiles. They include families such as the DuPonts, Whitneys, Harrimans, Rockefellers, Mellons, Manvilles, and Fords. This segment of the upper class has had a long tradition of social intercourse with European nobility, Eastern Ivy League schools, and the New York City social and debutante life. Because both their social and economic activities are international, they tend to be internationally-minded. For the most part, they are white Protestants. Since membership is based upon lineage, the upper-upper class has an almost caste-like character. A person is born into it, though females occasionally can enter through marriage. Occupation-wise, the upper-upper-class person works at some profession (the Protestant ethic is too strong in this country to indulge a leisure class) and serves on numerous boards of directors in banking, business, and education. He or she is usually a product of private schools, an Ivy League college graduate, and listed in the *Social Register* and *Who's Who*.

The Lower-upper Class

Since the 1920s, new business opportunities have accounted for additions to the upper class. Investments in Texas oil, the space industry, electronics, communications, real estate, and so on, have produced a *nouveau riche,* which includes such names as Hunt, Murchison, Getty, Hughes, Giovanni, Kaiser, and Kennedy. The older industrial aristocracy regards this group as upstarts, and they have not been fully admitted into the upper-upper class. It is only when their children and grandchildren attend the finer prep schools and the Ivy League colleges, and are socialized into what one sociologist has characterized as "graceful living,"[10] do they become members of the upper-upper class (provided, of course, that they have still managed to retain some of their wealth.) A perfect example of this type is the late President John F. Kennedy. Although the son of one of the country's richest men, and elected to the highest political office in the land, John Kennedy was not considered a member of the upper-upper class. Indeed, his sister Patricia Kennedy, who was at the time married to actor Peter Lawford, was once not allowed to buy into an exclusive upper-upper-class co-op on New York City's posh Sutton Place. Jacqueline Bouvier Kennedy Onassis, on the other hand, although coming from a family nowhere near as wealthy as the Kennedys, by virtue of the "oldness" of her family is a member of the upper-upper class. The Kennedy children, Caroline and John, are upper-upper-class, since they represent the third generation of wealthy Kennedys.

The Upper-middle Class

The upper-middle class has historically been the backbone of the community because of its civic participation and support of cultural affairs. The typical upper-middle-class person is a well-to-do, self-employed professional, or the owner or manager of a large business establishment. Here occupation and education are the key defining variables. Upper-middle-class persons are concerned with individual success, and their career is the most important determinant of their status. Education helped them get where they are and they want the same thing for their children, who, in turn, are expected to achieve in school and, later on, in some profession or high-status occupation.

Although they may enroll their children in private schools, they will send them to what is perceived as a ''good'' public school, ''good'' being defined as academic-achievement oriented. They are also quite likely to take an active part in their children's education; many suburban school board members come from this stratum.

The Lower-middle Class

For the lower-middle-class person, occupation and education are also the key variables. However, he or she differs from his or her upper-middle-class counterpart in that the lower-middle-class individual does not have as much personal wealth. Although he or she is college educated and works at a white-collar job, because he or she is salaried, he or she cannot usually look forward to living comfortably in his or her own lifetime. The lower-middle-class person is also characterized by extreme status consciousness, stressing respectability above all else.

Since in many instances those below them on the stratification ladder, (in particular, highly skilled blue-collar workers) often make more money than they do, status has to be stressed to preserve their tenuous middle-class identity. Many lower-middle-class families, therefore, will move to the suburbs, believing that their children will receive a better education and thus enhance their opportunity to advance occupationally and solidify the middle-class status of the family. With their upper-middle-class counterparts, education is seen as the pathway to economic achievement, and they will try to do everything they can to ensure their children's success in school. However, because they do not have the power or the influence of the upper-middle-class parent, their impact upon the educational system is nowhere as great.

The Upper-lower Class (Working Class)

The lower class is comprised of the working class (upper-lower) and the subworking (lower-lower). The working class is perhaps in the most difficult position of all in the United States. They have little access to a college education and receive no training in the higher cultural forms. They are, therefore, literally cut off from the mainstream of American culture.

Although upper-lower-class workers in many instances earn as much or more than their lower-middle-class correspondents, they internalize a completely different value system. This comes about because of the blue-collar nature of their job and their lack of higher educational achievement. Often, the more successful will brag about how much more money they make than "a college guy they know"; nevertheless, they somewhat resent their limited educational opportunities and usually feel uncomfortable around educated people. Initially they have high expectations for their children, but do not have the power nor the resources to actively see to it that their children succeed in the educational system. Usually, only their most academically talented children eventually achieve success. The working-class person is forced to rationalize away his or her other children's failure by pointing to how they're "doin' all right" without a college degree, although secretly, they still want their children to go on to college. Since they have little or no control over their children's education, they cannot fulfill their wishes for a better life for their offspring.

The Lower-lower Class

The lower-lower-class individual is at the very bottom of the class structure. He or she is characterized by a low prestige occupation, is semi-skilled at best (unemployed at worst), takes home a low salary, and has little education and virtually no power to control his or her own or his or her children's destiny. Schools were hostile places for the lower-lower-class person when he or she was a child, stamping him or her as inferior, and he or she sees the same thing happening to his or her children. The person accepts this judgment because he or she has never been exposed to any other.

CONFLICT AND THE PUBLIC SCHOOLS

The view of public education to be presented stresses the elements of conflict and the potentials for friction between the various classes, groups, and political interests that are instrumental in shaping the public schools. In particular, the discord between the middle class and lower class, and the inequalities that result from the domination of the schools by the middle class, will be focal points of examination. The upper classes in the United States have little to do with the everyday workings of the public schools. Upper-class children do not, except under unusual circumstances,[11] attend public schools. They are enrolled, instead, in elitist private schools where upper-class values prevail.[12] The influence of the upper class on American education is therefore most felt at the national level, where priorities are set.[13] The upper classes, those in positions of power, define what passes for reality in any society;[14] they formulate the values that ensure the view of society as legitimate. The public schools carry out the mandate of the powerful, and the dissension in education manifests itself over access to middle-class status. Education has rarely provided entrance into the higher circles of power,[15] but a college degree is a definite passport to the middle class.[16] There is much that is wrong with middle-class life, with its emphasis on conformity and social striving; but a quick glance at mortality rates, illness, and other general measures of the quality of life show that a middle-class individual leads a far better life than does a lower-class one.

Briefly, then, our thesis is that public schools—along with their obvious function of transmitting, from one generation to the next, knowledge and skills necessary to be an adult member of society—serve two other fundamental and inseparable purposes: (1) they keep lower-class students from competing equally with middle-class students; and (2) they serve to legitimate the political and social system. In order to understand public education, we must see it as a competitive struggle for social and economic rewards. It is essentially a tug-of-war between the middle and lower classes, with the upper classes literally above the battle. A brief historical look at the origins of public education will show how the relationship of bureaucracy and social class are essential to an understanding of the role of the public schools in the United States.

The Beginnings of Free Education in America: 1776–1830[17]

Although Thomas Jefferson devised a plan in 1779 which called for the free education of all white children in the state of Virginia, there was great opposition to what was considered the radicalness of Jefferson's proposal. In particular, Jefferson's notions that the best and most capable students, not the well-born, should receive the most education, and that performance in school should be substituted for birth in choosing America's future leaders, did not sit well with Virginia's elite. For the most part, the years immediately following the Revolutionary War were characterized by a general lack of interest in any educational reform; the conclusion to be drawn from Jefferson's inability to create interest in a democratic educational system is that change was not desired by the Colonial ruling class.

In general, when children received formal education during this period, they did so in district schools, a term used to denote the one-room rural or village schoolhouse of the late eighteenth and early nineteenth centuries. A district was a legal entity only for the purposes of schooling; its boundaries were defined by the distances children could reasonably be expected to travel to and from school.

The major characteristic of the district school was the virtually complete control of education by an extremely small political unit. It was a prime example of what we call today "community control." Power over the schools resided with the parents (including lower-class ones) and the first clashes were generated over parental efforts to regulate their children's education. For many citizens of the time, involvement in school matters was their only opportunity for political participation, and they jealously guarded their rights. So seriously did they take their prerogatives that this era in American educational history is characterized as one of constant conflict between the schoolmaster on the one hand, and the students and parents on the other; the latter usually won, since they held the power of the purse. This dissidence (as we will show in some of the following chapters) is still indicative of the schools today; the major difference today is a shift in those who occupy the positions of power. In any event, the political nature of the schools and the role of power was established early in the history of the United States.

The schoolmaster represented outside knowledge, which in turn stood for outside authority. He symbolized standards and values other than those of the local community. Each time the students humiliated the master or drove him away from the district (the factual and fictional accounts of the period give abundant evidence of the commonality of this occurrence), the community triumphed over the outside world, if only symbolically. If our interpretation of the legitimizing function of American education is correct, it would stand to reason that this community triumph over external authority would not be tolerated for long. Legitimation is a societal phenomenon and community control would have to be replaced by centralization. And, indeed, this is just what the Common School Movement sought to accomplish.

The Common School Movement: 1830–1880

The Common School Movement had three fundamental goals: (1) to provide a free elementary school education for every American white child; (2) to create a trained educational profession; and (3) (most importantly) to establish some form of state control over local schools. This last aim was crucial, for without central control the other two goals could not be realized.

The most widely advertised and popularly appealing aspect of the common school reform era was its massive efforts to increase school attendance. If children were to learn to accept authority and to be controlled and socialized, the majority of poor children (who needed it most) had to attend schools. The historical evidence is quite clear in this respect. Industrialization and urbanization undermined traditional means of social control and legitimacy. Whereas the small communities had been characterized by both formal and informal means of social control, the large developing cities mitigated against the informal. American society was at the time politically dominated by the Whig party. The Whigs, a group of politicians and their businessmen supporters, did not trust the "masses" to voluntarily conform to America's moral standards. Faced with the demise of the personal network of social control that had typified the local community, and seeking to ensure that individuals living in a large impersonal urban environment would promote the general welfare of the society, the Whigs looked to the schools as the institution which could effectively and efficiently internalize a sense of control and social duty in the urban population. It was quickly realized that bureaucracy provided a sure means of combining these priorities with education.

As the schools became larger and larger, the administrative tasks of running them increased in complexity accordingly.[18] Superintendents in large cities had hundreds of schools to coordinate. Hierarchies vested with specific authority were established. Roles and duties were defined to avoid possibilities of conflict, and subordinates were expected to grant obedience to their superiors. In order to perfect these hierarchies, educators argued that it was necessary to build and develop career lines within the schools. If education was to become an attractive "profession," incentives such as promotions within ranks, tenure, pensions, and so on, were needed. Further reinforcement came from the dominant ideology of the society. Educators began to justify the bureaucratization of education by using the example of industry as a standard. School systems were often described as factories, and metaphors based on the corporation and the machine became a part of the educational rhetoric.

Thus, the priorities of the professional educators who ran the schools coincided with the leaders of the society. The argument advanced for bureaucracy shifted to efficiency and effectiveness rather than social control. Bureaucracy became an educational fact of life, so much so that Michael Katz writes:

> In the third quarter of the nineteenth century, increasingly complex administrative problems, reinforced by the nepotism and politics that afflicted school practice, made rationalization and coordination a necessity for urban school systems. Faced with this need, schoolmen (and some laymen as well) justified their organizing principles by analogies from industry, which they believed had successfully solved the same basic problem: the management of large numbers of people performing different tasks. The process of bureaucratization within education was so thorough and so rapid because of the schoolmen themselves, who saw in the new organizational forms the opening up of careers and a parital solution to the problem of regulating behavior within the occupation.[19]

Educators, in their haste to bureaucratize education, met with little opposition since influential laypersons agreed with their goals. Bureaucracy, as we shall see throughout this work, gave (and continues to give) differential advantage to the children of the affluent.

In sum, the goal of the Common School Reform Movement was an effort to find an effective substitute for the mechanisms of social control and secularism that characterized the preurban, preindustrial, stable community. Bureaucracy was quickly seen as an efficient means of accomplishing this. And since it coincided with the efforts of educators to coordinate and run the schools, in the process providing a means toward achieving "professionalization," it became an entrenched form. However, we must not lose sight of the underlining factor here: the major goal of the common school was to improve moral and social consensus in a heterogeneous population, and bureaucracy was the most efficient mechanism for fulfilling this task. Whether or not the Common School Movement attained its purposes is open to debate; what is not, though, is the creation of conflict as one group sought to coerce another to do its bidding. Due to the wealth of documentation concerning the role of the schools in the North, we will concentrate on this region in order to show the intensity of this struggle over access to public education.

The Common Schools in the North

During the fifty-year span from 1840 to 1890, a great many of the characteristics of present-day schools were established. As stated before, one avowed purpose of expanding the role of the public schools was to correct the perceived antisocial behavior of poor children and thereby bring harmony and order to urban America. We must bear in mind, too, that the earliest high schools and secondary schools were not intended for the lower classes.[20] It was the middle-class child, whose family could afford the lack of his or her income, who attended the high school, and its curriculum was tailored to him or her. The dissent in the early stages, then, revolved around the elementary or primary schools. Only in the latter part of the nineteenth century did it reach the high schools.

One of the more interesting characteristics of schools of this time was the amount of support they received from the Protestant middle class. The schools were seen by Protestant parents as a means of guaranteeing the separation of their children from lower-class children (many of whom were Catholic), and at the same time providing them with an advantage in making their fortunes. No conspiracy was necessary; simply wanting to help one's child was enough to keep the system going. One did not have to agree with others to keep lower-class children from succeeding; one had only to make sure that one's own child was getting the advantage. Since thousands of middle-class parents were in positions to maintain their children's status in school, we can easily see how the present system of educational inequality originated.

The dissonance at this time was extremely intense because something else had been added to the struggle between classes: religion. The contest for control of the school involved the established middle-class Protestants and the new lower-class, immigrant, largely Catholic population. The Protestants wanted to be certain that their children would better, or at least maintain, their status, while Catholics, wanting the same for their children, had to cope with the added burden of hostility and religious prejudice. The complex problems of Catholic immigration and assimilation demanded a specific type of Catholic—one who would not identify with the outside, secular, and Protestant life. Both groups thus marshalled what resources they could. The battle over control of the New York City school system can be taken as representative of this Protestant–Catholic opposition.

By 1825, the Public School Society, which grew out of the earlier Free School Society, operated eleven free schools serving almost 20,000 children. The Public School Society, although composed largely of Protestants, was upset that Catholic children were staying away from the schools. The Catholic Church, in turn, argued that the public schools were using public monies to support sectarian Protestant education, and therefore the Catholic Church was also entitled to public monies for its own schools. The Church held that no single curriculum could inculcate acceptable moral and religious values for both religious groups. Therefore, Catholic control over their children's curriculum was necessary, something that could best be accomplished in locally controlled schools supported by public money. Due to the unequal power base of the two groups, the Catholics lost out and were forced to build a parochial school system with their own money. This pattern reflected Catholic education up until the late 1960s, when lack of financial support and interest among parishioners forced the closing of many Catholic schools.

The Protestant victory helped to ensure a middle-class Protestant nature for the public schools; their values were solidly embedded in the educational system and have remained so to this day. Right from the start the battle lines were drawn between the middle and lower classes as they fought to control public education. Religious differences added to the bitterness of the struggle. Legitimacy was extremely difficult to establish as long as lower-class Catholics viewed the conflict in religious terms. The open Protestant nature of the schools would have to be secularized if lower-class Catholics who sent their children to public schools were to accept the socialization process as legitimate. While this eventually happened, the history of this neglected strife remains to be written, and obviously such an attempt is beyond the scope of this work. However, we would like to discuss one last example of the historical process of dominance by the middle class over the lower class—the rise of special education programs in the schools.

The Growth of Special Education: 1880–1920

One of the more important educational trends of the late nineteenth and early twentieth centuries was the growth of special education. "Special education" means "schooling designed for specific groups of children in recognition that the roles they would play in American society would probably be different from those available to other children."[21]

It is our contention that the primary motivation for the rise of special education was the middle class' belief that it would help improve the schools' efficiency in the moral training–social control of the lower classes. Here we go beyond the usual revisionist Marxist arguments that the growth of special education resulted primarily from increasing industrialization and a weakened apprentice system in the United States.[22] Such an explanation misses the fact that with the very limited exception of vocational training,[23] the other types of special education—hand training, manual training, and industrial education—did not prepare the student to fill skilled vocational roles. Of more importance was the belief that special education would attract poor children to the schools, thereby ensuring that their morals could be reshaped. Special education was thought to be far more attractive to poorer students (both economically and intellectually—though both were usually joined in most educators' minds) than were the traditional intellectual subjects. Felix Adler, president of New York's Ethical Culture Society, for instance, wrote in 1888 that manual training was more effective than traditional subjects because "history, geography, and arithmetic are not interesting as a rule, to young children, especially not to young children of the class with which we are now dealing. These listless minds are not easily roused to an interest in abstractions."[24] Two decades later, the Dean of Stanford's School of Education, Ellwood P. Cubberly, summed up the mood of the country with his observation that urban schools would have to abandon "the exceedingly democratic idea that American Society was devoid of classes and begin to educate the various classes according to their special needs."[25]

The theory that the children of the poor were more able to work with things than to memorize books and abstractions quickly became an educational fact of life. Special education programs, directed by middle-class educators for lower-class children, from their inception produced a restrictive type of education by further limiting the future educational opportunities of the poor. Arguing from a purely economic perspective misses the point. The reformers who instituted and advocated special education were in no way threatened by the students who were to be trained in special education courses. Nor is the argument that big business imposed a special type of training to create a more submissive labor force any more acceptable. Special education programs were for the most part technologically valueless to American industry. Graduates of these programs were not even useful in breaking strikes, for most strikes occurred among skilled tradesmen whose number was never great enough to satisfy industrial needs and whose skills made them vital to the industrial process. Church and Sedlak have summed up quite well the reasons for the growth of special education. They write that its development and popularity in the schools

> resulted from no conspiracy or plot to keep down the poor. The advocates of extending a limiting education to the blacks and the poor and the working classes were motivated by fear of the dangerous classes and by concern for the welfare of the whole society, and they were propelled by an arrogance that they knew what was best for society and for certain individuals in it. These people feared the poor, the black, and the workingman as a threat to social order and moral order, but not as a threat to their own economic status. They were arrogant because they sought to impose their moral and social values on other people and because they sought to predict the lives of individuals and to force them to follow these paths by limiting their educational opportunities. They were arrogant because they thought that imposing their own moral values on others in school was more important then enabling people to seek their own values in life.[26]

The argument for special education was an argument shaped by the arrogance of power. The middle classes, having won previous battles, were now convinced they knew best. However, because all decisions based upon naked power can ultimately prove unpredictable and ineffective, legitimacy had to be quickly established. The powerless had to feel an obligation to obey, not resist, those whose interests were not favored had to come to accept their position of subjugation. One way to accomplish this (the way used by the schools, as we shall see in the chapters to follow) was to socialize everyone to accept those values that supported the status quo.

While the above historical analysis is obviously selective (something that we hope will be remedied in the rest of this work), it does introduce the basic tension that resulted from the middle class' attempt to control public education. By stressing centralized authority and advocating bureaucratic structure as the best and most rational way to educate large masses of children, the middle class originated an ideology which enabled the school to become a primary mechanism for establishing social control and legitimacy in the society. Since the upper class was not threatened by such a development, this particular interrelationship of power, bureaucratic structure, and social class was established early and still persists today.

SUMMARY

In this chapter, we have tried to show that our society is characterized by the increasing growth of the administrative structure of bureaucracy. In order to understand the "bureaucratic ethos," we must see it in conjunction with the variable of power. This is accomplished by asking the question: whose interests are best served by bureaucratization? Such a question ultimately leads to an analysis of the relationship between bureaucracy and social stratification or inequality. By taking this direction we see bureaucracy not as a historical inevitability as Max Weber argued, but rather as the manifestation of the values of those in power as they seek to ensure and preserve their position of dominance. In particular, we noted that the middle class has historically dominated public education in the United States—that the class–schooling relationship is vital to any understanding of American education.

We then presented an overview of the class structure in the United States. A three-tiered strata system—upper class, middle class and lower class, with each divided into an upper and lower part—was seen as best approximating the system of stratification in the United States. A brief description of the six strata were offered, along with their attitudes toward education.

Throughout, we stressed the elements and conditions of potential and real conflict between the various classes, groups, and political interests which are instrumental in shaping the public schools. Manifestations of this strife were noted during three historical periods: (1) the beginnings of free education, 1776–1830; (2) the Common School Movement, 1830–1880; and (3) the growth of special education, 1880–1920.

The first period, 1776–1830, was initially characterized by the district school, a term used to denote the rural or village schoolhouse. This type of decentralized school district system predominated until the 1820s, when it was replaced by the Common School Movement. Late eighteenth-century and early nineteenth-century public education was typified by tension between the schoolmaster, who represented outside knowledge, and the townspeople. Since the latter held the pursestrings, they triumphed, but their victory over outside authority challenged the legitimacy function of the schools and the centralized Common School Movement began to grow as an alternative.

The Common School Movement, lasting from 1830 to 1880, had three basic goals: (1) to provide free education for every American white child; (2) to train educational professionals; and (3) to establish state control over local schools. This last goal was the most important, since the common school was envisioned as an instrument which could provide moral and social consensus for a heterogenous population.

Lastly, we looked at the growth of special education from 1880 to 1920. This too, was seen as arising out of middle-class society's belief in the efficacy of the schools as an agent for the moral training of the lower classes. From its inception, the movement for special education was symbolized by a moral arrogance which held that middle-class educators knew what was best for lower-class students.

In short, in this chapter we have argued that the interrelationship of power, bureaucracy, and social class is an historical development, and must be taken into account if we are to understand the role of education in the United States. What follows is an examination of the everyday workings of the public school and its relationship to power, bureaucracy, and social class. Throughout, we will stress a sociological perspective that is thoroughly grounded in a historical framework, believing that the present educational institution cannot be fully understood without a knowledge of the structural conditions from which it emerged.

NOTES

1. Joseph Bensman and Arthur J. Vidich, *The New American Society: The Revolution of the Middle Class.* Chicago: Quadrangle Books, 1971, p. 21.

2. Robert Nisbet, *The Sociological Tradition.* New York: Basic Books, 1966, pp. 145–146.

3. For an extended critique of Weber's views on bureaucracy, see Alvin W. Gouldner, "Metaphysical Pathos and the Theory of Bureaucracy," *American Political Science Review, 49* (1955), pp. 496–507.

4. William J. Chambliss, "Introduction," in William J. Chambliss (ed.), *Sociological Readings in the Conflict Perspective.* Reading, Mass.: Addison-Wesley, 1973, p. 25.

5. Celia S. Heller (ed.), *Structural Social Inequality.* New York: Macmillan, 1969, p. 4.

6. The view of stratification used here is based on Hans H. Gerth and C. Wright Mills, *Character and Social Structure.* New York: Harcourt, 1953/Harbinger Books, 1964.

7. Ibid., p. 307.

8. See Max Weber, "Class, Status, Party," in Hans H. Gerth and C. Wright Mills (eds. and trans.), *From Max Weber: Essays in Sociology.* New York: Oxford University Press, 1958, pp. 180–195.

9. This conception of the class structure in the United States owes a great deal to Bensman and Vidich, *The New American Society.*

10. Joseph Kahl, *The American Class Structure.* New York: Holt, Rinehart and Winston, 1967, pp. 187–193.

11. Politicians, for example, will sometimes send their children to public schools in order to show they are "just plain folks." Amy Carter, the daughter of President Jimmy Carter, who attends a local Washington, D. C. public school, is an obvious example.

12. Very little has been written about upper-class education by sociologists. This is true of analysis of the upper class in general, since, unlike the lower classes (who have been almost "studied to death"), they have the power to limit inquiry into their lives. For selective information on upper-class education, see E. Digby Baltzell, *The Protestant Establishment.* New York: Random House, 1964, pp. 335–352; and C. Wright Mills, *The Power Elite.* New York: Oxford University Press, 1956, pp. 63–68, 106–107, and 128–129.

13. For a discussion of how national priorities in education are set, see Joel Spring, *The Sorting Machine*. New York: McKay, 1976.

14. For an analysis of how those in positions of power define reality for a society, see Antonio Gramsci, *Selections from the Prison Notebooks,* edited and translated by Quintin Hoare and Geoffrey Nowell Smith. New York: International Publishers, 1971; and C. Wright Mills, "The Cultural Apparatus," in Irving Louis Horowitz (ed.), *Power, Politics and People: The Collected Essays of C. Wright Mills*. New York: Ballantine Books, 1964, pp. 405–422.

15. Former Secretary of State Henry Kissinger would be an exception to this rule.

16. For an analysis of how Catholics use Catholic colleges for this purpose, see Joseph A. Scimecca and Roland Damiano, *Crisis at St. John's: Strike and Revolution on the Catholic Campus*. New York: Random House, 1968.

17. We have relied heavily on Robert L. Church and Michael W. Sedlak, *Education in the United States: An Interpretive History*. New York: Free Press, 1976, for the historical sections that follow.

18. The following description of the institutionalization of bureaucracy in public education is based upon Michael B. Katz, *Class, Bureaucracy and Schools: The Illusion of Educational Change in America*. New York: Praeger, 1975, pp. 66–73.

19. Ibid., p. 72.

20. See in particular the standard work on the development of the high school in America, Edward Krug, *The Shaping of the American High School*. New York: Harper & Row, 1964.

21. Church and Sedlak, *Education in the United States*, p. 192.

22. See, for example, Paul C. Violas, *The Training of the Urban Working Class*. Chicago: Rand McNally, 1978.

23. For a documentary history of vocational education in America, see W. Norton Grubb and Marvin Lazerson (eds.), *American Education and Vocationalism: A Documentary History*. New York: Teachers College, 1974.

24. Quoted in Church and Sedlak, *Education in the United States*, p. 221.

25. Ellwood P. Cubberly, *Changing Conceptions of Education*. Boston: Houghton Mifflin, 1909, pp. 56–57.

26. Church and Sedlak, *Education in the United States*, p. 221.

II

Conflict in the Schools

3

The Student

The traditional view of the school in the United States is one in which the institution of public education was conceived to provide (and continues to provide) the means to guarantee an open and free society. Children who have the ability to succeed will do so, thereby insuring this open-class society. Upward social mobility, the "great American dream," can become a reality for every student who has the intellectual ability and is willing to work hard and make the sacrifices necessary to achieve success. Albert Shanker, head of the nation's largest teachers union local, writes that the "public schools have, by any reasonable standard, enjoyed great success. . . . Masses of immigrants, the poor, the illiterate have been educated and, through education, have achieved unprecedented upward social mobility."[1]

How accurate is this picture of the schools—what the revisionist historian Colin Greer has sarcastically labeled the "great school legend" (the professional educator's view that "once upon a time there was a great nation which became great because of its public schools")?[2] Not very! For once we look beyond the rhetoric, a very different picture emerges. Much closer to reality, as we shall see, is the conclusion reached by historian David Tyack, who, in surveying the origins of urban education, states that in spite of "frequent good intentions and abundant rhetoric about 'equal educational opportunity,' schools have rarely taught the children of the poor effectively—and this failure has been systematic, not idiosyncratic.''[3]

Before we begin our analysis, certain concepts we will be using—*education, schooling,* and *socialization* —must be defined in order for the reader to better understand the interrelationship between schools and society.

Education

Education can be either informal or formal. Informal education denotes ''patterns of education taking place within the family or neighborhood, or even within the school, under special situations such as field trips or extracurricular projects, where the usual forms of structured classroom instructions are not operative.''[4] The emphasis here is upon learning, which can take place anywhere. Formal education on the other hand, refers to what occurs in a designated institution whose basic purpose is the accomplishment of educational tasks—for example, a school. Although we will refer from time to time to informal education, our primary concern is with formal education. For our purposes, then, ''formal education'' will be used synonymously with schooling.

Schooling

A school is a relatively permanent organization which includes teachers, administrators, and students. Teaching is the principal activity of the school. ''Schooling,'' therefore, refers to the experience of attending a school. Schooling encompasses the various things that happen to people in school and the myriad activities they engage in while in attendance. Activities such as teaching, inadvertent learning, and such other nonlearning activities as obtaining a diploma or degree, being graded or evaluated, meeting friends, keeping children off the streets, providing free health care to students, and so on, are integral parts of the process of schooling.[5]

When we speak of education in the United States we are talking about schools. In particular, we are concerned with the socialization process that occurs in schools.

Socialization

Socialization refers to the process through which persons ''acquire the social patterns of the groups to which they belong and what the content of these patterns actually is.''[6]

Families and schools jointly socialize children into adult roles. For the most part, families and other nonschool groups are concerned primarily with familial and friendship roles. Schools, on the other hand, are most concerned with roles relating to work and public life. In an ideal situation, school socialization should build upon the initial and concurrent socialization experiences provided by the family; however, schooling is far from an ideal situation. In actuality, some of the most important educational problems originate in the conflict between the expectations of the home and school. A primary example are those educational objectives which are usually attainable for middle-class children but are often not accomplished by lower-class children.[7]

In keeping with the sociological perspective, when we talk of socialization, we mean the process whereby individuals learn the behaviors required for the performance of social roles. Socialization in schools is seen as a primary mission, a deliberate attempt to formally transmit the dominant behavior and value patterns of the larger American society to the younger generation.[8]

As we will show throughout this work, the school socialization process differentially affects different groups. Those in positions of power define role expectations and subsequently have an easier time meeting these expectations. School achievement and school failure, in this view, are both integral parts of a larger socialization process. Being a student in this country is largely a role-playing activity. As Sarene Boocock states:

> What children who fail to "make it" in school lack is role-playing skill, not the desire to succeed, and because they do not know how to play the role of student, they are less likely to do things that will lead to success.[9]

Since role-playing is first learned in the family, the logical place to begin our analysis of role-playing, socialization, and schooling is there. We will now focus upon the family as it affects success or failure in the schools.

THE FAMILY AND THE SCHOOLS

The family into which a child is born is a major determinant of his or her success in school. For the most part *the* most powerful predictor of school performance is the social class or socioeconomic status (SES) of the student's family. Countless studies have documented this relationship, a relationship which seems to exist no matter what measure of SES is used:

> It holds with a variety of achievement—aspiration variables, including grades, achievement test scores, retentions at grade level, course failures, truancy, suspensions from school, dropout rates, college plans, and total amount of formal schooling. It also predicts academic honors and awards, elective school offices, extent of participation in extracurricular activities, and other indicators of "success" in the informal structure of the student society. It holds, moreover, even when the powerful variables of ability and past achievement are controlled.[10]

Another important family characteristic which has an important effect on school performance is family size. Lower-class families are usually larger, and lower-class children often start school verbally disadvantaged because of their limited contact with adults. This social class—verbal disadvantage relationship has been documented by the English educational sociologist, Basil Bernstein, and will be more fully covered in Chapter 6.

SES is also related to a number of attitudinal variables which may intervene in the SES−school performance correlation. For instance, the communication of a certain set of values by middle-class parents, as well as an outlook on life that incorporates educational and occupational success, in turn produces higher actual achievement when the child gets to school.[11] In an early study, Herbert Hyman found that higher-status parents were more likely to perceive a college education as essential to economic success and advancement, whereas this was not the case for lower-status parents.[12] A few years later, Bernard Rosen found that middle-class individuals tended to show higher "need achievement"; this manifested itself in a value system and childrearing practices which he labeled as "achievement syndrome." The major characteristic of this syndrome was an orientation toward success in school and in later life.[13] By far the most comprehensive study of the relationship between social class and values for children has been carried out for the past two decades by Melvin Kohn and his associates at the National Institute of Mental Health.

Kohn's work shows that socialization techniques are related to the values and attitudes that are endemic to certain kinds of occupations.[14] According to Kohn, middle-class occupations differ from working-class occupations in at least three significant ways. First of all, middle-class occupations require skill in handling ideas and personal relationships, whereas working-class occupations are characterized by skill in handling objects and they require little talent in interpersonal interactions. Second, middle-class occupations permit self-direction; working-class occupations are usually much more closely supervised and more heavily routinized. Third, middle-class occupations are individual-oriented; working class occupations are group-oriented. These differences in types of work are in turn reflected in shared class value systems, into which children are socialized. This explains why middle-class parents, who value independence, initiative, and individuality, tend to teach their children to be responsible, self-reliant, and striving, while working-class parents, who value security and order, teach their children to be conforming and obedient. Kohn refers to these two different value orientations as "conformity" and "self-direction."[15] Middle-class parents relate to their children in terms of internality, with behavior evaluated on the basis of motives and underlying attitudes. Working-class parents, on the other hand, interact with their children in terms of externality, and judge their children's behavior by its consequences. Most importantly, Kohn stresses that parents' behaviors with their children reflect those attributes that are viable in their own lives. Working-class life requires conformity, authority, and rigidity, while middle-class life demands initiative, self-expression, and independence. The overall implication of Kohn's studies is that individual personality traits and values affect the occupations people obtain and, conversely, their job experiences affect their personalities and values. In terms of their relationships to their children, the higher SES parent wants his or her child to understand the world around him or her and to make sense of it through his or her own efforts. The lower SES parent, on the other hand, is mainly concerned with avoiding trouble by meeting the demands of those in positions of authority. These values are subsequently translated into success or failure in the schools, with middle-class children coming out on top at the expense of their lower-class counter-parts.[16]

As was stated before, of almost equal importance is the internal life of the family. Such considerations as parental expectations, modes of communication, distribution of power, and childrearing practices all contribute to academic achievement. Unfortunately, though, the evidence here is not as clear cut as it is with SES because very little research on family socialization directly links it with the school system. Informal education obviously plays a large role in the process and tends to create subcultural variations in socialization, which in turn affects motivation and achievement. However, until more evidence becomes available regarding informal education and socialization, we have to agree with Boocock who states: "The particular combination of social motives most conducive to high achievement and the particular patterns of socialization most likely to produce them have not been clearly established."[17] Keeping this in mind, we can now look at what the research on these other familial factors does show.

Parental Aspirations

Children who achieve tend to come from families that have high expec-tations for them. Joseph A. Kahl, for example, found that parents were the major influence upon academic achievement of students. Boys who had college aspira-tions had parents who were not satisfied with their own status and had therefore applied continuous pressure on their children to do better.[18] Parents who themselves either looked to their own middle-class values or who strived to emulate these values were more likely to instill them in their children. Once students acquired the motivation to achieve, their social-class background did not hold them back, but the initial acquisition of an achievement orientation was class-linked.

Another important contribution to academic achievement is a high level of parent—child interaction, especially in the form of positive adult response to the mastery of approved tasks.[19] A third variable that must be considered is the position of family members with respect to one another. The evidence seems to indicate a positive relationship between academic achievement and a relatively equalitarian family structure,[20] a situation most often found in the middle-class family.

Perhaps most important of all are behavior standards. Every individual acquires, in addition to language, those standards of behavior which determine how he or she will act in social situations, including the school classroom. Conformity has often been noted as a characteristic of high-achieving children. In this view, the high-achieving child has internalized the values of adults and therefore is treated preferentially. The middle-class child here is clearly at an advantage since, as we will show in the next chapter, teachers are predominantly middle-class and rarely question their own values.

Basically, although there is relatively little class difference among families in their attaching of a value to achievement (all parents want their children to achieve and recognize formal education as an important means), there is a class difference in the translation of these values into a workable set of life goals and strategies for attaining them. Parents of children who achieve in school successfully communicate this to their children and, more importantly, teach them the behaviors needed to fulfill these expectations.[21]

Thus, by the time they enter school, some children are already at a disadvantage. In particular, the lower-class child is immersed in a vicious cycle.

> Arriving at school without the speech patterns, the self-control and good manners, and the familiarity with books and other educational paraphernalia of his better prepared peers, the disadvantaged child will probably draw more inexperienced or incompetent teachers. Consequently he will perform poorly (and his performance will get lower relative to his middle-class age mates the longer he stays in school), get into more and more serious trouble, and leave school earlier, thus fulfilling teachers' and society's expectations for him—and guaranteeing that he will remain at the bottom of the social ladder.[22]

School roles, like all roles, are defined by those in power. Children (usually from the lower class) whose parents are in no position to challenge the values of the school start out at a disadvantage and never fully catch up. Indeed, the initial handicap of lower-class students widens over the years of schooling. School achievement, from the sociological perspective, is a role like any other, and those who are powerless do not achieve success. We can see this same principle at work in another area, one which transcends class—that of sex roles.

SEX-ROLE SOCIALIZATION

Sex, like race, is an attribute which is given to a child at birth, is highly visible, and, except under highly unusual circumstances, is permanent. Sex in our society is a role, and children are socialized into appropriate sex roles. In relation to education, boys and girls have different patterns of performance in school, and their experiences outside of school also differ in ways that affect academic motivation and achievement. What follows is an examination of the ability and personality characteristics which involve both sex and academic performance. We will then show how this affects the socialization of boys and girls with respect to achievement in general and school behavior in particular.

School Performance

The most interesting finding concerning sex and school performance is that certain specific skills are sex-related. Sex-role differentiation appears quite early; the evidence suggests that the thinking patterns of males and females are different, at least by the time both are old enough to be tested.[23] For instance, girls do better on tests of memory, and this superiority is especially clear at about the age of seven,[24] while boys tend to do better on tests which require spatial and mathematical ability.[25] Two questions need to be asked concerning these differences. First, how important are they for learning? Second, what are the implications for school achievement? The answer to the first is that sex-related differences in thinking are not very important. Schools are organized around the premise that learning is not entirely (or even primarily) a result of genetic or maturational abilities. Verbal, mathematical, spatial, and conceptual skills can be taught. This is not to imply that success in teaching these abilities is independent of the child's already developed readiness. However, if any group of children have not acquired certain intellectual skills that other children of their age possess, it is reasonable to assume that at least part of the problem lies in the teaching they have encountered.[26]

As to the second question, the answer must be analyzed in relation to a pronounced degree of discrimination against female students. Quite simply, the social conditions of schools are set up to reinforce sexual discrimination. As Patricia Sexton points out:

> The major discriminatory practices of elementary and secondary schools, aside from the aggravated pattern of male dominance in them, are probably to be found mainly in the schools' failure to encourage qualified female students to pursue studies and careers in nontraditional areas, such as science, math, technology, and the outright exclusion of females, at least in the past, from schools and courses of study that have been available to males.[27]

If girls are, on the average, less skilled in spatial and mechanical tasks, does this mean that fewer women should be admitted to programs in engineering, architecture, medicine, or dentistry?[28] This is presently the case, but, conversely, men are not discriminated against in professions that require skills in language, linguistic, and verbal skills. Obviously favoritism is at work here. Even more importantly, because men have been found to be more aggressive,[29] should they be in dominant political positions? As Maccoby and Jacklin state:

> There is nothing inevitable about male achievement of all available leadership positions. As women acquire the relevant competencies, and as these competencies become known to themselves and others, groups will less and less be formed on the initial assumption that the male members will have more of the needed skills. Leadership roles should thus gradually become more equitably distributed. There will no doubt continue to be groups in which physical strength, or agression-based dominance, will be the means of seizing leadership, or in which these traits are needed in a leader if the group is to achieve its goals. In such cases, we would expect leadership to gravitate to males. But in groups where leadership is achieved and held through skill in setting available goals, in planning, organizing, persuading, conciliating, and conveying enthusiasm, we see no reason for a sex bias.[30]

Yet incipient discrimination is found in elementary and secondary schools in the form of stereotypic definitions of authority and leadership roles. Males are believed to be better suited for leadership roles, and both teachers and students are socialized to accept these stereotypes. For instance, it has been well documented that teachers tend to have more interactions and longer conversations with the boys in their classrooms,[31] and that teachers see them as being the dominant sex in their classrooms.

In short, males dominate much of American society and its public school system. School administration, local and state boards of education, the U.S.

Office of Education, the National Education Association (NEA), the American Federation of Teachers (AFT), administration and boards of trustees in higher education—indeed, all groups that make, effect, or carry out policy in the public schools are overwhelmingly led and staffed by males.[32] Females have historically played a subordinate role and have learned this role in the family and in school. Girls are generally more compliant, conforming, and suggestible than boys, tending to conform more readily to directives from parents and teachers than do boys.[33] Outside of the evidence that boys have better spatial relations skills and girls better language acquisition skills, no real differences between the sexes can be explained by either biological or psychological variables,[34] yet girls achieve less than boys. The relationship between sex roles and school performance is explained by socialization, and can be summarized as follows:

> The structure of the student role and the educational system in general is in some important respects incongruent with sex-role expectations and performance, for *both boys and girls*. For boys, the feminine atmosphere of the school and the emphasis upon obedience and conformity, instead of upon more active learning, overshadow their first years in school, and they do not catch up with girls in performance until the clear linkages of academic achievement with occupational and other kinds of adult success make school and learning more relevant. For girls, intellectual interests and potentialities are increasingly repressed as they come to represent unfeminine competitiveness.[35]

The onesidedness of this differential achievement has led one writer to state: "The school is one institution that both perpetuates the myth of women's inferiority and helps to transform the myth into a reality."[36]

Because the whole issue of sex-role socialization is so controversial and important to any understanding of the contemporary experience in schools, we will devote a whole chapter (Chapter 11) to it. Suffice it to say for now that we believe that differences in achievement, both in school and in society, are not explained by any theory of innate differences. Girls do not achieve as much as boys because they are not expected to. Males are in positions of power and define societal expectations. The schools merely reinforce these already existing expectations. The schools as agents of socialization reinforce sexual stereotyping. Achievement, or lack of it, is reducible to role-socialization. This becomes even more obvious when we look at the literature on the effects of teacher expectations on school achievement.

TEACHER EXPECTATION EFFECTS ON SCHOOL ACHIEVEMENT

The major thrust of the literature having to do with teachers' expectations is centered around judgments teachers make about students and some of the results of these judgments. The teacher establishes the social-role structure of the classroom; students perceive this role, act out the role, and in so doing become locked into it.[37]

In essence, the teacher-assigned role becomes a self-fulfilling prophecy.[38] For as countless studies have shown, the major distinguishing characteristic of the student role is "passivity,"[39] which brings with it an acceptance of expectations. The good student is one who listens attentively to the teacher, does not disturb the class, and is receptive to the teacher's wishes. In a study of over 200 high school seniors, Bowles, Gintis, and Meyer found that the most rewarded personality trait was perseverance. This was followed in rank order by dependability, consistency, identification with school, empathy with orders, punctuality, deferment of gratification, external motivation, predictability, and tactfulness. Perhaps even more important were their findings concerning those personality traits which were most penalized. Creativity led the list, followed by aggressiveness and independence.[40]

In general, teachers make value judgments about children quite early, sometimes within the first week or month of the school year,[41] and on the basis of such factors as race, status of parents, and personal appearance.[42] All of these ideally should have nothing whatsoever to do with the child's ability to learn and achieve. Middle-class teachers' prejudgments that lower-class and minority students will be less successful academically than middle-class children can determine the entire school future of the child.[43] A recent case in point concerns an attitudinal study of high school teachers in Fairfax County, Virginia, an affluent suburb of Washington, D.C., and reputedly one of the best school systems in the nation. A questionnaire administered showed that the teachers had lower academic expectations for black students than for white students. More than half of the teachers questioned said they believed that minority students were not adequately prepared to take advanced academic courses.[44] The findings so troubled the county's top school administrators that they labeled the study "confidential" and asked school board members not to discuss it publicly.[45]

Authority is always on the side of the teacher and the teacher can impose his or her standards on students. The battle is unequal and usually comes out one way. At best, students develop strategies to cope with their subordinate positions. It is obvious, then, that teachers are extremely important in defining the attitudes and values of those who sit in their classrooms. Basically, teachers are engaged in a form of labeling behavior. The labeling perspective which originally developed in the study of crime and deviance[46] is an extremely useful device for identifying individuals who do not adapt themselves to the accepted behavior codes of the dominant group.

Social scientists who consider themselves labeling theorists see deviance in terms of social definitions. Deviance is a relative phenomenon, occurring when others (usually in positions of authority who have the power to enforce their definitions) define an action as deviant. The deviant is labeled, is allowed little if any chance to offset the label, and ultimately comes to accept the label as a definition of self. As Nanette Davis states, the basic premise of labeling theory is "that societal reaction in the form of labeling or official typing, and consequent stigmatization, leads to an altered identity in the actor, necessitating a reconstitution of self."[47] Although, obviously, the bulk of work done on the labeling perspective has been in criminology and deviance, nevertheless a small but growing body of literature does exist that applies this theoretical perspective to schools.

The Labeling Perspective and Schools

One of the earliest applications of the labeling perspective to schooling is Aaron Cicourel and John Kitsuse's *The Educational Decision-Makers* (1962).[48] Cicourel and Kitsuse investigated the process by which students came to be defined, classified, and recorded in the categories used in their high school records. They were particularly interested in how definitions and procedures were applied to students differentiated and labeled as "college material," "academic problems," "trouble-makers," and so on. They concluded that school counselors' judgments of students on the basis of a student's biography, social class, and "social type" were even more important in predicting school achievement than were the student's demonstrated ability and performance.

Perhaps the most famous study of all those in this perspective is Rosenthal and Jacobson's classic *Pygmalion in the Classroom* (1968).[49] It should be noted here that this work differs from the bulk of the "labeling theory" literature in that its primary purpose is to show the positive effects of labeling. In the Rosenthal and Jacobson study, all children in a lower SES elementary school in San Francisco were given a nonverbal intelligence test described to teachers as a test which would predict and identify academic "bloomers" or "spurters." One out of every five children was then randomly designated as a "spurter." This information was then given the teachers in the school. This "white lie" about the "blooming potential" of students who were no different than their peers constituted the total intervention of Rosenthal and Jacobson. Eight months later, all of the children were given the same test again. The results were startling. Depending upon the grade level, average gains of up to twenty-seven points in IQ scores were reported. Interesting attitudinal changes were also noted. The teachers rated the "spurters" as more curious, more interesting, more appealing, and generally better adjusted than their nonspurter peers.

In short, Rosenthal and Jacobson showed that teacher expectations played an exceedingly large role in the educational achievement of elementary school pupils. The other studies that we will examine look at the opposite side of the coin—school failure—and how teacher expectations are related to it. The first of these is by Ray Rist.[50]

Rist observed a group of black children in an urban ghetto school from the time they began kindergarten in September of 1967 until the end of the second grade, in order to analyze the impact of teacher expectations and social interactions on the social organization of a class. He was particularly interested in the relationship of teachers' expectations of potential academic performance to the social status of the student.

Rist's major finding was that

> the development of expectations by the kindergarten teacher as to the different-
> ial academic potential and capability of any student was significantly deter-

mined by a series of subjectively interpreted attributes and characteristics of that student. The argument may be succinctly stated in five propositions. First, the kindergarten teacher possessed a roughly constructed "ideal type" as to what characteristics were necessary for any given student to achieve "success" both in the public school and in the larger society. These characteristics appeared to be, in significant part, related to social class criteria. Secondly, upon first meeting her students at the beginning of the school year, subjective evaluations were made of the students as to possession or absence of the desired traits necessary for anticipated "success." On the basis of the evaluation, the class was divided into groups expected to succeed (termed by the teacher "fast learners") and those anticipated to fail (termed "slow learners.") Third, differential treatment was accorded to the two groups in the classroom, with the group designated as "fast learners" receiving the majority of the teaching time, reward-directed behavior, and attention from the teacher. Those designated as "slow learners" were taught infrequently, subjected to more frequent control-oriented behavior, and received little if any supportive behavior from the teacher. Fourth, the interactional patterns between the teacher and the various groups in her class became rigidified, taking on caste-like characteristics, during the course of the school year, with the gap in completion of academic material between the two groups widening as the school year progressed. Fifth, a similar process occurred in later years of schooling, but the teachers no longer relied on subjectively interpreted data as the basis for ascertaining differences in students. Rather, they were able to utilize a variety of informational sources related to past performance as the basis for classroom grouping.[51]

On the basis of such sources of knowledge as an interview with parents, a report by the school social worker which provided a tentative list of those children whose families were on welfare, and the teacher's past experience with older siblings, the children were broken into groups eight days after the start of the year. "Fast learners" were seated at table 1, and those children who "had no idea of what was going on in the classroom" were seated at tables 2 and 3. Rist believes that those children chosen to be seated at table 1 closely fit the teacher's "ideal type" of successful child. The reference group she used, according to him, was a black–white, well-educated middle class. The teacher had determined what constituted a "fast learner" by using as the basis for her judgment those attributes most desired by educated members of the middle class. These characterists were: (1) ease of interaction among adults; (2) high degree of verbalization in Standard American English; (3) the ability to become a leader; (4) a neat and clean appearance; (5) a family that is educated, employed, living together, and interested in the child; and (6) the ability to participate well as a member of a group.[52]

The teacher ascribed a high status to a certain group of children who fit in with her preconceived notions of what was necessary to be a "fast learner." She then proceeded, during the course of the year, to respond favorably to this group (table 1) and negatively to the other groups. In Rist's words:

> The organization of the kindergarten classroom according to the expectation of success or failure after the eighth day of school became the basis for the differential treatment of the children for the remainder of the school year. From

the day that the class was assigned permanent seats, the activities in the class-room were perceivably different from previously. The fundamental division of the class into those expected to learn and those expected not to permeated the teacher's orientation to the class.[53]

The first-grade experience for the children was more of the same. Here, again, the children were divided into three groups, this time tables "A," "B," and "C." Those children placed at table "A" had all been at table 1 during kindergarten. No student who had been at table 2 or 3 in kindergarten was assigned to table "A." All of tables 2 and 3 (with one exception) were placed at table "B," with table "C" consisting of those children who were repeating the first grade. Rist refers to this seating arrangement as a "caste phenomenon"[54] since there was absolutely no upward mobility into the high ability or "fast learner" group for any of the "slower" students.

The second grade also perpetuated the original kindergarten classification scheme. The second-grade teacher divided the children into three ability groups called "Tigers," "Cardinals," and "Clowns." As before, no student who had not sat at table "A" in first grade was assigned to the high-ability "Tiger" group. At this point, school policy reinforced the teacher's views; no child could demonstrate competence at a higher reading level and advance because all children had to continue at the pace of his or her reading group. The "self-fulfilling prophecy" was in full operation; a "slow learner" had no option but to continue as a "slow learner," no matter what his or her performance.[55] Thus, on the basis of a single teacher's judgments, made eight days after entering kindergarten, children were locked into a student role that proscribed success or failure for them throughout their school career. They were "labeled" early and the school system perpetuated the initial judgment of the kindergarten teacher. Labeling is also prevalent in a study of the English school system, reported by Hargreaves, Hester, and Mellor.[56]

Although this study was carried out in Great Britain, we can easily generalize to America's public schools. The authors found that "appearance, conformity to discipline role aspects, conformity to academic role aspects, likeability, and peer group relations,"[57] were the most important variables in "typing" students. Hargreaves et al. then build upon this to develop a theory of labeling or, to use their word, "typing."

> The theory proposes that pupils are typed or formulated by teachers in three stages. The first stage, that of "speculation," begins when the teacher first comes to know about and/or to meet the pupil for the first time. The third stage, that of "stabilization," marks the point at which the teacher has a relatively clear and stable conception of the identity of the pupils. He "knows" the pupil; he understands him, he finds little difficulty in making sense of his acts and is not puzzled or surprised by what he does or says. The second stage, that of "elaboration," stands between the other two states. . . . These stages should not be regarded as highly discrete or distinct stages that can easily be distinguished. Although the stages do occur in a sequence, they do not refer to distinctive periods of time. A stage is characterized by certain problems and

processes. The stages fuse into each other, both in the sense that they can overlap in time and in the sense that processes from different stages can and do occur at the same point in time.[58]

Applications of the Hargreaves position can be found in recent studies of American schools. Francis Ianni and his associates at the Horace Mann—Lincoln Institute document the use of "sorting," which is similar to labeling and typing. In studying the social organization of a multiracial New York City high school, they found that students are sorted into perspective groupings largely by racial or ethnic identification. Chinese students, for example, were perceived as bright, studious, academically oriented, and highly motivated, whereas black students were seen as being generally poor students lacking both motivation and ability.[59]

Further evidence of the ethnic and racial dimension of the labeling perspective can be found in Jane Mercer's work on the prevalence of mental retardation in the elementary schools of Riverside, California.[60] Mercer found that "mental retardate" is an acquired role like such others as "talented," "slow," and "average." More Mexican-American and black children were placed in classes for the mentally retarded. In many instances these classifications did not correspond to IQ and other objective tests.

Labeling also plays a prominent role in Gerry Rosenfeld's study of a Harlem elementary school.[61] Rosenfeld found that teachers assumed that the lower-class black students were "unwilling to change" and "were of little worth as they were." Teachers believed that their students could not be worked with; that they were not ready for learning. Thus, if a student failed it was always his or her fault, never the teachers', given the insufficient human material with which they had to work. Failure was tied to the cultural milieu of the school. Rosenfeld's conclusions are summed up in the following statement:

> The examination of Harlem School has revealed that the requirements for being a student were much more stringent than were the requirements for being a teacher. And the penalties for failure in the student role were much more harsh and longer lasting than the penalties for failing to teach. The teacher—learner relationship was not reciprocal; rather, it placed an altogether incommensurable burden on the child. It placed him at a disadvantage in the strivings toward reasonable life chances. Problems unsurmounted in the classroom made for compounded problems in later years, diminishing the skills with which his education purportedly prepared him.[62]

Basically, then, the labeling system asserts that when one party in a relationship is disproportionately powerful, he or she is able to label those in subordinate positions. Equally important is that this is accomplished while maintaining the appearance of justice and rationality. Because all decisions based upon power can ultimately prove unpredictable and inefficient, legitimacy has to be established. Students who are labeled "slow learners" and who are not allowed to achieve in school must come to accept this label. This is accomplished via the use of the individualistic perspective, a stress upon individual responsibility for success or failure. Children fail because there is something wrong with them, not with the schools. They must be socialized to accept their position of inferiority. The schools have been fairly successful in linking the concept of individualistic responsibility to the legitimacy process. Students are socialized to accept the values of the status quo, which is said to provide equal opportunity for all. If they fail to achieve in school and society, no one can then say they did not have the opportunity to achieve.

SUMMARY

We have tried to show in this chapter that failure and achievement on the part of students is best seen as role behavior. Students achieve, not because of any innate superiority but due to the social class background of their parents. Children fail by the same token, because they were born to lower-class parents.

In short, those without power, those least likely to define the situations in which they find themselves, are more likely to be forced to accept a negative or inferior role. Under this conflict perspective girls tend to achieve less than boys, not because they are less ''bright'' than boys but because fewer women are in positions of power in our society and in our schools. It is the same for lower-class males and anyone else whose role behavior is defined and reinforced by those in superordinate positions. Conflict and power, not innate abilities, define the role of student, as well as the role of teachers and administrators who compromise the social system of the school, as we shall see in the next two chapters.

NOTES

1. Albert Shanker, ''The Big Lie About the Public Schools,'' *The New York Times,* May 9, 1971, U.F.T. Column.

2. Colin Greer, *The Great School Legend.* New York: Viking, 1971, p. 3.

3. David B. Tyack, *The One Best System: A History of American Urban Education.* Cambridge, Mass.: Harvard University Press, 1974, p. 11.

4. Seymour W. Itzkoff, *A New Public Education.* New York: McKay, 1975, p. 13.

5. Ibid., p. 12.

6. Audrey James Schwartz, *The Schools and Socialization.* New York: Harper & Row, 1975, p. xiv.

7. Ibid., p. xv.

8. Ibid., p. 1.

9. Sarene Boocock, *An Introduction To The Sociology of Learning.* Boston: Houghton Mifflin, 1972, p. 76.

10. Ibid., p. 36.

11. Ibid., p. 37.

12. Herbert H. Hyman, ''The Value Systems of Different Classes: A Social Psychological Contribution to the Analysis of Stratification,'' in R. Bendix and S.M. Lipset (eds.), *Class, Status and Power.* New York: Free Press, 1953, p. 438.

13. Bernard C. Rosen, ''The Achievement Syndrome: A Psycho-cultural Dimension of Social Stratification,'' *American Sociological Review, 21* (1956), pp. 203–211.

14. Melvin L. Kohn, ''Social Class and Parent–Child Relationships: An Interpretation,'' *American Journal of Sociology, 68* (1963), pp. 471–480.

15. Melvin L. Kohn, *Class and Conformity.* Homewood, Ill.: Dorsey Press, 1969.

16. For an exception, which questions the relationship of SES and school achievement, see Ralph H. Turner, *The Social Context of Ambition*. San Francisco: Chandler, 1964.

17. Boocock, *Sociology of Learning,* p. 60.

18. Joseph A. Kahl, "Educational and Occupational Aspirations of 'Common Man' Boys," *Harvard Educational Review, 23* (1953), pp. 186−203.

19. See in particular L. F. Cervantes, "The Isolated Nuclear Family and the Drop-out," *Sociological Quarterly, 6* (1965), pp. 103−118; and Bernard S. Rosen and R. D'Andrade, "The Psycho-social Origin of Achievement Motivation," *Sociometry, 22* (1959), pp. 185−217.

20. See Glen H. Elder, "Family Structure and Educational Attainment," *American Sociological Review, 30* (1965), pp. 81−96; and Fred L. Strodtbeck, "Family Interaction, Values and Achievement," in David C. Mc Clelland et al. (eds.), *Talent and Society.* New York: Van Nostrand, 1958, pp. 135−194.

21. Boocock, *Sociology of Learning,* pp. 75−76.

22. Ibid., pp. 76−77.

23. Ibid., p. 81.

24. See H. Amster and V. Wiegand, "Developmental Study of Sex Differences in Free Recall," *Proceedings,* 80th Annual Convention, American Psychological Association, 1972; E. Felzen and M. Anisfeld, "Semantic and Phonetic Relations in the False Recognition of Words by Third and Sixth-grade Children," *Developmental Psychology, 3* (1970), pp. 163−168; and E. G. Sitkes and C. E. Meyers, "Comparative Structure of Intellect in Middle- and Lower-class Four-year-olds of Two Ethnic Groups," *Developmental Psychology, 1* (1969), pp. 592−604.

25. M. E. Backman, "Patterns of Mental Abilities: Ethnic, Socioeconomic and Sex Differences," *American Educational Research Journal, 9* (1972), pp. 1−21; T. A. Gerace and W. E. Caldwell, "Perceptual Distortion as a Function of Stimulus Objects, Sex, Naivete, and Trials Using a Portable Model of the Ames Distorted Room," *Genetic Psychology Monographs, 84* (1971), pp. 3−33; I. G. Sarason and J. Minard, "Text Anxiety, Experimental Instructions and the Wechsler Adult Intelligence Scale," *Educational Psychology, 53* (1962), pp. 299−302; and P. S. Very, "Differential Factor Structures in Mathematical Abilities," *Genetic Psychology Monographs, 75* (1967), pp. 169−207.

26. Eleanor E. Maccoby and Carol N. Jacklin, *The Psychology of Sex Differences.* Stanford, Calif.: Stanford University Press, 1974, pp. 127−128.

27. Patricia Sexton, *Women in Education.* Bloomington, Ind.: Phi Delta Kappa Educational Foundation, 1976, p. 64.

28. For example, 98 percent of all Bachelors of Engineering degrees and 91 percent of all Bachelors of Architecture degrees awarded in 1975−1976 were awarded to men. Ninety-six percent of all graduating dentists and 84 percent of medical doctors in 1974 were also men. *Digest of Educational Statistics.* Washington, D.C.: U.S. Department of Health, Education and Welfare, 1977−1978, pp. 110, 115.

29. See F. A. Pedersen, and R. Q. Bell, "Sex Differences in Preschool Children without Histories of Complications in Pregnancy and Delivery," *Developmental Psychology, 3* (1970), pp. 10−15; P. K. Smith and K. Connolly, "Patterns of Play and Social Interaction in Pre-school Children," in N. B. Jones (ed.), *Ethological Studies of Child Behavior.* London: Cambridge University Press, 1972, pp. 65−95; and L.A. Serbin, K.D. O'Leary, R.N. Kent, and J.A. Tonick, "A Comparison of Teacher Response to the Pre-academic and Problem Behavior of Boys and Girls," *Child Development, 44* (1973), pp. 796−804.

30. Maccoby and Jacklin, *Psychology of Sex Differences,* p. 370.

31. Ibid., p. 135.

32. See Sexton, *Women in Education,* pp. 55−60.

33. Maccoby and Jacklin, *Psychology of Sex Differences,* p. 272.

34. Ibid., pp. 303−374.

35. Boocock, *Sociology of Learning,* p. 95.

36. Bonnie Cook Freeman, "Female Education in Patriarchical Power Systems," in Philip G. Altbach and Gail P. Kelly (eds.), *Education and Colonialism.* New York: Longman, 1978, p. 207.

37. Thomas W. Collins and George W. Noblitt, "The Process of Interracial Schooling: An Assessment of Conceptual Frameworks and Methodological Orientations," in National Institute of Education,

The Desegregation Literature, A Critical Appraisal. Washington, D. C.: U. S. Department of Health, Education and Welfare, 1976, p. 91.

38. Doris R. Entwisle and Murray Webster, Jr., "Expectations in Mixed Racial Groups," *Sociology of Education, 47* (1974), pp. 301−318.

39. See in particular Philip Jackson, *Life in Classrooms.* New York: Holt, Rinehart and Winston, 1968.

40. Samuel Bowles, Herbert Gintis, and Peter Meyer, "The Long Shadow of Work: Education, the Family and the Reproduction of the Social Division of Labor," *Insurgent Sociologist, V* (1975), pp. 12−13.

41. See Nathaniel Hickerson, *Education for Alienation.* Englewood Cliffs, N. J.: Prentice-Hall, 1966; and Ray C. Rist, "Student Social Class and Teacher Expectations: The Self-fulfilling Prophecy in Ghetto Education," *Harvard Educational Review, 40* (1970).

42. Ray C. Rist, "The Milieu of a Ghetto School as a Precipitator of Educational Failure," *Phylon, 33* (1972), pp. 348−360.

43. Philip L. Alsworth and Roger R. Woock, "Ocean Hill, Brownsville: Urban Conflict and the Schools," *Urban Education, 4* (1970), pp. 25−40; and Kenneth B. Clark, "Clash of Cultures in the Classroom," in Meyer Weinberg (ed.), *Integrated Education—Learning Together.* Chicago: Integrated Education Association, 1964, pp. 18−25.

44. Athelia Knight, "Teacher Attitudes on Blacks Sparked Va. Dispute," *The Washington Post,* May 9, 1978, p. C-1.

45. Ibid.

46. The labeling theory in criminology and deviance can be traced to the works of Howard S. Becker, *The Outsiders.* New York: Free Press, 1963; Edwin Lemert, *Human Deviance, Social Problems and Social Control.* Englewood Cliffs, N.J.: Prentice-Hall, 1967; and Frank Tannanbaum, *Crime and Community.* Boston: Ginn, 1938.

47. Nanette J. Davis, "Labeling Theory in Deviance Research: A Critique and Reconsideration," *Sociological Quarterly, 13* (1972), p. 460.

48. Aaron Cicourel and John Kitsuse, *The Educational Decision-Makers.* Indianapolis: Bobbs-Merrill, 1963.

49. Robert Rosenthal and Lenore Jacobson, *Pygmalion in the Classroom: Teacher Expectations and Pupils' Intellectual Development.* New York: Holt, Rinehart and Winston, 1968.

50. Rist, "Student Social Class and Teacher Expectations."

51. Ibid., pp. 72−73.

52. Ibid., p. 81.

53. Ibid., p. 82.

54. Ibid., p. 90.

55. Ibid., p. 94.

56. David H. Hargreaves, Stephen K. Hestor, and Frank J. Mellor, *Deviance in Classrooms.* London: Routledge, 1975.

57. Ibid., p. 17.

58. Ibid., p. 145.

59. Cited in NIE, *The Desegregation Literature,* p. 152.

60. Jane R. Mercer, *Labelling the Mentally Retarded.* Berkeley, Calif.: University of California Press, 1973.

61. Gerry Rosenfeld, *Shut Those Thick Lips: A Study of Slum School Failure.* New York: Holt, Rinehart and Winston, 1971.

62. Ibid., p. 94.

4
Teachers

The position of "teacher" is a role, and like any other role has appropriate behavior patterns and a normative structure attached to it. The role of teacher, therefore, is not dependent upon the personality of its occupant. Just as the personality of any individual is seen as being constant over time regardless of the various roles he or she acts out, so the role associated with a position is seen as basically similar for the different individuals who may fill it. Personality and role are not, however, always unrelated. On the one hand, certain individuals may be attracted to a particular role because they perceive it as being one which will satisfy their personality needs. On the other hand, the effect of constantly playing a role usually insures that an individual's personality is influenced by his or her behavior in that role. The role of teacher is an excellent example of just this. Individuals bring with them certain characteristics and, in turn, once socialized they take on specific characteristics which together form the total role of teacher. Therefore, our analysis of the role of teacher will be in two parts: the first will be a description of such background characteristics as educational attainment, sex, attitudes toward teaching, social-class background, and political preferences prospective teachers bring with them. The second part will consist of a historical analysis of the role of teacher, tracing its development from Colonial times to show how these antecedents have profound implications for the present. By combining these two perspectives we will gain a greater insight into what it means to be a teacher in the United States.

BACKGROUND CHARACTERISTICS OF THE PUBLIC SCHOOL TEACHER[1]

Educational Background

Our teachers are highly educated. The nondegree teacher has almost disappeared in the 1970s; 99 percent of teachers hold a bachelor's degree and over one-third have a master's degree or higher. Of particular importance is that over three-quarters of all teachers received their bachelor's degree (75.5 percent) and master's degrees (79.1 percent) from public institutions. We can infer from this that teachers overwhelmingly attended institutions that cater to the middle class, since public-supported institutions have for a long time performed this function.

TABLE 4–1   HIGHEST DEGREE HELD[2]

	Total			
	1961	*1966*	*1971*	*1976*
Less than bachelor's	14.6	7.0	2.9	0.9
Bachelor's	61.9	69.6	69.6	61.6
Master's or six years	21.3	23.2	27.1	37.1
Doctor's	0.4	0.1	0.4	0.4

Sex

The latest figures available concerning the sex of teachers shows that women teachers outnumber men teachers by a two-to-one margin. More men, however, teach in secondary schools than do women. Out of a total teaching population of 2,155, 455, women account for 1,432,580, or 66 percent of the total, while men number 772,868 (34 percent). Further breakdowns into elementary and secondary teaching show that of a total of 1,175,980 elementary school teachers, 978,557 (83 percent) are women and only 197,423 (17 percent) are men. As for secondary school teachers, men constitute 525,445 (54 percent) and women 454,023 (46 percent) of the 979,468 total.[3]

The figures for leadership roles, however, present a different picture; only about 15 percent of principals and one-half of 1 percent of superintendents are women. Approximately 19 percent of elementary school principals are women, but less than 4 percent of junior high and 3 percent of senior high school principals are women.[4] These figures point to a male-dominated school system where women are primarily subservient. As Patricia Sexton states:

> Male dominance in school leadership ensures that: Males make all the important decisions in the school system, decisions that undoubtedly perpetuate sex stereotypes and inequalities; women by their exclusion are denied vocational opportunities and access to high prestige and high salary jobs for which many are qualified; the most damaging of all sex stereotypes, that only males are capable of high level leadership, is thereby confirmed in the minds of the young

and of the general public. Both males and females are socialized to believe and advocate male dominance.[5]

Furthermore, such a system of male dominance reinforces a basic conservatism among teachers. First of all, beginning male teachers have little or no intention of ending their careers as classroom teachers. One government-sponsored study showed that 71 percent of beginning male teachers intended to leave the classroom; 51 percent hoped for a higher ranking position within the schools, and the rest (20 percent) anticipated leaving teaching altogether.[6] Male teachers clearly desire to attain an administrative position, which, as will be shown in the next chapter, is a role whose location in the bureaucratic structure makes for extreme conservatism. Anticipatory socialization, the aspiring toward a higher rank and the internalizing of role expectations, thus acts to create a conservative male teacher.[7]

Generally speaking, women teachers have different ambitions than men teachers. Teaching allows women to facilitate what Dan Lortie has called ''in-and-out plans.''[8] Teaching allows women to leave for a while, then reenter the occupation and only lose incremental earnings for the period they were away. Lortie also points out that the ''in-and-out'' pattern is premised on the assumption that no major technical changes are likely to take place while one is away; so those who leave for a time (married women in particular) may, consciously or not, have a stake in a slow rather than rapid change in teaching techniques.[9]

In short, young men are pushed to conservatism by being forced to emulate administrators as models. Women are kept from positions of authority, and because married women may leave, they often are not really committed to educational innovation. Lortie has summed up this type of conservatism. He writes:

> There is a clear congruence between teachers' preferences and conservatism of outlook. What teachers consider desirable change can be summed up as ''more of the same''; they believe the best program of improvement removes obstacles and provides for more teaching with better support. They want arrangements to ''unleash'' their capacities. Their approach is implicitly conservative; in assuming that current instructional tactics are adequate if properly supported, the blame for deficiencies is laid upon the environment. Remedies lie in changing the environment, not in finding more efficacious ways to instruct.[10]

Attitudes toward Teaching

Occupational characteristics attract people to a given line of work. The characteristic that attracted teachers more than any other is the desire to work with young people. Seventy-one percent of those in the NEA sample listed this as one of their three main reasons for entering teaching. (It was the only reason chosen by a majority of teachers). Next was interest in subject matter, which was stated by 38 percent. The value of education to society closely followed (34 percent). As would be expected, a much larger proportion of secondary than elementary teachers have been drawn to teaching by an interest in a subject matter (59 percent of secondary school teachers choose this). This, however, was still second to the desire to work with young people (66 percent).

TABLE 4–2[11]   REASONS FOR CHOOSING TO TEACH, BY SEX

	Total	Men	Women
Desire to work with young people	71.4	71.0	71.6
Interest in subject matter	38.3	50.3	32.3
Value of education to society	34.2	29.8	36.3
Long summer vacation	19.1	20.9	18.1
Influence of family	18.4	10.9	22.1
Job security	17.4	23.4	14.5
Influence of a teacher	5.5	6.9	4.8
Financial rewards	4.3	4.3	2.0
Employment mobility	3.0	4.5	2.3

Teachers are thus attracted to teaching by the lure of ''psychic rewards'' (''getting through to a student,'' ''teaching a student to read'') rather than extrinsic rewards (usually monetary). Although there is nothing wrong with such aspirations (indeed, they are among the most noble in our society), a tendency to overact, to become a moral agent, has been noted as a characteristic of teachers. The result of a study of five towns in Florida shows that:

> Although some respondents stressed the desirability of independence of mind, most allusions to moral outcomes and citizenship emphasized compliance and obedience. Connecting compliance with classroom norms to future citizenship authenticates the teacher's control efforts. Thus discipline becomes more than mere forbidding and ordering; the dross of classroom management is transformed into the gold of dependable citizenship. Whereas some critics of schools cry ''oppression'' at teacher dominance of classrooms, these respondents see it as preparing citizens for the Republic.[12]

An unrelated but perhaps even more important reason for the stress placed on psychic rewards is that teachers are hindered in attempts to collectively organize to change conditions of their work. If their basic rewards come from their interaction with their students, they are more likely to attempt to change only their immediate environment (their classroom) rather than the school or the society it reflects. Society, too, has an interest in seeing that teachers look to other than financial aspects: that of keeping the cost of schooling down. (As we shall see in Chapter 8, this has been changing as teachers organize and demand extrinsic rewards—a situation that has produced a great deal of conflict.)

Social-class Background

Using a social class index based upon father's occupation (which, though far from precise,[13] is still useful), the NEA survey shows that more than half (53.7 percent) of all teachers come from blue-collar working-class or farm backgrounds. Moreover, 61.1 percent of all men teachers and 49.9 percent of women teachers come from a working-class background (see Table 4-3).

TABLE 4–3 FATHER'S OCCUPATION[14]

	Total %			Sex						School Level					
				Men			Women			Elementary			Secondary		
	1961	1971	1976	1961	1971	1976	1961	1971	1976	1961	1971	1976	1961	1971	1976
Farmer	26.5	19.3	15.2	22.0	16.3	10.9	29.5	20.9	17.1	30.3	23.0	15.7	21.7	15.3	14.5
Unskilled worker	6.5	8.4	9.9	8.7	9.6	11.8	5.4	7.8	9.0	6.2	8.0	8.8	6.8	6.8	11.1
Skilled or semi-skilled worker	23.4	25.7	28.6	30.3	34.3	38.4	20.2	21.2	23.8	21.4	23.4	26.7	25.9	28.3	30.5
Clerical or sales work	7.1	5.5	5.7	7.3	6.1	4.7	7.1	5.2	6.3	7.3	4.9	6.2	6.9	6.2	5.3
Managerial worker or self-employed	22.0	22.1	20.5	22.1	24.9	19.2	21.6	22.5	21.1	21.6	22.5	21.8	27.6	21.7	19.1
Professional or semi-professional worker	14.5	18.9	20.1	11.8	17.0	15.0	15.7	19.8	22.6	13.2	18.2	20.8	16.1	19.6	19.4

Teaching can, therefore, be viewed as a definite upward mobility step for men (slightly less so for women), and teachers can easily be classified as highly likely to manifest what Richard Hofstadter has labeled "status anxiety."[15] Briefly stated, "status anxiety," or "status politics" as the phenomenon is also referred to, is seen as instrumental in understanding any group which desires to improve or maintain its status. Essentially the process manifests itself, to use one example, in a group's out-middle-classing the middle class; in a word, becoming "superpatriots." Those who have just moved into the middle class are not yet secure in their position and they overidentify with their new class.[16] Although the notion of "status anxiety" or "status politics" by itself is not enough to generalize to a conservative outlook among teachers, when taken with other findings—in particular, their own statements about their political beliefs—a picture of a conservative person emerges.

Expressed Political Behavior

Teachers as a group are usually seen as basically middle-of-the-road in political preference. However, when asked about their political philosophy, teachers show a definite trend toward the conservative side; 62 percent consider themselves conservative and only 38 percent consider themselves liberal.[17] In light of the previous characteristics shown, this expressed conservatism should come as no surprise. Whether or not it represents a predisposition to conservatism or whether it is a learned political behavior is difficult to ascertain from the available data. Suffice it to say, for now, that teachers are basically conservative and, as we shall now see, have been so since the beginnings of the public schools in this nation.

THE HISTORICAL ROLE OF THE TEACHER IN AMERICAN SOCIETY

A basic premise in this discussion is that the major role of the teacher is that of subordinate, a position which carries with it the expectations of docility and passivity. Teachers have historically been forced into a conforming, conservative role, and in most instances have gone along with the second-class citizenship such a position entails. The following excerpts from a teacher's contract illustrate what was quite commonly expected of the teacher fifty years ago.

> I promise to take a vital interest in all phases of Sunday-school work, donating of my time, service, and money without stint for the uplift and benefit of the community.
> I promise to abstain from all dancing, immodest dressing, and other conduct unbecoming a teacher and a lady.
> I promise not to go out with any young men except in so far as it may be necessary to stimulate Sunday-school work.
> I promise not to fall in love, to become engaged or secretly married.
> I promise not to encourage or tolerate the least familiarity on the part of any of my boy pupils.

I promise to sleep at least eight hours a night, to eat carefully and to take every precaution to keep in the best of health and spirits, in order that I may be better able to render efficient service to my pupils.

I promise to remember that I owe a duty to the townspeople who are paying my wages, that I owe respect to the school board and the superintendent that hired me, and I shall consider myself at all times the servant of the school board and the townspeople.[18]

The contract presented above is obviously written with a woman teacher in mind; and the generally held view of teaching is that it is and always was a woman's occupation. Historically, however, this was not the case. Teachers in Colonial America were usually men. Women teachers, who constituted a minority, taught primarily in "dame's schools," in which pupils came to the teacher's home.

It was only as public education expanded during the nineteenth century that schools became staffed primarily by women. By 1870, for example, women outnumbered men teachers by approximately 123,000 to 78,000.[19] This feminization of teaching is best explained economically, since women could be and were hired for less money than men. Teaching was also highly attractive for women since they did not have as many alternatives open to them as did men. The major employment options for women were domestic service, employment in factories, and extensions of such female functions in the home as laundering and baking. It was not until the twentieth century that office opportunities, and such other "feminine" occupations as nursing, social work, and library positions became readily available to women. Equally importantly, women were considered to be more malleable and conforming, according to the Victorian image of nineteenth-century woman.

A parallel consideration was the community's continuous belief that they could dictate the private lives of the teacher. From the first inception of public schools, communities took the position that the school was theirs to control, not the educators'. As David Tyack points out, "with no bureaucracy to serve as a buffer between himself and the patrons, with little sense of being part of a professional establishment, the teacher found himself subordinated to the community."[20] Thus, sex-role expectations for females coincided quite nicely with the public's desire to control as many aspects of schooling as possible. For example, a woman's right to retain her job after marriage was not established until 1904, when a married school teacher in Brooklyn, New York, was finally reinstated by the courts with back pay, after having been dismissed when it became known she had married. The court ruled that marriage "was not misconduct."[21]

After this a married woman could be employed in the New York City schools, but in 1913, a married teacher in the Bronx, Mrs. Bridget Pexitto, was dismissed for having become pregnant. Principals were ordered by the Board of Education and Superintendent to search out any other teachers who might be "showing." It was only after Mrs. Pexitto took the case to the State Commissioner of Education that she was rehired. Perhaps a *New York Times* editorial best summed up the general community sentiment toward the rights of teachers when it stated that it believed the school system was a:

victim of that comparatively new and disturbing malady called feminism. Time was when women married and took up the conjugal relation expected thereafter to devote themselves to the care of their home and training of their children. This woman is representative of a new order. She claims the right to hold her place in the public service when she is obviously unfit to perform the duties attached to it. . . . There are plenty of widows and women with living husbands well fitted to serve as teachers. But the action of the Board of Education in the case of Mrs. Pexitto was in the public interest.[22]

While things have obviously gotten better for teachers, in many school districts they are still treated as less than first-class citizens. Indeed, it is questionable as to whether teaching affords the same civil rights as do other occupations. Fischer and Schimmel call attention to how controls are surreptitiously used to revoke the Bill of Rights for teachers.

A known history of social dissent, though peaceful and lawful, is commonly viewed with suspicion by hiring authorities. Screening committees and administrators are concerned with the efficient functioning of their schools. They tend to view social activists as potential troublemakers who will interfere with the smooth running of a "tight ship." Viewed with suspicion is a history of activism in "peace movements," "Black power," "Women's liberation," "World Federalism," and perhaps most suspect of all, "Gay Liberation."

Open support of similar causes by teachers often leads to harassment, disciplinary actions, and at times, dismissal. Most teachers do not fight unwarranted disciplinary action, choosing rather to negotiate a quiet resignation with a positive letter of recommendation that makes possible a new job and, therefore, economic survival in some other community. Most administrators would rather "settle" the matter in the same way in order to avoid public controversy, which might endanger the next bond issue. Thus, in a way both teachers and administrators contribute to the erosion of civil rights.[23]

Given the current job shortage in education and the fiscal predicament in which most communities now find themselves, a very real "chilling effect" permeates our schools. It is the brave teacher, indeed, who, faced with the prospect of unemployment, will take a controversial stand. Teachers, quite simply, are in positions of subordination. Although they would like to claim the same status and rewards as professionals do in our society, they cannot. A look at the whole question of professionalism will bear this out.

PROFESSIONALISM

Numerous writers have defined the conditions under which an occupation may legitimately be refered to as a profession.[24] We have taken from the literature on professionalism what we consider to be the most important characteristics of professionalism and present them below:

1.   A unique, definite, and essential social service.

2. A long period of specialized training.
3. A broad range of autonomy for both the individual practitioners and the occupation as a whole.
4. An esoteric body of knowledge to be used in performing the service.
5. A comprehensive self-governing organization of practitioners.
6. Control over entry into the profession.

Of the six, the only characteristic that we can accept is the first one. Teaching is obviously a unique and essential social service. However, when we come to the next five we doubt very much that teaching meets their criteria.

A Long Period of Specialized Training

Two kinds of schooling are involved in work socialization—*general schooling* and *special schooling*. Compared with occupations in general, teaching requires relatively long general schooling, with a bachelor's degree as a minimum requirement. Special schooling for teachers, on the other hand, is not as long as that found in such professions as medicine, law, or engineering. Also, education as a specialized subject of study simply has not been characterized by any intellectual rigor; at best it has borrowed from other disciplines. (This will be more fully discussed when we look at the fourth criterion of professionalism.)

Compared with crafts, professions, and highly skilled trades, arrangements for what Dan Lortie has referred to as a "mediated entry"[25] (a process whereby an individual is gradually taught what is expected of him or her) are generally undeveloped for teaching. The only major device available is "student" or "practice" teaching, which is short and fairly casual. Indeed, a striking feature of teaching is the abruptness with which full responsibility is assumed. A young man or woman is a student in June and a full-fledged teacher in September.

Lacking a long period of specialized training, teachers learn their jobs by themselves in actual teaching situations. Such institutionalized experiences as "workshops" and "in-service" courses are available to teachers, but are generally thought to have little significance in learning to be a teacher.

In short, the kind of training teachers receive leaves a great deal of room for the emergence and reinforcement of idiosyncratic experience ("individualistic socialization"). Teachers, themselves, overwhelmingly claim that they learned to teach by experience and by trial and error in the classroom,[26] resulting in subjective problems for them. Those in other lines of work, when they come to doubt their proficiency and the value of the service they offer, usually have something to fall back on to help them regain their self-confidence. If they have perceived their expertise (or for that matter, their ignorance) as jointly shared, the individual burden is greatly reduced. A doctor, for example, can take comfort from his or her compliance with the normal expectations of his or her occupation—he or she can feel that everything possible within "the state of the art" was done. The doctor can thus cope with the death of a patient by sharing the weight of failure and guilt; his or her inadequacy is part of a larger inadequacy of medicine. He or she can also take comfort in the belief in the advancement of medical science, feeling that in the future such events will be eradicated. Teachers can derive little consolation from this method; a lack of specialized training coupled by an individualistic conception of practice exacerbates the burden of failure.[27]

The Remaining Criteria

We believe that the third criterion, autonomy, is directly dependent upon the last three, and therefore must be seen in conjunction with them. If teachers do not have an esoteric body of knowledge, a comprehensive organization of practitioners, and control over entry into the profession, they will not have a broad range of autonomy, either as individuals or as members of the occupation as a whole. We will therefore look closely at items 4, 5, and 6 and how they affect teacher autonomy. Fortunately, our task is made easier by a study by Jill Bystydzienski which brilliantly analyzes these aspects of teacher professionalism.[28]

Knowledge, Organization, Control and Autonomy in Teaching

In the first half of the nineteenth century, educators interested in improving the American public school system began to focus on the preparation of elementary school teachers as a significant problem. In 1823, a Congregationalist minister, Samuel R. Hall of Concord, Vermont, established a private academy for the training of prospective teachers. The Reverend Hall gave a series of lectures on "schoolkeeping," admitted a few children for the purpose of having a class to demonstrate on, and is generally acknowledged to have written the first widely used text on education, *Lectures on Schoolkeeping,* to be published in America.[29]

On July 3, 1839, the first state normal school opened at Lexington, Massachusetts, with three young female students and the Reverend Cyrus Peirce of Nantucket as principal.[30] A second school opened two months later at Barre, Massachusetts, and a third one a year later at Bridgewater, Massachusetts. It was this school at Bridgewater that was to have a profound effect on teacher education as its graduates took jobs all through New England.

Some famous educators of the time, among them Horace Mann and Henry Barnard, began to champion the establishment of these normal schools. Such schools, they believed, could overcome the inadequate preparation of prospective teachers and in the process teachers could be taught to be "professionals."

It was fitting that Massachusetts was the site of the first state-supported schools for the exclusive purpose of preparing teachers, because Massachusetts since colonial days had been a leader in the public schooling movement. In 1647, Massachusetts had passed the first law for the purpose of promoting general education for the common people. This has been called the "Old Deluder Law" because of the first phrase of the law: "It being one chief object of that old deluder, Satan, to keep men from the knowledge of the scriptures."[31]

Normal schools grew rapidly and by the Civil War all of the northern states were involved in improving the common schools by improving teaching. By

1875, state normal schools were located in twenty-five states from Maine to California.[32] Educators, however, were divided among themselves concerning both how teachers should be trained and what constituted "professionalism." One group believed that a so-called "strictly professional" education should take place after some general liberal arts preparation and then should consist of instruction in methods of teaching, classroom governance, and pedagogy.[33] Others argued that the distinction between liberal or academic studies and the "strictly professional" was a false one and advocated simultaneous instruction in both as a means toward achieving professionalism among teachers.[34] The debate became particularly intense toward the turn of the century, when it was discovered that many graduates of liberal arts colleges were going into secondary education without any preparation in the "science of education." This esoteric body of knowledge was considered by the teacher training advocates to consist of "theories" or "principles of learning."[35] Although no general agreement was reached as to what this new "science" was to entail, specifically, for the most part the "theories and principles" consisted of ready prescriptions on how to handle students and teach specific subject matter. Intellectual content was borrowed from established disciplines, in particular, psychology. Unlike the legal profession, whose esoteric body of knowledge was indisputably the written law, and doctors (who by the end of the nineteenth century had embraced not only substantial knowledge of the human body but also some diagnostic and healing techniques), teachers were still searching for that particular domain which would define more precisely that activity they had to offer to society called "teaching."

In short, nineteenth-century advocates of "professional" training for teachers were in general agreement that an esoteric body of knowledge was an essential ingredient if teachers were to obtain professional status. The fact that such a body of knowledge, this hoped-for "science of education," did not develop and does not exist today was and is a major obstacle that accounts for the failure of teachers to professionalize their occupation. Equally important was their failure to develop a "comprehensive self-governing organization of practitioners."

The Growth of the National Education Association

Even if a group does develop its own body of knowledge, unless it can bargain effectively in the economic market of our capitalistic society, it will not be successful in securing a position of prestige for its members. Conversely, though, it is conceivable for an occupational group to "mystify" the extent to which it may actually hold a unique body of knowledge, as long as it collectively has the power to do so.[36]

The educators who came together in 1857 to form the National Teachers Association (changed to National Education Association [NEA] in 1870) seemed to be very much aware of the role a strong organization could play in the professionalization of teachers. The constitution, drawn up at the first meeting in Philadelphia, contained a preamble which still stands today as the expression of purpose: "To elevate the character and advance the interests of teaching, and to promote the cause of popular education in the U.S. . . . ."[37] One of the educators who addressed the small group which gathered in Philadelphia that year was William Russell. Speaking on what professionalism meant, Russell advocated that, with a state-granted charter, the NTA examine and pass upon applicants for membership. Those who passed would then be issued a certificate which would serve as legal evidence of competency to teach. Teachers would thus claim the right, set up proper standards, and assume responsibility for admitting and rejecting candidates. The state and the public, Russell observed, would gladly accept such an assumption of responsibility by the teaching "profession."[38]

The following year, at the NTA's annual meeting in Cincinnati, its president, Zalmon Richards, in his inaugural address, similarly argued that teaching had to become a profession, one in which its own members set standards and passed upon the applications of candidates for admission. Teachers should weed out "incompetents," and existing normal schools should be upgraded with the help of the NTA, Richards asserted.[39]

The founders and leaders of the Teachers Association thus strongly advocated the creation of a self-regulating organization which would have strong and effective control over the teaching occupation, would gain respect and confidence of both state and public, and in the process, raise the status of teachers. These lofty goals, however, never progressed beyond the rhetorical stage. Quite likely the major reason for the Association's failure to become an effective vehicle for professional control and autonomy for public school teachers was its inability, from its inception, to adequately reflect the interests of teachers and develop an organizational structure which would represent and promote these interests.

On the whole, the Association was an elitist group. For example, women, who constituted a majority of teachers, were excluded from membership at first, and only in 1866 were they admitted to the NTA. It then took several decades for women to win positions of leadership and full participation within the Association. (In 1910 Ellen Flag Young, Superintendent of Chicago's public schools, was elected the first woman president of the NEA.)

This elitism was also enhanced by the fact that secondary and elementary school teachers received very different preparation. Only a minority of the latter were trained in normal schools (most were only high school graduates), whereas secondary teachers tended to be liberal arts college graduates and looked down at their elementary counterparts.

Further, the organizational structure lent itself to fragmentation, particularly in the proliferation of specific departments which tended to separate different groups of educators, with an attendent chauvinism related to the specific group. For example, the Department of Kindergarten–Primary Education established in 1884 had little or nothing in common with the National Science Teachers Association (established in 1895) or the Department of Vocational Education (founded in 1875). Not only did the specific departments meet separately outside the realm of the annual NEA meetings, but even during the annual convention, members of specific departments tended to congregate and socialize with each other rather than intermingling with other groups.[40]

Clearly, the various groups of educators which became part of the Association, having had differential educational preparation and not perceiving specific job situations or contexts to be similar, saw little in terms of common interests among the membership groups. The departmental organization of the NEA further reinforced these perceived differences. Yet despite these splits in the NEA between men and women, primary and secondary teachers, and various specialists, there admittedly were enough fudamental interests on the part of all teachers to have provided a foundation for unification if the NEA leadership had not been so short-sighted.

To be sure, convention speakers and annual resolutions from 1857 on did from time to time make pronouncements in favor of better pay, status, working conditions, pensions, and tenure, interests which could have united teachers. However, such pronouncements, particularly during the first fifty years of the NEA's existence, were mild and relatively infrequent. They were not designed to bring definite results, largely being educative and admonitory rather than proclamations of intended action.[41] The philosophy adopted by the leadership of the NEA during its first fifty years thus seems almost to have deliberately excluded teacher welfare issues, as well as political involvement, from the policies of the Association. The prevailing belief among the NEA's leaders was that all educators, including classroom teachers, should first establish themselves as professionals. By this they meant not only the development of an organization but also a relevant body of knowledge. Hence, the activities of the NEA consisted of keeping educators informed about the "state of the science of education," rather than attempting to set standards or to improve teacher welfare.

It should be of no surprise, then, that the leaders were by and large drawn from the ranks of administrators, particularly superintendents, as well as college professors—two groups whose economic and social status was far above those of classroom teachers; and for whom welfare and related issues were of no immediate concern. This implies that the leadership of the NEA was simply not concerned about the plight of public school teachers, failing to recognize that economic issues are fundamentally tied to the process of professionalism in a capitalist society. For an occupational group to become a profession, it must bargain on the market for higher economic gains, and its success or failure in this determines, in the long run, its social status. The failure of the NEA to deal equally with economic realities and educational or knowledge concerns resulted in a loosely structured organization of educators who perceived few common goals and interests among themselves. Leadership of the NEA in the nineteenth century involved a great deal of lipservice to the setting of standards and regulations by educators, but these intentions were not followed up by any action. A review of the *Proceedings* of the NEA in the latter half of the nineteenth century reveals a preoccupation on the part of its participants with petty organizational details, annual excursions and free dinners given for them by their convention hosts, and matters dealing with school and classroom management. Resolutions dealing with standards and teacher welfare were generally tabled, and if adopted, were never followed through. A comparison with the *Proceedings of the American Medical Association,* which was founded at about the same time, indicates a much more favorable attitude on the part of physicians to adopt resolutions dealing with setting of standards and frequent designation of committees to carry out such resolutions.[42]

In 1880, the NEA approved the formation of its National Council of Education. The Council consisted of fifty-one prominent educators and was seen as "a national authority, a court of last resort to which educators could appeal, a body competent to formulate principles and courses of study."[43] Wesley, the NEA's official historian, refers to the Council as "the guardians of correct thinking" for educators.[44]

Those who organized the Council decided that in order to unify educators a strong organization had to exist, one which would establish "standards of good taste, truth, correct thinking, right answers and the best that had been taught and said."[45] These lofty ideals proved to be as impractical as they sound. Founded to provide a service similar to that of the *Journal of the American Medical Association,* the Council succumbed to elitism and devoted most of its meetings (until 1920 when it was turned into a delegate organization) to debates and vague pronouncements. Neither in word nor in deed did the Council become a source of authority on standards for classroom teachers.

In short, classroom teachers, with little power, were excluded from positions of leadership in the NEA. Administrators and college professors, who had little in common with teachers and whose concerns were rather abstract, simply did not reflect the practical interests of most teachers. Hence, the prominence and social prestige of the NEA leadership did very little to elevate the status of teachers.

It took a long time before the NEA actually became an authentic voice of public school teachers. In the meantime, however, failing to secure autonomy, teachers became increasingly subjugated to other forms of control, specifically control by the state.

THE GROWTH OF STATE CONTROL OVER PUBLIC SCHOOL TEACHERS IN THE TWENTIETH CENTURY

Unlike the American Medical Association or the American Bar Association, the National Education Association did not play an active role in the developing of licensure for its members. Because it was more concerned with esoteric and organizational matters, the NEA leadership left certification totally up to state governments. By the time the Association had realized its mistake and had tried to mend its ways, state educational agencies had established firm control over admission into the occupation, including educational requirements and setting of standards for public school teachers.

The trend toward state control over public schools began as early as 1839, when several states created the office of chief school official (state superintendent of schools). Eventually, state school boards and state departments of education were established. At first, state educational administrators concerned themselves primarily with financial problems. Gradually, in the face of demand from both the general public and teachers themselves, they began to establish boards of examiners to devise tests of competence and generally oversee the certification of teachers, thereby establishing certain uniformities. At the turn of the century, state certification became the most prestigious credential for teachers. Usually granted for life, they differed from county and local licenses, which only allowed individuals to teach for a limited period of time, after which the certificates had to be renewed.

This use of examinations as a basis for the granting of state licensure for teachers was to be short-lived. In the first decade of the twentieth century, the practice came under increasing attack from large numbers of educational and lay groups. Gradually examinations were replaced by college and university preparatory programs for high school teachers, and eventually for elementary teachers as well. In the process, state agencies acquired the power to dictate to teacher preparatory institutions the length of study, and the types and number of courses required for certification. States also took on the responsibility for the legal accreditation of institutions for the education of teachers. By contrast, lawyers and doctors, through their professional associations, developed their own standards and requirements for licensure, which were then "legalized" through state approval.

One extremely important influence on state control of teacher preparation and certification was the civil service movement. Initiated in 1883 with the creation of the National Civil Service Commission, the movement articulated a need to organize the rapidly growing public service area. It sought to define the status of its employees, to clarify their rights and obligations, and to generally provide "objective" means for their selection. Because they were not actually state employees, teachers were not formally absorbed into the civil service system. Nevertheless, in controlling the certification process, states applied civil service procedures to teachers. This is particularly apparent in the detailed and specific classification of positions and specific prescriptions of requirements for preparation. (It is possible that this specificity of requirements and classification of positions by the state has led to teachers' "being treated increasingly more like bureaucrats than professionals.")

It was only toward the middle of the twentieth century that the NEA became more concerned with standard setting and certification. In 1946 it established the National Commission on Teacher Education and Professional Standards and, in 1948, the American Association of Colleges for Teacher Education. These organizations had as their purpose the raising of standards of teacher preparation. As various students of this development have pointed out, their effort in this direction has been very limited.[46] Coming on the scene as late as they did, all they could do was take on an advisory role to state educational agencies. The chance to gain any substantial control over the process of preparation and certification of teachers was long gone.

By the 1950s the trend toward state control over teacher preparation and certification was firmly established. Since then, despite attempts by NEA-sponsored groups to make major revisions in the credential structures for teachers (for example, placing more responsibility for preparation of teachers on educators in preparatory institutions), attempts to gain more control over the licensure process by the occupation itself have not been successful. Even though most states have been involved in periodic revisions of their credential structure for teachers, a close look at case studies of changes in certification structures of several states indicates that the general trend has been toward more specificity of requirements and more control by central state agencies. Hence, the general results of certification revisions have been to strengthen the civil service features of teacher preparation and certification rather than professional aspects, such as more autonomy by the occupation to set its own standards and requirements.[47]

The certification process for teachers has thus been in sharp contrast to licensure in other occupations, specifically such professions as law, medicine, architecture, and dentistry. Whereas the purpose of licensure for the latter is the identification of those qualified to practice, the actual purpose of certification in education has been a civil service process designed to regularize employment and remuneration from public school funds. In summary, whereas such professions as law and medicine through the development of certification standards have established a power base within their professional group, teachers have not. This lack of the establishment of an effective, autonomous teachers association has allowed state educational agencies to control the occupation. It is thus quite clear that the role of the teacher is not that of "autonomous professional."

At best, teachers are "semi-professionals." Etzioni has described what is meant by this term.

> Their training is shorter, their status is less legitimated, there is less of a specialized body of knowledge, and they have less autonomy from supervision than "the" professions.[48]

By claiming a professional status they do not possess, teachers are merely deluding themselves. As long as they eschew the political fact of life that power is not given but must be taken or at least bargained for from a position of strength, the role of the teacher will continue to fall far short of the professional status they desire. (We will see in Chapter 8 how the growth of teacher unions and militancy have begun to effect changes in the struggle of teachers to gain power.)

It is evident that teachers have historically played a subservient role. This lack of power manifests itself in a particular type of political behavior, a conservatism fueled by the socialization process teachers undergo.

THE SOCIALIZATION OF TEACHERS

Teachers have endured a long selection and socialization process that started way back in kindergarten, and which has effectively rendered them "safe." If we assume the usual pattern of attendance in elementary and secondary school, the teacher enters college with an extraordinary familiarity with his or her expected role. All high school graduates have spent approximately 10,000 hours in close contact with teachers. Persons whose aspirations and characteristics are dissimilar to the teachers with whom they come into contact are not likely to choose teaching as an occupation. Those who do come to choose teaching, therefore, do so on the basis of fairly accurate information as to what is expected of them. Former teachers, thus, play a large part in the development and encouragement of the ambition to teach, introducing an important sense of self-perpetuation into the recruitment process.[49]

This process is further reinforced, once the teacher begins the job, by the relatively unstaged career lines involved in teaching. The major opportunity for making status gains lies in leaving classroom teaching for full-time administration. The primary benefits and rewards of teaching do not come from teaching, but are the result of seniority and further education; in short, the incentive system in education is not organized to respond to effort or talent. As stated previously, few beginning teachers expect a long future in the classroom. Men expect to leave, and women see their participation as contingent on external factors. Most men work for promotion, and if they fail, must resign themselves to classroom teaching as a terminal status. Young single women hold off their commitments until they leave to marry or conclude that they will not marry. Married women are the most satisfied.[50] Basically, teaching is an occupation where men see themselves as unsuccessful, and because of the relatively low salaries attached to teaching, take outside employment to supplement their income.[51] At best, teaching is a ''job'' to them. Unmarried women have the most commitment to teaching but often are passed over for promotions to supervisory positions,[52] something that should breed resentment, particularly in this day of women's rights movements. Married teachers are relatively satisfied because a flat career line permits them to come and go with no serious loss of status.[53] Such a milieu does not generate any commitment to innovation or change; it merely reinforces the conservative attitude that teachers have been found to have.[54] As Harmon Zeigler, one of the best known students of the political behavior of teachers, states:

> The conservatism apparent in teachers is best understood, perhaps, by considering them as advocates of the interests of the middle class. Teachers prefer to do regular rather than radical things, and they do not encourage their students to participate in politics other than in the most accepted and established fashions. This interpretation is based upon the assumption that teachers charged with the responsibilities of injecting system maintenance values into the educational subculture encourage their students to become good citizens, and in so doing, do not offer students an alternative to acceptance of the *status quo*.[55]

Not only are teachers very conservative, they tend to become even more so the longer they teach.[56] And serious questions can be raised as to whether these conservative values of teachers are so supportive of the status quo that they become inimical to democratic practices. Clyde Nunn, for example, asks whether undergraduate schools of education are adequately preparing prospective teachers to accept such basic democratic values as tolerance of others and respect for the rights of minorities.[57] Nunn, replicating an earlier study by Selvin and Hagstrom of students at the Berkeley campus of the University of California, found that although support of civil liberties at the university was far from overwhelming, those students majoring in elementary and secondary education were so low in supporting basic civil liberties (as measured by a questionnaire which paraphrased the Bill of Rights) as to lead to the sarcastic conclusion that schools of education were "something other than 'hotbeds of democracy' in encouragement of support for civil liberties, even those pertaining to academic freedom."[58] Nunn's findings represent further substantiation in a long line of research which has documented the basically conservative nature of our nation's schools.[59]

Teachers, then, socialized toward conservatism, have this conservatism reinforced while on the job. The end result is a willing acceptance of the status quo, which is (as was stated earlier,) bureaucratically structured and predominantly middle-class-oriented. In the end, the acceptance of the status quo results in teachers' giving up much of the autonomy that could insure their professional status.

Robert Dreeben has reported on certain aspects of this. Using data from a national sample of principals and teachers,[60] he concluded that teachers tend, somewhat, to be negatively disposed to autonomy. That is "teachers *favor* (more than they approve) principals' efforts to maintain control and surveillance over teachers' activities."[61] So unexpected were these results that Dreeben writes: "For teachers to expect the principal to know what is going on in most classrooms most of the day . . . implies a kind of omnipresence that almost denies privacy."[62]

It has always been held, too, that secondary school teachers are more "professional" than their primary school counterparts, and hence demand more on-the-job autonomy. But Dreeben's findings question even this. He found "no clear-cut picture of teachers' desire for autonomy"[63] on the secondary school level.

Teachers go through a process of "double socialization"; first in schools of education where they are taught to be passive, docile, and politically conservative, and on job where they learn to accept a lack of automony and the authority of their supervisors. As Lortie states: "The system of self-selection based on familiarity, selection within training institutions and schools, supplemented by the tenure testing point, produces sufficient homogeneity to reduce strains which would otherwise be placed on the control system of schools."[64]

Further, the individualistic socialization process described previously supports the general conservatism of teachers in indirect ways. The lack of potency in the formal socialization system means that earlier conservative influences are not systematically offset in the course of induction. Teachers do not acquire any new standards which can be used to reverse earlier impressions, ideas, and orientations. Nor do their working conditions supplement low impact training with a general conception of teaching as an intellectual possession. In short, conservatism is endemic to the general role of teacher.

SUMMARY

The job of "teacher" was seen as a role, and was analyzed: (1) in terms of background characteristics that individuals bring to it; and (2) the external and historical characteristics that also define any role.

Concerning background characteristics, it was pointed out that although women teachers outnumber men by two to one, men hold most of the positions of power in teaching. This system of male dominance reinforces a basic conservatism among teachers. Males aspire toward administrative positions (which are seen as being conservative and bureaucratic), and women engage in "in-and-out plans," which allow them to leave and reenter teaching, fostering an interest in slow change in teaching techniques. Another reason for this conservatism is that teaching represents a rise in class for many teachers (more than half have fathers who were blue-collar workers). By seeking to improve their status, they overidentify with the middle class.

Conservatism among teachers was then shown to have had historical antecedents. From the first, teachers have been forced into a position of subordination. Although teachers claim to be professionals, which would allow for autonomy and in turn offset their subordination, a close look revealed that teachers were far from being professionals. They lack: (1) a long period of specialized training; (2) autonomy; (3) an esoteric body of knowledge; (4) a comprehensive self-governing organization; and (5) control over entry into the occupation. Of the major criteria of professionalism, teachers only meet one—they perform a social service.

Lastly, we focused on the socialization process of teaching, a process which begins in kindergarten and, for all intents and purposes, renders teachers "safe."

NOTES

1. Much of the following description of the American Public School Teacher is based on the latest available national study of teachers conducted by the National Education Association's research division, entitled *Status of the American Public School Teacher: 1975–1976*. Washington, D.C.: National Education Association, 1977.

2. Ibid., p. 11.

3. *Digest of Educational Statistics*. Washington, D.C.: U.S. Department of Health, Education and Welfare, 1977–1978, p. 50.

4. Patricia Sexton, *Women in Education*. Bloomington, Ind.: Phi Delta Kappa Educational Foundation, 1976, p. 58.

5. Ibid., p. 57.

6. W. S. Mason, *The Beginning Teacher*. Washington, D. C.: U. S. Department of Health, Education and Welfare, Office of Education, 1961.

7. For a work which deals with the consequences of "anticipatory socialization" (socialization into a role before the person occupies it), see Robert K. Merton, *Social Theory and Social Structure*. New York: Free Press, 1963.

8. Dan Lortie, *School-Teacher*. Chicago: University of Chicago Press, 1976, p. 88.

9. Ibid.

10. Ibid., p. 209.

11. NEA, *Status of the American Public School Teacher: 1975—1976,* p. 281.

12. Lortie, *School-Teacher,* p. 113.

13. For a more precise index based on occupation, see Peter Blau and Otis D. Duncan, *The American Occupational Structure.* New York: Wiley, 1967.

14. Composite table from *Status of the American Public School Teacher: 1970—1971.* Washington, D. C.: National Education Association, 1972, p. 61; and NEA, *Status of the American Public School Teacher: 1975—1976,* p. 127.

15. Richard Hofstadter, "The Pseudo-Conservative Revolt Revisited: A Postscript," in Daniel Bell (ed.), *The Radical Right.* Garden City, N.Y.: Doubleday/Anchor Books, 1964, pp. 97—104.

16. For an analysis of this phenomenon in American politics, see Seymour Martin Lipset, "The Sources of the Radical Right," in ibid., pp. 307—372. For an application of this concept to Catholics, see Joseph A. Scimecca and Roland Damiano, *Crisis At St. John's: Strike and Revolution on the Catholic Campus.* New York: Random House, 1968; and for an application to Italian-Americans, see Joseph A. Scimecca and Francis X. Femminella, "Italian-Americans and Radical Politics," in Francis X. Femminella (ed.), *Power and Class: The Italian-American Experience Today.* New York: American-Italian Historical Association, 1973, pp. 12—19.

17. NEA, *Status of the American Public School Teacher: 1975—1976,* p. 61.

18. Quoted in Louis Fischer and David Schimmel, *The Civil Rights of Teachers.* New York: Harper & Row, 1973.

19. David B. Tyack, *Turning Points in Educational History.* Waltham, Mass.: Blaisdell, 1967, p. 470.

20. David B. Tyack, *The One Best System: A History of American Urban Education.* Cambridge, Mass.: Harvard University Press, 1974, p. 19.

21. Philip Taft, *United They Teach.* Los Angeles: Nash, 1974, p. 12.

22. Quoted in ibid., pp. 13—14.

23. Fischer and Schimmel, *The Civil Rights of Teachers,* p. 8.

24. See in particular Myron Lieberman, *Education as a Profession.* Englewood Cliffs, N.J.: Prentice-Hall, 1956; William Goode, "The Librarian: From Occupation to Profession," *Literary Quarterly, 31,* October 1961, pp. 306—320; Everert C. Hughes, "Professions," *Daedalus, 92,* Fall 1963, pp. 655—668; and Eliot Friedson (ed.), *The Professions and Their Prospects.* Beverly Hills, Calif.: Sage, 1973.

25. Lortie, *School-Teacher,* p. 59.

26. Ibid., p. 60.

27. Ibid., p. 81.

28. This section is based on Jill M. Bystydzienski, "The Status of Public School Teachers in America: An Unfulfilled Quest for Professionalism," unpublished Ph.D. dissertation, State University of New York at Albany, 1979.

29. Charles A. Harper, *A Century of Public Teacher Education.* Washington, D.C.: National Education Association, 1939, p. 13.

30. Ibid., p. 26.

31. Ibid., p. 10.

32. Ibid., p. 72.

33. Richard Edwards, "Normal Schools in the United States" (1865), in Merle L. Borrowman, (ed.), *Teacher Education in America: A Documentary History.* New York: Teachers College, 1965, pp. 74—83.

34. John Dewey, "The Relation of Theory to Practice" (1904), in Borrowman (ed.), *Teacher Education in America,* pp. 140—171.

35. Borrowman, "Liberal Education and the Professional Preparation of Teachers," in Borrowman (ed.), *Teacher Education in America,* p. 25.

36. T. Johnson, *Professionalism and Power.* London: Macmillan, 1972.

37. Edgar B. Wesley, *The NEA: The First Hundred Years.* New York: Harper & Row, 1957, pp. 22—23.

38. National Teachers Association *Proceedings, 1857–1870.* Washington, D.C.: National Education Association, pp. 15–24.

39. Ibid., pp. 35–45.

40. Wesley, *NEA,* pp. 274–278.

41. Ibid., p. 336.

42. Bystydzienski, "The Status of Public School Teachers in America."

43. NEA *Proceedings,* 1880, p. 17.

44. Wesley, *NEA,* p. 262.

45. Ibid., p. 265.

46. See James B. Conant, *The Education of American Teachers.* New York: McGraw-Hill, 1963; and L. B. Kinney, *Certification in Education.* Englewood Cliffs, N.J.: Prentice-Hall, 1969.

47. Bystydzienski, "The Status of Public School Teachers in America," Chap. 3.

48. Amitai Etzioni, preface to Amitai Etzioni (ed.), *The Semi-Professions and Their Organization.* New York: Free Press, 1969, p. v.

49. Dan Lortie, "The Balance of Control and Autonomy in Elementary School Teaching," in ibid., p. 10.

50. Lortie, *School-Teacher,* pp. 82–108.

51. NEA, *The Status of the American Public School Teacher, 1975–1976,* pp. 43–48.

52. *Digest of Educational Statistics,* p. 52.

53. Lortie, *School-Teacher,* p. 99.

54. Lortie, in ibid., p. 100, does argue, however, that this lack of commitment on the part of teachers enhances their autonomy because it reduces the capacity of supervisors to exert influence over individual teachers. We would maintain just the opposite: that without any real commitment, teachers will go along with the status quo in the school.

55. Harmon Zeigler, *The Political Life of American Teachers.* Englewood Cliffs, N.J.: Prentice-Hall, 1967, pp. 21–22.

56. Ibid., p. 23.

57. Clyde Z. Nunn, "Support of Civil Liberties among College Students," *Social Problems, 20* (Winter 1973), pp. 303–310.

58. Ibid., p. 309.

59. See Edgar Litt, "Civic Education, Norms and Political Indoctrination," *American Sociological Review, 28* (February 1963), pp. 69–75; Willard Waller, *The Sociology of Teaching.* New York: Wiley, 1965; and Zeigler, *The Political Life of American Teachers.*

60. Robert Dreeben, *The Nature of Teaching.* Glenview, Ill.: Scott, Foresman, 1970. Dreeben's previously unpublished data is from Harvard University National Principalship Study, directed by Neal Gross.

61. Ibid., p. 72.

62. Ibid.

63. Ibid., p. 73.

64. Lortie, "The Balance of Control and Autonomy in Elementary School Teaching," p. 11.

5

The Principal

The contemporary public school has evolved from the one-room schoolhouse described in Chapter 2 to the mammoth bureaucratic organization found in urban areas.[1] The school itself (as well as the school system in which it is located) is characterized by hierarchies of power and authority, standardized programs, and routine procedures for secondary and elementary instruction. David Goslin has described the effects which the development of this bureaucratic structure has had on the school.

Among the responses of school systems to pressures for the provision of more complex educational services and the necessity for the maintenance of greater control over the educational process has been (1) an increasingly fine division of labor, both at the administrative and teaching levels, together with a concern for allocating personnel at those positions for which they are best suited and a formalization of recruitment and promotional policies; (2) the development of an administrative hierarchy incorporating a specified chain of command and designated channels of communications; (3) the gradual accumulation of specific rules of procedure that cover everything from counseling and guidance to school-wide or system-wide testing programs and requirements concerning topics to be covered in many subjects such as history, civics, and social studies; (4) a de-emphasis of personal relationships between students and teacher and between teachers and administrators, and a consequent reorientation towards more formalized and affectively (emotionally) neutral role relationships; and finally (5) an emphasis on the relationship of the total organization and the processes going on within the organization. In general the movement, particularly at the secondary school level, has been in the direction of the rational bureaucratic organization that is typified by most government agencies and many business and industrial firms.[2]

The school, like any other bureaucratic organization, has rules and regulations which must be obeyed if the organization is to function smoothly and efficiently. It can be said then that the school is in the power business, making sure that rules are carried out. The bureaucratic principles of centralization and standardization are used as mechanisms of social control. Central administration clearly controls the major decisions. The superintendent and his or her central staff formulate institutional policy, departmental budgets, hiring procedures, tenuring procedures, and so on. The principal's office is usually responsible for selection of required textbooks and the setting of discipline policies. Teachers' decision-making power is confined to situations within the classroom such as selection of supplementary reading materials, determining what concepts are to be taught, teaching methods, and homework assignments.[3] Centralization is supplemented by a second type of control mechanism, standardization—the application of uniform policies and practices throughout a school district. School systems across the nation employ such uniform procedures and practices as textbooks, standardized tests, curriculum guides, reward systems, and even attempts to control the personal lives of its members.[4]

In particular, the standardization of curriculum produces tension and conflict between teachers and administrators. The job of the administrator is to coordinate the various parts of the system, while teachers are under direct daily pressure from their students and from the local community to adjust to the unique qualities, special problems, and specific social situations of their students. Because teachers work in self-contained classrooms, they are insulated from the demands of the larger school system; but they are forced to pay the price of becoming caught between pressure from both their students and the school administration, which must carry out the policy of the central administration.[5]

As for the students, standardization is so pronounced that numerous writers have pointed to the similarities between schools and prisons.

> Like prisoners, students typically must obtain permission to use the library, to get a drink of water, and to use the restroom. They seldom have choice over what they will study or do in the course of a day. They must remain in the building during specific hours. Their grooming and manners and clothing are subject to close inspection and approval by the teachers in charge and, frequently, policemen are hired to patrol the hallways.[6]

The school is thus responsible for the production of a more or less uniform product (a literate student). The longer the educational process and the more complicated the skills the school is expected to inculcate, the more difficult is the task of making sure a student emerges with the proper qualifications. The result is the development of an enormously complex administrative structure.

The bureaucratically structured school has specific implications for students, teachers, and administrators who function within its setting. Since Chapters 3 and 4 were concerned with students and teachers, in this chapter we will concentrate specifically on the role of the elementary and secondary school principal. In particular, we will examine the part power and domination play in defining the principal's role.

THE ROLE OF THE PRINCIPAL

Schools are organized hierarchically, defining roles and expectations for teachers and administrators alike. Specifically, teachers are subordinate to principals, who are, in turn, subordinate to superintendents. Although, as was shown in the previous chapter, teachers are not professionals, the fact that they like to think of themselves as such (thereby desiring autonomy) ensures that a potential conflict situation is endemic to the bureaucratically run school. Teachers must either learn to accommodate themselves to a relatively powerless position or find ways to assert autonomy. School administrators are thus called upon to deal with the professional aspirations of teachers while concomitantly carrying out their managerial operations. Also, given that schools are ultimately responsible to the school board and outside community, administrators constantly try to make things run smoothly, or at least to give that impression. Outside intervention in the running of schools has been a historical reality, and administrators are well aware of this. What we have then is a highly volatile situation arising out of the professional aspirations of teachers and the managerial functions of school administrators. A major theme of this chapter is that the principal is so caught up in trying to alleviate this strife that he or she loses sight of his or her historical role as "principal teacher" or educational leader, and for all intents and purposes has become a bureaucratic manager. This role, that of administrative manager, is characterized by a primary emphasis upon the smooth running of the school. By focusing almost exclusively upon the overseeing and supervising of programs mandated by the central administration, the educational leadership role of the principal is neglected almost to the point of nonexistence.[7]

A recent textbook on the principalship lists the major duties involved in the administrative – managerial role:

a. Maintaining adequate school records of all types.
b. Preparing reports for the central office and other agencies.
c. Budget development and budget control.
d. Personnel administration.
e. Student discipline.

f.   Scheduling and maintaining a schedule.
g.   Building administration.
h.   Administrating supplies and equipment.
i.   Pupil accounting.
j.   Monitoring programs and instructional processes prescribed by the central office.[8]

This view of the position of "principal" can be contrasted with the educational leader role, which carries with it the expectations of effectively improving the teaching functions of staff to insure the achievement of the educational goals of the school. In short, the educational leadership role of the principal sees him or her building a cohesive and effective atmosphere in which everyone "pulls together" to achieve an optimal teaching and learning experience. If done properly, the total school functions in a harmonious relationship with everyone defining, interpreting, and establishing school goals. However, this is an emphasis that most principals pay lip service to, but rarely achieve. Few principals, given that they are under the direct control of a central administrative system, can develop an environment in their school which will enhance the talents of teachers. In the end the administrative duties have to be performed. As long as the primary emphasis of the bureaucratic structure is on creating and maintaining a smoothly running school, this administrative role takes precedence. Ultimately, there are just too many constraints upon the principal; there are too many administrative duties he or she must perform and too little time to fulfill all of them. The principal is by definition, in a bureaucratically run school system, the chief administrator of his building and is thereby held accountable for all managerial details. Central administrations all too often place priority on a "well-run" school and judge its smooth operation in terms of whether reports are handed in on time, the building and grounds are kept up, supplies and equipment are accounted for, and usually most important of all, given "the bureaucratic mentality,"[9] whether or not personnel problems are handled at the building level or passed on.

The community (having themselves been socialized in schools), if it does not see a well-run building, also has a tendency to lose confidence in the principal, something that a principal who realistically wants to keep his or her job or eventually move on to a better one cannot let happen. This is of particular importance to the principal who aspires to the role of school superintendent. The principal would thus be caught in a bind if he or she tried to emphasize a real educational leadership role. The result then is, as one writer states, ". . . that principals as a group are relatively unimportant as a force in making American education the kind of dynamic, creative vehicle for maximizing human potential it is capable of becoming."[10] While we would wholeheartedly agree with this judgment, we would be remiss if we did not state that we feel that this is an unfortunate occurrence. Principals can do otherwise, but as long as they are educational managers and not instructional leaders they will continue to push paper and not affect people. This becomes even more unfortunate given evidence that principals could really make a difference in educational policy. An important national study which points this up was carried out by Neal Gross and Robert Herriott, and is worth summarizing in some detail.

EDUCATIONAL LEADERSHIP AND THE SCHOOL PRINCIPALSHIP[11]

Gross and Herriott started with the basic assumption that an executive of a professionally staffed organization (principal) conforms to a definition of a role that stresses his or her obligation to improve the quality of staff performance. They designated this behavior Executive Professional Leadership (EPL). They then proceeded to test their assumption with a national sample of principals in forty-one cities with populations over 50,000. All in all, 501 principals and 3,367 teachers constituted the sample of what they refer to as the National Principalship Study.

The authors concentrated on elementary school principals because their definition of EPL was directly related to the efforts of a principal to influence the performance of teachers, and elementary school principals typically interact more directly and closely with teachers than do junior and senior high school principals. EPL was measured by asking 1750 teachers in the 175 elementary schools in the national sample how frequently their principal engaged in such behavior as giving teachers the feeling that their work was important; getting teachers to upgrade their performance standards in the classroom; offering constructive suggestions to teachers in dealing with their major problems; treating teachers as professional workers; bringing to the teachers' attention educational literature that would be of value to them in their jobs; and displaying a strong interest in improving the quality of the educational program.

Of particular importance was the relationship between a principal's EPL, teacher morale, and teacher and student performance. Gross and Herriott found all three to be positively correlated with a high EPL. In fact, the relationship was strong enough for the authors to state that "there is apparently some truth in the aphorism, 'as the principal, so the school.' "[12] In short, data from the National Principalship Study lends support to those who would criticize the trend to the ascendancy of the managerial role of the principal. Principals can conceivably make an important educational contribution, but do not. Why, then, the overwhelming emphasis upon the administrative–managerial role at the expense of the educational leadership one, when there is evidence that the latter can be a force conducive to the improvement of teaching and learning? Our answer to this question is that political concerns take precedence over educational ones. Administrators, involved in a conflict situation both with teachers and the community, seek to preserve their position of power. We can see this by looking at the growth of the educational administrator's role and how administrators have been more concerned with reinforcing their superordinate position than they have been with educational goals. Three examples are offered to support this assertion: (1) the rise of progressive education; (2) the accountability movement; and (3) the embracing of systems analysis.

THE GROWTH OF THE EDUCATIONAL ADMINISTRATOR ROLE

Although it is extremely difficult, if not impossible, to pinpoint the exact date for the appearance of the public school principal, it is generally held that the first such positions emerged in large urban school systems during the first half of the nineteenth century. As Paul Pierce points out, the duties of the "head teachers" or "headmasters" in the middle of the nineteenth century were largely confined "to discipline, routine administrative acts, and grading of pupils in the various rooms."[13]

Gradually, though, the role of the principal evolved as schools became larger and the need for someone at the building level to coordinate such functions as grade reporting, record keeping, and building maintenance became apparent. A head or principal teacher was thus designated to oversee these duties while continuing to teach either full or part time. At the secondary levels the task of maintaining discipline and control was quickly added to the emerging role definition of principal.

During the latter part of the nineteenth century, the administrative responsibilities of principals in large cities began to change gradually from overseeing routine clerical duties to running the school. The principal became "the directing manager, rather than the 'presiding teacher,' of the school."[14]

By the turn of the century, the powers of the principal had expanded rapidly. Principals now "had the right to direct teachers, enforce safeguards to protect the health and morals of pupils, supervise and rate janitors, require the cooperation of parents, and requisition educational supplies."[15] Principals were thus clearly recognized as the legitimate administrative heads of schools, and as such were officially responsible for the instructional programs offered therein. Specifically they were usually told by superintendents to:

> keep teachers working "in union" on "the same general plan." They were encouraged to maintain a uniformity of progress throughout their schools. Courses of study insuring continuity of materials and teaching manuals specifying details of method were to be followed closely. Principals were expected to know what each class was doing at any hour. Inspection and examination were the chief devices of principals in maintaining this lock-step progress.[16]

The superintendency had been established much earlier, in the 1830s. "In 1837 Massachusetts created a state board of education and appointed Horace Mann as its full-time secretary."[17] For all intents and purposes Mann was Massachusetts' state superintendent of schools. An energetic and erudite advocate of reform, Mann called for the establishment of a superintendent's position to clean up the "sad" state of the Boston schools. Although Mann and his followers' reforms were resisted due to the political nature of the Boston school board, a superintendent was finally appointed in Boston in 1851. Whether Mann's efforts hastened or hindered the establishment of a superintendency in Boston is debatable, but his call for reform clearly had important effects elsewhere. Before 1843, only five cities had superintendents of schools; by 1860, nineteen more cities established the office.[18]

After the Civil War, with the growth of urban populations, superintendencies increased rapidly. By 1876, approximately 150 cities had established the office of superintendent.[19]

By the turn of the twentieth century, administrators were a rapidly growing and expanding force in public education. But as with all newly enfranchised groups they were characterized by extreme "status anxiety." Insecure in their new position, they overidentified with the middle-class professional and business groups which dominated public education, and they sought above all else to solidify their newly won position in the hierarchy of the school system. One way this could be accomplished was through their attachment to those prevalent ideologies which allowed them to cling to power by embracing the managerial aspects of their role. This, in turn, relegated the educational leadership role to the secondary status it has today. One such ideology was that of "progressive education," an educational viewpoint which was beginning to become quite powerful at the beginning of the twentieth century.

Educational Administrators and the Rise of Progressive Education[20]

Progressive education is best defined as an educational perspective which holds that "the child rather than what he studies should be the center of all educational effort."[21] It first attracted serious attention in the United States just after the Civil War. By the turn of the century it became more and more popular, continuing to grow until it reached its greatest popularity just after World War II. It was only with the Sputnik controversy that progressive education fell out of favor, as influential critics attacked it for somehow being responsible for America's falling behind in technological and scientific expertise.[22]

It is David Swift's contention that progressive education fit in quite nicely with administrators' desires to establish themselves as professionals. For example, one of progressive education's most basic administrative contributions was its flexibility.[23]

The school had become a large, complex organization with administrative problems resembling those found in any large bureaucracy. Problems such as demonstrating efficiency, legitimizing managerial authority, enhancing control over personnel, reducing intrastaff tensions, and increasing employees' versatility were plentiful.[24] Progressive education made it easier for the administrator to cope with these situations by strengthening his or her authority. It did this in a number of ways. First of all, it bolstered the principal's authority in evaluating teachers. Progressive education deemphasized grades. Whereas judging teachers by the measured academic performance of their pupils could be reduced to a routine clerical matter of interpreting statistics, progressive education enabled the administrator to rate the teacher on a number of criteria, thereby offering him or her more opportunity for exercising discretion.

Secondly, progressive education reduced the status of the specialists under the principal. Progressive education's depreciation of traditional academic knowledge meant that there were fewer teachers who could claim that they knew more than their supervisors. The principal might not have been an expert in subject matter, but then, neither was the teacher. As scholarship became more and more subordinated to the pupil's overall development, the subject matter expert became less important and less able to challenge the administrator's authority.

A third way consisted in the hiring of "locals," as opposed to "cosmopolitan"[25] teachers. By reducing the importance of specialists in subject matter, teachers who had broad, general knowledge could be hired. Such teachers tended to be more concerned with the teaching of children than with a discipline which would orient them to others outside the school. Their career line thus lay within the district; it was there that they sought promotion and recognition. They were, therefore, less likely to challenge the authority of the principal and more likely to demonstrate loyalty to the school board.

A fourth way in which progressive education facilitated the principal's job was via human relations. The techniques useful for controlling students could also be used to manipulate teachers. The notion of a democratic classroom softened the image of an authoritative education hierarchy. Administrators no longer issued commands; instead, they made "requests" or "suggestions." This made it easier for the principal to form a direct and personal relationship with each teacher. In this manner, the chances of resentful teachers joining together to question his or her authority was greatly reduced.

Fifth, progressive education removed a potential source of interstaff tension. When teachers were evaluated on the basis of their students' numerical progress, intense competition among the staff was likely to occur. Administrators could now remind teachers that they were "all in the same boat," that they must cooperate. Such a situation was directly in the interest of the principal, since the school is always vulnerable to outside influence, and manifest conflict in the school would invite attention and possible intervention.

Sixth and last, progressive education made teachers more interchangeable and hence easier for an administrator to move around, particularly if he or she wanted to reprimand a tenured teacher. A generalized method of instruction enabled a principal to shift teachers from a sixth grade to a first grade, a third to a fifth, or whatever he or she desired.

Swift sums up the argument in the following manner:

> The school's responses to growth and complexity were influenced by the management practices of American industry, which stressed economic efficiency and human relations. These responses were facilitated by progressive education. It gave the school an opportunity to redefine its goals in terms which would provide greater flexibility and security for the organization and also for its managers. In addition, it enabled administrators to cope with the problems of efficiency, authority, control, conflict and versatility.[26]

Thus, a very important reason for the acceptance of progressive education by educators was the help it offered to administrators in controlling teachers. Lest we convey the impression that progressive education was forced upon unwilling teachers, certain qualifications must be offered. There was some differential acceptance on the part of teachers. Elementary teachers for the most part quickly accepted progressive education for three major reasons: (1) it reduced academic demands to the point where many teachers and other personnel could satisfy the minimal requirements of their jobs; (2) it aided in pupil control, a crucial problem for individual teachers as well as for the school; and (3) it supported teachers' claims to professional status.[27]

Secondary teachers of subject matter, on the other hand, were more likely to resist progressive education. By wrapping themselves in the respectability of an academic discipline they could draw status from the recognized field. Also, discipline problems were less of a concern to secondary school teachers because problem students were usually channeled into less demanding courses. And lastly, because the secondary school teacher had some claim to expertise, he or she was less likely to be told what to do by the principal.

One other extremely important function served by progressive education needs mentioning: it effectively deferred attacks upon the competence of the public schools by shifting the school's emphasis from subject matter to the pupils themselves. It would thus only be a small step to blame lower-class students for the failure that had always occurred.

The rise of progressive education is a clear example of how an ideology was incorporated into public education less for its pedagogical appropriateness than for the function it performed in enabling one group (administrators) to control another (teachers). Our next example, the current emphasis upon accountability in education and its historical antecedent in the turn-of-the-century "efficiency" in the educational movement, will further illustrate the importance of power in understanding educational policy.

Conflict and Accountability

One of the most recent, though not by any means new, movements in public education is that of accountability. Accountability is both a movement and a group of related ideas currently being recommended for implementation in the schools. Among these ideas are, for example, the notions that: (1) all (or at the very least, most) educational objectives should be stated in behavioral terms; (2) requirements that teaching be competence- or performance-based should be established; (3) a method of educational evaluation which is limited to only what can be observed and measured should be devised; and (4) techniques of behavioral control which depend on an assumed instrumental relationship between means (generic behaviors) and ends (behavioral objectives) should be implemented.[28]

Although accountability has many glaring weaknesses—in particular, its insistence on only considering that which can be measured as learning—it nevertheless has received great support from administrators. Again, as with the case of progressive education, this acceptance has less to do with its educational worth than with its potential for control. Accountability in education thus "is not primarily a pedagogical movement. It is an administrative system, and as such it is impervious to arguments which are based on educational concerns. Accountability works administratively; that is, it does present a way of rewarding certain activities and punishing others.''[29]

The current popularity of accountability can be traced to what has been called the bible of the accountability movement, Leon Lessinger's *Every Kid a Winner* (1970).[30] Lessinger, in this work, stresses the rights of students to learn and the rights of the taxpayers to know what educational results take place to compensate for the increasing tax dollar spent on education. Lessinger's assumption is that once the school (or the teacher) knows that it is being held responsible for education, it will facilitate and bring about learning. Learning is linked to its costs, and therefore must be stated in quantifiable terms which are then broken down into cost statements. Or, as Lessinger writes, ''Once the output of schools is measured in proven learning instead of resources allocated or teaching done, the next step is to relate learning to its cost.''[31] Lessinger's emphasis is quite similar to one that appeared at the beginning of the twentieth century, the trend in educational administration that has been described by Raymond Callahan as the ''cult of efficiency.''[32] Callahan has cogently argued that the acceptance of the business ideology in education (cost efficiency) on the part of educational administrators was directly related to the fact that educational administration was in its infancy and, as such, administrators were extremely vulnerable. Educational administration had no theoretical base, no rationale on which to base its claim for acceptance. Given their perceptions of their own powerlessness in the face of criticism from the society, they readily embraced business values. As Callahan says:

> . . . I was not really surprised to find business ideals and practices being used in education.
> *What was unexpected was the extent, not only of the power of the business-industrial groups, but of the strength of the business ideology in the American culture on the one hand and the extreme weakness and vulnerability of school-men, especially school administrators, on the other.* I had expected more professional autonomy and I was completely unprepared for the extent and degree of capitulation by administrators to whatever demands were made upon them. I was surprised and then dismayed to learn how many decisions they made or were forced to make, not on educational grounds, but as a means of appeasing their critics in order to maintain their positions in the school.[33]

Efficiency in education was to provide both a better and a cheaper education. Budgetary concerns took precedence over educational matters. Subjects which did not traditionally fit into the ''3Rs'' were to be ignored. Taylorism, which was sweeping the business community, was translated into education. The emphasis in the schools was on per pupil cost, schools were referred to as ''plants,'' and the ''investment per pupil'' became the key concept in judging efficiency. Decisions as to what should be taught were made upon financial and not pedagogical grounds. Management of education was to become not only financially efficient but scientific as well. One of the earliest and most influential advocates, John Franklin Bobbitt, drew parallels between management and worker in industry and the administrator and teacher in the school, in the process building up the authority of the administrator at the expense of the teacher. If the administrator was powerless against the public at large, at least he or she could assert his authority over his or her teacher. The influence of Bobbitt's views seem to be inversely correlated with his unrealistic basis for a ''science'' of education. Bobbitt's perception of education was so narrow and mechanical that instead of turning for guidance ''to the psychologist, the social psychologist, and the sociologist, he cited the achievements of the Harriman Railroad Corporation.''[34] The magic wand was ''scientific management'' and administrators sought to wrap themselves in the magician's cloak. As was the case with progressive education, administrators were motivated by political and not educational reasons.

Although ''efficiency'' and ''accountability'' are not synonymous, nevertheless the former was a definite antecedent of the latter, and as such, both movements lack an educationally valid conceptual base; both make exaggerated claims for success. In short, they offer rhetoric instead of substance. For example, Lessinger offers a promise of educational opportunity to the poor.[35] However, upon close inspection, we see that contained in this approach is an inherently conservative bias—one that takes the political makeup of the society as the natural order of things.[36] Accountability, instead of helping the poor, ''prevents analysis of the influence of social and economic factors on school success by forcing educators to concentrate on measuring and testing learning in a social vacuum.''[37] Advocates of accountability refuse to look to the social structure, to a sociological perspective, for the root of the problems of the poor. What they offer is a variant of the individualistic perspective. It is now not the child who is at fault but the teacher. Teachers, in a particularly vulnerable position given the rising costs of education, are made the scapegoats for a system that has never worked.

Public school administration is dominated by a bureaucratic mentality. Administrators have jealously guarded their hierarchical authority, effectively excluding teachers from controlling their work conditions and from achieving true professional status. This is so in spite of the current growth and militancy of teachers unions. The teachers unions power base is stronger in the community than in the classroom (something that will be discussed in Chapter 8). And even this power is being threatened by the accountability movement. It seems too much of a coincidence that the accountability movement gained strength just when teachers were beginning to make power gains through their collective actions. Martin et al. give voice to this suspicion:

> We suspect that accountability will be seen as a means of stabilizing the teacher labor market by selecting out and firing teachers. This process serves a three-fold purpose not only for astute administrations but also for the corporate system as a whole. On the one hand, it assuages the angry inner-city parents who feel their children are getting inferior schooling; it leads these parents to believe something significant is being done for ''equal opportunity.'' At the same time, it reinforces the image of the teacher as the problem, and by using the teachers as scapegoats, continues to divert attention from the real sources of the power of inequality. Finally, it provides a stabilizing barrier to effective class-consciousness by teachers while claiming objectivity, fairness, and univ-

ersality of standards. In this way accountability can be used to stall the growing power of teacher unionism and to further constrain schools from becoming sources of individual self-discovery for both students and teachers.[38]

The accountability movement is basically a political movement. Economic and political forces provide the major thrust behind its acceptance. The rhetoric of holding down costs underlies a strain toward the maintenance of the hierarchical structure present in the school.

Accountability is designed to combat the quest for teachers' power, to prevent them from achieving autonomy in their work. To this end, administrators keep making the important "educational decisions," and accountability and cost efficient exponents seek to design an even more rigidly bureaucratic system than the one we now have. The accountability movement, if unchecked, has the potential to hinder teachers from taking collective action necessary to overcome their subordinate role in the school. In this manner, any power gains made by teachers can quickly be erased with an appeal to fiscal stringency; any inroads toward professionalism and the autonomy that goes with it can easily be checked by calls for accountability and efficiency. If there was a viable technology of learning, one that accurately lent itself to measurement, then the push toward accountability might have some validity. But as Daniel Griffiths, Dean of New York University School of Education, has stated, "No one has as yet related a teacher's behavior to a student's learning. There is some doubt that this will ever be done."[39] The movement for accountability must be seen for what it is—a power play to limit teachers' autonomy while increasing their responsibility.

Again, we can see how educational problems are reducible to power relations as administrators seek to control teachers. To repeat, it is no accident that the accountability movement seeks to make teachers the scapegoats for the failure of the lower classes (something that has characterized American public education since it began) just at a time when teachers are beginning to assert themselves via collective action.

One more example, the near-total embracing of "systems analysis" by administrators, will reinforce our contention that power and dissent define schooling in the United States.

Systems Analysis and Administrators

The systems approach, or "systems analysis" (terms which will be used interchangeably), is seen by administrators and educators in general as an answer to the problems that plague American education today. Perhaps because educational administrators have no scholarly discipline of their own, having traditionally borrowed from the social sciences, they have embraced systems analysis because it offers a way to bring various specialities together. Building upon the basic assumption of the interrelatedness and interdependence of all parts in a system, systems analysis in education becomes a means for planning at all organizational levels. In fact, the systems approach concerns itself primarily with the nature of decision-making, and hence, we will argue, this explains its appeal.

Educational administrators have come to view systems analysis as a source of what they consider to be a solid foundation for making decisions. Administrators, when called on to justify policies and recommendations, have a ready-made system for substantiating their claims. Armed with diagrams and flow charts as well as a specialized jargon, they can explain that which they seek to initiate. Obviously, the systems approach advocates would not agree with this description of what sociologists would call the "priestly role," preferring to see themselves instead as objective analysts. A closer look at systems analysis, however, shows an essential conservative bias of this approach.

Although systems analysis is not a set, established viewpoint with definite, clear-cut rules, nearly all systems approach models include the following features or elements: (1) some type of design for taking a particular action; (2) a description of possible alternatives; and (3) some form of evaluation procedure.[40] The concept of model is basic to the systems approach, for usually problems are too complex to cope with by ordinary inspection or common sense. Phenomena are approached in terms of interconnections and linkages, and possible behavior patterns are simulated in the model. An example of a general systems model is given below.[41]

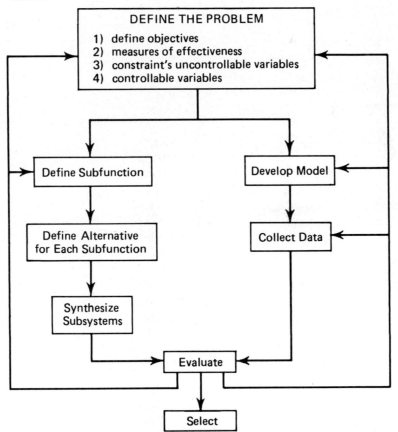

One of the more interesting aspects of the systems approach is its almost unqualified acceptance by educators. Claiming that it works on a practical level, they tend to scoff at what they consider to be mere academic criticisms. Such an atheoretical position masks the real problems that occur in the selection of one perspective over another. For example, when we inspect the systems approach a bit more closely, we can see that it bears little relation to reality. Our criticism, here, goes beyond the general one leveled at all efforts to construct reality—that is, that no model can fit reality precisely. What is involved here is not a choice between models, or between having a model and having no model, but a blind acceptance. In their desire to show that they are, above all else, practical, educators have simply borrowed wholesale one view from science and social science, overlooking the problems inherent in applying an analytical construct to an actual situation. In short, while it looks nice on paper to include uncontrollable variables in the systems model, these variables greatly reduce predictive power.

This uncritical usurpation overlooks, too, that human beings are not nerve endings or atomic particles; they possess free will which enables them to choose alternatives.[42] Such analogical thinking is inherently limited, forcing research into inappropriate paths which can only produce inaccurate findings about social beings.[43]

Another important condemnation of systems analysis revolves around the technical problems providing measures of its central concepts. For instance, how does one measure persistance or input demands to cope with stress? Or as Jerone Stephens phrases it: "It does seem reasonable . . . that feedback and systems mechanisms should be found in systems that continue to exist, but the problem occurs, at least partially, because they (Systems Analysts) do not specify any range, except system survival . . . within which the system remains despite disturbances."[44] This leads us to the complex question of system survival and change; we would argue that systems analysis, like functionalism, because of its preoccupation with system persistence (or maintenance, to use the functionalist's term), leads to the adherence of policy views supportive of the existing status quo. This conservative viewpoint manifests itself because, as M. L. Goldschmidt has stated, systems analysts like their functionalists counterparts tend "to see anything which exists, particularly if it has existed for a long time, as functional and system-sustaining and, hence, good."[45]

It is this inherent conservative bias that has been responsible for the receptivity toward the systems approach among educators. Systems analysis fits in with the management orientation of the superintendents and administrators who make the day-to-day decisions concerning educational policy. In the end, the decision to use systems analysis is a political one, and educators who claim that education is free from political consideration are at worst manipulative and deceptive and are at best naive. Because it focuses upon systems operations in abstract terms, rather than upon behavioral patterns of individuals or groups, systems analysis ignores and tacitly sanctions important aspects of political life. Outside of the Marxists, educators with few exceptions have blindly refused to confront the political implications of systems analysis.[46] In short, this method of handling educational problems coincides quite nicely with the bureaucratic role of the school principal.

SUMMARY

The principal or school-level administrator engages in role behavior just as do teachers. A potential source of conflict in the schools relates to the different definition of roles for teacher and administrator. In spite of their generally subordinate position, some teachers do insist on a professional status, which should carry with it a certain amount of autonomy over their work experience. Since schools have become more and more of a bureaucracy, a possible strain can arise between the teacher who conceives of himself or herself as a professional and the principal who views himself or herself as an organizational, or in this case, educational, manager. Blau and Scott, for example, have shown that although professional and bureaucratic modes of organization have many common principles, there is a basic source of conflict between "professional expertise" and "bureaucratic discipline"; that is, the control structure of the professions is fundamentally different from the hierarchical control exercised in a bureaucratic organization.[47] The ultimate justification for a professional's action is the professional's knowledge and expertise; whereas, the ultimate justification for a bureaucratic action is consistency with the rules and regulations of the organization as approved by the hierarchy.[48] As we have seen, the balance between teacher autonomy and administrative authority clearly favors the latter. Most, if not all, of this authority comes from the bureaucratic nature of the principal's role, in spite of the rhetoric that postulates a dual role for the principal as administrative manager and instructional leader. Principals and administrators in general have been quick to embrace educational ideologies that enabled them to maintain their power and authority over teachers. The incorporation of such educational ideologies as progressive education, accountability, and systems analysis into America's schools must, therefore, be seen more in terms of one's group's (administrators) attempt to dominate another group (teachers) than as an educational decision. The relationships that exist between administrators and teachers is thus related to a larger framework of power and conflict, dominance and subordination.

NOTES

1. Not all sociologists would agree with this description of the contemporary school as a rigid bureaucratic structure. For example, Charles Bidwell, in "The School as a Formal Organization," in James G. Marsh (ed.), *Handbook of Organizations*. Chicago: Rand McNally, 1965, pp. 972–1022, sees schools as characterized by a "structural looseness." However the history of administrative emphasis upon efficiency and the contemporary trend toward management by objectives supports our depiction.

2. David Goslin, *The School in Contemporary Society*. Glenview, Ill.: Scott, Foresman, 1965, p. 133.

3. Ronald G. Corwin, *Education in Crisis: A Sociological Analysis of Schools and Universities in Transition*. New York: Wiley, 1974, p. 20.

4. Ibid., p. 21.

5. Ibid., p. 24.

6. Ibid., pp. 22–23.

7. Obviously, not all principals neglect the educational-leadership role; however, the educational administrator or manager represents the ideal type today.

8. William H. Roe and Thelbert L. Drake, *The Principalship*. New York: Macmillan, 1974, p. 13.

9. For a review of the empirical evidence for the existence of the "bureaucratic personality," see Leonard V. Gordon, *The Measurement of Interpersonal Values*. Chicago: Science Research Associates, 1975.

10. Thomas B. Stone, "The Elementary School Principalship—Toward the Twenty-first Century," in *Selected Articles For Elementary School Principals*. Washington, D.C.: National Education Association, Department of Elementary School Principals, 1968, p. 21.

11. This section is based on Neal Gross and Robert E. Herriott, *Staff Leadership in Public Schools*. New York: Wiley, 1965.

12. Ibid., p. 61.

13. Paul R. Pierce, *The Origin and Development of the Public School Principalship*. Chicago: University of Chicago Press, 1935, p. 12.

14. Ibid., p. 211.

15. Ibid.

16. Ibid., p. 214.

17. Raymond E. Callahan, "The American Board of Education, 1789–1960," in Peter J. Cistone (ed.), *Understanding School Boards*. Lexington, Mass.: Lexington Books, 1975, p. 21.

18. Ibid., p. 24.

19. Ellwood P. Cubberly, *Public School Administration*. Boston: Houghton Mifflin, 1916, p. 59.

20. This section relies heavily on David W. Swift, *Ideology and Change in the Public Schools: Latent Functions of Progressive Education*. Columbus, Ohio: Merrill, 1971.

21. Burton Fowler, quoted in ibid., p. 4.

22. See in particular Hyman G. Rickover, *Education and Freedom*. New York: Dutton, 1959.

23. Swift, *Ideology and Change in the Public Schools*, p. 66.

24. Ibid., p. 83.

25. For an analysis of "locals" and "cosmopolitans" in organizations, see Alvin W. Gouldner, "Cosmopolitans and Locals: Toward an Analysis of Latent Social Roles—I," *Administrative Science Quarterly, 2* (December 1957), pp. 281–306; "Cosmopolitans and Locals: Toward an Analysis of Latent Social Roles—II," *Administrative Science Quarterly, 2* (March 1958), pp. 441–480.

26. Swift, *Ideology and Change in the Public Schools*, pp. 93–94.

27. Ibid., p. 146.

28. Don T. Martin, George E. Overholt, and Wayne J. Urban, *Accountability in American Education: A Critique*. Princeton, N.J.: Princeton Book Company, 1976, p. 3.

29. Ibid., p. 32.

30. Leon M. Lessinger, *Every Kid a Winner: Accountability in Education*. Palo Alto, Calif.: Science Research Associates, 1970.

31. Ibid., p. 9.

32. Raymond E. Callahan, *Education and the Cult of Efficiency*. Chicago: University of Chicago Press, 1962.

33. Ibid., Preface.

34. Ibid., p. 92.

35. Lessinger, *Every Kid a Winner*, pp. 6–8.

36. For an excellent critical review of Lessinger, see Martin Levit, "The Ideology of Accountability in Schooling," *Educational Studies, III* (Fall 1972), pp. 133–140.

37. Martin et al., *Accountability in American Education*, p. 45.

38. Ibid., p. 60.

39. Daniel E. Griffiths, "Intellectualism and Professionalism," *New York University Education Quarterly, V* (Fall 1973), p. 2.

40. John Pfeiffer, *New Look at Education: Systems Analysis In Our Schools and Colleges.* New York: Odyssey, 1968, pp. 46.

41. Ibid., p. 32.

42. Obviously, educational behaviorists would not accept this view. We would argue, though, that they too have uncritically accepted physical science models without considering the more recent developments in the physical and biological sciences which call mechanistic models into question. For an elaboration of this position, see Floyd Matson, *The Broken Image: Men, Science and Society.* Garden City, N.Y.: Doubleday/Anchor Books, 1966.

43. See John G. Gunnell, "Social Science and Political Reality: The Problem of Explanation," *Social Research, 35* (1968), pp. 159–201.

44. Jerone Stephens, "The Logic of Functional and Systems Analysis in Political Science," *Midwest Journal of Political Science, 13* (1969), p. 374.

45. M.L. Goldschmidt, "Democratic Theory and Contemporary Political Science," *Western Political Science Quarterly, 19* (1966 Supplement), p. 7.

46. Important exceptions are Frederick M. Wirt and Michael W. Kirst, *Political and Social Foundations of Education,* rev. ed. Berkeley, Calif.: McCutcheon, 1975; and Frederick M. Wirt (ed.), *The Polity of Schools.* Lexington, Mass.: Heath, 1975. However, we would argue that the pluralist assumptions they hold represent a conservative bias. For an elaboration of this position, see William Connolly, (ed.), *The Bias of Pluralism.* New York: Atherton Press, 1969.

47. Peter Blau and Richard W. Scott, *Formal Organizations.* San Francisco: Chandler, 1962, pp. 59–74.

48. For an analysis of how a bureaucratic structure stifles educational innovations in an elementary school, see Harry L. Gracey, *Curriculum or Craftsmanship.* Chicago: University of Chicago Press, 1972.

6

Conflict and Legitimacy within the School

The bureaucratization of American society is one of the fundamental developments of the twentieth century, and bureaucracy represents the dominant form of organization in the public schools.[1] The bureaucratically run school is the battleground for the various groups which comprise it. Conflict is generated between administrators, teachers, and students as they act out their roles in a large-scale organizational structure.

Over and above this role conflict is another level of conflict, one that pervades the entire system of public education and sets the tone for interorganization tensions—that of class conflict between the middle class and the lower class. Given the greater power, status, and resources at their disposal, the middle class is better able than the lower class to pursue their own interests in the schools. The conflict normally expected to occur when two parties are of unequal strength is effectively diffused as the lower classes are socialized to accept the educational system as legitimate. By controlling the making of rules and their promulgation, by defining what is accepted as pedagogically sound, the middle class is able to see to it that the schools protect their and their children's interests. We reiterate the assumption made earlier that the upper classes in America have little to do with the everyday workings of the public schools. Upper-class children are enrolled in expensive and exclusive private schools, which are also dominated by middle-class values through their middle-class headmasters and staffs. James McLachlan, in a comprehensive study of America's elite private schools, offers support for this position:

> For most of their history these schools have consciously educated their students to avoid, abjure, and despise most of what are traditionally thought to be aristocratic or upper-class values and styles of life. They have worked instead to *prevent* the development of aristocratic attitudes. They have tried to inculcate their students with what are usually thought to be classically "middle-class" values: self-restraint, rigid self-control, severe frugality in personal style, and the ability to postpone immediate gratifications for larger future ends. How successful they have been in this is another matter: like all educational institutions, private boarding schools have been faced with the inherent conflict between the values that the school wishes to transmit and those that its students bring with them from their homes and communities.[2]

The middle class is firmly in control of American education. The upper class has left the day-to-day running of the schools to the middle class because education does not pose any threat to the power structure. Educators can be left to their own devices.

We therefore differ with the Marxist interpretation which sees the schools as simply reflecting upper-class goals and values.[3] Instead, in this chapter, we focus upon the general conflict found within the schools, tension which is endemic to any bureaucratically run organization. Class opposition, when it is introduced, is seen in relation to the middle-class domination of the lower class and its attempts to impose the stamp of legitimacy on this unequal situation. Education provides access to the middle class and is therefore best analyzed as a struggle at this level.

CONFLICT IN THE SCHOOL: TEACHER VERSUS ADMINISTRATOR

The social forces that have produced the bureaucratization of American society have also created alternative forms of organization, among them the principles of professionalism. In the schools, this had produced a fundamental tension between the teacher, who regards himself or herself as a professional, and bureaucratic principles of organization, which are embodied in the educational manager role of the principal described in the preceding chapter.

Daily issues of confrontation revolve around the amount and direction of authority teachers should have over the selection of textbooks, methods, and curriculum development. The bureaucratic school does not support the self-conception of the teacher as one who possesses the expertise to make decisions; original thought can only be superficially followed in any large-scale organization. Standardization of position and superordination−subordination by rank are the primary concerns in a bureaucracy. Although teaching is not a profession, as we saw in Chapter 4, nevertheless a number of teachers are seeking to professionalize their occupation, resulting in a conflict situation as the two ideological positions, professionalism and bureaucracy, become defined as antithetical. An implicit assumption, then, is that when teachers seek to achieve more and more control over the policies that govern their work, they come into direct conflict with the bureaucratic school, which is designed to control and standardize work and otherwise constrain the authority of employees.[4]

Conflict theory stresses the tensions inherent in the very fact of differentiation within social structures. Conflicts arise between persons and groups located in different parts and competing positions within the system.[5] Priority is assigned to the variable of power. Tensions are extremely likely to occur when power is unequally distributed among various segments of an organization. Any attempt to shift the balance of power will tend to facilitate overt conflict.

By focusing upon conflict at the school or organizational level, we minimize the problems that arise in the schools as a result of the characteristics of individuals; we see the system as the producer of conflict. For example, as we stated before, friction is inherent in the differentiation of roles within the school. There is a fundamental contradiction between the subordinate status of teachers within the school and the perception of themselves as professionals with rights and obligations related to the improvement of education. Professional responsibilities require a certain amount of latitude and autonomy for coping with problems that arise. A professional is also primarily responsible to his or her colleagues who are seen as the only ones capable of evaluating him or her. As Ronald Corwin states:

> These principles are inconsistent with the fact that teachers are hired and evaluated by administrators to do a specific job; they are also inconsistent with many of the standardized requirements, a centralized decision-making system, close supervision, and task oriented rules under which schools operate.
>
> The teacher, therefore, inherits with the job inconsistent expectations about his proper role in education. The fact that he is an employee establishes one set of obligations; the fact that he is a professional employee compounds the situation by establishing competing expectations and standards. If he attempts to straddle both roles simultaneously, he can expect to experience some turbulence during his career.[6]

An incompatibility arises between bureaucratic and professional principles, which in turn becomes a potential source of conflict. Historically, given the socialization process of teachers, administrators have been able to neutralize any overt conflict by stressing managerial−employee roles. However, given the recent militancy of some teachers, conflict is generated when the more active teachers refuse to accept this role relationship.

In short, for some teachers there is a constant struggle to function in relation to the demands of both professionalism and bureaucratization. Administrators, on the other hand, have stubbornly refused to acknowledge these conflicting demands on teachers. For the most part, they are happy to define their role as it was a hundred years ago, before urbanization changed the face of this nation. Superintendents and school boards, too, have refused to acknowledge the fact that the educational system is rapidly changing. By continuing to insist upon reviewing each decision and suspiciously regarding the demands of teachers for more authority as insidious plots, they tend to exacerbate an already tense situation.[7]

The major conflicts between teachers and administrators are thus usually reducible to power and authority issues. In general, a sizable number of teachers feel they do not have enough authority. Administrators, on the other hand, are often dogmatic and dictatorial in their use of control, believing wholeheartedly in their decision-making prerogatives and jealously guarding them.[8] It must be reiterated here, though, that while some teachers want more prestige, the majority seem resigned to their role as subordinates, and this remains a major reason for their failure to achieve more power.[9] This partly explains why conflict is usually kept to a minimum in the schools, or is at least kept under control. Indeed, most teachers express strong loyalty to their administrators and their communities.

> Approximately two-thirds or more agree that teachers in their schools should adjust their teaching to the administration's view of good educational practice; are obedient, respectful, and loyal to the principal; look primarily to administration's judgment for guidance in case of community disputes (controversies over a textbook or a speaker); are completely familiar with written descriptions of the rules, procedures, manuals, and other standard operating procedures connected with running a classroom; and would not publicly advocate a position on the place of religion in the school if it differed greatly from the community's majority opinion.[10]

A majority of teachers also tend to believe that their principal is better qualified than they are to judge what is best for the school, and in general accept the rules and regulations set forth by the school administration.[11] It is, thus, only the willing compliance of the majority of public school teachers that has kept the conflict in the schools at a manageable level.

It must be borne in mind, too, that although the public schools have been bureaucratized, the process has not been entirely consistent or uniform in its development. A number of discrete practices have arisen which complicate even further the potential conflict between teachers and administrators. However, in nearly every school a delicate balance exists between teachers' practical solutions to everyday problems which arise in their classrooms and the pressures on them to comply to bureaucratic rules and regulations. Add to this a significant minority of teachers that can be classified as dissatisfied and alienated,[12] and the tinderbox nature of the school could easily result in an explosion.

To summarize, the almost universal administrative response to teachers' desires for autonomy is a reliance upon the educational—manager role and a subsequent tightening of bureaucratic controls, something which can only aggravate the already existing conflict. The end result is role-structured antagonism within a bureaucratic organization. The more administrators hide behind rules and regulations, the more they fuel a potentially dangerous situation. Can this be changed? Perhaps, but at present it seems that teachers and administrators are on a collision course as they jockey for power within the school.

TEACHER VERSUS STUDENT CONFLICT[13]

Teacher–student conflict, like teacher–administrator conflict, revolves around authority relations in the school. Here, too, the confrontation takes the form of institutionalized dominance and subordination and follows a specific pattern. First of all, teachers are adults and represent a different value-structure than that of children. The teacher stands for the established social order in the school, whereas students have only a negligible interest in the structure.

> Teacher and pupil confront each other with attitudes from which the underlying hostility can never be altogether removed. Pupils are the material in which teachers are supposed to produce results. Pupils are human beings striving to realize themselves in their own spontaneous manner, striving to produce their own results in their own way. Each of these hostile parties stands in the way of the other; in so far as the aims of either are realized, it is at the sacrifice of the aims of the other.[14]

In the reciprocal roles of teacher–student, the teacher represents established authority, and digressions from this order on the part of the student must be dealt with. Much of the teaching–learning process, too, is a boring routine of acquiring skills and competencies, and students react negatively to this reality. Such a situation produces a fairly inflexible amount of role behavior on the part of the teacher, and has far-reaching effects on his or her personality.

> The details of the carrying of authority are worked out with minute perfection; the teacher's voice and the expression of his face are formalized and forced to conform to the necessitites of the authority role. Likewise, there is an internal adaption to the conditions of teaching such that the teacher's personal dignity depends upon the teacher's role, one comes to think of himself not only as a teacher but as *the* teacher.[15]

In short, because teachers are placed in the position of having to force children to learn, unpleasantness and tension are the rule. The expectations of the teacher and the expectations of the students in his or her charge are quite different, and therefore conflict often results. Yet, it must be pointed out that, as with the conflict between teachers and administrators, the situation usually does not reach the stage of overt conflict. This is of particular importance when we consider how little the lower class is getting from the schools. While some lower-class children, in particular those who manage to internalize and manifest middle-class values, do succeed in the schools, the overwhelming majority of lower-class children receive an education that at best can be described as abysmal.[16] The job of the school becomes one of convincing the lower classes that their failure is their own fault, that they were given a fair chance and did not have what it takes to succeed. It is not the system which is at fault but the individual. The system's legitimacy must be maintained, and the schools practice a form of socialization that attempts to do just that.

SOCIALIZATION IN THE SCHOOLS: LEGITIMACY AND INDIVIDUAL RESPONSIBILITY

Public schools are set up to preserve middle-class hegemony. ("Hegemony," as defined by social scientists, refers to the process dominant groups use to get nondominant groups to accept domination.) The socialization process becomes a legitimizing process by emphasizing what Richard Sennett and Jonathan Cobb have called "the badge of individual ability."[17] By stressing an individualistic perspective, schools socialize children to accept the reasoning that their failure or their success is solely dependent upon their own ability. Given that the self is a social creation (derived essentially out of the socialization experience as the person integrates the various roles he or she is called upon to play), the acceptance of the individualistic perspective becomes essential for the acceptance of the legitimacy of the schools. Although it is debatable as to whether the family or the school is *the* most important primary agent of socialization, no one would argue that the educational experience is not *a* primary agent of socialization. The academically successful are given a positive self-image based on the belief that they succeed on their own merits.[18] Obviously, these persons would be extremely reluctant to question this ideology of individual ability, which would entail questioning an integral part of their very image of self. For example, teachers, the socializing agent with whom the student has the most day-to-day contact within the schools, have been academically successful by accepting the socialization process, and when they get to "the other side of the desk," they almost instinctively impose those values they themselves internalized upon their students. Teachers and students alike are playing roles; their behavior revolves around expected norms. In this way, educational failure can be understood as role behavior, a label like any other label.

However, it is of paramount importance that lower-class individuals' failure be seen by them as caused by their own lack of ability. For if they think otherwise they would not believe that the system is a legitimate one, that is has provided equal opportunity for them. Individuals who accept the role of educational failure based upon their own shortcomings do not look to the society and its class structure for the locus of their problems. They turn inward instead. Obviously, the schools are not solely to blame for this misperception. Our whole society is geared in this direction. Pop psychology books constantly tell us how to change *our* personalities, how to overcome *our* flaws, how to succeed by really trying. By changing *one's* self (or if one has trouble doing it alone, by seeing a therapist) one can eventually overcome *one's* individual inadequacies. What is not stated, though, is that upper-class people are successful because they were born to be successful, that they have dominant personalities because they have been giving orders all their lives; or that middle-class individuals received the education that "got them where they are today," for the most part because their parents were educated.[19] There is a wide gulf between the powerful and the powerless; between the educated and noneducated in our society. The shame of the schools is that they have done nothing to alleviate this; indeed, by their refusal to critically confront the individualistic perspective, they have reinforced this view. On this point the schools are implicated in a conspiracy, a conspiracy of inaction.

Teachers do not purposely denigrate their students, lock them into a role of failure. They are not agents of capitalism whose goal is to provide a differentiated labor force.[20] It is much more complex than that. Tied in with the socialization process is a whole network of power and status relationships. Public education, as it has evolved in the United States, may very well be a tool of the bourgeois capitalist class, as some critics have argued, but this is only because we live in a corporate capitalist society. Education could just as easily be a tool of a socialist state, or any other type of government. The basic problem of public education is that it is conservative; that is, it conserves or supports whatever power arrangements have evolved in the society at large. Education is ultimately dependent upon power arrangements, not economic ones. Accordingly, the ideal is always far removed from the real. Our schools are supposed to serve all children equally regardless of color, creed, and so on, but they do not because children from the middle classes have traditionally started with an advantage, and given the conservative nature of the schools, little is done to change this. The achievement values middle-class children acquire from their families are the same as those stressed by the schools. A situation of mutual support enables them to excel in academic achievement. Teachers prefer teaching children from the middle class, children who are perceived as better behaved and brighter than children from poorer families. Even though middle-class children do not always fully meet their teacher's expectations, their misbehavior tends to be interpreted as a natural consequence of their brightness or at worst an indication that they are spoiled. They are not perceived as threatening the authority of the school or basic values of the teacher.[21] Thus the correspondence of middle-class children's values with the schools' values virtually insure the academic success of the middle-class child. The lower-class student, on the other hand, suffers the consequences of not having his or her prior values in line with what is expected of him or her in the school. He or she is discriminated against as the school does virtually nothing to help him or her succeed. When he or she does succeed, he or she must overcome a number of handicaps. He or she must usually be the best of the lower class, whereas in the middle class the student only has to be average. In a word, the lower-class student is powerless to offset long-established educational relationships. The implications of this are obvious. Students who are powerless suffer from a poor self-image, which they internalize as their own fault, and eventually come to see themselves as less than worthwhile human beings. They become, for all intents and purposes, second-class citizens, devoid of autonomy and control over their own lives. As one student of urban education put it:

> We have managed to engage the brighter students, to alienate them (sometimes inadvertently) from their original group, and to entice them into the kingdom by the promise of acquisitive success. But the vast majority of ghetto dwellers remain uncalled and unreaching; powerless and ultimately hopeless. The large society decided to whom and to how many the right of choice will be offered. This is quite different from the notion (supposedly "basic" to American ideology) that choices and freedom are the rights of all.[22]

Millions of lower-class children are characterized by powerlessness and a depressed self-image. Ultimately they become submerged in what the exiled Brazilian educator Paulo Freire calls a "culture of silence."[23]

The middle class controls public education and seeks to preserve this position of dominance because education in America has replaced property as a guarantor of middle-class status. The period directly following the Civil War saw a great shift away from owning the property one worked at (being an individual entrepreneur), and toward the centralization of property. The result is that today the overwhelming majority of people work for some type of centralized bureaucratic structure. No longer able to insure their children's middle-class status by passing their property on to them, they seek to solidify their status by passing education on to their children. The middle class thus uses education as a birthright for their progeny; it replaces property they no longer own. If the lower class received the same amount of education, it would depreciate education's value. This creates a clear case of conflict. The middle class has definite interests to maintain, and are in a position to protect them. They use their relative power, status, and resources to assure their children's academic success. This is why middle-class school districts allocate so much more money for their students than do lower-class districts. Educational policies and programs are set up to provide every advantage for the middle-class child. The deck is stacked against the poor and powerless. IQ tests which measure middle-class values are still taken as evidence of intelligence, when there is more than sufficient documentation to establish a positive correlation between IQ and socioeconomic status;[24] the schools stress middle-class verbal skills at the expense of lower-class speech patterns. This latter change, based on the work of the British sociologist of education, Basil Bernstein, is just beginning to be taken up by American sociologists and deserves special attention.

BASIL BERNSTEIN: CLASS AND LANGUAGE CODES

Basil Bernstein has investigated the language patterns of the children of the working class, comparing them to middle-class children. He found a clear pattern of demarcation between the two, a demarcation that reinforces educational failure among the lower class.

Bernstein distinguishes two codes in speech patterns, what he calls a "restricted code" and an "elaborated code." A restricted code arises in the lower and working classes where the experience of children is closely shared, and subsequently the need to verbalize is reduced. The speech structure is simplified and the range of verbal alternatives is limited with meanings tending to be descriptive rather than analytical or abstract. The characteristics of an elaborated code are just the opposite: complex speech structure, wide range of alternatives, an emphasis on analytical and abstract meanings.[25] Bernstein notes that children from the middle classes "learn to scan a particular syntax, to receive and transmit a particular pattern of meaning, to develop a particular (verbal) planning process, and very early to orient toward the verbal channel," whereas children from the lower classes who are "limited to a restricted code will tend to develop through the regulation inherent in the code."[26] Although generalization and concrete descriptive statements can be transmitted in a restricted code, they involve a very low order of conceptualization. The middle-class-dominated schools are based on elaborated codes and children who already possess this speech pattern have a distinct advantage. According to Bernstein, they have access to both the elaborate and restricted code, where children from the lower classes are familiar only with the restricted code. Evidence of basic language differences between the middle class and lower classes have come from other societies as well. Pierre Guiraud, for example, found that French working class language was characterized by the use of "exaggeration, redundant terms, tautologies, repetitions, and illogical derivations."[27] Anselm Strauss and Lenore Schatzman have also noted the difference in articulation skills between the lower and middle classes in the United States.[28]

The difference between the two classes can be summarized by the following table:[29]

TABLE 6–1

	Lower Class	Middle Class
Perspective	Fixed perspective; rigid description.	Use of several standpoints and alternative interpretations.
Organization	Lack of clear referents; few qualifications; segmented organizational framework; little grasp of context of event if more than one action is involved.	Frequent qualifications and illustrations; clear narrative even when narrative is complex; unitary framework of organization.
Classification and relation	Relative inability to use categories for people and acts since the speaker tends not to think in terms of classes; imprecise use of logical connections.	Rich, conceptual terminology; frequent classifications and use of logical categories.
Abstraction	Insensitivity to abstract information and questions.	Sensitivity to generalization and patterns.
Use of time	Discontinuous; emphasis on the particular and ephemeral.	Continuous; emphasis on process and development.

The implications for education are obvious. The middle-class child begins with a clear-cut advantage and keeps it as he or she goes through school. The schools, therefore, primarily geared to middle-class standards and expectations, do very little, if anything, to offset this benefit. And even those educators who accept Bernstein's general conclusions tend to distort them in practice. Equating restricted code with such terms as "linguistic deprivation" or even labeling the student as a "nonverbal child," they divert attention away from the school, to the families and the cultural deprivation of the children. Bernstein, however, wants to show how schools can compensate for society by bringing "parents within the educational experience of the schoolchild."[30] If the parent can be included, can be brought in to help the child; if the content of the learning is drawn from the child's cultural background, lower-class children might very well be educated too. However, as we will argue throughout, the basic conflict between the middle class and the lower classes in the schools precludes any real cooperation between the schools and lower-class parents. The interests of the middle class takes precedence over those of the lower class because of the differentiated power structure in the society. To truly include lower-class parents in the educational process of their children would necessitate a shift in power. While this is a viable alternative, and one with which we will deal more fully in the last chapter when we offer some solutions, at this point we must stress that the connection between restricted language codes and public education is a political one; it is based on power relationships. This interrelationship bears further analysis.

RESTRICTED CODES, POLITICAL LEGITIMATION, AND THE SCHOOLS

The connection between language and socialization on the one hand, and the process of legitimation on the other, has never been fully analyzed by social scientists. A recent exception, whose major focus is theoretical and therefore still awaits empirical validation, is Clauss Mueller's *The Politics of Communication* (1973). One of Mueller's central concerns is the analysis of how political integration applies to the lower classes, who can neither articulate their own interests nor perceive social conflicts. They have, in his words, "been socialized into compliance . . . they accept the definitions of political reality as offered by dominant groups, classes, and governmental institutions."[31] This has taken place through the use of a type of restricted language code. According to Mueller, "the type of language an individual internalizes influences his cognitive development as well as his perception of himself and his environment."[32] For example, if a lower-class student linked his or her failure in school to the fact that he or she was born into a specific class, he or she would be much more likely to place the blame for his or her failure on the educational institution than would a student who did not see this class relationship. Indeed, Mueller goes even farther, arguing that the absence of sufficient conceptual development and of specific value predispositions, which relate to socialization and language codes, prevent the individual from attaining any real understanding of the political code of the society he or she is born into.[33]

Drawing heavily upon the works of Bernstein and the German sociologist and philosopher Jurgen Habermas,[34] Mueller takes Habermas' notion of "distorted communication" and extends it to show how any alternatives to the political system are precluded. By "distorted communication" it is meant "all forms of restricted and prejudiced communication that by their nature inhibit a full discussion of problems, issues and ideas that have public relevance."[35]

The lower-class child, because of exposure to a restricted language code and a rigid socialization pattern,[36] tends to view political structure as static and comes to abide by the perceptions of external authorities.[37] The impact of primary socialization is never overcome for the lower-class child; the schools do nothing to offset the passive political perspective the child is exposed to. The process for the middle-class child, however, is different. As Mueller points out:

> An elaborated code and flexible person-oriented socialization techniques make for a self-differentiated individual whose linguistic and cognitive abilities and sense of autonomy allow for reflection upon political institutions. Such a person can consciously choose to support or oppose the political system and articulate interests other than those which are predefined. His ability to handle symbols and his consciousness, which can be verbalized, enable him to comprehend policies and institutions with which he is confronted and be cognizant of the problems his society is facing.[38]

Differential socialization thus works to insure the legitimacy of the system. Lower-class youths, because they are taught to accept their failure as caused by their own individual inabilities, blame themselves rather than the school structure. They accept the system because their restrictive code does not permit them to construct any defense against dominant legitimations.[39] Middle-class youths, on the other hand, with their elaborated code, can question the system. However, realistically, because middle-class youths are successful, such questioning would imply a renunciation of a good part of their sense of self-worth. For middle-class students to accept that they are in college because they were born middle-class and not because, as their teachers have told them all along, "You're so smart," is rare indeed. And since only the best of the lower and working youths succeed, their self-esteem, like that of middle-class youths, is tied up with academic success. Thus, it becomes apparent how difficult questioning the legitimacy of the system is. The result is very little political reflection as the socioeconomic arrangement of the society is basically accepted. The schools are in the business of political socialization and they do a good job in helping to support the status quo.

POLITICAL SOCIALIZATION: LEGITIMACY ESTABLISHED

A simple definition of political socialization has been offered by Dawson, Prewitt, and Dawson, and will be used here. According to them, "Political socialization is concerned with the personal and social origins of political outlooks."[40] Schools have generally taken upon themselves the task of socializing future citizens. The following statement by a superintendent of schools illustrates this acceptance:

> The public school is the greatest and most effective of all Americanization agencies. This is the only place where all children in a community or district, regardless of nationality, religion, politics, or social status, meet and work together in a cooperative and harmonious spirit. . . . The children work and play together, they catch the school spirit, they live the democratic life, American heroes become their own, American history wins their loyalty, the Stars and Stripes, always before their eyes in the school room, receive their daily salute. Not only are these immigrant children Americanized through the public school, but they, in turn, Americanize their parents, carrying into the home many lessons of democracy learned at school.[41]

In reality, however, what actually occurs in school is somewhat different, for political socialization is closely related to domination and control. Specifically, the selected interests of the middle class are exercised over those of the lower class. Such a process is called the "hegemonic theory of political socialization."[42] As an example, in a capitalist country, it is obviously in the best interests of property owners to convince those who do not own property that private ownership (even when it is in the hands of a small group) is important and legitimate. As long as nonowners accept the notion of private ownership, they accept the rules and values by which they are dominated. Along these lines, the subordinate group must also believe that they too have a chance to get into a dominant position. The socialization process is a political one, and the values of individual success and failure are directly linked to the political values taught in the schools. To question the one is to question the other, and the schools seek to limit such questioning. In short, the schools are organized around the process of getting subordinate groups to accept the social values that insure their own subordination.

The family has defaulted from the process of playing any prominent role in political socialization and the schools have stepped in. In fact, as R. W. Connell has stated:

> it appears from a substantial body of evidence that processes within the family have been largely irrelevant to the formation of specific opinions. It appears that older and younger generations have developed their opinions in parallel rather than in series, by experiences in a common way of life.[43]

Parents are not likely to provide a political education for their children. When children are exposed to political issues, it usually occurs in a school civics course or somewhere else in the curriculum. It seems, therefore, that families exert much less political influence than they could. Outside of providing an attachment to a particular political grouping (Democrats or Republicans), politics is not given a high priority in the typical American family. Parents make little effort to articulate their own positions, nor do they push their children toward adopting them. This absence of political education in the family leaves the field wide open for the schools.[44]

Schooling and Political Socialization

The curriculum is potentially one of the primary instruments of political socialization. All students receive formal instruction in the nature and (too often) the glory of the established order. James Coleman has offered a useful distinction between *civic training* and *political indoctrination*. Civic education is that part of political education that emphasizes how a good citizen participates in the political life of his or her nation. Political indoctrination, on the other hand, concerns the learning of a specific political ideology intended to rationalize and justify a particular regime.[45] Although the official position of the schools purports to emphasize the former to the exclusion of the latter, in practice the distinction between the two is often blurred. In particular, this can be seen by focusing upon the political actions the student is exposed to in the classroom.

The child is exposed early to such rituals as saluting the flag, singing patriotic songs, and honoring national heroes. The importance of these ceremonies becomes obvious when we focus upon the amount of time and resources allocated to them. Teachers are compelled, either by law or by strong social norms, to spend valuable school hours on classroom activities that stress patriotic values.[46]

These rites are important politically for a number of reasons. First, rituals can be seen as the acting out of a sense of awe toward what is symbolized by the ritual. Basic feelings of patriotism and loyalty are instilled by the expression of devotion.[47] As Hess and Torney state: "The feelings of respect for the pledge and the national anthem are reinforced daily and are seldom questioned by the child."[48] Submission, respect, and devotion are associated with these acts.[49] The rituals "establish an emotional orientation toward country and flag though an understanding of the meaning of the words and actions has not been developed. These seem to be indoctrinating acts that cue and reinforce feelings of loyalty and patriotism."[50] Secondly, schools maintain political loyalties which have been established in the family, and introduce new ones. Third, and perhaps most important of all, rituals emphasize the collective nature of patriotism. Saluting the flag and singing the national anthem, are group activities.[51] "We-feelings" of a specific nature are reinforced. There is a general feeling of identification with others who are part of a benevolent whole. Nationalism, partisanship, and identification with a legitimate political group are more meaningful when they are experienced as part of a collectivity, and the ritual life of the school revolves around such a collective experience.[52]

On the whole, though, it is the teacher who is the primary political socializing agent for the child. The teacher represents *the* authoritative spokesman of society, for the teacher is usually the first model of political authority the beginning student encounters. The uniqueness of the teacher's authority can be seen by comparing the parent and the teacher.

> When a child responds to his parent as an authority figure, he does not separate the role from the incumbent of the role. He keeps the same parent permanently. Consequently, parents are very personal authority figures; they

dispense rewards and punishments in what often appear to be idiosyncratic and even capricious ways. The public school teacher as an authority figure, on the other hand, is much more like a political authority. The child learns that the authority role and incumbent of the role are separate factors. He learns that he should obey any incumbent who happens to occupy the role "teacher." Further, he discovers that rewards and punishments from authorities are affected by identifiable constraints that operate on the particular person in the role. The teacher, like the policeman, president, or mayor, is part of an institutional pattern, a constitutional order.[53]

In particular, the elementary school teacher is extremely important. Laurence Wylie, who observed a French village school, makes an important point concerning the role of the teacher in reinforcing authoritativeness in the schools.

> The four-year-old and five-year-old children . . . learn important lessons. They learn to sit still for long periods. They learn to accept the discipline of the schools. . . . They are not encouraged to express their personality. On the contrary they learn that their personality must be kept constantly under control.[54]

Evidence from American schools supports this linking of obedience with political learning.[55]

In sum, the ideals expressed about political socialization in the schools is often quite different from actual occurences. The stated goals of education imply the formation of citizens who can take an active role in a democratic society. Ideally, the student comes to learn about the political context of his or her society and is able to recognize existing conflicts and problems.[56] The underlying implication is that children who come from backgrounds where their parents are apathetic or unknowledgeable about political matters are afforded the opportunity to acquire knowledge about the real workings of the political system—to engage in serious thinking about politics and social problems. The picture that emerges from studies of the political socialization of children in the schools is, however, quite different from this ideal, and lends empirical support to our views concerning the role of legitimation in public education. David Easton and Jack Dennis, for example, conclude that "in the American system the child becomes tightly linked to the structure of authority."[57] Robert Hess and Judith Torney, in one of the best-known and comprehensive studies of political socialization (they interviewed over 12,000 elementary students in the United States), conclude that:

> *Compliance to rules and authority is the major focus of civics education in elementary schools.* . . . Teachers of young children place particular stress upon citizen compliance, deemphasizing all other political topics. The three items rated as more important than basic subjects (reading and arithmetic) by a majority of second- and third-grade teachers were *the law, the policeman,* and the child's *obligation to conform* to school rules and laws of the community. This

concern with compliance is characteristic of teachers of all grades. . . . Political socialization at early age levels emphasizes behavior that relates the child emotionally to his country and impresses upon him the necessity for obedience and conformity.[58]

Textbooks are bland affairs, reflecting a picture of a smoothly working political system with little or no conflict and inequality.[59] Indeed, if conflict is mentioned at all it is seen as something to be overcome so that things will again run smoothly. Consensus is the byword, and ideological controversy is to be avoided at all costs. However, because conflict is always implicit, the process does not always run as smoothly as educators would want. Audrey James Schwartz describes what can happen when a conflict between idealized values taught in the schools contradicts the experiences of the students.

> Rather than articulate disputed—and potentially disruptive—values that could become rallying points for dissent, these values remain implicit. A prime concern of the "new left" student movement in the late 1960s, for instance, was the apparent contradictions among common social values, particularly those relating to constitutionally protected civil rights. The young people's awareness that explicit value premises, such as, "government of laws, not men," are not always honored stimulated overt conflict directed at bringing official behavior into line with values that are deliberately taught. As a result of efforts to reduce discrepancies of this kind by force, many universities suffered serious tangible and other damage.[60]

It is interesting to note, here, that these "new left" activists (a very small minority of students) were for the most part, middle- to upper-class:[61] children less exposed to a restricted language code and distorted communication.

A certain pattern, thus, clearly emerges from the literature on political socialization: children internalize fairly similar attitudes toward authority as do their parents.[62] Schools, in a word, teach legitimacy.

There is, however, some evidence that the legitimacy of the school itself is being challenged. We are referring here to the recent controversy over violence and vandalism in the schools. Although it would be stretching the point to see this challenge as a revolt against political indoctrination, nevertheless the disregard for authority and the general feeling of alienation which are seen as causing these physical attacks on the school and those within it may conceivably represent a type of challenge to the legitimacy of the school and to the society at large.

Violence and Vandalism in the Schools

Although student misbehavior, lack of interest and attention, disrespect for teachers and authority, and antisocial school behavior in general have long been problems in American education, in recent years their coverage by the mass media has heightened considerably, thereby solidifying their status as genuine social problems. In particular, public concern has focused on the mounting evidence of school crime and vandalism. In light of this concern, and the lack of systematic data available to assess or describe the problem, the Ninety-third Congress passed the ''Safe School Study Act'' in 1974. This act mandated that the Secretary of Health, Education and Welfare (HEW) conduct a study to determine the seriousness of school crime, in terms of the number and locations of schools affected, the cost involved, the means of prevention, and the general effectiveness of these means.[63]

In response to this legislation, the National Institute of Education (NIE) surveyed more than 4000 schools during 1976 and 1977 in order to ascertain the seriousness of the problem of crime and disruption in schools. The NIE found that while acts of violence and property destruction increased from the early 1960s to the 1970s, both increases tended to level off after the early 1970s.[64]

In spite of this stabilizing trend, the problem in the second half of the 1970s was still of considerable enough magnitude to warrant concern. For example, 11 percent of students reported having something worth more than $1 stolen from them in any given month.[65] This figure represents about 2.4 million of the nation's students. And concerning acts of violence, 1.3 percent of secondary students reported being attacked in any one month; this represents some 282,000 students.[66] Figures for teachers are comparable. Twelve percent of the nation's 1.1 million teachers (approximately 130,000) have something stolen from them worth more than $1 in a typical month, and an estimated 1 percent are physically attacked at school during a period of a month, with 19 percent of these attacks requiring treatment by a doctor.[67]

The most widespread antisocial acts, though, are against the school itself, and may very well be symptomatic of a climate of alienation,[68] a climate that transcends class boundaries: both lower- and middle-class students are taking their frustrations out on the schools. According to the NIE study:

> The vandalism syndrome . . . seems likely to involve students, who care about school, but are losing out in the competition for grades and leadership positions, or who perceive grades as being unfairly manipulated for disciplinary purposes. Denied what they consider fair and adequate rewards by the school they take aggressive action against it.[69]

Violence in the schools, on the other hand, is seen as being perpetrated by students who are apathetic about grades, who have given up on school, and who feel they have little control over their lives.[70] And, unlike popular belief, race and ethnicity (of both students and schools) are not necessarily related to violence and vandalism.

MYTHS CONCERNING RACIAL–ETHNIC STEREOTYPES

Three assumptions are generally made concerning the relationship between racial–ethnic status and violence in schools:

TABLE 6-2 ESTIMATED NUMBER OF SCHOOLS REPORTING SPECIFIED TYPES OF OFFENSES TO POLICE BY LOCATION AND LEVEL: U.S. SUMMARY, SEPTEMBER 1, 1974–JAN. 31, 1977[1]

	ALL SCHOOLS				ELEMENTARY				SECONDARY			
	TOTAL	Metro-politan Center	Metro-politan Other	Non-metro-politan	TOTAL	Metro-politan Center	Metro-politan Other	Non-metro-politan	TOTAL	Metro-politan Center	Metro-politan Other	Non-metro-politan
Rape	219	50	100	68	110	10	69	30	109	40	30	38
Robbery	3,607	1,350	1,137	579	1,306	708	367	230	1,761	641	770	349
Assault	7,528	3,150	2,936	1,441	2,858	1,542	934	381	4,670	1,607	2,202	1,060
Personal theft	14,064	3,888	5,881	4,295	6,719	2,140	2,771	1,807	7,345	1,747	3,109	2,488
Burglary	32,215	8,360	13,017	10,837	21,958	6,058	8,735	7,164	10,257	2,301	4,282	3,673
Arson	3,518	1,297	1,514	705	1,445	709	477	258	2,072	588	1,037	447
Bomb	6,320	1,848	2,717	1,753	2,826	1,028	1,060	737	3,493	820	1,656	1,076
Disorderly conduct	7,888	2,320	3,168	2,399	3,703	1,335	1,366	1,001	4,184	914	1,801	1,397
Drug abuse	9,938	1,918	5,095	2,924	2,453	307	1,523	622	7,485	1,611	3,572	230
Alcohol abuse	4,961	879	2,285	1,795	1,212	759	652	300	3,748	620	1,632	1,495
Weapons	4,193	1,715	1,753	724	1,585	721	653	210	2,608	993	1,100	513
Number of schools reporting one or more offenses	46,349	11,422	19,156	15,710	30,245	8,137	17,541	9,566	16,104	3,284	6,615	6,204
Percent of schools reporting one or more offenses	49	61	50	42	41	56	41	34	72	82	81	61

1.   that the risks of violence are greater in minority (nonwhite) than in white schools;
2.   that court-ordered desegregation contributes to school violence; and
3.   that most violence in schools is interracial.[72]

It was found, though, that: 1) the proportion of minority students in a school is not a cause of the general level of school violence; 2) court-ordered desegregation is associated with slightly higher levels of violence in schools, but this quiets down after the initial conflict; and (3) the majority of attacks against students are not interracial.[73]

Ultimately, the NIE study came to the conclusion that violence in schools was not class- or race-oriented but had to do with students' feelings of control over their lives. "Schools in which students feel they have little control over what happens to them have more violence."[74]

It is still too early to determine whether or not this represents a real threat to the legitimacy of the schools. For now, all we can say is that the feeling of powerlessness is a universally uncomfortable one, and in light of this the potential for conflict and violence in the schools creates an exceedingly precarious situation.

SUMMARY

We have attempted to show in this chapter how schools tend to neutralize the conflicts that might arise in the everyday situation of educating children. Specific areas of friction, those between teachers and administrators and teachers and students were focused upon, with the resulting conclusion that the subordinate group in each case was socialized to avoid an overt conflict situation.

In particular, we are concerned with the overriding dissension in the schools, that of the class conflict between the middle and lower classes. It was shown that the emphasis upon the individualistic perspective, along with overt political socialization, tends to keep a lid on this rivalry. We looked at the work of Basil Bernstein and Clauss Mueller, who showed that language and language codes are used to preserve the status quo. We then focused upon the general relationship between schooling and political socialization. Finally, we raised the question as to whether the recent rise in violence and vandalism represented a threat to the legitimacy of the schools.

Since we have concentrated on conflict within the school in the last four chapters, we will now expand our analysis a bit in the next two chapters to include strife in the school district. Chapter 7 will be concerned with the struggles for dominance between school boards and superintendents, and Chapter 8 with the conflict between teachers and school boards and superintendents.

NOTES

1. This is not true of private schools, in particular the "upper-class" private boarding school. For example, Caroline Persell writes: "On the basis of available information; the formal and informal structure of the private boarding school appears to be dramatically different from that of the large, urban

bureaucratic educational system attended by so many lower-income and minority students.'' *Education and Inequality*. New York: Free Press, 1977, p. 52. See also James McLachlan, *American Boarding Schools: A Historical Study*. New York: Scribner, 1970.

   2. McLaughlan, *American Boarding Schools*, pp. 11−12.

   3. See for example, Samuel Bowles and Herbert Gintis, *Schooling in Capitalist America*. New York: Basic Books, 1976; and Martin Carnoy and Henry M. Levin, *The Limits of Educational Reform*. New York: McKay, 1976.

   4. Ronald G. Corwin, *Militant Professionalism: A Study of Organization Conflict In High Schools*. New York: Appleton, 1970, p. 13.

   5. Ibid., p. 22.

   6. Ibid., p. 47.

   7. Ibid., p. 55.

   8. Ibid., p. 110.

   9. Ibid., p. 111. See also Dan Lortie, *School-Teacher*. Chicago: University of Chicago Press, 1976.

   10. Corwin, *Militant Professionalism*, p. 234.

   11. Ibid, p. 224.

   12. National Education Association, *Status of the American Public-School Teacher: 1975−1976*. Washington, D.C.: National Educational Association, 1977, pp. 291−292.

   13. This section owes a great deal to Willard Waller, *The Sociology of Teaching*, New York: Wiley, 1965. Although originally published over forty years ago (1936), this work remains to this day the best descriptive analysis of the everyday conflicts and role expectations experienced by teachers.

   14. Ibid., p. 196.

   15. Ibid., p. 326. For a more contemporary analysis of the phenomena, see Gerald Levy, *Ghetto School*. New York: Pegasus Press, 1970.

   16. See Bowles and Gintis, *Schooling in Capitalist America;* Carnoy and Levin, *The Limits of Educational Reform;* Levy, *Ghetto School;* and Ray C. Rist, ''Student Social Class and Teacher Expectations: The Self-fulfilling Prophecy in Ghetto Education,'' *Harvard Educational Review,* 40 (1970), for quantitative and qualitative documentation for this statement.

   17. Richard Sennett and Jonathan Cobb, *The Hidden Injuries of Class*. New York: Vintage Books, 1973.

   18. Feelings of self-confidence have been shown to be related to achievement in schools. See in particular James S. Coleman et al., *Equality of Educational Opportunity*. Washington, D.C.; U.S. Office of Education, 1966; Sandra Peterson-Hardt, ''The Relationship Between Self-Esteem and Achievement Behavior Among Low Income Youth.'' Unpublished doctoral dissertation, Syracuse University, 1976; Bernard C. Rosen, ''The Achievement Syndrome: A Psychological Dimension of Social Stratification,'' *American Sociological Review,* 21 (1956), pp. 203−211; Audrey James Schwartz, ''A Comparative Study of Values and Achievement: Mexican American and Anglo Youth,'' *Sociology of Education, 48* (4) (Fall 1971), pp. 438−442; and Alan B. Wilson, ''Sociological Perspectives on the Development of Academic Competencies in Urban Areas,'' in A. Harry Passow (ed.), *Urban Education in the 1970s: Reflections and a Look Ahead*. New York: Teachers College, 1971, pp. 120−140.

   19. See Bowles and Gintis, *Schooling in Capitalist America,* especially Chapter 4.

   20. See Bowles and Gintis, *Schooling in Capitalist America;* and Carnoy and Levin, *The Limits of Educational Reform,* for sophisticated analyses using the Marxist perspective.

   21. Howard S. Becker, ''Social Class Variation in the Teacher−Pupil Relationship,'' *Journal of Educational Sociology, 25* (April 1952), pp. 451−465; and Audrey James Schwartz, *The Schools and Socialization*. New York: Harper & Row, 1975, pp. 103−104.

   22. Stanley Charnofsky, *Educating The Powerless*. Belmont, Calif.: Wadsworth, 1971, p. 7.

   23. Paulo Freire, *Pedagogy of the Oppressed*. New York: Herder and Herder, 1970.

   24. For a collection of the most important readings concerning the uses and misuses of IQ tests, see N. J. Block and Gerald Dworkin (eds.), *The I. Q. Controversy*. New York: Pantheon, 1976.

   25. See Basil Bernstein, *Class, Codes and Control,* Vol. I. London: Routledge, 1971.

   26. Basil Bernstein, ''Elaborated and Restricted Code: Their Social Origin and Some Consequences,'' *American Anthropologist, 66* (December 1966), p. 65.

   27. Pierre Guiraud, *Le Français Populaire*. Paris: Presses Universitaires de France, 1965, p. 79.

28. Anselm Strauss and Lenore Schatzman, "Social Class and Modes of Communication," *American Journal of Sociology, 60*(4) (January 1955), pp. 329–338.

29. Clauss Mueller, *The Politics of Communication*. New York: Oxford University Press, 1973, pp. 53–54.

30. Basil Bernstein, "Education Cannot Compensate for Society," in D. Rubenstein and C. Stoneman (eds.), *Education For Democracy*. Hammondsworth, England: Penguin Books, p. 107.

31. Mueller, *The Politics of Communication*, p. 9.

32. Ibid., p. 17.

33. Ibid.

34. See in particular Jurgen Habermas, "Toward a Theory of Human Communicative Competence," in Hans P. Dreitzel (ed.), *Recent Sociology,* No. 2. New York: Macmillan, 1972, pp. 115–148.

35. Mueller, *The Politics of Communication*, p. 19.

36. There is a vast literature on the rigid socialization patterns of the lower class. See in particular Melvin L. Kohn, *Class and Conformity*. Homewood, Ill.: Dorsey Press, 1969.

37. Mueller, *The Politics of Communication*, p. 84.

38. Ibid., pp. 84–85.

39. Clauss Mueller, "On Distorted Communication," in Dreitzel (ed.), *Recent Sociology,* No. 2, p. 107.

40. Richard E. Dawson, Kenneth Prewitt, and Karen S. Dawson, *Political Socialization,* 2d ed. Boston: Little, Brown, 1977, p. 1.

41. Quoted in Robert A. Dahl, *Who Governs?* New Haven: Yale University Press, 1961, pp. 317–318.

42. Dawson et al., *Political Socialization,* pp. 24–31. A competing model of political socialization, and one which is most likely used by the majority of political scientists, is systems analysis. For a summary of the use of systems theory in political socialization, see Dawson et al., *Political Socialization,* pp. 17–24.

43. R. W. Connell, "Political Socialization and the American Family: The Evidence Reexamined," *Public Opinion Quarterly, 36* (1972), p. 330.

44. Dawson et al., *Political Socialization,* p. 134.

45. James S. Coleman (ed.), *Education and Political Development*. Princeton, N.J.: Princeton University Press, 1965, p. 226.

46. Dawson et al., *Political Socialization,* p. 146.

47. Ibid., p. 147.

48. Robert D. Hess and Judith V. Torney, *The Development of Political Attitudes in Children*. Garden City, N.Y.: Doubleday/Anchor Books, 1968, p. 123–124.

49. Dawson et al., *Political Socialization,* p. 148.

50. Hess and Torney, *The Development of Political Attitudes in Children*, p. 124.

51. Dawson et al., *Political Socialization,* p. 148.

52. Ibid, pp. 148–149.

53. Ibid, p. 148.

54. Laurence Wylie, *Village in the Vaucluse*. Cambridge, Mass.: Harvard University Press, 1957, p. 57.

55. See especially Robert Easton and Jack Dennis, *Children in the Political System: Origins of Political Legitimacy*. New York: McGraw-Hill, 1969; Hess and Torney, *The Development of Political Attitudes in Children;* and Kenneth P. Langston, *Political Socialization*. New York: Oxford University Press, 1971.

56. Mueller, *The Politics of Communication*, p. 79.

57. Easton and Dennis, *Children in the Political System,* p. 287.

58. Hess and Torney, *The Development of Political Attitudes in Children,* p. 126.

59. Freshman and sophomore students of mine have stated seeing the famous "How a Bill Becomes a Law" film when they were in high school. The film, an animated cartoon, shows a bill running from one branch of government to another. Lobbyists and interest groups were never mentioned by their social studies teacher. For a contrast between the political system we profess to have and the real one, see Michael J. Parenti, *Democracy For The Few,* rev. ed. New York: St. Martin's, 1977.

60. Schwartz, *The Schools and Socialization,* p. 8.

61. See Kenneth Kenniston, *Young Radicals.* New York: Harcourt, 1968; and Richard E. Flacks, "The Liberated Generation: An Exploration of the Roots of Student Protest," *Journal of Social Issues, 23* (July 1967), pp. 52–57. These two writers, a psychologist and a sociologist respectively, point to the middle- and upper-class origins of the 1960s radicals.

62. See Easton and Dennis, *Children in the Political System;* Hess and Torney, *The Development of the Political Attitudes in Children;* and Lanston, *Political Socialization.*

63. National Institute of Education, *Violent Schools—Safe Schools: The Safe School Study Report to the Congress,* Vol. I. Washington, D.C.: U.S. Department of Health, Education and Welfare, 1978, p. 1

64. Ibid., p. 2.

65. Ibid., p. 3.

66. Ibid.

67. Ibid.

68. For works which deal with alienation in schools, see Barry Anderson, "School Bureaucratization and Alienation From High School," *Sociology of Education, 46* (Summer 1973), pp. 315–334; and S.V. Dillon and J.A. Grant, "Schools and Alienation," *The Elementary School Journal, 76* (May 1976), pp. 481–490.

69. NIE, *Violent Schools—Safe Schools,* p. 9.

70. Ibid.

71. Ibid., p. B-3.

72. Ibid., p. 6.

73. Ibid.

74. Ibid., p. 8.

7

School Boards and Superintendents

As we have shown, schools are political entities and, as such, must be seen in relation to the communities and interests they serve. "Community" is used here in the educational sense—that is, it is synonymous with "school district." Thus, a community can either be a large city or a small rural area. Its boundaries can range from one like New York City—with over a million pupils, a centralized board of education, numerous local school boards, and over sixty thousand teachers and administrators—to a small township with a few hundred students, a three-person board, and perhaps a dozen teachers.[1]

Because it is a political entity, the school district is characterized by conflict and power struggles among the people of the community (theoretically, through their representatives, the school board); superintendents and administrators; and teacher organizations.[2] Today, the major power struggle in the educational community is between teacher organizations on one side, and school boards and superintendents on the other. This conflict ranges from disagreements over salaries in the suburbs to struggles over decentralization in the cities. Given the historical lack of a power base for teachers, such a contest represents a relatively new development. A new alignment of forces has begun to take shape, and the old antagonists, superintendents and school boards, have now joined forces to take on the

113

"new kid on the block." The history of public education in the United States can thus be seen as competition between various groups for control over the schools.

Initially, members of the local communities were in charge. Gradually, as towns grew larger and centralization took place, school boards, as representatives of the community, came to power. With more growth and greater centralization, superintendents, in the name of reform, eroded the power of school boards. Finally, teachers, primarily through teachers' unions, have reached a position where they can now challenge school boards and superintendents; in many large cities, teachers are involved in a struggle with the local community, who, by advocating decentralization, want to take back some of the newly won power of teachers. The control of public education, as will be shown in Chapters 7 and 8, has come full circle.

Conflict and the struggle for power have always been present in the public schools. What has changed is the participation of teachers, who have now established enough of a foundation to realistically fight for a position of dominance. One of the more interesting aspects of this struggle is that, with few exceptions,[3] educational scholars have historically failed or refused to see the political nature of the schools. It was only in 1967, when Laurence Iannaccone chided educational administrators and political scientists for neglecting the political nature of education,[4] that any real focus upon power emerged. The recognition of the "politics of education" is therefore a relatively recent development. However, because of the still pervasive general influence of functionalism and systems analysis, the overwhelming majority of scholars who have turned to the "politics of education" continue to view the schools as smoothly functioning entities in a pluralistic society.[5] Conflict, when it is studied, is seen as something to be managed. The ahistorical basis of the functionalist model has narrowly defined the scope of investigation. A look at the historical development of school boards and their relationship to superintendents, teachers, and the people of the community will further illustrate this.

THE SCHOOL BOARD: A PECULIARLY AMERICAN INSTITUTION

As Raymond Callahan has pointed out, "the pattern of having public schools directed and controlled by elected lay officials at the local district level is uniquely American."[6] Its origin lay in colonial New England and then spread to all parts of the country.

> In 1647, the government of Massachusetts Bay Colony passed a law requiring all towns of a certain size to establish and maintain schools, and placed the responsibility for compliance in the hands of local officials. In the early years the decisions necessary for operating these semipublc schools, such as selection of teachers, were made in town meetings. Then, as time passed and the population grew, the management of the schools was delegated to a committee of the local government. The final step in the process was to have elected officials

whose sole responsibility was the management and control of public schools, and these officials, whether they were designated as "school boards" or "school committees," were largely separate from and free of control of the local government.[7]

In 1789, Massachusetts passed an extremely important piece of legislation, one that set the stage for the first comprehensive state educational system.[8] This law required every town in the state to support an elementary school. Towns were also required to certify teachers and authorized to employ a special committee to look after the schools. In 1826, the original law was amended and the establishment of a school committee was made obligatory. Boston was one of the first towns to implement the law and created an elected school committee consisting of twelve members (one from each ward).[9] Not all cities followed the lead of Boston, though. New York City, for example, did not have an elected school board until 1847.[10] As stated previously, Horace Mann was appointed secretary to the Massachusetts state board of education in 1837, and, for all intents and purposes, was state superintendent of schools. From 1837 until his resignation in 1848, Mann was, without question, the most well known and influential educator in the country.

Mann was quick to criticize the Boston schools and, shortly after his appointment, recommended that the schools be supervised by a professional superintendent. Mann's first open conflict came with the publication of his 1843 *Annual Report*. During the spring of 1843, Mann had traveled to Europe at his own expense, observing schools in England, Ireland, Scotland, France, Prussia, and Saxony.[11] His annual report, almost 200 pages long, contained his observations and stated his conclusion that the Prussian school system was the best in Europe and the English the worst. Mann attributed the excellence of the Prussian schools to its system of supervision. The next year, Mann sought to transform the Boston school system into one similar to the Prussian one by getting people, sympathetic to reform, elected to the school board. To this end, Mann encouraged his friend and fellow reformer, Samuel Gridley Howe, to run. Howe, along with several other like-minded reformers, was elected. Being a man of action, Howe quickly began to analyze the Boston school system. A committee, under his leadership, administered tests to students and found that the Boston school system was a disgrace. The committee placed the blame for the poor state of the system directly on the twenty-four-man, ward-elected school board, which was in charge of administering the schools. Howe's committee recommended the appointment of a superintendent of schools to oversee the educational process, thereby offsetting the influence of the school board. Although the committee had no intention of abolishing the school board, they still met with such vigorous opposition that Howe and most of his fellow reformers were not nominated for reelection in 1845.[12] But the idea for reform was strong and a fulltime superintendent of schools was appointed six years later.

The idea of ward school government was also popular in regions other than New England. In fact, in 1799 Thomas Jefferson had unsuccessfully proposed to the Virginia House of Burgesses that the ward be a unit for the division of cities and counties and for the supervision of the free education system. According to one historian, Jefferson later "expanded his early idea of the ward as an educational unit to the ward as a unit of general government, and from 1810 to the end of his life, the establishment of a general system of public education in Virginia and the subdivision of its counties into wards were his two great objectives."[13] Jefferson, fearing the corrosive effect of urbanization on a republican form of government, advocated ward government as an alternative, and as the country expanded westward, so did the ward concept.

In the end, however, the ward concept lost support. As city schools grew in size and number, the complex arrangements for managing the schools gradually began to consume all the time of at least one member of the school board.[14] For example, the Public School Society of New York City, the philanthropic organization which maintained pauper schools in the early nineteenth century, appointed one member of its board of trustees to visit the families of the poor to persuade them to send their children to school. Five years later this person was appointed general business agent for the society, and when the society was consolidated with the public schools of New York City, he became the assistant superintendent of schools.[15]

After the Civil War, as the urban population rapidly increased, the problems of administering public schools expanded proportionally. School boards coped with this growth in two ways: (1) they hired a fulltime superintendent; and (2) they enlarged the membership of the board.[16] Despite the fact that school boards deemed it necessary to appoint fulltime superintendents, they generally refused to grant them any real powers. Superintendents obviously resented this, and their discontent continued to mount until it resulted in public struggle for power with the school boards at the end of the nineteenth century.

Starting about 1870, the issue of how much authority superintendents should have was hotly debated. The objective of such well-known superintendents of the time as John Philbrick, Thomas Bucknell, Andrew Draper, and William Maxwell (to name just a few), was literally to change the power structure of the schools. They viewed themselves as educational "experts" who could see to it that the best educational programs were introduced into the schools and carried out. In the large cities, they spoke of driving out corrupt "gutter politicians" who were using the school boards and schools for their own political and economic ends.[17]

By 1895, the struggle between school boards and superintendents had broken out into open conflict. A subcommittee, chaired by Andrew S. Draper, Superintendent of Schools in Cleveland, Ohio, was appointed, in 1893, by the Department of Superintendence of the National Education Association to study the organization of the schools. It reported the following in February of 1895:

> It is not in doubt. All who have had any contact with the subject are familiar with it. It is administration by boards or committees, the members of which are not competent to manage professional matters and develop an expert teaching-force. Yet they assume, and in most cases honestly, the knowledge of the most experienced. They override and degrade a superintendent when they have the power to do so, until he becomes their mere factotum. For the sake of harmony and the continuance of his position he concedes, surrenders, and acquiesces in

their acts, while the continually increasing teaching-force becomes weaker and weaker and the work poorer and poorer. If he refuses to do this, they precipitate an open rupture and turn him out of his position. Then they cloud the issues and shift the responsibility from one to another. There are exceptions, of course, but they do not change the rule.[18]

School board members did not take Draper's charges lying down. William George Bruce, a Milwaukee journalist and school board member, had founded the *American School Board Journal* in 1891 to serve school board members, and now used the *Journal* to fight back. In a series of articles, editorials, and cartoons, Bruce stressed the notion that the schools belonged to the people and not to professional educators. In his attacks on what became known as the Draper report, Bruce did, however, tend to blur the issues. The whole question of legislative versus administrative powers was left unresolved, and to this day, remains so.

While the battle over control of the schools was being waged in the pages of educational journals, the struggle repeated itself in thousands of school districts throughout the United States, as superintendents following Draper's lead sought to establish control over their school districts. But Bruce had succeeded in mounting enough opposition to thwart the superintendents' drive for control over school boards. In the end, school boards held the power to hire and fire, and they used it. As a result, a number of prominent superintendents found themselves out of work. Callahan has summarized the outcome of the conflict.

> The evidence indicates that after 1895 changes were made in city school systems in the direction of implementing most of the recommendations made by the Draper committee. Schools *were* largely removed from partisan politics. School boards *were* reduced in size. Superintendents *were* gradually given the power to hire teachers, select textbooks, and control the educational program generally. But two of the basic recommendations were not put into effect. One was the idea of separating the business and instructional aspects of the superintendency. . . . The other major recommendation not achieved was that of making the superintendent independent. As long as the school board retained, as it did, the power of appointment and dismissal of the superintendent, she or he could not be independent. And the major outcome of the confrontations of 1895 was that the American tradition of having its public schools controlled by elected officials was maintained.[19]

The attack by superintendents on the school boards ostensibly failed and in the years that followed, superintendents switched tactics, concentrating instead on educating and persuading selected school board members as to what the proper role of the superintendent should be. They were helped, too, by the reform movements of the early nineteenth century. The system of ward-dominated politics was being challenged by middle- and upper-class citizens' groups. Changes in the school system followed changes in the political system, as the control of the schools shifted from ward-based school boards to central boards. This change resulted in a shift of power:

from the working class (who by the 1880s ''captured'' many city wards) to the upper class and to more cosmopolitan professionals who claimed to be revolted by disclosures of inefficiency and corruption. Henceforth, the schools would be run by a ''guardian'' class who because of their own superior education presumably knew what kind of schools should be maintained. They wanted teachers to be loyal to their elite values rather than those of the ward boss. Thus, the control of schools passed from the ''people'' to the tiny minority of owners and college graduates who wanted the schools to preserve and protect their way of life.[20]

The movement to control the schools took on elitist tendencies, as lay responsibility declined in the face of reform and centralization. These changes effectively succeeded in taking power away from the lower and working classes. Reformers in the name of ''taking the schools out of politics'' effectively substituted their own brand of middle-class politics by removing the control of school governance away from the neighborhood level.[21]

School boards rapidly became dominated by middle-class and business interests. Scott Nearing, a radical economics professor who had been fired from the University of Pennsylvania, was, in 1917, one of the first to document this trend. His conclusion that school boards were unrepresentative of the general population and that the lower classes were being almost totally excluded from control over the schools was based on a sample of nearly one thousand school board members in 104 cities with populations of over 40,000.[22] Five years later, George Strubble reached basically the same conclusions when he studied 959 school board members and found that 350 were bankers, merchants, or business executives, and only 54 were from what he called the laboring classes.[23] The criticism of school board representation that proved to be the most influential was that of George Counts, a professor of Educational Administration at the prestigious Teachers College, Columbia University, who published his classic *The Social Composition of School Boards* in 1927. Counts found that some 32 percent of school board members were proprietors of stores and banks. Professional men represented 30 percent, and those in management and supervision constituted 14 percent. Only 8 percent were of the laboring class, whereas they represented 60 percent of the population of the cities at the time. To be more specific, out of the 2,943 town and city board members studied, 486 were merchants, 335 lawyers, 266 doctors, 183 manufacturers, and 180 were bankers.[24] Subsequent follow-up studies have confirmed Counts' conclusions. In 1962 Alpheus White undertook a study for the Office of Education, and found that 34.5 percent of board members were in business as owners or managers, and 27.4 percent were engaged in professional or technical services. Manual workers— skilled, semi-skilled, and unskilled—represented 8.5 percent of board members, almost exactly the same figure that Counts had found thirty-five years earlier.[25] A 1966 Gallup poll reported that 65 percent of school board members were engaged in business and professions.[26] A review of the findings on school board members would show a typical member to be a ''middle-aged male professional, married with children in the public school, and active in the organizational and associational life of the community.''[27] The more recent national studies generally reinforce this

TABLE 7–1   OCCUPATIONS OF MALE MEMBERS OF PUBLIC BOARDS OF EDUCATION IN THE UNITED STATES[28]

Occupation	District Boards	County Boards	City Boards	State Boards	College and University Boards	All Boards
	%	%	%	%	%	%
Proprietors	2	18	32	18	33	21
Professional service	1	22	30	53	41	29
Managerial service	*	5	14	2	5	5
Commercial service	*	3	6	*	1	2
Clerical service	*	2	6	1	*	2
Manual labor	1	4	8	*	0	3
Agricultural service	95	44	2	2	9	30
Ex officio	0	2	*	24	11	7
Unknown	1	0	2	0	0	1
Total	100	100	100	100	100	100
Number of members	2545	299	2943	252	351	6390
Number of boards	974	58	509	39	42	1622

stereotype.[29] One such study by Zeigler and Jennings is summarized in Table 7-2 below.

During the 1930s Counts' book was discussed and debated by educators and school board members. In 1933, Charles Judd, Dean of the School of Education at the University of Chicago, became so angry over the corruption that characterized the Chicago Board of Education and their meddling and interference in the running of the Chicago public schools, that he publicly advocated the elimination of school boards.[30]

Although Judd's proposal created quite a stir in education circles, he received little overt support. Superintendents, who could be fired by school boards and who remembered what had happened in the 1890s, remained silent on the issue. But perhaps the person who did more than anyone else to ensure that Judd's views never advanced beyond the talking stage was Jesse Newlon, a colleague of Counts' at Columbia. Newlon, a former superintendent of schools in Denver, and a past president of the National Education Association, argued in his book *Educational Administration As Social Policy* (1934) that school boards should be made more representative, rather than be abolished. He warned that school boards should not be too large and should be "nominated by a council created for that purpose, in which important groups and the public as a whole would be represented."[31]

The question of whether or not school boards should be abolished or stripped of their power was finally settled in 1938. In June of that year, George Strayer, head of the Department of Educational Administration at Teachers College, Columbia University, issued a statement sponsored jointly by the National Education Association and the American Association of School Administrators. The

TABLE 7–2   SOCIAL AND ECONOMIC COMPANIONS BETWEEN BOARD
MEMBERS AND GENERAL PUBLIC[32]

Characteristics	General Public	Board Members
Sex:		
Males	48%	90%
Females	52	10
Race:		
Whites	89	96
Nonwhites	11	4
Age:		
Under 40	37	24
40–59	39	63
60 and over	23	13
Education:		
Less than 12 grades	41	7
12 grades	32	22
1–4 years of college	23	47
Graduate and		
professional school	4	25
Income:		
Under $7,500	56	10
$7,500–19,999	39	54
$20,000 and over	6	36
Occupation:		
Professional and		
technical	16	34
Managers, officials and		
proprietors	14	32
Farmers	5	13
Clerical and sales	11	9
Craftsman and foreman	19	8
Operatives	16	2
Service workers and		
laborers	11	3
Other	8	—
Home Ownership:		
Yes	66	93
No	34	7
Religious Preference:		
Protestant	74	85
Non-Protestant	26	15

Table 7-2 continued

Characteristics	General Public	Board Members
Church Attendance:		
Weekly	38	61
Less than weekly	62	39
Political Party:		
Democrat	46	40
Independent	30	16
Republican	24	44

document, entitled *The Structure and Administration of Education in American Democracy,* proposed the structure, organization, and administration of public schools. Strayer devoted almost a third of the book to local school administration, and advocated straight out that the final authority over public education in a democartic society must rest with a lay board.[33]

Strayer repeated a number of recommendations that had been made many times before. School boards should be small and elected, not appointed. They should be removed from partisan politics and should serve without pay. They should also be legislative bodies, turning over the executive function to the superintendents. As Callahan says: "With Strayer's endorsement, these ideas became the 'conventional wisdom' regarding the organization and functioning of school boards, and they continued to be accepted and adopted all over the country."[34] Two of Strayer's recommendations, though, were neither accepted nor adopted, and subsequently precipitated much of the conflict that characterized education in the 1960s. These two recommendations were: (1) that teachers be given a voice in the development of educational policy; and (2) that school boards consult with and be sensitive to all segments of the community.

School boards have neither willingly given teachers a say in policy nor listened to minority groups. Because of this (and other reasons, which will be elaborated upon), they have paid a price in increasing conflict and, more importantly, in the erosion of their power base. Their position of control has been so diminished that the most recent and comprehensive national study of public school governance found that school boards have largely ceased to exercise their policy-making functions; that, for the most part, they do not govern but merely legitimize the educational policy recommendations of the school superintendent.[35] There appears to be two primary reasons, other than the ones mentioned previously, that have led to the subordinancy of school boards:(1) educational problems have become so complex as to render board members almost completely dependent upon the superintendent; and (2) federal and state recommendations have greatly reduced the parameters of the educational decisions school boards can make. Concerning the first, our interpretation is that systems analysis has again served a political function. By couching educational problems in systems techniques, superintendents and administrators have overly complicated the process of education. This is not to argue that education has not become more and more complex over the years as findings accumulate in such areas as educational psychology, sociology, guidance, and curriculum. However, given that superintendents lack both a first-rate education[36] and substantive educational technology, we cannot help but question how much expertise they really do have. As for the second reason, fiscal constraints have become so demanding that in the words of one writer:

> Though figures vary from district to district, a good estimate for the average community is that 75 percent of the school budget goes for salaries. Here again the states lay down limitations, some fixing the minimum salaries, some establishing ratios between the pay of teachers and that of principals, and at least one, Delaware, determining the whole salary schedule. What the state doesn't decree has become more and more the product of hard collective bargaining between the board and the various maintenance unions, teacher's unions, and teacher's associations.
>
> Beyond the overwhelming item of salaries, a district budget usually allots about 10 percent to the bonded debt, 5 percent to transportation, insurance, and the like. Since none of these items permits much leeway, the range that remains for option is something like 5 percent of the entire budget.[37]

It seems, then, that school boards have lost in their power struggle with superintendents. Interestingly enough, a number of scholars have decried this, as a subordination of the will of the people. For example, William Boyd, after stating how school boards have become inclined to defer to the expertise of the superintendent, writes:

> But here we find outselves again faced with the tension between democracy and efficiency. For how can the "best" decisions on public policy (in education or other realms) be made. By the people, by the "experts," or by some delicate combination thereof?[38]

The only problem with Boyd's analysis is that, as has been documented previously, school boards have not been representative for at least sixty years, and it is questionable whether superintendents are all that "efficient." Education has no technology that can be demonstrated to be efficient; indeed, as we saw in Chapter 5, efficiency is a term borrowed from the business world, which has little or no meaning for education.

The only thing we can say with any certainty is that there has been a decided realignment of power in the control of the schools—away from the school board to the superintendent. However, this does not represent any shift in power away from the middle-class dominance of the schools; for, if anything, the superintendent is just as conservative, just as socialized into middle-class values as is the typical school board member.

THE SCHOOL SUPERINTENDENT

As we have intimated all along, the role of the school superintendent has changed from that of the scholar-teacher to that of educational manager.

Although the term "superintendent" is sometimes used in connection with the chief state school officer, we use the term here only in connection with the chief executive officer of a board of education in an operating school district. This designation is consistant with the structure of the educational institution in the United States. With the exception of Hawaii, each of the the other states has organized schooling and school districts with boards of education as the administrative agencies for these districts. Except for the very small districts, boards of education have employed a "chief school officer" or superintendent to oversee the district.

Historically, the creation of the superintendency is related to the reorganization of school districts. When school districts were organized into one-room schools, as was the case in New England, the local board of education could adequately handle any administrative problems that might arise. However, when many of these districts were combined into city-wide school districts toward the middle of the nineteenth century, the management of these larger districts tended to become much too demanding for a board of education comprised of citizens who had volunteered a part of their time to public service.[39]

As cities began to grow rapidly, the one-room schools located in wards grew also. The result was that all the schools within each city needed to be coordinated. More importantly, the cities had to allocate financial resources to these schools, and volunteer lay board members found the demands of their time so great that they sought assistance. City councils began to take the initiative in creating the office of superintendent and selecting someone to fill it. The first city superintendent of schools was appointed by the Buffalo Common Council on June 9, 1837.[40] One month later the mayor and aldermen of Louisville, Kentucky appointed the second superintendent.[41] By 1860, twenty-seven cities or city school districts had established the position of superintendent.[42]

The establishment of superintendencies in noncity areas did not occur until the beginning of the twentieth century. Noncity schools were usually one-room rural schools. When they were organized it was at the county level. Utah was one of the first nonurban states to move toward large consolidated school districts in 1915.[43]

Two movements affected the organization of school districts outside the major cities. The first of these was the famous Kalamazoo decision which incorporated the high school into the common school system of the country.[44] Both city and rural districts had to consider how they could best make a high school education available to those of high school age. More recently the growth of suburbia has led to the growth of noncity school districts. Rural, consolidated, and suburban school boards have followed the model of the city and appointed local superintendents of schools.

The office of the superintendency developed in four stages. At first, the office was essentially a clerical one—board members needed someone who could relieve them of minor details. Often, the first superintendents were not trained educators. As educational programs became more complex, board members began to rely more and more on the superintendent for assistance with educational matters. In this second stage, the superintendent was chiefly an educator, and was often a scholar of note.

With continued growth, boards of education frequently found it necessary to hire a superintendent of business as well as a superintendent of education. A dual administrative organization evolved: an executive for business and one in charge of education; both reported directly to the board of education. Dissatisfaction with this dual supervisory network resulted in the third stage: the superintendent as business manager. Superintendents were now expected to be budget experts, managers of property, school plant specialists, and coordinators of elections to pass tax levies and bond issues. Because of these other responsibilities, they usually neglected educational and instructional purposes to concentrate on business issues.[45]

The last stage, that of the suprintendent as chief executive and chief professional advisor—one who has made the board dependent upon him—is occurring now. It consists of a realignment of power arrangements in terms of those who control public education, but represents no real societal power shift, since the superintendent is a strong representative of middle-class values. A profile of the school superintendent will quickly establish that he or she [46] is no threat to the middle-class dominance of public education.

PROFILE OF THE SUPERINTENDENT

Various American Association of School Administration Yearbooks from 1920 on provide descriptive profiles of superintendents. Taken together, they show increases in average age at assuming the superintendency and in amount of education. The most recent and comprehensive study of the school superintendent is by Richard Carlson,[47] and an interesting picture emerges from Carlson's synthesis of the research on superintendents.

Demographic Characteristics

School superintendents in the United States are almost exclusively white and male. Black and female superintendents are few and far between. Superintendents come from large families and overrepresent the first born in sibling order. Given the contrasting opinions of psychologists concerning size of families and birth order, it is perhaps best to repeat what Blau and Duncan found: "The chief advantage enjoyed by men either first or last, as well as by only children, is their better education."[48]

Size of Home Town

Superintendents overrepresent small towns and underrepresent the largest cities, with 57.5 percent of them coming from towns of 10,000 or less. This finding is in general agreement with the finding that teachers usually come from small towns and rural backgrounds.

Socioeconomic Class

School superintendents come from the lower and middle classes. As a professional group they are therefore upwardly mobile. Table 7-3 compares them with other occupational groups in terms of family status.

The percentage of superintendents who are children of professionals is extremely low and represents a profession that is truly open to all levels of the society. This availability, however, carries with it definite personal habits of conservatism. For example, one study in the mid-1960s showed that all superintendents in Oregon were married and only 2.4 percent of superintendents had ever been divorced.[49] Given that the divorce rate has been calculated at anywhere from thirty-three to forty percent, superintendents either show a remarkably happy married life, or a fear of deviating from any societal norm. Given the wealth of evidence concerning tension and role strain among superintendents,[50] the latter seems a more likely interpretation. As Carlson states:

> Board members are opposed to superintendents who are either bachelors, widowers, or divorcees. . . . One can infer from the data that the career of the superintendent depends on entry into the blissful state of matrimony and that the

TABLE 7–3   CORRELATION BETWEEN OCCUPATIONAL GROUPS AND PROFESSIONAL STATUS OF FATHER[51]

Occupational Groups	*Percentage Whose Father's Occupation Classified as Professional*
School superintendents	11.0
D.D.S. students	25.1
M.D. students	31.1
American business elite	14.0
High-level civil servants	28.3
U.S. senators	22.0
U.S. representatives	31.0
All professional workers	15.3
1961 college graduates	23.9
Military executives	18.0

man should strive, in order to maximize his occupational opportunities, to keep his wife from separating herself from him by death or divorce.[52]

Religion

Affiliation with an organized religion has a definite connection with the career of a superintendent. In a national sample of superintendents, 75 percent indicated that they attended church weekly.[53] School superintendents are also most likely to be Protestant.[54] This reflects the fact that school board members are overwhelmingly Protestant. For example, Jennings and Zeigler report that 85 percent of board members are members of the Protestant faith. [55]

Political Party Affiliation

The most recent study on party affiliation (1967) showed that 45 percent of superintendents considered themselves Republicans, 34 percent Democrats, and 20 percent Independent. A Gallup poll in the same year reported that 42 percent of the general public considered themselves Democrats, 31 percent Independents, and 27 percent Republican.[56] Superintendents were thus much more Republican than was the general public at the time.

SCHOOL SUPERINTENDENTS: AN OPEN ELITE

Carlson sums up his profile of the school superintendent as follows:

> The material on career contingencies of the superintendency . . . seems to support the judgment that the superintendency constitutes a relatively open elite. The barriers for entry into the occupation seem to present few obstacles: the superintendents came from the small towns and rural areas, and from large lower- and middle-class families; relatively few of their fathers were professionals. Though formal educational requirements exist, they do not seem to present a real challenge or to restrict entry seriously. Most school superintendents obtain less than the full amount of formal education available; and there is no reason to believe that they possess distinguished academic records, that they took their basic college education at institutions of distinction, or that they possess relatively basic intelligence. All of this is not to say that superintendents have no ability, skill, or basic competence. The point is, relatively speaking, the superintendency seems to be an open elite.[57]

The school superintendent, despite this seeming lack of distinction, has nevertheless tended to dominate the school board. According to N. O. Kerr, the relative ignorance of the community and the new school board members about the workings of the school system have tended to relegate the school board into ''rubber stamps'' for the approval and ''legitimation'' of policies developed by the superintendent.[58] Evidence in the years since Kerr's study has tended to overwhelmingly support his conclusions.[59] In particular, Zeigler and Jennings, in the first systematic analysis of the governing of American schools, state that the disparity between authority (as vested in school boards) and leadership (enacted by superintendents) "violates a fundamental principle of democratic institutions."[60] Although the school board is legally the policy-making body for the school district and has the formal power to hire and fire its superintendent, it does not transform its *de jure* authority into *de facto* decision-making power.[61] David Minar has identified this uneven pattern of assertion as the distinction between the *rank authority* of the school board and the *technical authority* of the superintendent.[62]

To the reasons for this shift in power, we can add the following ones. School boards have difficulty in exerting their authority because they are multimember bodies, which can range from three to fifteen members, although five to seven is the usual number. The committee structure explicit in such an arrangement mitigates against effective, efficient, and swift decision making. Moreover, in many instances, members may not be fully aware of the authority vested in the board.[63] Educational writer and critic James Koerner sums it up this way:

> The role of school board members is perhaps the most ill-defined in local government. The individual board member has no legal power, though the board itself is considered a corporation. The board's rights and responsibilities are rarely spelled out by the state except in the most general terms, and the board rarely undertakes to define them itself. The board's entire role and that of its individual members is simply an accretion of customs, attitudes, and legal precedents without much specificity. Many school board members . . . move in a sea of confusion about their powers.[64]

Another important reason for superintendent control of school board is that educational administrators have worked diligently to reinforce the tendency of lay persons to regard the superintendents' professional qualifications with deference.[65] As political scientist Thomas Eliot notes, the American Association of School Administrators has been instrumental in perpetuating this show of esteem. He cites the following bit of advice given by the AASA to school board members:

> Curricula planning and development is a highly technical task which requires special training. . . . Board members do not have and cannot be expected to have the technical competence to pass on the work of expert teachers in this field. . . . Nor can the board pass on specific textbooks.[66]

The superintendent, then, seems to be firmly in charge of the public school system. The struggle for power has thus shifted from that between superintendents and school boards to one where these two former antagonists have joined forces under the leadership of the superintendent to do battle with teacher organizations. Since the 1960s, teachers' organizations have become more and more militant and have reached a point where they are now in a position to challenge superintendents and school boards for control of the schools. It took teachers a long time to achieve this status and, given the nature of public education, their position (as we shall see in the next chapter) is an extremely tenuous one, one that is constantly subject to attack.

SUMMARY

In this chapter we saw that conflict and struggles for power in the schools have existed from the beginning of public education's history. One of the earliest and most intensive struggles concerned school boards and superintendents. In particular, the end of the nineteenth century witnessed one of the fiercer battles. The result of this struggle tended to negate the power of the superintendent. The school board's power to hire and fire proved to be too strong a resource and superintendents were forced to acquiesce. From then on superintendents began to use other tactics to erode the power base of the school boards. At present superintendents have been so successful in doing this as to have produced an almost complete role reversal, with school boards having become subordinate to them.

We also argued that this ascendency of the superintendent has done little to alter the middle-class dominance of the schools. The superintendent is, if anything, even more conservative than the school board members he theoretically is accountable to. The result has been a merging of forces by these two old opponents as they now prepare to do battle with teacher associations, which have become increasingly more militant since the 1960s.

NOTES

1. Although everyone has heard of small towns with populations under one hundred, their school system is usually consolidated into a larger district.

2. A possible fourth power component, mayors, have (for purely pragmatic reasons) generally stayed out of the battle for control of public schools. As Joseph M. Cronin states; "Mayors win very few open battles with big-city school boards. Most mayors sense this and suppress the temptation to change the school system." *The Control of Urban Schools*. New York: Free Press, 1973, p. 175.

3. See David Easton, "The Function of Formal Education in a Political System," *The School Review*, 65 (1957), pp. 304–316; and T. H. Eliot, "Toward and Understanding of Local School Politics," *American Political Science Review*, 52 (1959), pp. 1037–1051.

4. Laurence Iannaccone, *Politics in Education*. New York: The Center for Applied Research in Education, Inc., 1967.

5. See in particular Frederick M. Wirt and Michael W. Kirst, *Political and Social Foundations of Education*, rev. ed. Berkeley, Calif.: McCutcheon, 1975.

6. Raymond E. Callahan, "The American School Board, 1789–1960," in Peter J. Cistone (ed.), *Understanding School Boards*. Lexington, Mass.: Lexington Books. 1975, p. 19.

7. Ibid.

8. Stanley K. Schultz, *The Culture Factory: Boston Public Schools, 1789–1860*. New York: Oxford University Press, 1973, p. 11.

9. Callahan, "The American School Board, 1789–1960," p. 19.

10. Carl F. Kaestle, *The Evolution of an Urban School System: New York City, 1750–1850*. Cambridge, Mass.: Harvard University Press, 1973, p. 104.

11. Callahan, "The American School Board, 1789−1960," p. 21.

12. Ibid., p. 23.

13. Samuel P. Huntington, "The Founding Fathers and the Division of Power," in Arthur Maas (ed.), *Area and Power*. New York: Free Press, 1959, p. 176.

14. Cronin, *The Control of Public Education,* p. 52.

15. Ibid.

16. Callahan, "The American School Board, 1789−1960," p. 25.

17. Ibid.

18. *National Education Association Proceedings, 1895.* Quoted in Callahan, "The American School Board, 1789−1960," p. 30.

19. Callahan, "The American School Board, 1789−1960," p. 34.

20. Cronin, *The Control of Urban Schools,* pp. 57−58.

21. Ibid., p. 11.

22. Scott Nearing, "Who's Who on Our Boards of Education," *School and Society,* January 20, 1917, pp. 89−90.

23. George Struble, "A Study of School Board Personnel," *The American School Board Journal,* XV (October 1922), pp. 48−49, 137−138.

24. George Counts, *The Social Composition of School Boards.* New York: Arno Press, 1969, p. 62.

25. Alpheus L. White, *Local School Boards: Organizations and Politics,* Office of Education Bulletin, No. 8. Washington, D.C.: U.S. Government Printing Office, 1962.

26. Cited in Robert Bendiner, *The Politics of Schools.* New York: Harper & Row, 1969, p. 13.

27. Peter J. Cistone, "The Recruitment and Socialization of School Board Members," in Cistone (ed.), *Understanding School Boards,* p. 54.

28. Counts, *The Social Composition of School Boards,* p. 52.

29. National School Boards Assocaition, *Women on School Boards.* Evanston, Ill.: The Association, 1974.

30. Callahan, "The American School Board, 1789−1960," p. 39.

31. Jesse Newlon, *Education As Social Policy.* New York: Scribner, 1934, p. 242.

32. L. Harmon Zeigler and M. Kent Jennings, *Governing American Schools: Political Interaction in Local School Districts.* North Scituate, Mass.: Duxbury Press, 1974, p. 28.

33. George Strayer, *The Structure and Administration of Education in American Democracy.* Washington, D.C.: National Education Association, 1938.

34. Callahan, "The American School Board, 1789−1960," p. 41.

35. Zeigler and Jennings, *Governing American Schools.*

36. For substantiation of this assertion, see Neal Gross and Robert E. Herriot, *Staff Leadership in Public Schools.* New York: Wiley, 1965; and Richard O. Carlson, *School Superintendents: Careers and Performance.* Columbus, Ohio: Merrill, 1972.

37. Bendiner, *The Politics of Schools,* p. 36.

38. William L. Boyd, "School Board−Administrative Staff Relations," in Cistone (ed.), *Understanding School Boards,* p. 104.

39. Thomas M. Gilland, *The Origin and Development of the Powers and Duties of the City School Superintendent.* Chicago: University of Chicago Press, 1935, Chap. 2.

40. Theodore L. Reller, *The Development of the City Superintendency of Schools in the United States.* Philadelphia: Published by the author, 1935, p. 82.

41. Ibid.

42. Ibid.

43. Roald F. Campbell, Lavern L. Cunningham, and Roderick F. McPhee, *The Organization and Control of American Schools.* Columbus, Ohio: Merrill, 1965, p. 190.

44. *Stuart v. School District No. 1 of Kalamazoo,* 30 Michigan 69 (1874).

45. Campbell et al., *The Organization and Control of American Schools,* p. 191.

46. The phrase *he or she* has been used throughout this work for stylistic reasons, so as to offset sexism in language. We wish, however, to underscore that the superintendency is one of the most sexist professions in the United States. In the hundred-year period between 1870 and 1970, only six women (3 percent) have been superintendents in the twenty-five largest United States cities. Additionally, June Marr

found that nationally .2 percent of superintendents were women. And they were, for the most part, located in small nonmetropolitan districts. "Survey of Women Superintendents," unpublished seminar paper, Stanford University (June 1973), cited in Larry Cuban, *Urban School Chiefs Under Fire.* Chicago: University of Chicago Press, 1976, p. 181.

47. This section is based on Carlson, *School Superintendents.*

48. Peter Blau and Otis D. Duncan, *The American Occupational Structure.* New York: Wiley, 1967, p. 307.

49. Carlson, *School Superintendents*, p. 22.

50. See Thomas Funicello, "Role Strain among School Superintendents." Unpublished Ed.D. dissertation, State University of New York at Albany, 1976.

51. Carlson, *School Superintendents*, p. 22.

52. Carlson, *School Superintendents*, p. 27.

53. M. Kent Jennings and L. Harmon Zeigler, *The Governing of School Districts.* Eugene, Ore.: Center for the Advanced Study of Educational Administration, University of Oregon, 1969, p. 3.

54. According to Carlson, *School Superintendents*, p. 29, 90 percent of Oregon's superintendents are Protestant and 87 percent nationally are Protestant.

55. Jennings and Zeigler, *Governing School Districts*, p. 3.

56. E. S. Hickcox and R. J. Snow, "Profile of Superintendents of Schools," in Lee Deighton (ed.), *The Encyclopedia of Education, 8.* New York: Macmillan and Free Press, 1971, pp. 545−555.

57. Carlson, *School Superintendents*, pp. 35−36.

58. N. O. Kerr, "The School Board as an Agency of Legitimation," *Sociology of Education, 38* (1964), pp. 34−59.

59. See Cistone, "The Recruitment and Socialization of School Board Members"; Keith Goldhammer, *The School Board.* New York: The Center for Applied Research in Education, Inc., 1964; and Zeigler and Jennings, *Governing American Schools.*

60. Zeigler and Jennings, *Governing American Schools*, p. 4.

61. Ibid., p. 148.

62. David Minar, "Community Characteristics, Conflict, and Power Structures," in Robert S. Cahill and Stephen P. Hensley (eds.), *The Politics of Education in the Local Community.* Danville, Ill.: Interstate Printers and Publishers, 1964, pp. 132−133.

63. Zeigler and Jennings, *Governing American Schools*, p. 148.

64. James D. Koerner, *Who Controls American Education?* Boston: Beacon Press, 1968, p. 122.

65. Zeigler and Jennings, *Governing American Schools*, p. 150.

66. Eliot, "Towards an Understanding of Public School Politics," p. 1037.

8

Teacher Power

April 11, 1962—the day the United Federation of Teachers (UFT) went out on strike against the New York City School System—represents the turning point in the relationship between teachers and superintendents and school boards. Although the 1962 strike was not the first by any means (between 1940 and 1962 there had been over 100 work stoppages in the United States), after the UFT walkout teacher strikes occurred with increasing frequency. Teachers, long regarded as docile, feminized, obedient, and generally content with their relatively low status and pay, began to assert themselves in the early 1960s. They entered the power struggle for control over the schools and the conflict began. Teachers became, in a word, militant.

MILITANCY AMONG TEACHERS

The aggressiveness of teachers is integrally related to the bureaucratization of education and the desire on the part of teachers to be considered professionals. Bureaucratization is a set of procedures for controlling the work situation and supervising employees. Professionalism, on the other hand, as we saw in Chapter 4, is based on

131

a desire for autonomy and authority. Bureaucracy and professionalism, thus, tend toward diametric opposition, in the process generating tension over the competing definitions of authority. For example, sociologist Ronald Corwin, in his study of twenty-nine schools and over 1500 teachers, found that five of the ten highest-ranking sources of friction between teachers and administrators concerned issues of authority.[1]

The crux of the authority problem revolves around the fact that teachers feel excluded from the policy- and decision-making process. Teacher organizations are levers which can be used for providing access for teachers into educational policy areas. Thus, teacher organizations (both unions and NEA affiliates) are not only concerned with such bread-and-butter issues as salary and fringe benefits; they have also demanded a say in matters such as class size, standards of employment, educational programs, and curriculum development.

Lest the reader get the wrong impression concerning teacher militancy, we must reiterate what was stated in Chapter 4. The majority of teachers are overwhelmingly supportive of the status quo in education. Militant teachers, then, represent a minority of all teachers. This raises an interesting question: who are the militants? Although very little has been written on the background characteristics or predisposition of militant teachers, some generalizations can be drawn. First of all, male teachers are more likely to be militant than female.[2] Militant teachers are also more likely to be under forty years of age than their nonmilitant colleagues.[3] Furthermore, given the general liberalism of Jews, Jewish teachers tend to be more militant than their Protestant and Catholic counterparts.[4] Militant teachers are more likely to come from working-class backgrounds and consider themselves Democrats.[5] Lastly, it is important to mention that although militant teachers are a minority, they tend to be overrepresented in leadership positions and can often count on the backing of the majority of teachers.[6]

It is clear that by the 1960s the dimension of militancy was in the air, as teacher organizations began to play at power politics. School boards and administrators were forced to make concessions to teachers. As we have done throughout, we turn to the past to get a clearer picture of the present.

TEACHERS ASSOCIATIONS AND UNIONS: A BRIEF HISTORY

Teacher militancy can be traced to the growth of teacher unions, in particular the American Federation of Teachers (AFT), which is affiliated with the AFL−CIO. The National Education Association (NEA) has taken more extreme positions as it has been forced to compete with its more militant rival. In the growth of both these organizations and their struggles between themselves can be found the beginnings of teacher militancy.

The NEA

Before the emergence of teacher unions, the professional society was dominant. In 1830 a number of local and regional groups established the American Institute of Instruction as a national center. The institute came under the domination of university faculty members, however, and quickly lost the support of elementary and secondary school teachers. Two other unsuccessful efforts were made to establish a national association before the founding of the National Teachers Association in 1857. The organization soon changed its name to the National Education Association (NEA) by which it is known today.[7] Membership in the NEA was open to teachers, superintendents, principals, and other supervisors. The stated purpose of the organization was to elevate "the character and advance the cause of popular education in the United States."[8] However, when the call went out to organize teachers in 1857, invitations were mailed not to classroom teachers, but to presidents of numerous state education associations which had begun to flourish in the early nineteenth century. Ten presidents accepted, and, all in all, a total of forty-three educators attended the first meeting of the NTA in Philadelphia.[9] Few of them, however, were classroom teachers.

At first, the group was quite small, ranging between two hundred to three hundred members in its first decade. It was only in the 1870s that the NEA became larger when a merger was arranged with the National Association of School Superintendents and the American Normal School Association.

From the start, the NEA was dominated by a disproportionate number of college and supervisory personnel, who as Marshall Donley, Jr., states, "had a tendency to talk a lot and do little."[10]

From its inception, the dominance of superintendents and administrators in the NEA tended to push questions of salaries, pensions, and other matters affecting teachers as employees into the background. Any unionization of teachers was vehemently opposed. It was widely held that any affiliation with the labor movement (which was made up of manual workers) would threaten the "professional" status of teachers. This opposition to unions was not only found among administrators and board members but among rank-and-file teachers as well. The pursuit of improved wages and other economic benefits was generally perceived as a form of unprofessional conduct.[11]

For the most part, the NEA found itself in a paradoxical situation, torn between a genuine concern for improving conditions for teachers, but either unwilling or unable to accomplish anything until the general goal of better schooling had been met.[12]

The NEA thus made very little headway in achieving any power for teachers in the nineteenth century. Limited membership, abstract discussions and debates, a commitment to overall improvement in the schools before teachers' benefits could be improved, and a dominance by supervisors all combined to produce a staid, conservative organization. It was not until the beginning of the twentieth century that any real sparks of teacher militancy could be seen. Of particular importance was the formation of the Chicago Teachers Federation in 1897.

The Chicago Teachers Federation

The first teacher's unions in this country were begun in San Antonio, Texas, and Chicago just before the turn of the century. The Chicago Teachers Club, which eventually became the Chicago Teachers Federation, was started by two women, Catherine Goggin and Margaret Haley. Margaret Haley, the acknowledged leader of the CTF, fought to bring teachers into the mainstream of progressivism in the city of Chicago by forming an alliance with the labor movement and with liberal and radical reformers. She and the CTF consistently fought for higher salaries, pensions, and tenure for Chicago's teachers. The Chicago organization was ahead of its time as it struggled against the centralization of power in the schools and supported such issues as women's suffrage and child labor legislation. The CTF also instigated legal suits against Chicago's utility companies, the powerful *Chicago Tribune,* and a number of large corporations to force them to contribute their legal share of school taxes.[13]

Although Haley's CTF was the earliest teacher's organization to win and exercise any real authority, in the end it succumbed to more powerful forces. Initially, as a mark of solidarity, the CTF had included supervisors and principals among its membership. When it was discovered, however, that the supervisors had been awarded a raise and that rank-and-file teachers had not, the CTF associated itself with the American Federation of Labor (AFL). This affiliation was viewed as a threat by the educational establishment. In 1915, Chicago's Board of Education quickly adopted the Loeb Rule (named after businessman and school board chairman, Jacob Loeb). Under this rule employment as a teacher in Chicago schools could be denied to any member of the CTF as long as the union was linked with organized labor. Teachers were required to state in writing that they would not be members of the AFL during their employment in the Chicago public schools.[14]

Not only did the CTF regard this as an assault upon them, but the famous labor leader of the early twentieth century, Samuel Gompers, and local Chicago union leaders were appalled. Officials of Chicago and other Illinois labor federations wrote a letter to the governor of Illinois claiming ''that the corporate elite on the board were attacking the labor movement and trying to use the schools to 'create for them a body of trained, efficient, and somewhat servile workers' at the lowest cost in taxes.''[15] Gompers had come to Chicago from Cleveland to help the CTF in their fight, fresh from a successful battle over an antiunion ruling where the Cleveland superintendent of schools had blacklisted union teachers. But Gompers soon found that Chicago was different. At first an injunction against the Loeb ruling was obtained, but the next year the board, under Loeb's chairmanship, refused to rehire sixty-eight teachers, most of whom were prominent in the CTF and who had good to superior teacher ratings. The Illinois Supreme Court upheld the ouster, maintaining that the board had "the absolute right to decline to employ any applicant for any reason or for no reason at all."[16]

Margaret Haley and the CTF were forced to compromise with Loeb and the Chicago school board, and subsequently withdrew from the Chicago Federation of Labor. Two years later Margaret Haley also left the NEA, where she had also been a strong advocate of teacher rights. Around the turn of the century, Haley had been instrumental in the founding of the National Federation of Teachers (NFT), a loosely organized alliance of local teacher federations. Originally organized in 1899 and reorganized in 1901, the NFT limited its membership to classroom teachers. It had met concurrently with the NEA and had unsuccessfully tried to move the NEA away from its conservative posture. In Boston in 1903, Haley had started a campaign to turn the NEA into an organization which would work for better conditions for all teachers in general and women teachers in particular. Women teachers had even less power than men teachers in the NEA and Margaret Haley fought battles on two fronts.

In 1910, Haley combined forces with leaders of New York's militant Interborough Association of Women Teachers to plan strategy for the election of Ella Flag Young. The nominating committee recommended a man, but for the first time in history a woman stood up to give a minority recommendation. The hundreds of women wearing Ella Flag Young buttons had done their politicking well; in the vote that followed, Young received 617 of 993 votes of the active members. The press called the outcome a "triumph without parallel in the history of women's organizations." During Young's administration and that of the next four presidents—all endorsed by Haley—the NEA paid increasing attention to classroom teachers, endorsing higher salaries, equal pay for equal work, women's suffrage, and advisory teacher's councils. In 1913 the NEA approved a new organization advocated by Haley, the Department of Classroom Teachers, a group that stemmed from the League of Teachers Associations (composed largely of urban women elementary teachers).[17]

On the whole, though, in spite of such women as Margaret Haley and Ella Flag Young, the NEA basically continued the same role it had played in the nineteenth century. As we stated, Margaret Haley withdrew from the NEA in 1918 and concentrated instead on preserving gains won by the CTF by cultivating alliances with local Chicago and Illinois politicians.[18] She clearly saw the political nature of school dominance and acted accordingly.

As a rule, during the first two decades of the twentieth century, teachers continued to be poorly paid and ill-prepared, and received little respect from the society they served. Indicative of the low status of the American public school teacher was the reaction of the New York City Superintendent of Schools, when asked in 1905 if there were any conditions which might justify a teacher in complaining about his superior. "Absolutely none," was his answer.[19] Teachers did, however, manifest some militancy. In 1918, the teachers of Memphis, Tennessee walked out demanding a 33⅓ percent salary increase. The Memphis school board countered with an offer of ten dollars more a month and the strike was halted.[20] For the most part though, the legacy of militancy begun by the CTF was passed to New York City.

The UFT

In 1916, the New York City Teachers Union affiliated with the American Federation of Teachers (AFT) as Local 5. With the application of the Loeb Rule and the withdrawal of Margaret Haley and the CTF, a vacuum in the leadership of the AFT was created; and Local 5, beset with internal problems and no direction from the National, floundered about. The AFT, for example, did nothing to offset the interrogations in New York City of teachers about their personal beliefs and the books they read or assigned to their students. When the United States entered World War I, the New York City Board of Education instituted teacher loyalty oaths. Henry Linville, a founder and then president of Local 5, alone protested the oath. Linville questioned both the utility and fairness of a loyalty oath, citing the lack of evidence that teachers had been guilty of any disloyal statements or treasonable acts. The request for the loyalty oath then proved to be preliminary to a much more extensive inquiry authorized by the Board and conducted by Associate Superintendent of Schools John L. Tildsley. Three teachers questioned by Tildsley about their opinions, books read and recommended to students, topics assigned, and their general classroom behavior were brought up on charges of "conduct unbecoming a teacher."[21] So authoritarian had been the process that John Dewey, the eminent philosopher and educational theorist, pronounced the evidence against the teachers to be

> absolutely nothing but charges about [the teachers'] private views and private opinions; and these views were not expressed within any school, but were brought out, taking it at their worst . . . in a purely private and personal hearing. I don't know what this is called in 1917, but it used to be called the Inquisition.[22]

The New York Local 5 also had to contend with an attempted Communist Party takeover campaign. Linville and Abraham Lefkowitz (another founder of the Teachers Union) were so fearful of the Communist threat that they asked the AFT to revoke the charter of Local 5, thereby allowing them to form a new local which would exclude Communists. After numerous hearings and investigations and even despite the urgings of AFL President William Green, the AFT delegate assembly, influenced by large blocks of Communist votes, voted to reject Linville's and Lefkowitz's request. The two men, along with about 700 of their followers, quit the TU and, in 1935, founded the unaffiliated Teachers Guild.[23] Without Linville and Lefkowitz, the TU, as well as the AFT, fell completely into the hands of the Communists.

In 1940, when George Counts succeeded in gaining control of the AFT, the TU charter was revoked and the Linville–Lefkowitz Teachers Guild was granted a new charter.[24] Although the Teachers Guild, as a chartered local of the AFT and AFL, could call upon the assistance of local and state labor leaders, the Teachers Guild up until 1960 "had to settle for grudging and strictly limited recognition by the school board."[25] What effectiveness the union had depended upon its appeals to the community, the legislature, and to school authorities. At best it was reduced to arguing solely on moral and educational grounds for what it wanted. It was in no position to do otherwise.

During the 1950s, another New York City group, the High School Teachers Association (HSTA), quickly became militant.

> In 1959, a group of 800 evening high school teachers, under the direction of Roger Parente, the secretary of the HSTA, struck for one month. The strikers were successful in closing down all evening high schools in the city; and the strike resulted in a substantial salary increase without reprisals. Because of the strike's success, it was HSTA, the sponsoring organization, that was catapulted into a position of prominence—though the Guild, too, had supported the strike, even participating in the picketing.[26]

Within a few months of the settlement of the evening school strike, the Teachers Guild threatened to strike. However, when it asked for HSTA support, a split developed within the HSTA over whether the organization should honor Guild picket lines in the event of a strike. A faction of the HSTA, led by Parente and HSTA vice-president Samuel Hochberg, wanted to support the Guild. Another faction, headed by Emil Tron, HSTA president, regarded the Guild's threatened strike as a power play and refused to support it. Tron's group won out, and the Parente and Hochberg faction quit the HSTA and formed the Committee for Action through Unity (CATU); shortly afterward, the Committee merged with the Guild. The new organization became the United Federation of Teachers, Local 2 of the AFT, AFL-CIO.[27] Charles Cogan of the Guild was chosen president of the UFT, and Samuel Hochberg its deputy-president.

Almost immediately after its formation, the UFT called for a May 15, 1960 strike. The strike was forestalled by the Board of Education, which promised to hold a collective bargaining election and to permit a dues checkoff for the UFT. The Board lagged in implementing its promises and the UFT called a strike for November 7, 1960. Almost 5000 teachers stayed out of school in support of this one-day strike and the Board of Education, under pressure from organized labor and New York City Mayor Robert Wagner, promised to appoint a fact-finding committee.[28] The next year, the Board, acting on the recommendations of the fact-finding committee, conducted a referendum to determine whether or not teachers wanted collective bargaining. Teachers approved collective bargaining by a vote of over 3 to 1 and a collective bargaining election was set for December 1961. Three groups were on the ballot: the UFT, the TU, and the Teachers Bargaining Organization (TBO)—an amalgam of organizations put together by the NEA. The UFT received almost two-thirds of the votes cast.[29]

The UFT entered into collective bargaining with the New York City

Board of Education. However, when salary negotiations broke down, the UFT again threatened to strike. By a slight majority vote a strike was called for on April 1, 1962. "Pickets appeared in front of schools and 20,558 teachers—51 percent of the teaching staff—responded to the strike call."[30]

The strike was halted after one day by a court injunction and the next day the Governor of New York, Nelson Rockefeller, met with Mayor Wagner, Superintendent of Schools John Theobald, members of the Board of Education, and representatives of the UFT. It was agreed that an extra 13 million dollars would be given to New York City in state aid for teachers' raises. Governor Rockefeller also asked that no reprisals be initiated against those who struck. This proposal was accepted by the Board of Education, and Superintendent Theobald instructed principals not to question teachers who had been absent from school on the day of the strike.[31]

The UFT had wrested some power from the New York City School Board and Superintendent. It had won an important victory that went well beyond the raises teachers had been given. In the aftermath of the strike, the union victory proved to be the biggest single success in the history of teacher organizations in the United States.[32] The UFT quickly became the largest local teachers union in the country. Its victory spurred teachers unions all over the nation, and perhaps most important of all, it forced the NEA to change certain of its positions concerning teacher militancy. This change in the NEA would prove to have a great impact on the majority of America's teachers.

NEA and Unionism

When faced with its resounding defeat in New York City, the NEA placed its major effort on combatting teacher unions in other large cities. At first, the NEA simply attacked the concept of a strike as highly unprofessional. Gradually, it began to take a more positive tone, emphasizing "professional negotiations" and urging school boards to consult regularly with local NEA representatives. By 1962, the NEA began to use the concept of sanction (a kind of blacklisting of school districts), and passed the following resolution:

> The National Education Association believes that, as a means for preventing unethical or arbitrary policies and practices that have a deleterious effect on the welfare of the schools, professional sanctions should be invoked. These sanctions would provide for appropriate disciplinary action by the organized profession. The National Education Association calls upon its state associations to cooperate in developing guidelines which would define, organize, and definitely specify procedural steps for involving sanctions by the teaching profession.[33]

Within two months of the passage of this resolution, the Utah Education Association applied sanctions for two days against the Alpine, Utah, School District. By the end of 1962, local NEA teacher groups in at least fifteen states had applied sanctions against school districts.

It was in 1962, too, that a scattered number of school boards began grudgingly to recognize the right of local teacher groups to negotiate for their members. Long Beach, California, teachers, for example, won this right for themselves. But perhaps the most significant achievement as far as the NEA was concerned occurred in Denver, Colorado, where the school board agreed to negotiate with the Denver Classroom Teachers Association. This was the first time a large-city NEA affiliate had been offered negotiation rights.[34] By the middle of 1963 NEA affiliates had won over twenty negotiation rights in seven states.[35] But real power was denied the NEA as long as it continued to advocate the use of sanctions and eschew the strike.

The Failure of the Sanction

So pleased with itself over the use of sanctions in Utah, the NEA applied this weapon against the state of Oklahoma in 1964. It achieved some success when state-supported levies to local school districts were initiated, something which Oklahoma teachers had been advocating for two years. Three years later, however, the results were quite different when the NEA sought to impose sanctions against the state of Florida. The National NEA had investigated school conditions in Florida at the request of the Florida Education Association (FEA). An NEA committee had reported that taxes and politics were the basis for inadequate education in Florida. The previous year had been a gubernatorial election year in Florida and Claude Kirk who subsequently became governor, had, when campaigning, promised massive improvements in education in 1967. Upon election, Kirk reversed himself and called for budget cuts in education. The Florida NEA imposed five sanctions which called for:

> 1) censure of the governor for "lack of leadership for a positive school system"; 2) national circulation of notices that Florida schools were not satisfactory for teaching; 3) national notice to business and industry of these conditions; 4) national notice to individuals outside the state that they would be acting unethically to accept teaching positions in the state; and 5) statewide notice that individuals not presently employed in the Florida School System who accepted such employment would be subject to charges of unethical conduct.[36]

Governor Kirk chose to ignore the NEA sanction, and when he vetoed an educational appropriations bill that resulted in loss of $150 million for Florida's schools, teachers in Broward County walked out and remained away from their classes for seven days. The Governor and the FEA were on a collision course; when Governor Kirk threatened to veto still another bill, the FEA called on its members to walk out. On February 19, 1967, 26,000 teachers throughout the state did not report to their classrooms. The very next day the state authorized the hiring of substitutes (many of them uncertified) to reopen the schools. As the walkout continued, the state refused to budge and the number of striking teachers dropped. In a number of Florida counties, school boards obtained injunctions which required that the teachers return. Faced with these conditions, all the NEA could do was urge that the public schools of Florida be closed to protect the safety and welfare of children of the state. In addition, the Southern Association of Colleges and Schools warned that Florida's schools could lose their accreditation because of the employment of un-qualified teachers.[37]

In the end, though, the NEA failed to accomplish what it had set out to do—to close Florida's schools. As Marshall Donley states:

> The Florida sanction by NEA, the association's longest involvement in such a statewide action in its history, was probably its last. A few years later, NEA officials made it clear that statewide actions of the Utah, Oklahoma, and Florida type would not be encouraged. The NEA assistant executive secretary who had directed the Florida effort was fired. Florida had taught NEA a lesson: The American public was not so fully on the side of its teachers that it would place their needs first. As a result, NEA turned away from sanctions and strengthened its use of more traditional mechanisms of labor unions: achieving contracts; getting the rights of teachers in writing; striking if necessary, but selectively, district by district. NEA learned, too, that the prestige of the national organiza-tion should not be put irreversibly on the line in any single struggle. NEA had learned to fight where it had to and in the way required, knowing now that if it lost one battle, it would survive to fight again.[38]

The NEA's use of sanctions had led to a dead-end, and the association was forced to fall back on the union tactic of the strike. During the next few years strikes by both NEA and AFT affiliates would break out in almost epidemic proportion around the country.

Strikes occurring in a relatively new setting—the college campus—also began to take place at around the same time and are worth noting. Professors' strikes can be traced directly to the organizing success of the American Federation of Teachers. The largest strike occurred in 1966 in the Chicago junior college system, when well over 600 faculty members, members of the Cook County Teachers Union, struck to protest the refusal of the junior college board to negotiate with the union.[39] However, the first and most dramatic strike against a university occurred at St. John's University in New York City.[40]

On December 15, 1965, thirty-one faculty members were fired by the St. John's administration. Of these, twenty-six belonged to the United Federation of College Teachers (UFCT), and included the chapter president. Three officers of the American Association of University Professors (AAUP) were also among the thirty-one. Union membership at the time had been approximately seventy-five, but in the wake of the firings membership doubled.

For the most part, the administration of St. John's University remained adamant in their position, that they could fire professors for whatever reasons they deemed important, in spite of a subsequent AAUP censure. In the end, this position won out and the UFCT was defeated. Those faculty who had struck and refused to return to St. John's took jobs elsewhere. Out of the defeat, however, a much stronger union arose as the UFCT used the St. John's strike as a learning experience and, under the leadership of Israel Kugler began to expand their position in the New York City University system.

The use of the strike as a weapon for teachers became established, and 1967 can be seen as the year when the NEA moved away from its no-strike position. Until 1967 strikes were not officially acceptable to the NEA under any conditions, though this obviously had not prevented local affiliates from walking out. During the 1967 NEA convention, however, the executive secretary-elect of the NEA stated: "The NEA will not encourage strikes, but if one occurs after all good faith efforts fail, we will not walk out on our local associations."[41]

The end of the 1960s thus saw hundreds of teacher strikes, most of them centered on three basic issues: higher pay, a greater say in school planning, and the right to organize. By the 1970s teacher militancy began to take on a new, and what came to be a much more important, dimension: the development of mechanisms to mediate differences between administrators, school boards, and teachers—the right of collective bargaining.

COLLECTIVE BARGAINING

Collective bargaining in education has been defined as:

> A set of procedures to provide an orderly method for teachers associations and school boards through professional channels to negotiate on matters of common concern, to reach mutually satisfactory agreement on these matters, and to establish educational channels for mediation and appeal in the event of impasse.[42]

Collective bargaining reduces, and in some cases eliminates altogether, the decision-making prerogatives that have historically been the province of school boards and administrators. Obviously, this is a major reason for the vehement resistance expressed by many boards of education and administrators toward collective bargaining.

There is a fundamental difference between the power of teachers before and after the right of collective bargaining has been secured. Without it, school boards could: (1) act unilaterally without consultation with teachers; (2) impose one-way communication; (3) always have the last word; (4) lack good faith; (5) ignore divergencies between policy and practice; and (6) generally retain a power relationship that was one-sided, paternalistic, and authoritarian. Using collective bargaining, however: (1) boards are required to consult with employees; (2) communication is two-way; (3) impasse procedures are provided; (4) good faith bargaining is mandated; (5) constant dialogue requires the board to discuss divergencies between policy and practice; and (6) the power relationships are bilateral, cooperative, and democratic.[43] Collective bargaining, then, is a means which teachers have used to gain some power. Teachers, in short, have become more aggressive, having digested the political lesson that in order to achieve any power one must fight for it. Because they have been involved in a power confrontation, much of what they have won has been at the expense of others. Foremost among those who have had to give up power to the militant teachers associations have been principals.

Collective Bargaining and the Changing Role of the Principal

Collective bargaining has produced profound role changes among administrators. Indeed, many administrators feel that they have been shunted aside by collective bargaining and made to feel like adversaries when they are not. School principals, in particular, have become concerned that their power has been curtailed so sharply and so rapidly that they can no longer exercise any educational leadership. (Militant teachers retort that the principals themselves gave up their leadership role when they embraced the managerial role). In any event, very real conflict exists at the school level between teacher organizations and principals. The principal's power is dependent, to a large extent, upon the degree of authority held by teachers. If teachers gain authority, principals lose some. During the last decade and a half principals have lost power not only to teachers but to central administrations as well. So stark has the transformation been that a number of educationists have stated that principals now operate from a powerless base. They are neither part of the administration nor a member of the teacher's organization. As Lutz, Kleinman, and Evans note:

> Many teachers realize that although their building principal functions in the formal organization as the communication link in the line between themselves and the central administration, they can more readily achieve their goals via the informal communication channels maintained among teacher organization leaders, chief administrators and board members. . . . [44]

Traditionally, if an individual teacher or group of teachers had a grievance, it would be discussed with the school principal. He or she would then either resolve it or pass it on to his or her immediate supervisor. With collective bargaining, this is no longer the case. Teachers with grievances communicate directly with a grievance committee of their association or union, which then brings them to the attention of the board of education or the superintendent. The principal, who formerly had control over this and other areas, now is faced with teachers who negotiate directly with higher officials. A power realignment has taken place in the everyday governing of the schools. Teachers now bargain over issues such as class size, length of school day, grouping policies, transfer of unruly students, and similar issues.[45]

Not only is the principal much less powerful than ever before, but is also caught up in an untenable position. He or she is a member of the administration; yet, in order to function, he or she must deal effectively with teachers. If he or she sides with management during a strike, he or she jeopardizes his or her relations with teachers. If he or she supports the teachers, he or she runs the risk of alienating the superintendent who has hired him or her and can fire him or her.[46] Principals have reacted to this dilemma in various ways. For example, the Michigan Elementary School Principals Association disaffiliated itself from the Michigan Education Association after the state labor relations board ruled that principals could not be represented by teacher groups at the bargaining table.[47] Principals in New York City at first joined a Teamsters local, and eventually the UFT. However, probably the most influential force in the alteration of the roles of teachers and principals in the collective bargaining process has been the courts.

Bargaining Law

In June 1968, the United States Court of Appeals for the Seventh Circuit ruled that the Constitution gave teachers the right to engage in union activities. Further, the court stated that a teacher could not be dismissed for exercising this right, whether tenured or not.[48] However, teachers' rights to strike have remained a bit limited in states where state laws deny this right to all public employees.

Perhaps the most famous of all such laws is New York State's Taylor Law, which was passed in 1967 and is still on the books today. The Taylor Law forbids public employees to strike and imposes penalties which include: (1) the losing of check-off privileges (dues which are taken directly out of the union member's paycheck); (2) jailing of union leaders; (3) the imposition of fines against the union; and (4) the loss of two days' pay for every day missed by the employee. It seems extremely unlikely that laws such as the Taylor Law can provide effective solutions to teacher—school board conflicts. Clearly, these statutes have failed to prevent strikes, and the antagonisms that have resulted have virtually crippled whole school systems. In addition, an unintended consequence of the Taylor Law has allowed stubborn boards of education in times of economic stringency to refuse to negotiate once a strike has been called, and to use the two days' pay fines to offset any eventual teacher raises. A case in point was the 1976 Schenectady (New York) Teachers Union strike. Teachers stayed out for eleven days, and the twenty-two days' pay they lost was only slightly less than the raises they were eventually able to negotiate. Furthermore, during the course of the strike many teachers, because of economic hardships imposed by the threat of the loss of two days' pay, had to cross picket lines manned by friends. Eventually, too, the union's leaders spent a number of days in jail. The end result of all this conflict were antagonisms between teachers who had "stuck it out" for the whole strike and those who had crossed the picket lines, and between the union and the school board. Such antagonisms run deep and will remain that way for many years to come. The Schenectady Teachers Union believes that the school board used the Taylor Law to try and break the union. The school board believes that the teachers used illegal means in order to receive pay raises the Schenectady tax payers could not afford. The question of who was right and who was wrong becomes lost in the bitterness that follows such a confrontation. There are no winners, and the losers are the children who must attend school in an atmosphere charged with resentment and hatred. Laws such as the Taylor Law thus carry with them a tremendous potential for harm. If any good at all is to come out of such acts, it may be the realization that teacher organizations cannot afford to fight among themselves if they are to achieve parity with school boards and superintendents. The possibility of a merger of NEA and the AFT has arisen, and although attempts have been unsuccessful to the present, such a merger may very well come about in the near future.

THE NEA AND AFT—TO MERGE OR NOT TO MERGE

The NEA and AFT have been in competition throughout the twentieth century, and the conflict between them reached its climax in the 1960s, when a pattern was established. Large city teachers organizations tend to affiliate with the AFT and the rest with the NEA. By 1978 the NEA claimed 1,800,000 members and the AFT 450,000. A national organization that could combine these two groups could bring even more power to teachers, and educational leaders are well aware of this fact. For instance, David Selden, the newly elected AFT president, stated in 1968, that the merger of the two organizations was the overriding goal of his administration.[49] By 1970 local affiliates of the two national teacher organizations had merged. But it was in 1972 that the largest merger occurred. Albert Shanker's powerful New York City teachers union merged with the New York State Teachers Association to form the New York State United Teachers (NYSUT).[50]

Merger talks also began in the next few years between the NEA and AFT, but up to now nothing has come of these talks—old conflicts take a long time to heal. The New York State merger also proved to be short-lived and in 1976, the UFT and its affiliates withdrew from NYSUT. A merger of the NEA and AFT, therefore, does not seem forseeable in the immediate future; but given the shrinking educational dollar and the cutbacks in jobs and services in education that has characterized the late 1970s, a merger of the two in the 1980s should never be considered an impossibility. Divided teachers are obviously not as powerful as united ones, and the NEA and AFT may realize that this is more important than their differences. Yet, in spite of this division, teachers have accrued enough of a power base to force a shift in the power structure of public schooling in America.

POWER IN THE SCHOOLS: THE SHIFTING BASE

The strike has become a genuine weapon for teachers. School boards and superintendents now have to listen seriously to teachers' demands. Teachers find themselves negotiating from a position of strength, and not weakness, as has historically been the case. As one writer put it:

> If the decade of sixties accomplished nothing else, it buried permanently the myth that teachers are self-sacrificing missionaries content to work for whatever

wages and under whatever conditions the patrons in a local community thought appropriate for such "service-minded folk."[51]

It is thus almost incontrovertible that teachers, through their collective action, have achieved some power within the public schools. What will they do with this power? Will they change the educational system? Or is their power only symbolic? These are questions that we hope will be answered in the 1980s. For now, all we can say without fear of contradiction is that teachers, like the school boards and superintendents they do battle with, are members of the middle class. Although they have asked for smaller classrooms, better working conditions, more educational resources, in the name of helping their students, little has been altered in the public schools. Lower-class children still fail at the same rate they always have; public schools are still the bureaucratic monsters they always were. What has simply occurred is that, like superintendents who challenged the school boards and won, teachers have challenged both and now must be reckoned with. They have flexed their muscles, have achieved a better position for themselves, and seek to hold on to it. Very little has changed, though, for the lower classes. The game is the same, only the players are different.

SUMMARY

The shift in power has been somewhat cyclical. First the local community, through its representatives (the school board) controlled the schools. Then, through reform and covert manipulation, superintendents usurped much of the power of the school boards. Now teachers have challenged superintendents for control. Although some basic changes in power relations have taken place in educational institutions, it must be reiterated that these changes have done little to alter the basic structure of education (at least since the reformers got the schools out of the hands of the lower classes and ward bosses). School board members, superintendents, and teachers are all solidly middle-class individuals, and whoever eventually wins the current battle will still be middle-class. Therefore, although changes have occurred, little if anything has been done to offset the essential middle-class orientation of the schools. The internal conflicts over who controls education have not helped the children of the poor nor addressed the issue of the legitimacy of the educational system. We will now examine the larger society, to discover whether its demands on public education have confronted some of these questions.

NOTES

1. Ronald G. Corwin, *Militant Professionalism*. New York: Appleton, 1970.
2. See Stephen Cole, *The Unionization of Teachers*. New York: Praeger, 1969; and William T. Lowe, "Who Joins Teachers Groups," *Teachers College Record*, 5 (April 1965), pp. 614–619.
3. See Cole, *The Unionization of Teachers;* and Corwin, *Militant Professionalism*.
4. See Cole, *The Unionization of Teachers;* and Mildred Kornacher, *How Urban High School*

Teachers View Their Jobs. Washington, D.C.: U.S. Office of Education Cooperative Research Project No. 5-8144, 1966.

5. See Cole, *The Unionization of Teachers*.

6. See Corwin, *Militant Professionalism*, pp. 327−328.

7. Edgar B. Wesley, *The NEA: The First Hundred Years*. New York: Harper & Row, 1957, pp. 8−24.

8. Philip Taft, *United They Teach: The Story of the United Federation of Teachers*. Los Angeles: Nash, 1974.

9. Marshall O. Donley, Jr. *Power to the Teacher*. Bloomington, Ind.: Indiana University Press, 1976, p. 10.

10. Ibid.

11. Taft, *United They Teach*, p. 4.

12. Donley, *Power to the Teacher*, p. 11.

13. David B. Tyack, *The One Best System; A History of American Urban Education*. Cambridge, Mass.: Harvard University Press, 1974, pp. 259−260.

14. Taft, *United They Teach*, p. 7.

15. Tyack, *The One Best System*, p. 263.

16. Ibid.

17. Ibid., pp. 266−267.

18. Ibid., p. 264.

19. Donley, *Power to the Teacher*, p. 17.

20. Ibid.

21. Taft, *United They Teach*, p. 19.

22. John Dewey, *Toward the New Education*. New York: Teachers Union, 1918, p. 121.

23. Cole, *The Unionization of Teachers*, p. 13.

24. Ibid.

25. Taft, *United They Teach*, p. 87.

26. Cole, *The Unionization of Teachers*, p. 18.

27. Ibid.

28. Ibid., p. 19.

29. Ibid.

30. Taft, *United They Teach*, p. 12.

31. Ibid.

32. Donley, *Power to the Teacher*, p. 49.

33. Quoted in ibid., pp. 68−69.

34. Ibid., p. 70.

35. Ibid., p. 76.

36. Ibid., p. 88.

37. Ibid., p. 91.

38. Ibid., pp. 94−95.

39. Ibid., p. 104.

40. For a more detailed analysis of this strike, see Joseph A. Scimecca and Roland Damiano, *Crisis At St. John's: Strike and Revolution on the Catholic Campus*. New York: Random House, 1968.

41. Donley, *Power to the Teacher*, p. 107.

42. *Professional Negotiations with School Boards–A Legal Analysis and Review: School Law Series, Research Report, 1965−R−3*. Washington, D.C.: Research Division, National Education Association, 1965, p. 15.

43. Chester M. Nolte, *Status and Scope of Collective Bargaining in Education*. Eugene, Ore.: Eric Clearinghouse on Educational Administration, University of Oregon, 1970, pp. 13−14.

44. Frank W. Lutz, Lou Kleinman, and Sy Evans, *Grievances and Their Resolution: Problems in School Personnel Administration*. Danville, Ill.: Interstate Printers and Publishers, 1967, p. 84.

45. Donald A. Myers, *Teacher Power–Professionalization and Collective Bargaining*. Lexington, Mass.: Lexington Books, 1973, p. 108.

46. Ibid., p. 109.
47. Donley, *Power to the Teacher*, p. 137.
48. Ibid., p. 138.
49. Ibid., p. 160.
50. Ibid., p. 167.
51. Myers, *Teacher Power—Professionalization and Collective Bargaining*, p. 1.

III

Conflict in the Society

9

Education and Inequality

Since this nation's founding, the public school, more than any other social institution, has been looked upon to provide access for upward social mobility. However, close inspection reveals that this commitment to "equal educational opportunity" (to use the current term) as a means for achieving success has been characterized more by rhetoric than results. Very little has been achieved by attempts to offset what we consider to be the discriminatory practices of the schools. Yet the belief in educational opportunity as a means of social mobility has proven hard to shake. When faced with contradictory evidence, people fall back upon the individualistic viewpoint so prevalent in American society—a perspective which not coincidentally they were socialized to accept in the schools. The lower-class poor and immigrant groups are taught to perceive the success of a few of their educated members as evidence that the group as a whole is witnessing a rise in status, that opportunity exists for all of them, and that formal education makes a difference in later life.[1] Only by rejecting this traditional attitude, only by turning attention to the progress made by the entire group, can the educational system's role in achieving equality be analyzed. For example, if opportunity is defined as the degree of openness or equality of access to valued things (in this case, education), then equality of opportunity would imply that a random member of a given stratum will

151

have the same chance or probability of ending up in a salaried profession as the random member of any other given stratum. But this is not the case. Sons,[2] particularly at the higher and lower ends of the ladder, tend to remain in the same broad occupational categories as their fathers. For example, a national study has shown that over 40 percent of the sons of self-employed professionals became professionals themselves, and 30 percent enter some white-collar occupation. In contrast to this, only about 5 percent of laborer's sons enter a profession and 15 percent some other white-collar job.[3] Moreover, as Charles Anderson points out: "These are crude categories and do not take into account the high probability that the laborer's mobile son enters a lower-status profession or business career than the professional's son (for example, possession of a teaching certificate as opposed to a Ph.D., and assistant manager of a small business as opposed to an executive in a large company)."[4]

Just as important, if not more so, is the opportunity to attend and graduate from college. Whereas a century ago an elementary school education put one in good stead, today, with the rampant "credential inflation," one needs a college degree if one is to have any real chance at social mobility.[5] The crucial questions are thus: who goes to college? and more importantly, who graduates from college?

INDICATORS OF EDUCATIONAL SUCCESS

The most important factor in explaining who goes on to college is a student's class background (his or her parents, education, occupation, and income). The higher a person's class background, the greater the probability that the person will attend college.[6] As Bowles and Gintis state:

> Even among those who graduated from high school in the early 1960s, children of families earning less than $3000 per year were over six times as likely *not* to attend college as were children of families earning over $15,000.
>
> Moreover, children from less well-off families are *both* less likely to have graduated from high school and more likely to attend inexpensive two-year community colleges rather than a four-year B.A. program if they do make it to college.[7]

Basically, the data show that the results of schooling correlate with social background. So too does scholastic achievement. For example, if the output of schooling is measured by scores on nationally standardized achievement tests, children of parents with high education outperform children of parents with low education by a wide margin. Among white high school seniors, those whose parents were in the top 10 percent in their class were on the average well over three grade levels ahead of those students whose parents were in the lowest 10 percent.[8]

These differences in scholastic achievement and inequalities in years of schooling are not a reflection of differing intellectual ability. For:

an individual in the ninetieth percentile in social class background is likely to receive five more years of education than an individual in the tenth percentile, . . . he is likely to receive 4.25 more years schooling than an individual from the tenth percentile with the same IQ. Similar results are obtained when we look specifically to access to college education for students with the same measured IQ. Project Talent data indicates that for "high ability" students (top 25 percent as measured by a composite of tests of "general aptitude"), those of high socio-economic background (top 25 percent as measured by a composite of family income, parents' education, and occupation) are nearly twice as likely to attend college than students of low socio-economic background (bottom 25 percent). For "low ability" students (bottom 25 percent), those of high social background are more than four times as likely to attend college as are their low social background counterparts.[9]

The relationship of social class to educational success is therefore extremely difficult to deny.[10] Defenders of the system are reduced to the assertion that things are getting better; and of course they are. But the important question is, how much better? Whereas graduation from high school is now becoming increasingly equal across class lines, enrollment in college is still class related. For example, one of the largest studies ever attempted—HEW's National Longitudinal Study of the high school class of 1972, based on a national sample of 18,143 high school seniors—showed that in the second year after graduation, only 45 percent of the lowest socioeconomic group, as opposed to 87 percent of the highest socioeconomic group, had attended some type of postsecondary school or college. More importantly, among those questioned who were in school at the time, 45 percent of the lowest socioeconomic group, and 72 percent from the highest group, were in four-year colleges and universities.[11] This would seem consistent with the data which shows that graduation from college is still dependent on one's social background.[12] In short, the evidence seems to indicate that parents' social status and their level of education is comparable to their children's. The correlation is so high that Bowles and Gintis say with confidence: "On balance, the overall data suggest that the number of years of school attained by a child depends upon family background as much in the recent period as it did fifty years ago."[13]

Yet, as we stated before, given its legitimation function, the belief in equal educational opportunity is a difficult one to change. Perhaps the most important challenge to this notion came in 1966 with the publication of James Coleman et al.'s study of the "Equality of Educational Opportunity." The report (hereafter referred to as the Coleman Report) was mandated by section 402 of the 1968 Civil Rights Act.

THE COLEMAN REPORT

In the Coleman Report, Coleman and his colleagues expected to find gross differences in the quality of schools attended by students from dominant and minority groups. They assumed that inequality in the age of school buildings, instructional facilities, class size, teacher background, and so forth, would account for differences in achievement among minority and nonminority students. However, after measuring these variables, as well as the backgrounds of the children, and comparing them to school achievement, Coleman came up with some unexpected findings. First, Coleman found that black and white schools were not as unequal as had been assumed. Second, he discovered that differences in relative school achievement were not reducible to differences in measured educational "inputs." What Coleman was saying, in effect, was that even unlimited spending on teacher training, school buildings, and new curricula would not reduce the relative difference in achievement levels of poor children. What did correlate, though, with differences in achievement among poor children was the socioeconomic status of children with whom they attended school. The child from a poor background or a low socioeconomic status did better in school if he or she attended school with children of a higher socioeconomic level. Put into a racial context (because black children are predominantly poor), black children will perform better in school if they are educated with middle-class white students. It was the peer group and not the schools which accounted for differential achievement.[14] Coleman's findings were disheartening to educators and social planners and they sought to ignore them as much as possible.[15]

Although the Coleman Report did not offer any final answers, it did raise serious questions about the traditional beliefs as to the causes of educational inequality. Coleman found that when academic achievement is the major criterion of educational opportunity, at least when standardized tests of mathematical and verbal performance are used, traditional standards make relatively little difference when compared to the social and economic composition of fellow students. In essence, Coleman changed the traditional way of thinking about the school. The message of the Coleman Report was that traditional assumptions about education no longer held. It would take much more than the provision of equal school facilities to offset the inequality in the society. Schools would now have to provide unequal "inputs" in order to guarantee equal "outputs." In particular, "compensatory" educational programs were given an impetus, one of the most important and most famous of which was the Office of Economic Opportunity's Head Start program. The Head Start program was a summer preschool program which involved professional educators, community workers, guidance counselors, and parents in a concerted effort to raise the cognitive skills of poor children. The program was designed to compensate for the deficient background of the lower socioeconomic student. Its title, though, was really a misnomer because poor children were not really given a head start; they were given a boost to enable them to start evenly. For the most part the program was judged a failure because although the children made gains at first, their gains were eventually nullified as they stayed in school. The problem that educators could or would not see was that the major focus of Head Start was on trying to change the child and not the middle-class school. Still, Operation Head Start did accomplish a number of significant things. Specifically, it called much-needed attention to the health and nutritional needs of children and created a mechanism through which many of their needs could be satisfied.[16] Most important of all, the involvement of poor parents in the program gave them necessary experience in dealing with the educational bureaucracy, experience that would later be translated into a cry for decentralization (something that will be dealt with in more detail in the last chapter).

Other attempts at improving the education of lower-class children ranged from "making the curriculum more relevant," to recruiting more lower-class teachers, to the forced integration of the schools through busing. The result of all these efforts are essentially the same as that of Head Start—very limited success, which was eventually offset by other factors. Levin and Carnoy have summed up quite well the end product of compensatory programs:

> By almost all observable standards, these programs failed to achieve their ostensible objectives. Test scores of disadvantaged children did not appear to improve despite the massive efforts in this direction.[17]

In general, the early 1970's were characterized by a sense of failure on the part of educators as they began to face the fact that the schools were not helping the lower classes achieve any real educational gains. It was in this climate that Christopher Jencks and his associates at the Harvard School of Education published the now famous *Inequality: A Reassessment of the Effect of Family and Schooling in America (1972)*.

JENCKS ON INEQUALITY

In *Inequality*, Jencks et al., reinterpreting much of Coleman's data, argued that the assumed correlation between educational advantage and economic success was more illusionary than real.

> The primary reason some people end up richer than others is not that they have more adequate cognitive skills. While children who read well, get the right answers to arithmetic problems, and articulate their thoughts clearly, are somewhat more likely than others to get ahead, there are many other equally important factors involved.[18]

One of these other factors, according to Jencks, was "luck." The media immediately condensed Jencks' study, and implied that his conclusion was that "schools do not make a difference." However, this is only a superficial interpretation which overlooks the fact that Jencks introduced a class-conflict position into his analysis. He saw poverty in class terms not in racial ones. Jencks was far more interested in eliminating the difference in wealth between the richest fifth of the population and the poorest fifth than between blacks and whites. The average black worker earns 50 percent less than the average white worker, but the average member of the richest fifth of the population earns 600 percent more than the poorest fifth.[19]

Jencks felt that only a redistribution of wealth would overcome inequality in American society. He closed his work with the following passage:

> The long-term direction of such progress seems clear. In America, as elsewhere, the general trend over the past 200 years has been toward equality. In the economic realm, however, the contribution of public policy to this drift has been slight. As long as egalitarians assume that public policy cannot contribute to economic equality directly but must proceed by ingenious manipulations of marginal institutions like the schools, progress will remain glacial. If we want to move beyond this tradition, we will have to establish political control over the economic institutions that shape our society. This is what other countries usually call Socialism. Anything else will end in the same disappointment as the reforms of the 1960s.[20]

Jencks' study, like the Coleman Report before it, was criticized on numerous grounds,[21] in particular for the measures used, the conclusions reached on the basis of the data, and for the omission of data which could lead to other conclusions.[22] More importantly, though, Jencks' was most severely criticized for leaving himself open to erroneous political interpretation. As Kenneth Clark sarcastically states:

> Jencks' contribution to the increasing social science litany of immobility and despair for minority-group youngsters is a significantly new and novel one. These children are not only blocked by their culture and their genes, but they are now also being blocked by the inherent meaninglessness of the schools. If education itself is of no value then there can be significance in the struggle to use the schools as instruments for justice and mobility. Jencks has closed the circle. The last possibility of hope for undereducated and oppressed minorities has been dashed. The social scientists have now provided policy makers with the invaluable rationale that, given the insignificance of schools as an instrument for translating the promises of democracy into reality, there is in fact no realistic need either to desegregate the schools, decentralize schools, equalize expenditures for schools, or for that matter, even adequately maintain schools.[23]

Indeed, Clark goes so far as to question Jencks' motives. He writes: "From the perspective of this observer, it is a matter of significance, not coincidence, that the closing of the circle of doom comes at a time in American history when Negroes and other dark-skinned minorities are increasing their demands for the reality of equal education."[24]

In any case, whatever the intentions of Coleman and Jencks, their work has been interpreted on political grounds, and have been cited as evidence that schools can do very little to effect social inequality. Both studies, however, state much more than that, raising certain fundamental questions about the structure of our educational system. In fact, lost somewhere in the rhetoric was Jencks' view that selection systems within schools do have a significant effect on inequality. But in the rush to interpret their findings politically (to support the status quo) the critical issues were somehow cast aside. These same political processes were at work in the immense amount of publicity accorded to two studies done by psychologists, Arthur Jensen and Richard Herrnstein, both of whom sought to blame inequality on the genetic inferiority of blacks.

ARTHUR JENSEN

Arthur Jensen, an educational psychologist at the University of California at Berkeley, argued in a 1969 article in the *Harvard Educational Review* entitled ''How Much Can Schooling Boost IQ?'') that the failure of the various compensatory strategies ''proved'' that blacks in the United States had an inherently inferior capacity for abstract reasoning.[25] Jensen's highly complex statistical analysis which stated that intelligence was 80 percent genetic or inherited was rejected by the overwhelming majority of psychologists, who called him to task for making inappropriate generalization and glossing over counterevidence which showed environmental influences on intelligence.[26] However, because education cannot be divorced from the political realm, Jensen's work was used to provide a rationale for the spending of less money on education. In essence, ''Jensen's argument provided a vent for many latent feelings that blacks were inferior and many, both educators and laymen, used his findings, or a tempered version of them, to explain what they understood to be the blacks' lack of success despite a decade's best efforts to help them.''[27]

RICHARD HERRNSTEIN

Richard Herrnstein's argument, first presented in *Atlantic* in 1971 and later expanded in book form as *IQ in the Meritocracy* (1973),[28] was even more political than Jensen's. Herrnstein's thesis is based on the hypothesis that differences in mental abilities are inherited and that people who are similar in mental ability are more likely to marry and reproduce, so that there will be a tendency toward long term stratification by mental ability (IQ). Success, in Herrnstein's view, requires mental ability, and social rewards depend on success. He concludes that hereditary meritocracy, or positions of prestige and power in the United States, is concentrated in groups with high IQs.

> The ties among IQ, occupation and social standing make practical sense. The intellectual demands of engineering, for example, exceed those of ditch digging. Hence engineers are brighter on the average. If virtually everyone is smart enough to be a ditch digger, and only half the people are smart enough to be engineers, then society is, in effect, husbanding its intellectual resources by holding engineers in greater esteem, and on the average, paying them more. The subjective scale of occupational standing that everyone carries around in his head expresses a social consensus both powerful and stable, particularly in the occupational choice of individuals.[29]

Herrnstein's conclusions can be criticized on a number of grounds. First of all, the IQ scores of children do not correlate with the scores of their parents. Two parents whose IQs are over 140, for example, will not necessarily have children whose IQs are in the same range. Their children can have higher or lower IQs, and the meritocratic caste system that Herrnstein postulates would not come about, since high-IQ parents may produce low-IQ children, and conversely, low-IQ parents may produce children with higher IQs than their own. Secondly, personality and motivational factors are important for success. Whereas children of high-IQ parents (given the present correlation with higher social class) would tend to have children with high motivation and personalities suited for success in our society, they may also produce children with low motivation and maladjusted personalities (given the expectations placed upon their offsprings). Thirdly, Herrnstein's argument is based on the premise that people choose occupations primarily for economic reward, and that job satisfaction plays little, if any, role in the process. Sewer workers, for example, make more money than do teachers. According to Herrnstein's argument, those with higher IQs sould gravitate toward the sewer-worker job. This is obviously not the case. Lastly, Herrnstein's argument is essentially politically conservative, one that supports the prevailing social arrangements. Noam Chomsky has pointed to this fallacy in Herrnstein's argument. Chomsky states that Herrnstein bases his judgments

> on a ranking of occupations which show, for example, that accountants, specialists in public relations, auditors, and sales managers tend to have higher IQs (hence, he would claim, receive higher pay, as they must if society is to function effectively) than musicians, riveters, bakers, lumberjacks and teamsters. Accountants were ranked highest among 74 listed occupations, with public relations 4th, musicians 35th, riveters 50th, bakers 65th, truck drivers 67th, and lumberjacks 70th. From such data, Herrnstein concludes that society is wisely "husbanding its intellectual resources" and that the gradient of occupation is a natural measure of value and makes practical sense.
>
> Is it obvious that an accountant helping a corporation to cut its tax bill is doing work of greater social value than a musician, riveter, baker, truck driver or lumberjack? Is a lawyer who earns a $100,000 fee to keep a dangerous drug on the market worth more to society than a farm worker or a nurse?[30]

The reasons that one occupation may be more prestigious or may receive greater reward has less to do with IQ than with variances in political power, organization into interest groups, and the ability of different social classes to remain on top. The reasons individuals move up, down, or remain the same on the occupational ladder has less to do with IQ than with the socioeconomic status of their parents. The public schools do little to change this; indeed, they can be said to reinforce this inequality in society. This is accomplished via the use of testing and tracking. Such a position can be made consistent with the findings of Coleman and Jencks, who concluded that many of the important effects of educational selection occur inside schools. As James Rosenbaum points out:

Coleman and Jencks probed the influence of schools on opportunity and inequality in society, and their results indicate that none of the many factors which they investigated (including resources, racial and social class composition, etc.) has a significant effect on students' cognitive outcomes, educational attainment, occupational status, or income. When Jencks states that "differences between schools are . . . relatively small compared to . . . differences within the same school" . . . many people infer that he is saying that nothing makes any difference. But that is not what Jencks concludes. Although he holds that most factors representing differences between schools do not have any effects, he also demonstrates that the selection system within schools (commonly called tracking) is the measurable factor that influences [educational] attainment . . . Coleman's and Jencks' studies point to selection within schools as a important determinant of school outcomes.[31]

Coleman and Jencks, because they used data based on large-scale survey techniques, could not appropriately analyze the differences within schools. The best method for doing this is the case study, and after a brief look at the history of testing and tracking, three case studies will be presented to show the mechanisms the middle class uses to triumph over the lower class in the schools—how the lower class is locked into its class position by public education.

EDUCATIONAL TESTING AND TRACKING

A useful definition of tracking is offered by Rosenbaum who defines tracking "as any school selection system that attempts to homogenize classroom placement in terms of students' personal qualities, performances and aspirations. Thus tracking is a general term that includes both ability grouping and curriculum grouping and emphasizes their social similarities."[32] On the basis of so-called objective tests, students are sorted into various programs or tracks, such as college preparatory, noncollege preparatory, general, business, or commercial, to cite some of the more popular names. Tracking is a fact of life in the majority of American high schools, in spite of the almost total lack of evidence supporting its positive educational effects. Instead, it has unquestionable administrative and managerial benefits.

Although the actual assignment of students to a specific track usually begins officially at the first year of high school, the procedures begin long before that. The end result is discrimination, whether intentionally or unintentionally, primarily against lower-class and minority students. A look at the evolution of psychological testing in the schools will bear this out.

The History and Politics of the Intelligence Test

The first usable test of general intelligence was published in France by Alfred Binet in 1905. Intelligence testing became popular through the importation of Binet's test to America by Louis Terman, Robert Yerkes, and Henry Goddard.

Although they considered themselves to be objective scientists, these three "pioneers of the mental testing movement shared a number of social−political views, as exemplified by the joint involvement in the turn-of-the-century eugenics movement."[33] Terman, Yerkes, and Goddard were in the forefront of the movement to provide a genetic interpretation of socioeconomic class differences in test scores. This manifested itself in the first practical effect of the testing movement, the restrictive immigration law of 1924. Prior to World War I, with the exception of certain groups classified as undesirables, immigration to the United States was unrestricted. But as early as 1912, Goddard was invited by the U.S. Public Health Service to Ellis Island to apply intelligence tests to newly arriving immigrants. Goddard administered tests and classified 83 percent of Jews, 80 percent of Hungarians, 79 percent of Italians, and 87 percent of Russians as feebleminded.[34]

Five years later, America entered World War I and some 200,000 intelligence tests were applied to inductees by Colonel Robert Yerkes. The data provided the first large-scale evidence that blacks scored lower than whites on measures of intelligence. It was also found that Latin and Slavic countries stood low, and the Poles did not score significantly higher than blacks.[35]

Yerkes' colleague, Carl C. Brigham, a First Lieutenant in the Psychological Division during the war, had a profound impact in promoting immigration restrictions. His book, *A Study of American Intelligence* (1923), based on a reanalysis of the Army inductee data, purported to show that Nordic draftees were superior intellectually to the Alpine, Mediterranean, and Negro races.[36] Alarmed by the fact that the Alpine and Mediterranean races constituted over 70 percent of the total immigration at the time, Brigham called for something to be done about this.

The political use of Brigham's book was swift and Congress passed the Immigration Act of 1924, which restricted not only the total number of immigrants but included the assignment of national origin quotas. Immigrants would be allowed into the United States proportionate to the number of their countrymen already here as determined by the Census of 1890. The 1890 census was chosen specifically because the large migratory wave of southeastern Europeans of the 1890s was not represented in its figures, and these "intellectually inferior" immigrants could be effectively excluded.

The dominant genetic or hereditarian position began to be less influential in the 1930s, as psychologists became more sophisticated in their techniques and began to confront the ideological biases in their measuring instruments.[37] Indeed, the shift toward an environmental position became so dominant that in 1930 Brigham renounced his early position, stating that his early linking of intelligence to race "was without foundation."[38] But the damage had already been done, at least as far as the educational institution was concerned—the intelligence testers had invaded the schools, transferring the army-induced tests to the student.[39] Intelligence testers claimed that on the basis of their tests they could assign students to the curriculum which best suited them for preparation for later life. And, to reinforce the intelligence tests and other student evaluation methods, two new educational institutions were created which would eventually lead to even more rigid tracking—vocational guidance and the junior high school.

VOCATIONAL GUIDANCE AND THE JUNIOR HIGH SCHOOL: THE INSTITUTIONALIZATION OF TRACKING[40]

The early vocational guidance counselors attempted to function as human engineers who would shape individual abilities to fit a particular slot in the society. This gave them a dual responsibility: the analysis of personal talents and the planning of educational programs for future vocations. The junior high school was designed to make this educational planning and guidance possible at an early age; its original purpose was the differentiation of students into separate courses of study according to ability and vocational goals. Vocational guidance was thus conceived of as a means of changing the general pattern of industrial development as students were expected to choose a vocation in the junior high school and follow an education program designed to prepare them for this occupation through high school. Of particular importance was the vocational guidance counselor, usually a trained psychologist who used a variety of tests to determine students' occupational abilities. Thus, the main argument for the existence of the junior high school was that it facilitated the differentiation and educational guidance of students. The guidance counselor was the key to the system, as he or she selected a course of study for the student from the general curricula available.

Both the vocational guidance movement and the rise of the junior high school were based on the assumption that interests, abilities, and aptitudes stabilized and became fixed during the adolescent period. Such a conception of adolescence clearly affected education, providing further justification for separating the upper years of elementary school into a school with a different type of education. It also meant that the vocational guidance counselor would concentrate on socializing adolescents.[41]

Many people still retain this notion of the fixed quality of personality characteristics and interests, in spite of the denial by educators. Out of the differential curriculum and vocational guidance movement grew the tracking system we know today, a system that discriminates against the lower-class student.

TRACKING

One of the earliest and most comprehensive studies of the structure and process of tracking was August Hollingshead's famous *Elmstown's Youth* (1949). Hollingshead researched the social structure of Elmstown in depth and provided a comprehensive understanding of how it worked. In his words:

> *there is a functional relationship between the class position of an adolescent's family and his social behavior in the community* . . . we can conclude with confidence that adolescents who have been reared in families that possess different class cultures may be expected to follow different behavior patterns in the responses to situations they encounter in their participation in the community's social life. Furthermore, this study, if it has done nothing else, has demonstrated clearly that, for a complete cross section of a relatively homogeneous age and

sex group in one community in contemporary America, the home an adolescent comes from conditions in a very definite manner the way he behaves in his relations with the school, the church, the job, recreation, his peers, and his family.[42]

Hollingshead's finding concerning the interrelationship of class and tracking were so obvious and persuasive that few sociological studies undertaken since then have ignored the effects of social class and educational achievement.[43]

As was stated previously, large-scale surveys such as the Coleman Report and Jencks' *Inequality* cannot focus on the process of tracking within the schools. Only the case study approach can do this. Keeping this in mind, three case studies which probe different aspects and levels of the tracking process are presented. The first is Gerald Levy's description of "Midway Elementary School," a ghetto school in New York City's Bedford—Stuyvesant area. Although it does not concern tracking *per se,* it does show how the lower class is labeled as intellectually and socially inferior as soon as they first set foot in the public school. The second is a study of Grayton High School, a Boston area school, by James Rosenbaum. Here Rosenbaum analyzes a school where social class and race are controlled, and then shows that tracking is inextricably built into the system. Rosenbaum's study clearly indicates that tracking is not the result of any conspiracy, but is a mechanism of discrimination that is deeply embedded in the schools and that is used by the group which happens to be dominant. Power and conflict are the important variables; the need to dominate manifests itself in the schools despite the lack of class differentials. The same source of conflict is present as when superintendents struggled with school boards, or when both got together to battle with militant teacher groups. Without social class distinctions which make for a natural conflict situation, given the unequal distribution or power of the parties, other discrepancies arise. In the case of Grayton High School, guidance counselors tracked students indiscriminately, and in the absence of parents who did not exert themselves, effectively locked students into specific vocational roles. The third case study is a comparison of two schools, "Industrial City" High School, and "Academic Heights" High School, by Schafer and Olexa. They show that when class distinctions are present, class differentials make for a natural order of dominance and submission; lower-class children are discriminated against because they are not in any position to offset the process.

Pretracking in a Ghetto School[44]

Midway Elementary School, the ghetto school described by Levy, is an example of the role that teachers play in negatively labeling lower-class children. The new teacher comes to Midway with high expectations and ideals. He or she has every intention of becoming a good teacher. Levy designates the new teacher as an "acute teacher," and goes on to describe the process by which the "acute teacher" eventually becomes a "chronic teacher," one whose only concern is controlling students. Midway Elementary School represents an illustration of the political process of education. Teachers and administrators bring the values of their social class to the lower-class school. They soon discover, however, that their original intentions and political views are unimportant; they learn what the institution expects of them. According to Levy:

> American society defines its ghetto schools as the vehicle of lower class Black mobility. On schools is placed the burden of preparing ghetto youth for middle-class life. But those who believe in the public goals of ghetto education assume that society is prepared to absorb its lower classes. When ghetto education fails to accomplish its public goals these same people blame the inadequacy of the education if they are liberals and the inferiority of the children if they are conservative. Few educational ideologists focus on the political task of ghetto schools.[45]

Levy brilliantly describes just how this political process works. Half of Midway's staff are chronic teachers. They have taught in the school from one to thirteen years and have internalized a style and set of values which enables them to teach and operate in the school with a minimum of discomfort. They long ago accepted the notion that control precedes education, and genuinely believe that they are working for the best interests of the child. Thus, they can hit a student and reconcile this as being beneficial to the child.

Control is the dominant concern of the chronic teachers at Midway, even to the extent that it becomes a condition of self-esteem. Competence is judged by the staff in terms of how well one can control one's classes. Male teachers come to use control as a basic indicator of masculinity. Those teachers who can best control a class become models for the others to emulate. Midway gives the appearance of an army camp, with male teachers strutting around the halls with military carriage and bearing.

Acute teachers are advised early that his or her inability to control the children will be interpreted by administrators and other teachers as evidence of his or her inadequacy as a teacher. There is a certain truth to this dictum, for the teacher who loses control becomes dependent upon others to regain it. Those who are called upon to constantly help out others resent this intrusion because they must interrupt their own routines. Thus, helpless teachers quickly get a reputation for incompetence. They are seen by others as "not doing their job." Teachers who do not resort to methods of control soon run the risk of being "destroyed" as an effective teacher. The children, who have been previously socialized to accept authority from chronic teachers, see any deviation from the hard-line attitude of the school as a weakness on the part of the acute teacher and a chance to take advantage of him or her. An open conflict situation is immediately set up. And, as anyone who has had contact with young children knows, their energy and tenaciousness is almost limitless. Eventually, most of the acute teachers (21 out of 35, according to Levy) at Midway found themselves shouting at their classes, as they began to lose control of them. Acute teachers responded to this increasingly chaotic situation with feelings of personal inadequacy and unworthiness. Among some of the male teachers these feelings began to border on anxiety about their masculinity, as they compared themselves to the chronic male teachers who strutted around the school.

> Among certain teachers the initial experience with the children is destructive to the point where previous success, financial, academic, occupational and erotic, temporarily lose their salience. They talk about their inability to sleep nights worrying about what the children are going to do to them the following day. Their experience in Midway causes deep personal fear, even terror.[46]

Ultimately the conflict becomes so great that the "acute teacher" defines the situation as "them against me" and eventually closes ranks with the chronic teachers, now defining the situation as "them against us." Acute teachers who previously criticized and condemned chronic teachers for authoritarian, often brutal methods of control, begin to actively seek their advice. Chronic teachers, their own behavior now reinforced, freely give advice and share techniques with the new convert. The chronic teacher has been vindicated, his or her competence reinforced.

Midway School is characterized by a cycle of conflict so vicious that Levy uses the metaphor of war to describe it. The only issue is control. Children are hit, cajoled, manipulated in any way that will secure control. The children, in turn, respond by doubling their efforts to triumph over the teacher. The education process, if we can even refer to it as that, represents class warfare, with the lower class losing. And it is not only a struggle between teachers and children. Teachers are in conflict with administrators, administrators with parent groups, parent groups with teachers in a vicious cycle of acrimony and mistrust. Education does not occur for the lower classes at Midway; only the facade of education exists. Yet children are addressed as if learning was actually taking place. The ghetto school reinforces the failure of the lower class, and lower-class education becomes a giant con game. At the same time that children are being socialized to see themselves as failures, they are constantly urged not to give up. An invitation to success is built into the communication of failure, because teachers know that a child who has given up is totally uncontrollable. The hope for success is sustained. "The child is always given another chance to succeed on the condition that he conform to the values of the school."[47]

The school is a conflict-ridden milieu, one that reeks of failure, and although just about everyone involved comes to know this is so, the pretext of learning is still kept up. The legitimacy of the system must be secured. In lower-class schools like Midway, there exists a thin line between communicating failure and sustaining the myth of mobility, between preparing children for failure and holding out the hope of success. If this balance is not maintained, the lower classes might see that their failure is political and not idiosyncratic. Midway's inability to help move its students into the middle class stems from the political reality of American society. When Midway is seen in this light it becomes clear that

> the school's task is the exact opposite of its publicly stated purpose. In a time

when American society is unprepared to absorb its lower-class youth into the middle-class, Midway successfully serves the purpose of not training its children for middle-class life.

The children's experience in Midway is one of daily defeat and failure. But the children are not told that they are failing because they are lower-class Blacks and Puerto Ricans. They are not informed that their failure is institutionalized and semiautomatic. They are not advised of the political significance of their failure. They are informed that they are failing because they are not learning to read. For it is crucial to Midway's stability that it appears as if the children are failing because of what they fail to learn.[48]

Levy's case study of Midway Elementary School presents a bleak, despairing picture of how a ghetto school is used to keep the lower classes from achieving upward mobility, while trying to convince them that their lack of success is their own fault. It is a portrait of a system so conflict-ridden that one cannot help wondering how so many sociologists of education can continue to talk of smoothly running schools that are able both to educate and discipline their students simultaneously.

Tracking in Grayton High School[49]

Grayton High School was selected from the Boston metropolitan area because it reflected a socially homogeneous setting in which social class and racial differences would not complicate and interact with the school system. Grayton High School thus is composed of predominantly white, working-class, first- or second-generation Irish- and Italian-American students. Only 12 percent of the students come from upper-middle-class families.[50]

The two academic tracks at Grayton are college preparation and noncollege. Nearly 48 percent of the ninth-grade students used in Rosenbaum's sample are in the college track and 32 percent attend college after graduation.

Rosenbaum's findings indicate that tracking occurs even when social class distinctions are missing. Most importantly, he found that Grayton had an extremely rigid tracking system, with virtually no changes out of, and especially into, the college track from the noncollege track.[51] The main characteristic of Grayton's tracking system is stability, and the only mobility is downward. Rosenbaum described this system as a tournament with very simple rules—"when you win, you win only the right to go on to the next round; when you lose, you lose forever."[52]

Another interesting discovery was that no one indicator or variable explained initial track placement. Guidance counselors had a tremendous amount of leeway in assigning students to different tracks. Working-class parents rarely became involved in any track changes. "Because the parents generally had not gone far in school, they often feel that the guidance counselors know more about educational matters, and they just go along with the decision."[53] A possible explanation for the middle-class parents' lack of involvement is offered by Rosenbaum when he states that: "It seems likely that a professional or managerial occupation in a working-class community signifies different social characteristics than it does in an upper-middle-class community."[54]

The illusion of choice is maintained throughout. Grayton's students and their parents are led to believe that they had a real choice in the selection of a track, when in reality the data indicate that the decision was made solely by the guidance counselor, and in many instances, arbitrarily. The existence of the misconception of choice is of extreme importance because it indicates a belief in the legitimacy of the placement, enlisting students and parents in a system that offers them few real opportunities. In this manner coercion is avoided and conflict is effectively distilled. The deception that choice is present is much more effective than coercion. As Rosenbaum states in his conclusion:

> Rather than deny choice to lower-track students, the track system allows them to make choices based on inadequate or incorrect information. This kind of choice is far more insidious than coercion, for it leaves students more vulnerable to socialization processes that create academic and social obstacles to subsequent track changes, that divert students' attention from opportunity to consumption, and that leads them to accept voluntarily the low status and poor prospects of their track position.[55]

Although Grayton High School's tracking system does not favor middle-class students, it still manages to discriminate against lower- and working-class students by making them believe they have had a choice, and that any subsequent failure is their own fault. There is no evidence available from an all-middle-class high school, but it is hard to envision middle-class parents letting guidance counselors arbitrarily track their children into noncollege tracks which eventually lead to low-status jobs. Grayton High performs its legitimation function quite well, in the process managing to keep a good part of the working class in their place. This second function is more obvious in our last case study.

Tracking in "Industrial City" and "Academic Heights" High Schools[56]

"Industrial City" High School is located near the central business district of Industrial City, not far from the campus of a medium-sized midwestern state university. It occupies approximately two square city blocks. The economy of the community in which Industrial City High is located is dependent on the automobile industry. "Academic Heights" High School is housed in an overcrowded multimillion-dollar complex, completed in 1956. It is located near the edge of a community whose economy is based on the large state university located there. Academic Heights High has a 177-acre campus with many progressive features.

Industrial City High had a two-track system, college and noncollege; and Academic Heights had a four-track system: (1) Special Room (handicapped and retarded); (2) General, Business, and Industrial (for those who planned to complete their formal education with a high school diploma); (3) College Curricula (for those who planned to complete college); and (4) Advanced Placement (for students with exceptionally high academic aptitude).

Interestingly enough, Schafer and Olexa, like Rosenbaum, failed to uncover the actual dynamics of the process of assignment to a particular track. However, the end result of the selection system is clear enough. They state:

> Whatever the precise dynamics of the decisions, the outcome was clear in the schools we studied: coming from a white-collar family of the white race substantially increased a student's chances of entering the college-prep track. . . 83 percent of white-collar youth, compared to 48 percent of those from blue-collar homes, enrolled in the college-prep track. The relationship with race is even stronger: 72 percent of whites and 30 percent of blacks were assigned to college-prep track.[57]

Race and socioeconomic background were important influences on track assignment even after the effects of IQ and previous achievement were controlled for.

Also like Rosenbaum, Schafer and Olexa found an extreme rigidity in the tracking systems at Industrial and Academic Heights high schools. The initial track assignment decision was almost irreversible, with only 7 percent of those who began in the college-prep tracks shifting to the noncollege-prep tracks, and only 7 percent moving in the other direction.[58] This inflexibility questions the theoretical justification or rationale for tracking—that low-achieving students, when separated into homogeneous groups, will receive better instruction which will then prepare them to move on to higher tracks. Without this educational improvement and upgrading of low-track students, the track system, according to Schafer and Olexa, takes on the characteristics of a virtual caste system.[59]

One's track position also exerted a strong influence on dropping out of high school. The chances of students' dropping out were nine times greater if they were from the lower tracks than if they were in the college-prep tracks. In fact, track assignment was found to be more highly correlated with dropping out than was previous achievement, IQ or father's occupation.[60]

The tracking system simply did not produce the benefits its proponents claim for it. Indeed, in many instances just the opposite results were found. Noncollege-prep students experienced: (1) lower academic achievement; (2) greater decline and less improvement in achievement; (3) less participation in extracurricular activities; (4) greater initiation of mischief in school; (5) a greater tendency to drop out; and (6) greater involvement in delinquent acts than did college-prep students.[61]

Schafer and Olexa then asked how these findings can be explained. Although it is possible that students assigned to the college-prep track were brighter, more skilled academically, and better motivated toward achievement to begin with, a more likely interpretation given the data is that assignment to a lower track "confers on students a stigmatizing label which in turn erodes self-esteem and commitment to the goals and norms of the school."[62] In short, Schafer and Olexa concluded that the high schools they studied sort out and label working-class students for low-status occupations.

SUMMARY

In this chapter we have tried to show the extent of inequality in the nation's schools. Public schools, run by middle-class individuals with middle-class values, perpetuate an insidious system of inequality. Yet the belief in the existence of equal educational opportunity remains. One important reason for this is that much of the social science research which has dealt with inequality (such as the Coleman Report and Jencks' *Inequality*.) has been interpreted politically. Jensen and Herrnstein's work on the genetic inferiority of blacks was used to bolster the belief that success had little to do with the socioeconomic status of one's parents. Our position is just the opposite and we looked at the history of testing and the phenomenon of tracking to substantiate our argument. In particular, we focused on the history of the IQ test and how it was originally used to label specific groups as inferior, and subsequently produced restrictive immigration quotas. We then turned to the institutionalization of tracking, tracing its origins to the birth of vocational guidance and the junior high school. Three case studies of tracking (pretracking in an elementary ghetto school, a look at a Boston high school, and a contrast between two midwestern high schools) were offered to show how schools track students into educational success and failure.

NOTES

1. Robert L. Church and Michael W. Sedlak, *Education in the United States: An Interpretive History*. New York: Free Press, 1976, p. 437.

2. The literature on social mobility has almost exclusively dealt with males; hence the use of the word "sons" is merely descriptive.

3. Peter M. Blau, "The Flow of Occupational Supply and Recruitment," *American Sociological Review, 30* (August 1965), pp. 475–490.

4. Charles H. Anderson, *Toward a New Sociology*, rev. ed. Homewood, Ill.: Dorsey Press, 1974, p. 136.

5. See in particular Caroline Bird, *The Case Against College*. New York: McKay, 1975; and Richard Freeman, *The Over-Educated American*. New York: Academic Press, 1976. In spite of disclaimers, a college education still provides for future economic success. For substantiation, see Barry R. Chiswick, *Income Equality*. New York: National Bureau of Economic Research, 1974; and Jacob Mincer, *Schooling, Experience and Earnings*. New York: National Bureau of Economic Research, 1974.

6. Anderson, *Toward a New Sociology*, p. 139.

7. Samuel Bowles and Herbert Gintis, *Schooling in Capitalist America*. New York: Basic Books, 1976. p. 31.

8. Ibid., p. 32.

9. Ibid., pp. 32–33.

10. A recent exception is Richard A. Rehberg and Evelyn R. Rosenthal, *Class and Merit in the American High School*. New York: Longman, 1978. However, we would argue that due to the fact that

the authors studied seven suburban high schools with 99 percent white population, their study is not applicable beyond their sample.

11. The Research Triangle Institute, *National Longitudinal Study of the High School Class of 1972: A Capsule Description of First Follow-up Survey Data*. Washington, D. C.: U.S. Government Printing Office, 1976.

12. William L. Spady, "Educational Mobility and Access: Growth and Paradoxes," *American Journal of Sociology, 73* (November 1967), pp. 273—286.

13. Bowles and Gintis, *Schooling in Capitalist America*, p. 33. There is evidence though that the gap between whites and blacks is narrowing. See in particular Richard B. Freeman, *Black Elite: The New Market for Highly Educated Black Americans*. New York: McGraw-Hill, 1977; and William H. Sewell, Robert M. Hauser, and David L. Featherman (eds.), *Schooling and Achievement in American Society*. New York: Academic Press, 1976.

14. James S. Coleman et al., *Equality of Educational Opportunity*. Washington, D.C.: U.S. Office of Education, 1966.

15. See Daniel P. Moynihan, "Sources of Resistance to the Coleman Report," *Harvard Educational Review, 38* (Winter 1968), pp. 23—36.

16. Church and Sedlak, *Education in the United States*, p. 455.

17. Martin Carnoy and Henry M. Levin, *The Limits of Educational Reform*, New York: McKay, 1976, pp. 3—4. On a more positive note, the National Institute of Education's *Compensatory Education Study* does report some gains in reading and math scores for Title I students. See National Institute of Education, *Compensatory Education Services*. Washington, D.C.: National Institute of Education, U.S. Department of Health, Education and Welfare, 1977; and National Institute of Education, *Compensatory Education Study: Final Report to Congress*. Washington, D.C.: National Institute of Education, U.S. Department of Health, Education and Welfare, September 1978. However, whether or not these gains will be wiped out as has been the case in the past is an open question.

18. Christopher Jencks et al., *Inequality*. New York: Basic Books, 1972, p. 8.

19. Church and Sedlak, *Education in the United States*, p. 455.

20. Jencks et al., *Inequality*, p. 265.

21. For criticisms of the Coleman Report, see Samuel Bowles and Henry M. Levin, "The Determinants of Scholastic Achievement—An Appraisal of Some Recent Evidence" *The Journal of Human Resources, III* (Winter 1968), pp. 3—24; and Frederick Mosteller and Daniel P. Moynihan (eds.), *On Equality of Educational Opportunity*. New York: Vintage Books, 1972.

22. For example, Jencks did not take into account evidence on the relationship of family income and school achievement presented by Samuel Bowles and Herbert Gintis, "IQ in the Social Structure," *Social Policy, 3* (1972—1973) pp. 65—96.

23. Kenneth B. Clark, "Social Policy, Power, and Social Science Research," in *Harvard Educational Review* Editors, *Perspectives on Inequality, Reprint No. 8*. Cambridge, Mass.: Harvard Educational Review, 1973, p. 81.

24. Ibid.

25. Arthur R. Jensen, "How Much Can We Boost IQ and Scholastic Achievement?" *Harvard Educational Review, 39* (Winter 1969), pp. 1—123.

26. See in particular Leon J. Kamin, *The Science and Politics of IQ*. New York: Wiley, 1974. Kamin's investigation of Sir Cyril Burt's work eventually led to the conclusion that Burt, whose English twin studies had been a major buttress of the genetic inheritance of intelligence, was based on fabricated data. See also Boyce Rensberger, "Briton's Classic IQ Data Now Viewed as Fraudulent," *The New York Times*, November 28, 1976, p. 26.

27. Church and Sedlak, *Education in the United States*, p. 470.

28. Richard J. Herrnstein, *IQ in the Meritocracy*. Boston: Little, Brown, 1973.

29. Ibid., p. 124.

30. Noam Chomsky, "IQ Tests: Building Blocks for the New Class System," in Clarence Karier (ed.), *Shaping the American Educational State: 1900 to the Present*. New York: Free Press, 1975, p. 401.

31. James Rosenbaum, *Making Inequality: The Hidden Curriculum of High School Tracking*. New York: Wiley, 1976. p. 41.

32. Ibid., p. 6.

33. Leon J. Kamin, "Heredity, Politics, and Psychology," in Karier (ed.), *Shaping the American Educational State*, p. 368.

34. Ibid., p. 370.

35. Ibid., p. 371.

36. Charles C. Brigham, *A Study of American Intelligence*. Princeton, N.J.: Princeton University Press, 1923, p. 159.

37. For a description of how this change came about, see Russell Marks, "Race and Immigration: The Politics of Intelligence Testing," in Karier (ed.), *Shaping the American Educational State*, pp. 316–342; and also Marks', "Testers, Trackers and Trustees: The Ideology of the Intelligence Testing Movement in America, 1900–1954," unpublished Ph.D. dissertation, University of Illinois, 1972.

38. Charles C. Brigham, "Intelligence Tests of Immigrant Groups," *Psychological Review, 37* (March 1930) p. 165.

39. For an analysis of this process see Clarence Karier, "Testing for Order and Control in the Corporate Liberal State," *Educational Theory, 22* (Spring 1972), pp. 159–180.

40. This section relies heavily on Joel Spring, *Education and the Rise of the Corporate State*. Boston: Beacon Press, 1972, pp. 91–108.

41. Ibid., p. 100.

42. August B. Hollingshead, *Elmstown's Youth: The Impact of Social Classes on Adolescents*. New York: Wiley, 1949, p. 441.

43. Rosenbaum, *Making Inequality*, p. 9. However, Barbara Heyns, "Social Selection and Stratification within Schools," *American Journal of Sociology, 79* (May 1974), pp. 1434–1451, offers some evidence that the apparent social class biases in tracking are related to track placement only because of class biases in achievement test scores.

44. This section is based on Gerald Levy, *Ghetto School*. New York: Pegasus Press, 1970.

45. Ibid., p. xiii.

46. Ibid., p. 44.

47. Ibid., p. 89.

48. Ibid., p. 173.

49. This section is based on Rosenbaum, *Making Inequality*.

50. Ibid., pp. 22–25.

51. Ibid., p. 39.

52. Ibid., p. 40.

53. Ibid., p. 122.

54. Ibid., p. 26.

55. Ibid., p.196.

56. This section is based on Walter E. Schafer and Carol Olexa, *Tracking and Opportunity: The Locking-Out Process and Beyond*. Scranton, Pa.: Chandler, 1971.

57. Ibid., p. 34.

58. Ibid., p. 36.

59. Ibid.

60. Ibid., pp. 45–47.

61. Ibid., p. 51.

62. Ibid., p. 61.

10

Minority Groups and Education

Minority groups in the United States have been characterized by political powerlessness. Consequently, because education cannot be divorced from the political realm, ethnic groups have not usually fared well in the schools. By tracing the history of discrimination against black people (America's largest minority group), we will see how the pattern began and why it continues to this day. We will then point out how this pattern of prejudice extends to other minority groups, paying particular attention to Mexican-American, Puerto Rican, and American Indian children.

BLACK EDUCATION IN THE UNITED STATES: COMPULSORY IGNORANCE[1]

Early American educational policy for slave children has been called a system of "compulsory ignorance."[2] Most slaves never attended a school and their ignorance

171

was a primary instrument of enslavement. This procedure was an American adaptation; for West Africa, the native area of over half of the slaves, had had formal education for its inhabitants at least since the sixteenth century.

The first state to adopt a compulsory ignorance law was South Carolina in 1740. The law read:

> *Be it enacted,* That all and every person and persons who shall hereafter teach, or cause any slave or slaves to be taught to write, or shall use or employ any slave as a scribe in any manner of writing whatsoever, hereafter taught to write; every such person or persons shall, for every offense, forfeit the sum of one hundred pounds current money.[3]

During the next century similar laws were enacted in state after state. For example, in 1823, Mississippi outlawed the gathering of six or more blacks for educational purposes. In 1830, a law in Louisiana prescribed imprisonment of from one to twelve months for anyone guilty of teaching a slave to read or write.[4] Although the prospects for a free black to receive an education were better, they were hardly adequate.

The Education of Free Blacks

Free blacks in the South could receive an education through one or more of the following ways: (1) public schools; (2) secret and other private schools; (3) Sabbath schools; (4) apprenticeship; and (5) special treaty requirements.[5]

As can be seen from Table 10-1, a much higher percentage of free black children in the North attended school than in the South. However, it must be noted that nowhere in the North was the schooling of black children widespread or systematic. Even when there were statutes to provide schooling, they were more often ignored than implemented.

Black parents tried as best they could to press local and state authorities to provide public education for their children, but given their general state of powerlessness they were unsuccessful. As an alternative they began to establish private schools. Unlike white parents, who have sent their children to private schools because they were dissatisfied, for various reasons, with the public schools, black parents did not have the choice of being dissatisfied.

Although the individual private schools were sometimes aided by white abolitionists, the basic poverty of blacks insured that the schools could offer only the barest minimum in the way of education. "Often located in basements and spare rooms, lacking materials and books, and operating for as little as two months a year, the schools filled a small part of a great need."[6] Only publicly supported schools could have begun to confront the needs of black children, but white American society would not offer these services to the children of slaves. Meyer Weinberg has eloquently summed up the relationship of black children to the schools in the period preceding the Civil War:

TABLE 10-1 PERCENT OF FREE BLACK CHILDREN IN SCHOOL, BY STATE: 1850–1860[7]

State	1850	1860	State	1850	1860
Alabama	3.0	4.2	Louisiana	7.0	1.5
Arkansas	1.8	3.5	Maine	20.7	22.0
California	0.1	3.8	Maryland	2.2	1.6
Connecticut	16.4	16.0	Massachusetts	15.9	16.8
Deleware	1.0	1.3	Michigan	8.0	16.3
Florida	7.1	1.0	Minnesota		6.9
Georgia		0.2	Mississippi	0.0	0.3
Illinois	5.9	8.0	Missouri	1.5	4.3
Indiana	8.2	9.8	New Hampshire	14.0	16.2
Iowa	5.1	12.9	New Jersey	10.0	10.8
Kansas		2.2	New York	11.1	11.6
Kentucky	2.9	2.0	North Carolina	0.8	0.4
Ohio	10.0	15.5	Texas	5.0	3.1
Oregon		1.6	Vermont	12.5	16.2
Pennsylvania	12.1	13.3	Virginia	0.1	0.1
Rhode Island	15.0	13.5	Wisconsin	10.6	9.6
South Carolina	0.9	3.7	District of Columbia	4.2	6.1
Tennessee	1.1	0.7	Territories	1.4	0.7
Total	6.1	6.7			

For many generations, most blacks had been denied schooling by the dominant society, by masters in the slave society, or by public authority in the society of free Negroes in the North and South. Those for whom the doors of schools have been open had to rely on the benevolence of private charity or their own intensive efforts. Negroes had to struggle constantly for the right to learn, for the right to be taught in an equal and nonsegregated setting. The conspiracy to keep them in ignorance was pervasive. Most ironic of all, free Negroes were expected to pay taxes for schools they could not attend. Still, they hungered for learning and strove to achieve it in the face of a slavery that survived even in freedom. The claim of whites that Negroes were intellectually incapable of learning was refuted by the desperate attempt of whites to deny them schooling. Whites seemed to fear not that Negroes could not learn but that they would.[8]

Black Education After the Civil War

The early years after the Civil War were characterized by white terrorism against black schools. In some southern states teachers could only work under armed guard. The Ku Klux Klan ran roughshod, and numerous schools were burned to the ground; teachers were beaten and murdered.[9]

In general, the overall poverty of blacks and the overt suppression by whites combined to keep black education to a minimum. It was obvious, for those who chose to look, that blacks' receiving an education would hinge on their being accepted into the public school system. Equally obvious was that the establishment of such a system would be a political and not an educational decision. Indeed, it was only as the result of the national congressional elections of 1866 that any change occurred. The Republican party pledged itself to a program of justice for the freedman. Existing state governments were dissolved and blacks were given the right to vote. "Constitutional conventions held throughout the South in 1867 and 1868 produced basic documents which, among other things, gave the South its first free and universal public educational system."[10] By 1870, every southern state had created a public school system financed by a state fund, and by 1880 a third of all black children in the United States were enrolled in public schools.[11]

Although a number of states specifically forbade any discrimination towards blacks, states circumvented this by building dual school systems for whites and blacks. Segregation quickly became the rule.

Plessy v. *Ferguson* (1896): The Legitimation of Compulsory Segregation[12]

Between 1896 and 1899, the United States Supreme Court legitimized the principle of compulsory segregation, and the near inviolability of local and state control of public education.[13] In 1895, the Supreme Court docketed the case that would establish the "separate but equal" doctrine in constitutional law for the next sixty years.

Homer Plessy, who was one-eighth black and seven-eighths white, was arrested in Louisiana when he refused to ride in the "colored" coach of a railroad train as required by Louisiana law. He then instituted an action to restrain enforcement of the statute because it violated his constitutional rights. The defendant, Ferguson, was the Louisiana judge who conducted Plessy's trial.

Plessy's lawyers argued that state-enforced segregation labelled Negroes inferior. The Supreme Court, when it tried the case on appeal, disagreed, stating that such laws did not necessarily imply the inferiority of a race. Therefore, Plessy could not suffer any damage as a result of separation, provided that the facilities furnished were equal to those from which he was excluded.

Blaustein and Ferguson have summarized the implications of the *Plessy* v. *Ferguson* case:

> With the Plessy decision, the separate but equal formula became the law of the Constitution. *Plessy* v. *Ferguson* is cited again and again as the case which established this doctrine. And yet, oddly enough, there are no words in the Court's opinion which declare that segregation is to be permitted when equal facilities are provided. Such words were to come from later lower court decisions which attempted to give meaning to the Plessy principle. What happened in the Plessy case was that the judges upheld what they believed to be the "reasonableness" of the Louisiana transportation laws without providing

guidance for the other courts which had to decide these subsequent segregation cases. The principle propounded by the nine men of 1896—that a state could compel "reasonable" racial segregation—was strictly judge-made law, giving a hitherto unknown meaning to the Fourteenth Amendment. It was basic law, but it left unanswered two critical questions: What are the criteria for measuring equality? What is the proper judicial remedy where inequality is found to exist?[14]

Three years later in 1899, the Supreme Court heard its first school segregation case, *Cummings* v. *Board of Education*. The black plaintiffs had asked for an injunction closing the white schools of Richmond County, Georgia, until a separate school was provided for black children. They argued that under the separate but equal doctrine complete failure to provide a high school resulted in an obviously unequal situation. The Court, to the contrary, held that closing of white schools would not eradicate the wrong and thus dismissed the suit. By taking this view, the Court, in its first education case, not only avoided judging the validity of the separate but equal doctrine, but also refused to indicate appropriate standards for measuring equality.[15]

From 1900 on then, the doctrine of "separate but equal" quickly became institutionalized as the law of the land. And it would become obvious that separate was the important word, not equal. Black schools fell further and further behind white schools in the amount of expenditures allocated to them by local authorities. By 1910, as historian Henry Bullock has observed, "the Negro child's portion of the money spent for public education had fallen far below his proportional representation in the population."[16]

The pattern of inequality and segregation in the South initiated during Reconstruction was solidified in the first two decades of the twentieth century and maintained until the 1950s. Church and Sedlak have summarized this institutionalization of segregated education. They write:

> Segregated education rested on the Supreme Court decision in *Plessy* v. *Ferguson* (1896) that, so long as blacks received absolutely equal facilities, the fact that the facilities were separate constituted no violation of their civil rights. "Separate but equal" became the formula for justifying all segregated institutions in the South—from drinking fountains and railroad cars to schools."[17]

Legal Challenges to Segregation

In 1953, the NAACP submitted a long historical brief to the Supreme Court which was designed to show how the institutionalization of segregation had created an official caste system in the United States. The NAACP contended that the controlling political and economic interests in the South were convinced that the subjugation of the black race was essential to their survival. In *Plessy* v. *Ferguson* the Court had ruled that such subjugation through public authority was sanctioned by the Constitution, and thereby had sanctioned an archaic and provincial notion of racial superiority which for over fifty years had injured and disfigured an entire race.[18]

On May 17, 1954, the Supreme Court handed down its famous opinion in *Brown* v. *Board of Education of Topeka* (347 U.S. 483). The central contention of the plaintiffs was upheld:

> In the field of public education the doctrine of "separate but equal" has no place. Separate educational facilities are inherently unequal . . . we hold that the plaintiffs and others similarly situated . . . are, by reason of the segregation complained of, deprived of equal protection of the laws guaranteed by the Fourteenth Amendment.[19]

A year later the Court decided in *Brown II* (349 U.S. 294) that the defendants (Topeka Board of Education) would be required to "make a prompt and reasonable start toward full compliance."[20]

It became apparent in the years following the *Brown* decision that school boards did not intend to integrate "with all deliberate speed." In fact, a decade after *Brown,* some 90 percent of black children in the South still attended all-black schools, an increase of over 400,000 since 1956.[21] Another strategy was necessary; beginning about 1960, young blacks in the South began to turn away from the courts and to concentrate on electoral activity and large-scale nonviolent demonstrations. Joined by young, liberal whites and clergymen, they began to forge a civil rights movement. Although the South was the primary target, those who came of political age in the civil rights movement began to look toward the North, whose system of segregation, though better hidden was no less real.

Segregation in the North

Northern school boards had a ready defense for charges of segregation levied against them in the 1950s and 1960s. They laid the blame on residential segregation. In 1964, the federal government entered into the conflict. With the wave of national support for civil rights, Congress passed into law the Civil Rights Act of 1964. A number of students of desegregation have signaled this act as the beginning of the "administrative era" of school desegregation.

One of the most important aspects of the Civil Rights Act was Title IV, which required the Commissioner of Health, Education and Welfare (HEW) to provide technical assistance for local school boards which were in the process of preparing school desegregation plans. Title IV also authorized the Attorney General to bring desegregation suits on behalf of potential plaintiffs who could not afford to sue on their own. The resources of the Department of Justice were thus made available for desegregation litigation.

Title VI of the same act proscribed the withholding of federal funds for programs or activities which practiced or encouraged segregation in any form. Title VI ordered that:

> No person in the United States shall on the grounds of race, color, or national origin, be excluded from participation in, be denied the benefits of, or be subjected to discrimination under any program of activity receiving federal financial assistance.[22]

Title VI also provided the impetus for the establishment of offices within HEW which would be charged with determining compliance of school districts applying for federal funds. Because the administrative machinery of the public schools are located at the state and local levels, the withholding of funds was the only practical enforcement mechanism that the federal government could wield. The threat of denial of funds proved so much more effective in bringing about compliance than the case-by-case method of the judicial process that more black students attended desegregated schools in the first year after the implementation of the Civil Rights Act than during the previous ten years.[23]

The gains, however, were short-lived as the political process caught up with the exhuberance of the Civil Rights movement and the general good will toward President Lyndon Johnson. Johnson had been able to push through the Civil Rights Act, something his predecessor John Kennedy most likely would have had difficulty in accomplishing. But congressional support began to wane. By 1966, southern congressmen were able to mount an effective counterattack on the desegregation movement. Desegregation became an issue in the 1968 Presidential election as Nixon began to formulate his famous Southern strategy.

Finally, when Nixon took office in 1968, he reversed the trend toward strict enforcement of desegregation.

> The resources were disengaged and officials were encouraged by Nixon and by pressure from some Members of Congress not to press for enforcement. In Congress there continued to be efforts to limit the conditions under which HEW could withhold or cut off funds. The Justice Department's pro-desegregation stand was diverted and, in fact, the Department was used in the service of those desiring to delay desegregation. Justice lawyers went to the Supreme Court in the *Alexander* v. *Holmes* case to request a delay in the desegregation order.[24]

The whole enforcement procedure which had begun with such high hopes a few years before slowly began to crumble, and the 1960s view that desegregation was inevitable disappeared. The Ford administration continued the trend that had started under its predecessor. The Carter administration has begun to reverse the process somewhat, but the mechanisms established almost a decade ago are highly resistant. At this time, we can give Carter high marks for his attempts, but so far very little has been done to offset the negative Nixon years. However, the courts in the 1970s have replaced the short-lived "administrative era" that provided the framework for the desegregation of America's public schools and for the conflict generated by the decisions.

Legal Reform Again—Busing in the 1970s

As the Supreme Court began to deal with the question of implementation in accordance with their decision in *Brown,* it was only a matter of time before they had to rule on the question of busing. On April 20, 1971, the Supreme Court announced its decision that it had unanimously upheld the busing of students as a legitimate tool for desegregation in the *Swann* v. *Charlotte–Mecklenburg* case. At the same time, the Court also approved various techniques for rezoning school districts as a means to finally ending the dual school systems in the South. Seventeen years after it had interpreted inequality to mean segregation, the Court ordered busing as a means for desegregating one of the largest school systems in the South, the Charlotte–Mecklenburg County, North Carolina, school system.

Before the Supreme Court decision, Charlotte–Mecklenburg County, the forty-third largest school district in the country, had operated a dual system. The decision became a landmark one, not only because of the busing issue, but because it provided an opportunity for the Supreme Court to define in more precise terms just what it considered the scope and duty of school authorities and district courts in executing the *Brown* decision. Prior to *Swann,* the Supreme Court had shied away from dealing with the intricate details of segregation. Local school districts had largely been allowed to use a "trial-and-error" process in implementing desegregation. With the *Swann* decision the Supreme Court provided them with detailed criteria with which to proceed.[25]

The Charlotte–Mecklenburg school system in 1971 consisted of approximately 85,000 pupils in over 100 schools. About 71 percent of those pupils were white, and 29 percent, or roughly 25,000 were black. Of these 25,000, 21,000 attended segregated schools in Charlotte. In fact, 14,000 attended 21 schools which were 99 percent or more black. In 1969, Swann filed suit against the schools, and a two-year federal court battle began. The United States District Court for the Western District of North Carolina held the Charlotte–Mecklenburg school system guilty of discriminatory actions resulting from deliberate decisions to locate new schools in black residential areas. This was construed by the Court as a failure on the part of the school board to desegregate the schools. The District Court then ordered the school board to develop a plan for desegregation. The Court felt that the board was procrastinating and appointed Professor John Finger of the University of Rhode Island to prepare a workable desegregation plan. In February of 1970, both the board and Dr. Finger submitted their plans.[26]

The board's plan called for the closing of seven schools and the reassigning of their pupils. It proposed substantial assignment of blacks to nine of the systems ten high schools, producing 17 percent to 36 percent black populations in each. The projected black attendance at the tenth school, Independence, was 2 percent. The Finger plan adopted the school board zoning plan for senior high schools with one modification. It required that an additional 300 black students be transported from the black residential area of the city to the nearly all-white Independence High School.[27]

The importance of the Finger plan, and the Court's decision to implement it, was its support of the principle of busing to desegregate the schools. The Court held that the long-cherished concept of neighborhood schools must be abandoned if it did not guarantee racially mixed schools for children in predominantly minority neighborhoods. In the North, as well as the South, neighborhood schools were no longer seen as melting pots where children of different ethnic backgrounds could become ''Americanized.''[28] The *Swann* decision thus helped to discourage one-race schools by making it extremely difficult to maintain the dual district system when busing could rectify the imbalance. The Supreme Court was quite emphatic in this, giving the lower courts the right to order busing to achieve racial balance in school districts. The predominant issue was clearly busing, something that has a much deeper history than is usually acknowledged.

Busing[29]

In 1869, Massachusetts enacted the first law authorizing the spending of public funds to transport children back and forth to school. The vehicles used for this purpose were horsedrawn wagons and carriages. (Interestingly enough, horsedrawn pupil transportation lasted well into the 1920s; in 1928, for example, 12 percent of school transportation vehicles used in thirty-two states were horsedrawn).[30]

Today, school busing is the greatest single transportation system in the country. Yet the whole busing quesiton is clouded in confusion. Five of the more important myths are worth noting.

Busing Goes Against Tradition and Represents a Break with Past Approaches to Improving Education. Lost, here, is the fact that the first public transportation bills were passed in the nineteenth century, and by the end of World War II all the states had passed legislation on school busing.

Busing Is the Exception and the Neighborhood School Is Always the Most Desirable Institution. Recent surveys, however, show that over 40 percent of America's schoolchildren ride school buses each day.[31]

The Decision To Bus Has, Until Recently, Not Been Guided by Social Beliefs or Principles. Yet the history of pupil transportation offers the most conclusive refutation of this idea. The theory of busing is inseparable from the belief that education is required for the welfare of the society. Ironically, too, the experience in the South provides the most dramatic instance of the use of busing to support a set of social values. Without elaborate transportation facilities, the dual school system in the South would not have been possible.

Riding on the Bus Is Bad for Children. Although it is true that riding long distances on a bus can be a hardship for children, especially younger ones, it is interesting to note that the problem is rarely raised, except in instances were desegregation is involved.

Busing Is a Financial Burden on a Community. In a number of instances, busing has proven costly to schools. Yet the equation of busing with raised expenses is not automatic because, for example, the busing that eliminated the one-room schoolhouse provided a financial saving to the community, and busing for desegregation purposes often does the same.[32]

It is quite obvious that busing is a political issue and therefore impossible to look at in a purely educational way. This, however, does not prevent social scientists from analyzing the problem, and certain of their views will be presented.

TABLE 10–2   YEAR OF STATUTORY AUTHORIZATION FOR PUBLIC PUPIL TRANSPORTATION BY STATE, 1869–1919[33]

Date	State	Date	State
1869	Massachusetts	1903	Virginia
1876	Vermont	1904	Maryland
1880	Maine	1905	Oklahoma
1885	New Hampshire	1905	Utah
1893	Florida	1907	Missouri
1893	Connecticut	1908	West Virginia
1894	Ohio	1909	Colorado
1895	New Jersey	1910	Mississippi
1896	New York	1911	Arkansas
1897	Iowa	1911	Georgia
1897	Nebraska	1911	Illinois
1897	Pennsylvania	1911	North Carolina
1897	Wisconsin	1912	Kentucky
1898	Rhode Island	1912	South Carolina
1899	Kansas	1912	Arizona
1899	North Dakota	1912	Idaho
1899	South Dakota	1913	Tennessee
1899	Indiana	1915	Nevada
1901	California	1915	Alabama
1901	Minnesota	1915	Texas
1901	Washington	1916	Louisiana
1903	Michigan	1917	New Mexico
1903	Montana	1919	Delaware
1903	Oregon	1919	Wyoming

The Evidence on Busing

David Armor has been in the forefront of those social scientists who believe that busing does not lead to any improvement in the school achievement of black students. Armor looks at the results of busing in five areas: (1) academic achievement; (2) aspirations; (3) self-concept; (4) race relations; and (5) educational opportunities.[34] Of the five, Armor finds a positive effect of busing only in the last. He has summarized his findings as follows:

> It seems clear that from the studies of integration programs we have reviewed that four of the five major premises of the integration policy model are not supported by the data, at least over the one-to-five-year periods covered by various reports. While this does not deny the possiblity of longer-term effects or effects on student characteristics other than those measured, it does mean that the model is open to serious question.[35]

Thomas Pettigrew, Elizabeth Useem, Clarence Normand, and Marshall Smith were quick to point out that there were serious flaws in Armor's argument.[36] They felt that Armor had established unrealistically high standards by which to judge the success of school desegregation; he had used selective evidence, failing to mention at least seven studies which reached opposite conclusions; and that he had unfairly compared the achievement gains of black students in desegregated school with white gains, rather than with the achievement of black students in black schools.[37] As expected, Armor replied to his critics,[38] which increased the controversial nature of the evidence and ultimately subordinated it to the political nature of the debate, something that occurred in the Coleman Report—Jencks' *Inequality* dispute. In short, like other educational matters, the decision on busing was made on political grounds. This can be clearly seen in the recent conflict that took place over busing in Boston, Massachusetts.

Busing in Boston

One of the most conflict-ridden and violent episodes in the desegregation controversy was initiated in Boston on June 21, 1974, when Judge W. Arthur Garrity of the Boston Federal District Court ordered the Boston School Committee (Board of Education) to desegregate the Boston schools.[39] The District Court found that the Boston school system had been a segregated one. As Roger Abrams states:

> In 1971−1972, almost 85 percent of the approximately sixty thousand white students enrolled in the system were assigned to schools over 80 percent white; over 60 percent of the approximately thirty thousand black students were assigned to schools over 70 percent black.[40]

Or, in the words of the court itself: "Racial segregation permeates schools in all areas of the city, all grade levels, and all types of schools."[41]

The efforts to desegregate over the next few years was met with violent resistance as the School Committee of Boston and "white ethnic" groups sought to resist the court edict. So intense was the conflict that police had to be stationed at high schools in white neighborhoods when busloads of black children arrived. White parents refused to have their children bused away from the neighborhood school, in many instances keeping them at home as long as they could. It took almost three years before the conflict died down and only then because the Federal Court literally took over the functions of the School Committee. When faced with the prospect of integrated schools, white parents had chosen to fight as long as they could. Others, who could afford it, placed their children in private schools or moved from the city altogether, raising the specter of "white flight."

White Flight: Fact or Fancy

The notion of white flight holds that white parents, when faced with the prospect of integrated schools in the cities, either place their children in private schools or flee to the white suburbs. A familiar name in the debate over whether "white flight" actually occurs is James Coleman, author of the Coleman Report. From April 1975 through December 1975, Coleman was very much in the news. Newspapers carried such headlines as "A SCHOLAR WHO INSPIRED IT SAYS BUSING BACKFIRED"; "COURT ORDERED INTEGRATION RAPPED BY SOCIOLOGIST WHO STARTED IT ALL."[42] These headlines were based on a paper Coleman and two colleagues delivered to the American Educational Research Association on April 2, 1975, entitled "Recent Trends in School Integration," which concluded that in cities where desegregation had been ordered, white families removed their children from the public schools.[43]

Over the next six months, Coleman reiterated this theme in a number of papers, public statements, and media interviews. Many social scientists began to criticize Coleman's position on three grounds:

> First, they stressed the complexity of the so-called "white-flight" phenomenon and suggested the importance of variables that Coleman's work had not considered. Second, they questioned the scientific ethics of communicating opinions in the form of research results before any analysis was available for review by the social-science community. Third, the emphasized that even if Coleman's dire predictions of massive losses of white students were accurate, the appropriate policy response would be extensive metropolitan desegregation rather than the abandonment of constitutional protectives.[44]

These criticisms also noted that little if any court-ordered desegregation had occurred in the nation's largest central city districts between 1968 and 1970, the years covered by Coleman's data.[45] Robert Reinhold, a reporter for *The New York Times*, checked out this point by contacting each of the twenty school districts in question. Under Reinhold's by-line, the *Times* ran the story headlined, "COLE-

MAN CONCEDES VIEWS EXCEEDED NEW RACIAL DATA,'' on the first page. Reinhold writes that the heart of Coleman's argument is that integration in the years

> 1968−1970, led to a substantial exodus of white families in the following three years, 1970−1973, over and above the normal movement to the suburbs. However, a thorough check of all 20 cities—in which key officials were questioned by telephone—could find no court-ordered busing, rezoning or any other kind of coerced integration in any of the cities during the 1968−1970 period. Court suits were pending in many, but desegregation was limited to a few modest open enrollment plans, used mostly by blacks. If there was "massive and rapid" desegregation, as Dr. Coleman said, it could not have been due to court-imposed remedies.[46]

According to Reinhold, Coleman conceded that his public comments went beyond the data he had gathered, contending only that the overall implications of his remarks on white flight were still valid. Coleman later claimed he had been misquoted.[47]

Nor has the controversy abated in the last few years. Diane Ravitch, in a recent article (1978),[48] took issue with the statistical interpretations of Christine Rossell, whose 1975 article in *Political Science Quarterly*[49] was a major factor in discrediting the white flight thesis. Rossell then questioned Ravitch's qualifications, stating that it would be "just crazy to debate statistical analysis with a journalist."[50]

The whole issue shows again how scientific analysis becomes mired in controversy. In the end, decisions are made on political grounds. Busing is a conflict-charged situation; indeed, it may be the most delicate problem in education today, as communities try to resist what they consider to be harm to their children and to their position in society. The questions involved are part of the larger problem of power and powerlessness in society. This basic principle can further be seen in the manner in which other minority groups have been treated by America's educational system.

MEXICAN-AMERICAN CHILDREN

The history of Mexican-American children in the schools, like that of the blacks, has been primarily one of discrimination and exclusion. From the very beginnings of Mexican-American immigration to the United States, the Mexican-American was thought of as cheap, exploitable labor. As such, public education was not considered to be necessary for the Chicano, as it was for their Anglo neighbors. For example, in 1855 in New Mexico, the state with the highest proportion of Mexican-Americans, a law providing a tax for building schools for Mexican-Americans was proposed, but was then defeated in a referendum by the almost unanimous margin of 5,601 to 37.[51] In 1860, the result was the same. A school law was passed, but the provision for funds was defeated. Not until 1871 was the first public school instituted in New Mexico.[52]

Although the majority of people in New Mexico in the nineteenth century were Spanish-speaking, they had little if any control over public education. Nor did this condition change drastically when New Mexico became a state in 1912. Indeed, so obvious was the discriminatory practices that a specific section, Article X, Section 10, was written into the state constitution, so that Mexican-American children should not be denied the right to attend public schools. Given the powerlessness of the Mexican-American, this law was rarely if ever enforced.

Conditions in Texas were generally no better. By 1920, a pattern of deprivation and failure was built into the Texas school system. Compulsory attendance laws were not enforced, and Mexican-American children who did attend school were usually retained in the first grade for two or three years.[53]

Segretation was the general rule. Speaking of this practice in California, W. Henry Cooke states:

> Schools for ''Mexicans'' and schools for ''Americans'' have been the custom in many a Southern California city. It mattered not that the ''Mexicans'' were born in the United States and that great numbers of them were sons and daughters of United States citizens. It has been the custom that they be segregated at least until they could use English well enought to keep up with English-speaking children. Neither did it matter that many of them had a command of English nor that there was no legal basis for their segregation. Under a law enacted in 1885 and amended in 1893, it has been possible to segregate Indians and Mongolians in California's public schools. To many an administrator this included ''Mexicans.'' This pattern was followed because the majority groups in the local communities wanted it done that way.[54]

The personal cruelties of segregation were felt in many ways. ''In one part of Los Angeles County, Mexican-American and Anglo children attended the same school but were graduated on different nights.''[55]

The general pattern of segregation and discrimination persisted well into the middle of the twentieth century. At one point the process was so insidious that the Chicano children were used as pawns to get around the *Brown* decision outlawing segregated schools. When it became obvious that desegregation was unavoidable, federal courts in Texas accepted plans that integrated only blacks and Chicanos. The Mexican-American children were finally being treated as ''whites,'' but only because it allowed school districts to avoid the integration of Anglos with blacks.[56] Only when Mexican-Americans organized politically did they make any gains. They joined with the blacks in the civil rights movement and began to demand their rights.

Federal administrative action began in 1970, under authority of Title VI of the Civil Rights Act. School districts were assigned the obligation to provide special instruction whenever ''inability to speak and understand the English language excludes national origin−minority group children from effective participation in the educational program offered by a school district.''[57] In 1971 Massachusetts became the first state to require by law that school districts enrolling more than twenty pupils of non-English-speaking background must provide bilingual instruction.[58]

During the years 1968 to 1972, the U.S. Commission on Civil Rights conducted the most detailed survey yet made of Chicano education. The study, entitled, *The Mexican-American Education Study* focused primarily on schooling in the Southwest, where approximately 70 percent of all Spanish-surnamed students were attending school. The Commission found the following: 1) a high degree of segregation; 2) extremely low academic achievement; 3) a predominance of exclusionary practices by schools; and 4) discriminatory use of public finances.[59]

The Commission discovered that Mexican children start out in school fairly close to their Anglo counterparts in measured achievement of all kinds. They then begin to fall behind with each passing year. By the time they have reached high school, depending on the state, anywhere from 40 to 60 percent have dropped out. Those that remain in school are subjected to a rigid tracking system. As Thomas Carter states:

> Mexican-Americans are greatly overrepresented in the lower-ability tracks of every mixed school I have observed; Anglos are overrepresented in the middle- and high-ability tracks. In one Texas ''Mexican'' high school, which serves very low income families, only the low and average tracks were found. In other district schools three or more tracks exist, including the accelerated. Tracking at the elementary school level is increasing; secondary school tracking is general and well established. Many tracked or homogeneous first grade classes were observed.[60]

The tracking system in the Southwest serves as a device which effectively isolates Chicano youngsters. Some ''slow'' tracks in mixed schools are 100 percent Mexican-American.[61] The end product of all this is a system of pervasive inequality. The track system fails Chicano students, and in turn encourages them to reject the school. This rejection is then rationalized by educators as reflecting the failure of the Mexican-American home and culture. Teachers argue that one can expect little from such a background and then act as if this were an ironclad reality. The result is a vicious circle, perpetuated by those in positions of power at the expense of those subordinate to them.

A similar situation exists between the school system and another Spanish-speaking group—the Puerto Ricans.

PUERTO RICAN CHILDREN

Ever since Puerto Rico became a U.S. Colony in 1898, the record of American help in Puerto Rican education has been a poor one indeed. The American government continually exhorted Puerto Ricans to educate themselves, but unconditionally refused to contribute any funds for that purpose.[62] On the whole, opportunities for educating Puerto Rican children were exceedingly scarce. In 1899 in one rural district, San José, only 1.5 percent of children under ten years of age were in school.[63] High schools were the preserve of the wealthy. Between 1919 and 1937 for example, the proportion of all public students enrolled in high school jumped from 2 to 5 percent.[64]

From the start, the emphasis in Puerto Rican education was on Americanization, and English was to be the language of classroom instruction. Since the largest number of Puerto Ricans migrated to New York, it was there that the language problems were the most apparent. For instance, right after World War II, three-fourths of all Puerto Rican students entering school in New York did not speak English.

The schools converted the language problem into a learning barrier. Herman Badillo, the first Puerto Rican member of the House of Representatives, remembered his own school days:

> I know . . . how amazed all the teachers were at the remarkable improvement of my intelligence quotient as I went from one grade to another. . . . I did not have the heart to tell them that all that happened was that I learned to speak English.[65]

A study of Puerto Rican high schoolers at the High School of Commerce showed unmistakenly that IQ rose along with the length of attendance in the city schools.[66]

The Puerto Rican child's educational progress was thus dependent on his or her learning English, but since meaningful measures were never taken to solve the problem, the New York City school system effectively abandoned the average Puerto Rican child. Nor was the education of the approximately 40 percent of Puerto Rican students who attended schools outside New York City any better, with dropout rates extremely high in city after city.[67]

Student achievement of Puerto Rican students have consistently lagged behind that of their white counterparts. Meyer Weinberg has summed this up by writing:

> The public schools failed to "work" for the Puerto Ricans anywhere near as effectively as they had for many immigrant groups. Numerous Puerto Ricans believed school authorities were determined not to educate their children. Repeatedly and almost unanimously, Puerto Rican students testified to the animosity shown them by teachers and other school staff. The exclusion of Puerto Ricans from classroom duties and from the school board itself underscored the feeling.[68]

It was only when the Puerto Rican groups staged public protests, and joined with blacks who were suffering a common fate, did any semblance of change come about. For example, when these two groups openly demonstrated in 1970, the City University of New York instituted an open enrollment policy. However, when

New York City was hit with a financial crisis in 1976, the open enrollment plan was one of the first casualties. Any educational triumphs of the Puerto Rican community were, thus, extremely short-lived.

The last group we will look at are the American Indians, whose experiences in the schools are, if possible, even worse than those of the blacks, Chicanos, and Puerto Ricans.

AMERICAN INDIAN CHILDREN

The education of American Indian children can be described, with little fear of contradiction, as consistently oppressive. From the first, American Indians were looked upon only as heathens to be converted to Christianity. The Catholic Franciscans established the first schools for American Indians in 1528. The Anglicans in Virginia began to educate Indian children by 1609. King James I ordered that Henrico College in Virginia be built for the children of ''the infidels'' in 1617. However, as Katherine Iverson points out, ''hostilities in 1622 and 1644 ended the Virginians' sense of responsibility to educate Native Americans for more than a century, until the Brafferton Building for Indians was eventually constructed at William and Mary in 1723.''[69]

Indian education in the eighteenth century was primarily seen as a means of pacification. In 1775, when the Revolutionary War broke out, the Continental Congress donated $500 to Dartmouth College for the education of Indian youth as a conciliatory measure to the Northern tribes to prevent attack gainst the settlements in New Hampshire.[70] The situation did not improve during the early years of the nineteenth century. Few treaties between the U.S. government and the Indians provided for educational annuities for the tribes. If Indians wanted educational facilities, they were forced to use part of their yearly allowances for education.[71]

The federal government formalized its responsibility to the Indian nations by establishing the Bureau of Indian Affairs (BIA) in 1836 as part of the War Department. The BIA was shifted to the newly established Department of Interior in 1849.[72] Yet even under the authority of the Bureau of Indian Affairs, exploitation of Indian children was the rule. Hopi children away at boarding schools were often used as cheap labor in nearby or distant locations, especially during the summers. Students at the Sherman Indian School in Riverside, California, were sent to the Imperial Valley or San Bernardino to pick cantaloupes or work on dairy farms.[73]

The administration of Indian education was part of a general system of political patronage and corruption. The teaching staff in the Indian schools was generally unsatisfactory, with political appointees selected first.[74] In fact, it was not until 1916 that a standard curriculum was published by the Indian Service, and this was strongly vocational.

By 1920, a number of Indian communities started to engage in political activity. In 1924, Congress passed the Citizenship Act and Indians were finally proclaimed equal citizens of the United States and of the state in which they resided. The political activity of American Indians, however, at this time did little to alter to oppressive conditions of Indian education. Realizing this, the Institute of Government Research, at the request of the United States Department of the Interior, published a study of Indian education in 1928. Under the direction of Dr. Lewis Meriam, the document known as the Meriam Report was highly critical of the conditions that Indian children were subjected to. Margaret Szasz has summarized the report as follows:

> In 1928 the Meriam Report observed, ''Boarding schools are frankly supported in part by the labor of the students'' who, when they were as young as fifth graders, work for half a day and go to school for half a day. The children were put to work in the dairy or in the fields, usually to raise crops for the school itself. Their clothes and shoes were provided for by their own labor through long hours in the laundries, tailor shops, and leather shops. The Meriam Report suggested, ''The question may very properly be raised, as to whether much of the work of Indian children in boarding schools would not be prohibited in many states by child labor laws, notably the work in the machine laundries.'' Finally the report seriously questioned whether the ''health of the Indian children warrants the nation in supporting the Indian boarding schools in part through the labor of these children.''[75]

The Meriam Report made a number of suggestions ranging from keeping children with their families to upgrading the teaching staff, but few if any were acted upon. The only noticeable shift was toward more of an emphasis upon the use of public schools.

The basic legal framework for relations between public schools and Indian education was created by the Johnson–O'Malley Act of 1934, which granted federal funds to provide the best education available for Indians in the state. In reality, however, school districts tended to treat the money as a general aid to education rather than specifically for Indian children. Weinberg is extremely critical of the state role.

> A generation of JOM (Johnson–O'Malley Act) showed that the Bureau of Indian Affairs had abandoned Indian children to the states. In turn, the state education departments abandoned the children to the school districts. There, they were treated in accordance with historical patterns of discrimination and deprivations.[76]

Finally, in the late 1960s, Indians again began to assert themselves politically to attempt to offset the conditions of deprivation that American Indian children had been exposed to for centuries.

A special Senate subcommittee on Indian Education was formed on August 31, 1967, with Robert Kennedy as its Chair. The purpose of the subcommittee was to examine, investigate, and make a complete study of all matters pertaining to American Indian education.[77] Following the assassination of Robert Kennedy, leadership of the subcommittee passed first to Senator Wayne Morse and then to Senator Edward Kennedy, who directed the last stages of the final report. The Kennedy Report was a devastating criticism of federal policy toward the Indians. Citing the failure of the government to act on the recommendations of the Meriam Report in the forty years since its publication, the Kennedy Report stated that the "dominant policy of the Federal Government towards the American Indian had been one of coercive assimilation," a policy which had resulted in "disastrous effects on the education of Indian children."[78] Its main conclusion was that the result had been a "dismal record of absenteeism, dropouts, negative self-image, low achievement, and, ultimately academic failure for many Indian children."[79] The situation has improved very little since the Kennedy Report, and the 1970s have been described by one student of Indian affairs as years of "rhetoric."[80] But perhaps the gravest indictment was stated by Fuchs and Havighurst, who in writing about the Navajos, state: "The extensive education needs are emphasized by the fact that after a century of Federal education programs, the Navajos have produced only one doctor, one lawyer, one Ph.D. and several engineers."[81]

It is, therefore, an understatement to say that the education of American Indian children has been an abysmal failure, even more so than that of blacks, Mexican-Americans and Puerto Ricans. Generally, discrimination has been an integral part of the educational experience of powerless minority groups. However, it must be pointed out that this discrimination has not always produced the same results for all groups as it has for blacks, Chicanos, Puerto Ricans and American Indians. Asian-Americans, for example, have fared well within the educational system. (Asian-American children do about as well as white pupils on standard tests of school achievement.)[82] The explanation for this has to do with their value system, which is similar to middle-class, white American values. Their emphasis on family relations, their business ethic, and their belief in the efficacy of educational attainment[83] are compatible with the middle-class value structure of public schools. Asian-Americans have started small businesses and have saved their money, and because they value their children's future, they have invested time and money to support their children's education. In short, their success in the schools, like that of Jewish-Americans,[84] stems from the fact that their values do not conflict with the middle-class orientation of the schools, and they are therefore better able to offset any differential treatment experienced in the schools.

White ethnics, although they have also been discriminated against,[85] have also fared somewhat better than their nonwhite counterparts in the schools. This should not be taken to imply, as some have, that white ethnics have been accepted and assimilated into American culture and that they have been successful.[86] Such groups as Irish-Americans, Italian-Americans, Polish-Americans, and Slavic-Americans have at best made it into the working class and lower-middle class. And in many instances, Catholic ethnics have had to use parochial schools rather than public ones to reach the middle class.[87] Although these white ethnic groups are better off than their parents and grandparents, lower-class blacks, Puerto Ricans, Mexican-Americans, and American Indians (depending on their geographical location), they have not really succeeded in American society; theirs has been a scaled-down version of the American dream.[88]

In short, discrimination has been an ever-present factor in the conflict between powerful and powerless groups. The result has usually been a losing battle for the powerless. And even when they have achieved success, it has been limited.

SUMMARY

We have tried to show in this chapter the importance of discrimination in educational attainment. We focused first on the blacks, showing how their educational history can best be described as ''compulsory ignorance.'' It was only with the famous *Brown* decision in 1954, which banned segregation, that blacks began to make any gains in the schools. An even these gains were limited and resisted as school districts in both the South and North fought desegregation. In particular, the issue of busing proved to be the most volatile instrument of desegregation in the 1970s, as community after community objected to busing for desegregation purposes.

While communities violently fought against compulsory busing of children to insure racial balance (with the implicit support of government), social scientists debated whether or not busing caused ''white flight,'' the abandonment of the public schools by white parents. To this day, the issue of busing and the white flight thesis remain unresolved. The conflict generated as blacks sought to achieve equality in educational opportunity is still part of the contemporary situation.

We then examined the education of Mexican-American, Puerto Rican, and American Indian children. In each case we saw an historical process of discrimination and oppression equal to that of the blacks. In light of this we can come to only one conclusion: educational achievement is inextricably tied in with racial and ethnic prejudice in the United States.

NOTES

1. This section is based on Meyer Weinberg, *A Chance to Learn: The History of Race and Education in the United States.* New York: Cambridge University Press, 1977.

2. Weinberg attributes the first use of the term ''compulsory ignorance'' in 1865 to James Simpson of the Society of Friends in England. Simpson had visited Richmond, Virginia, and used the term to characterize the ''schools'' of slave children. W. E. B. DuBois used a similar term, apparently independent of Simpson, at the turn of the century. Ibid., p. 368.

3. Cited in Frank J. Klingberg, *The Appraisal of the Negro in Colonial South Carolina: A Study in Americanization.* Washington, D. C.: Associated Publishers, 1941, p. 69.

4. Weinberg, *A Chance to Learn,* p. 13.

5. Ibid., p. 15.

6. Ibid., p. 24.

7. Modified from Carter G. Woodson, *The Education of the Negro Prior to 1861*. Washington, D. C.: Associated Publishers, 1919, pp. 237—240.

8. Ibid., p. 39.

9. Descriptions of this terrorism can be seen in Vernon L. Wharton, *The Negro in Mississippi, 1865–1890*. New York: Harper Torchbooks, 1965; and Lawrence D. Rice, *The Negro in Texas, 1874–1900*. Baton Rouge: Louisiana State University Press, 1971.

10. Weinberg, *A Chance to Learn,* pp. 45—46.

11. Ibid., p. 46.

12. This section relies heavily on Albert P. Blaustein and Clarence C. Ferguson, Jr., *Desegregation and the Law: The Meaning and Effect of the School Segregation Cases*. New Brunswick, N.J.: Rutgers University Press, 1957, pp. 95—113. Reprinted in Charles A. Tesconi and Emmanuel Hurwitz, Jr. (eds.), *Education for Whom?* New York: Dodd, Mead, 1974, pp. 107—124. Subsequent page citations are from the reprinted version.

13. Weinberg, *A Chance to Learn,* p. 54.

14. Blaustein and Ferguson, *Desegregation and the Law,* p. 111.

15. Ibid., p. 113.

16. Henry Allen Bullock, *A History of Negro Education in the South: From 1619 to the Present*. Cambridge, Mass.: Harvard University Press, 1967, p. 179.

17. Robert L. Church and Michael W. Sedlak, *Education in the United States: An Interpretive History*. New York: Free Press, 1976, p. 443.

18. Leon Friedman (ed.), *Argument: The Oral Argument before the Supreme Court in Brown v. Board of Education of Topeka, 1952–1955*. New York: Chelsea House, 1969.

19. Quoted in Weinberg, *A Chance to Learn,* p. 87.

20. Ibid., p. 90.

21. Ibid., p. 93.

22. Quoted in Dorothy C. Clement, Margaret Eisenhart, and John R. Wood "School Desegregation and Educational Inequality: Trends in the Literature, 1960—1975," in *The Desegregation Literature: A Critical Appraisal*. Washington, D. C.: U. S. Department of Health, Education and Welfare, July 1976, p. 17.

23. Gary Orfield, "Congress, the President, and Anti-Busing Legislation, 1966—1974," in R. Stephen Browning (ed.), *From Brown to Bradley: School Desegregation, 1954–1974*. Cincinnati: Jefferson Law Book Company, 1975, p. 85.

24. Clement et al., "School Desegregation and Educational Inequality," p. 18.

25. Tesconi and Hurwitz, *Education for Whom?,* pp. 42—43.

26. Ibid., p. 43.

27. *Swann* v. *Charlotte–Mecklenburg Board of Education,* 402 U.S. 1, 15 (1971). Reprinted in Nicolaus Mills (ed.), *The Great School Bus Controversy*. New York: Teachers College, 1973, pp. 47—64.

28. Tesconi and Hurwitz, *Education for Whom?*. p. 45.

29. This section is based on Nicolaus Mills, "Busing: Who's Being Taken for a Ride?" in Mills (ed.), *The Great School Bus Controversy,* pp. 3—13.

30. Ibid., p. 4.

31. Ibid., p. 6.

32. Ibid., pp. 10—13.

33. J. F. Abel, *Consolidation of Schools and Transportation of Pupils,* Bulletin No. 41. Washington, D. C.: U. S. Department of Interior, 1923, p. 22.

34. David J. Armor, "The Evidence on Busing," *The Public Interest, 28* (Summer 1972), pp. 90—126. Reprinted in Mills (ed.), *The Great School Bus Controversy,* pp. 81—122. Subsequent page citations are from this version.

35. Ibid., p. 12.

36. Thomas F. Pettigrew, Elizabeth L. Useem, Clarence Normand, and Marshall Smith, "Busing: A Review of 'The Evidence'," *The Public Interest, 30* (Winter 1973), pp. 88—118. Reprinted in Mills (ed.), *The Great School Bus Controversy,* pp. 123—158. Subsequent page citations are from this version.

37. Ibid., pp. 124−125.

38. David J. Armor, "The Double Double Standard: A Reply," *The Public Interest, 30* (Winter 1973), pp. 119−131. Reprinted in Mills (ed.), *The Great School Bus Controversy*, pp. 159−173.

39. *Morgan* v. *Hennigan,* 379 F. Supp. 410 (D. Mass, 1974).

40. Roger I. Abrams, "Not One Judge's Opinion: *Morgan* v. *Hennigan* and the Boston Schools," *Harvard Educational Review,* Reprint Series No. 11. *School Desegregation: The Continuing Challenge.* Cambridge, Mass.: Harvard University Press, 1976, p.5.

41. *Morgan* v. *Hennigan,* 379 F. Supp. 410 (D. Mass, 1974), p. 424.

42. Cited in Thomas F. Pettigrew and Robert L. Green, "School Desegregation in Large Cities: A Critique of the Coleman 'White Flight' Thesis," *Harvard Educational Review, School Desegregation: The Continuing Challenge,* pp. 17−69.

43. James S. Coleman, Sara D. Kelly, and John A. Moore, "Recent Trends in School Integration." Paper presented at the Annual Meetings of the American Educational Research Association, Washington, D. C., April 2, 1975.

44. Pettigrew and Green, "School Desegregation in Large Cities," p. 27.

45. Ibid., p. 28.

46. Robert Reinhold, "Coleman Concedes Views Exceeded New Racial Data," *The New York Times,* July 11, 1975, p. 7.

47. See Pettigrew and Green, "School Desegregation in Large Cities," for a discussion of this controversy.

48. Diane Ravitch, "The 'White Flight' Controversy," *The Public Interest, 51* (Spring 1978), pp. 135−149.

49. Christine Rossell, "School Desegregation and White Flight," *Political Science Quarterly, 90* (Winter 1975−76), pp. 675−695.

50. Michael Knight, "Scholars in New Rift over 'White Flight'," *The New York Times,* June 11, 1978, p. 27.

51. Laurence Murrell Childers, "Education in California under Spain and Mexico and under American rule to 1851." Unpublished master's thesis, University of California at Berkeley, 1930, p. 52.

52. Weinberg, *A Chance to Learn,* p. 142.

53. Ibid., p. 147.

54. W. Henry Cooke, "The Segregation of Mexican-American Children in Southern California," in Wayne Moquin and Charles Van Doren (eds.), *A Documentary History of the Mexican-Americans.* New York: Praeger, 1971, p. 326.

55. Weinberg, *A Chance to Learn,* p. 158.

56. Ibid., p. 164.

57. Ibid., p. 175.

58. Ibid., p. 176.

59. Ibid., p. 177.

60. Thomas P. Carter, *Mexican-Americans in School.* New York: College Entrance Examination Board, 1970, p. 88.

61. Ibid., p. 92.

62. Weinberg, *A Chance to Learn,* p. 232.

63. Julian H. Steward, *The People of Puerto Rico.* Urbana, Ill.: University of Illinois Press, 1956, p. 253.

64. Lloyd E. Blauch and Charles F. Reid, *Public Education in the Territories and Outlying Possessions.* Washington, D.C.: U.S. Government Printing Office, 1939, p. 111.

65. Quoted in Weinberg, *A Chance to Learn,* p. 243.

66. Ibid., p. 243.

67. See Richard J. Margolis, *The Losers: A Report on Puerto Ricans and the Public Schools.* New York: Aspina, 1968.

68. Weinberg, *A Chance to Learn,* p. 258.

69. Katherine Iverson, "Civilization and Assimilation in the Colonized Schooling of Native Ameri-

cans,'' in Philip G. Altbach and Gail P. Kelly (eds.), *Education and Colonialism*. New York: Longman, 1978, p. 153.

70. Weinberg, *A Chance to Learn,* p. 180.

71. Ibid., p. 181.

72. Estelle Fuchs and Robert J. Havighurst, *To Live on This Earth*. Garden City, N.Y.: Doubleday, 1972, p. 5.

73. Weinberg, *A Chance to Learn*, p. 180.

74. Ibid., p. 207.

75. Margaret Szasz, *Education and the American Indians*. Albuquerque, N.M.: University of New Mexico Press, 1974, p. 20.

76. Weinberg, *A Chance to Learn,* p. 216.

77. Szasz, *Education and the American Indians,* p. 149.

78. Committee on Labor and Public Welfare, Special Subcommittee on Indian Education Report, *Indian Education: A National Challenge*. Washington, D.C.: U.S. Government Printing Office, 1969, p. 1.

79. Ibid., p. 21.

80. Weinberg, *A Chance to Learn,* p. 227.

81. Fuchs and Havighurst, *To Live on This Earth,* p. 267.

82. James S. Coleman et al., *Equality of Educational Opportunity*. Washington, D.C.: U.S. Office of Education, 1966.

83. Although they are usually lumped together, Japanese-Americans have done somewhat better than Chinese-Americans in the educational system. See Harry Kitano, *Japanese-Americans: The Evolution of a Sub-Culture*. Englewood Cliffs, N.J.: Prentice-Hall, 1969; Stanford M. Lyman, *Chinese-Americans*. New York: Random House, 1974; and Stanford M. Lyman, ''Contrasts in the Community Organization of Chinese and Japanese in North America,'' in Norman R. Yetman and C. Hoy Steel (eds.), *Majority and Minority: The Dynamics of Racial and Ethnic Relations,* 2d. ed. Boston: Allyn and Bacon, 1975, pp. 285–396.

84. Marshall Sklare, *America's Jews*. New York: Random House, 1971.

85. For example, see Carl Wittke, *The Irish in America*. Baton Rouge: Louisiana State University Press, 1956; and Joseph Lopreato, *Italian Americans*. New York: Random House, 1970.

86. See Andrew M. Greely, *Ethnicity in the United States*. New York: Wiley, 1974.

87. See Joseph A. Scimecca and Roland Damiano, *Crisis at St. John's: Strike and Revolution on the Catholic Campus*. New York: Random House, 1968.

88. Ibid., pp. 3–20.

11

Sex Roles and Education

As we stated in Chapter 3, we believe that differences between the sexes in achievement (both in school and in society) are best explained not by any theory of innate differences but by social role expectations. Girls achieve less than boys because they are expected to do so. Most positions of power in American society are male dominated and definitions of social reality mirror this authority structure. Schools are instruments of sex role socialization which reinforce sexual differentiation.

SEX ROLES

Upon birth, the child enters what has been called "society's first major tracking system"—his or her sex role.[1] As Ann Oakley states:

> In most maternity hospitals sex-typed comments on the behavior and appearance of new borns are aired within a few moments of birth. The male baby who has

an erection while being weighed is referred to jokingly as 'a dirty little man'; the female baby born with curly hair is told she is pretty, and some hospitals keep pink and blue blankets for girls and boys. All these responses mark the beginning of a gender learning process which is critically important for the child.[2]

By the time the child reaches three or four years of age, he or she has incorporated the concepts "male" and "female" into his or her conception of self.[3] At this age too, boys frequently and consistently choose traditionally masculine items on preference tests, while girls choose feminine items.[4] Possible interpretations of this phenomenon range from the notion that boys are more consistently and more strongly punished for cross-sex behavior (tomboys are acceptable, where sissies are not) to the view that "feminine" behavior is limited and uninteresting to the active, curious child.[5] In any case, for whatever the reasons, boys as they grow older continue to increase masculine-trait preferences, and girls continue to manifest ambivalence in their choices.

Sex roles, the sum of expected behaviors attached to the differing positions of being male or female, are learned quite early. It should be stressed, though, that personality characteristics considered appropriate for each sex in American society and the division of labor that usually accompanies these expectations are by no means matters of universal agreement. Sex roles vary considerably in different cultures. For example, Margaret Mead, in her classic study of three tribes of New Guinea, found that one group considered a gentle temperament the ideal for both sexes, another an aggressive temperament for both, and the third considered the model to be sensitive, emotional and dependent behavior for men, as opposed to aggressive and dominating behavior for women.[6]

Sex role expectations are thus socially induced. Human behavior patterns can not be traced to biological traits or instincts. Gender differences in personality are related to cultural conditioning—in a word, to socialization. We learn to be "masculine" or "feminine" according to our society's ideas about what male and female sex roles should be. This we hold, given even the psychological research which suggests that there are sex-linked differences attached to intellectual and cognitive abilities.

SEX-LINKED DIFFERENCES IN INTELLECTUAL AND COGNITIVE ABILITIES[7]

Although there are conflicting studies, certain patterns emerge. In Maccoby and Jacklin's recent comprehensive review of the literature, they found three areas where sex differences were fairly well established, those of verbal, mathematical, and spatial abilities. The first favors girls, while the second and third give boys an advantage.

Verbal Ability. Verbal ability is the generic term which includes vocabulary, speech fluency, language understanding, and reading achievement and comprehension. Studies using standardized tests tend not to reveal any consistent results favoring one sex over the other until the age of ten or eleven, when girls clearly begin to outscore boys.

Mathematical Ability. Mathematical ability includes arithmetic operations, mathematical reasoning, and achievement in such areas as algebra and geometry. From the age of four, when systematized tests can be constructed to tap mathematical ability, through early adolescence, there seems to be no real distinction. By about thirteen years of age, however, test results tend to favor boys.

Spatial Ability. Spatial ability ranges from competence in seeing relationships between shapes and objects to visualizing what a shape would look like if its orientation in space were changed. Very few studies find sex differences during early childhood. However, by the age of eight or nine, boys begin to move ahead, and by adolescence are clearly ahead.

Our conclusion that these abilities are not inherently sex-related is based on two premises. First of all, the studies cited by Maccoby and Jacklin are, as in other areas of psychological research, not definitive and conclusive, with different studies yielding dissimilar results due to differences in samples, research methods, definitions used, and so on. Secondly, and more important, we believe that the fact that the sex differences do not appear until the ages of eight or nine at the earliest represents the influence of the school environment, the socialization process boys and girls are exposed to. We of course realize that our interpretation is just that—an interpretation—but we offer it nevertheless, in light of our total view concerning the learning of roles in school achievement. As we have posited throughout, much of social science research is interpretive and we leave it to our readers to make up their own minds given this controversial topic. No matter what the final conclusion is, though, we feel that Maccoby and Jacklin place the debate in perspective when they write:

> If girls are, on the average, less skilled in visual–spatial tasks, does this mean that fewer of them should be admitted to graduate schools in engineering, architecture, and art? Should fewer men be admitted to training in languages, linguistic science, and creative writing, on the grounds that girls, with their greater verbal skills, are more likely to profit from advanced training? Here we must emphasize once again the overlap in the sex distributions. There are many girls with high-level visual–spatial skills. It is by no means self-evident that visual–spatial skill is the intellectual ability that is most needed by engineers, but even if it were, and even if the elusive sex-linked recessive gene carried the major part of the variance in these skills (which it probably does not), current estimates are that at least 25 percent of women have it, as compared with approximately 50 percent of men.[8]

There is no need, then, to discriminate in our education patterns for males and females, yet this is what we do, and as we will now show, have done historically.

SEX-ROLE SOCIALIZATION: A BRIEF HISTORY[9]

The historical antecendents of present day sex-role socialization can be traced to the early influence of the Church. In Colonial America the major concern of the Puritans was that children be able to read the Bible for themselves. Thus, both boys and girls studied reading, and such other basics as writing and arithmetic.[10] Beyond the elementary level, however, education was primarily the domain of boys. Boys almost exclusively went on to the secondary level and to college if their families could afford it.

Education for the most part consisted of what Paul Goodman calls "incidental learning,"[11] the process whereby parents teach children what they need to learn to become adults in the culture. In Puritan New England this began at about age six, when young boys were expected to mirror their fathers and young girls their mothers in everything from dress to manners. All chores were assigned according to sex. Boys were expected to help their father with planting, harvesting, building barns, and so forth, while girls emulated their mothers in such tasks as cooking, spinning, sewing, and candlemaking. Childhood was considered a time of preparation for adulthood, and since the major concerns of adult Puritans were religion, occupation, and marriage, it stands to reason that the socialization process would revolve around these three aspects of life.

The Puritans saw great religious significance in the choice of an occupation for a boy. God had a particular calling in mind for him. God called a man to a particular occupation by endowing him with the talent and inclination to pursue the occupation.[12] This idea of a calling did not apply to girls in the same way. According to Puritan theology, girls did not receive particular callings; rather, the general calling of each female was that of wife. It was simply taken for granted that women were designed to serve in a domestic capacity.[13] The idea that women were designed for only one kind of life's work, while men were suited to a variety of careers, prevailed until well into the nineteenth century.

Nineteenth-century socialization patterns also stressed clearly differentiated sex-role differences. In the home, children watched their parents fulfilling traditional sex-role functions, which were reinforced by biblical admonitions of early Christianity. The division of labor between the sexes (men in the world, women at home) was justified as being "God's will."[14]

In the first half of the nineteenth century, private secondary schools began to open for girls. They were called "seminaries" and were intended to prepare women to be better wives and mothers. Training for teaching school was also available in case the young girl had to work a few years before getting married, or if the "poor unfortunate" could not find a husband. In 1824, the first public high school opened for girls, but college was still off-limits.[15]

Sexual discrimination was quite pronounced. Books used in the schools exemplified male heroes whom boys were encouraged to emulate. The exploits of Spanish-American War hero Admiral John Dewey, clergyman Henry Ward Beecher, inventor Tom Edison, and multimillionaire businessman Henry B. Plant were found the most often in textbooks. Girls, on the other hand, were encouraged to pattern their lives after very different role models. Any girl who might look up to a nontraditional woman was immediately chastised for admiring "that which was not fitting to her sex."[16] In fact, one popular book warned young female readers against venerating Joan of Arc because her "masculine" attitude cast a shadow on her more womanly qualities. Her position as a military leader was seen as unsexing her. A much better model to follow was Queen Victoria, who never let her position as Queen overshadow her being a woman.[17]

For men, then, the emphasis was on doing; for women, on being. Women were expected to devote their energies exclusively to the family. The woman who did not marry was considered a sorrowful creature indeed. The role of a woman included being a ministering angel, a beautiful ornament, the preserver of morality, a submissive wife, a diligent housekeeper, and a trainer of children.[18]

Thus, we can safely characterize the history of sex-role socialization for women as extremely discriminatory and limiting. Men could choose what they wanted to be, while women were to be wives and mothers. This way of thinking persisted until the present, when it has begun to be challenged.

SEX-ROLE SOCIALIZATION AND DISCRIMINATION: THE MODERN ERA

Sex-role discrimination in the contemporary United States, though less visible than in Colonial America, is no less real. So subtle is this bias that it is often not even perceived by all parties concerned, by the females, their parents, or educators of both sexes. Indeed, it is very difficult to convince the public of school sexism because girls, unlike blacks and other minority groups, obtain high scholastic achievement. However, we do feel that there is enough evidence to conclude that a basic pattern does exist, and that it begins quite early. Carole Joffe, for example, has commented on how sex-role socialization starts as early as nursery school, where girls are complimented when they wear dresses, songs reinforce sexual patterns, and story books overrepresent males.[19] In particular, this trend toward the emphasis on males in school books has been of major concern to educators who oppose sex-role discrimination. As one study found:

> Since females comprise 51 percent of the population of the United States, one would expect them to be equally represented in the world of picture books. On the contrary they vary between 20 and 30 percent. There were five times as many boys, men, or male animals pictured as there were females.[20]

It was further found that not a single woman doctor could be located in any children's books surveyed; and although over 50 percent of women work in this country, only one picture book dealt with working mothers.[21]

Perhaps the most devastating criticism was made by a task force of the

Central New Jersey National Organization of Women (NOW), collectively called Women on Words and Images. Their study covered 134 books published by four-teen major U. S. publishing companies used in three suburban New Jersey towns. Based on close to 3000 stories, the following ratios were uncovered:[22]

Boy-centered to girl-centered stories	5:2
Adult male to adult female main character	3:1
Male to female biographies	6:1
Male to female animal stories	2:1
Male to female folk or fantasy stories	4:1

The study also found that boys were represented as showing more strengths and were pictured as being more competitive and aggressive, while girls were pictured as being passive, docile, and dependent.[23]

The usual reason given for the overwhelming representation of boys in children's literature is boys' lack of reading readiness in the primary grades. Boys, it is held, will only read stories about boys and not about girls. Women on Words and Images challenge this, stating:

> We seriously question this premise. We are convinced that if girl's stories were not so limp, so limited, so downright silly even, boys would cease to discrimi-nate between boys' and girls' stories. There would only be "good" or "bad" stories. (Harriet the Spy and Pippi Longstocking have no trouble making friends among boys as well as girls.)[24]

Even math books, which are supposed to be ideologically neutral, con-tain sex biases. Marsha Federbush, for example, found that elementary math texts indulged in sexual stereotyping. Whenever activities were pictured, it was automat-ically assumed that the most obvious and normal activities for girls were cooking, sewing, and watching boys, and for women, housewifery (which was depicted by the presence of an apron, mop, iron, broom or eggbeater).[25] Spelling and phonics books were no better.

Elementary school girls are thus socialized into a hidden curriculum of sexism. Along with being exposed to few, if any, heroic and positive female role models, they are expected to be docile creatures. They are reinforced for silence, neatness, and conformity. As Frazier and Sadker perceptively state:

> Owing to the teachers' bestowal and withdrawal of rewards and an environment that stresses docility, the elementary school directly reinforces the passivity that the young female student may bring with her from home. The result is a bizarre distortion of the learning process. Neatness, conformity, docility, these qualities for which the young girl receives good grades and teachers' praise have little to do with active intellectual curiosity, analytical problem solving, and the ability to cope with challenging material. For good grades and teachers' praise, the grade school girl relinquishes the courage that it takes to grapple with difficult

material. This naive young bargainer of seven or eight has made an exchange that will cost her dearly.[26]

The attitudes introduced in elementary school are then reinforced in the high schools.

SEX-TYPING IN SECONDARY SCHOOLS

One of the earliest studies to recognize the sexist bias in the high school was James Coleman's *Adolescent Society* (1961). Coleman found that high status for boys was achieved by their doing things. Athletic success was the most direct path, but there were alternative means, including academics. It was, however, a different story for girls. According to Coleman, in order to attain a high status, girls had to cultivate their looks, wear the right clothes, and wait until the football player or his equivalent, whose status was determined by his specific achievements, came along to choose her.[27] Thus, girls were socialized not to want to be remembered as a "brilliant student," but to want to be voted "most popular." Essentially, Coleman suggested that girls were caught in a "double-bind." They wanted to meet their parents' and teachers' expectations for good performance, but saw each achievement as threatening their feminine image, thereby making them unpopular with the boys. One result is that bright girls might do less than their best in school, whereas bright boys, without the same fear concerning the relationship between academic achievement and acceptance, are more likely to be top students.

Guidance counselors further perpetuate stereotypes, fostering them upon both the college-bound and the noncollege-bound. Counselors recommend different colleges to males and females, with males more likely to be told to apply to elitist institutions. Vocational choices take the form of discrimination in careers. Boys are geared to "masculine" and girls to "feminine" occupations.

The whole process becomes one which Pottker and Fishel, who borrowing the term from Erving Goffman, label as an educational example of "cooling the mark out."[28] As described by Goffman, the victim of a con game is called a mark. In order for the con to be successful, the mark must accept his or her losses without complaining or taking action against the operators of the con game. This is best accomplished by making the mark blame himself or herself. The process that the mark goes through in order that he or she not complain is called the "cool-out" or "cooling the mark out."[29] Burton Clark has also applied this concept to the community college system,[30] and we will have more to say about his application in the next chapter.

How does the "cooling out" process work for women? According to Pottker and Fishel:

> In Goffman's confidence game, certain facts are sometimes purposely misrepresented to the mark. In the school system, vocation and academic training

stresses to boys that they must choose a career or pick a vocation and so on, but this is not emphasized to girls. The assumption is that if girls do work, their work will be temporary and unimportant, and will terminate upon marriage. Schools also show what they consider men's work and women's work to be when they track *all* of the girls into home economics classes, and *all* of the boys into shop classes. Labor statistics show that today's schoolgirl will work at least twenty-five years, and that she will also find the monetary rewards of this work of great importance to her. Therefore, the misrepresentation of essentials she receives from her school will most likely harm her in later life.[31]

The female student is constantly exposed to sexist stereotypes as she wends her way through school. Stereotyping remains constant even when it is acknowledged that girls will enter the occupational world. Although they are exposed to information about all occupations, it becomes clear early on that they are expected to fill traditional "female" jobs—secretaries, nurses, dental hygienists, and teachers.

And for those who somehow manage to offset the pressures set by the school, there is an intensification of the cooling out process. Nonconforming females are taught to feel guilt.

> Guilt leads to a sense of insecurity, and once the mark is insecure, once her belief in herself is shaken, it becomes easier to cool her out. Guilt is employed by the school when the girl or woman shows signs of not having been properly cooled out already. How many women have been made to feel as if they would not be good mothers upon stating that they would rather continue teaching than stop work when pregnant? Instead of concentrating on the question of what constitutes a proper policy regulation, the school hints to the teacher that she is an abnormal and unnatural woman.[32]

This experience translates into the reality that the level of women's intellectual and creative potential is stilted, with a concomitant loss to society. What is interesting is that this has only recently been defined as a problem. Much of this shift is due to the pioneering work of psychologist Matina Horner, who posits the notion that women have been socialized to manifest what she labels "a fear of success."

FEAR OF SUCCESS AMONG WOMEN

Matina Horner argues that women are in a state of conflict in that although they feel it is acceptable, indeed expected, to do well in school, they also feel that it is unladylike to beat men at any task. The result is that women want to succeed but not too much.[33]

Horner's method of eliciting this conflict was to ask college students to write stories about highly successful members of their own sex. She then scored the stories in terms of unpleasant events or characteristics of the successful person. She found that most of the women subjects described unpleasant incidents and attributes in their stories about successful women, but only a small percentage of the male subjects gave similar descriptions of successful men. Studies building upon this technique with adolescent subjects offered support for Horner's thesis,[34] although acceptance of the concept has not been without criticism.[35]

Horner's basic contention is that most women have a motive to avoid success, which manifests itself in the form of anxiety about achieving success. Women expect such negative consequences as social rejection and/or feelings of being unfeminine as a result of succeeding. Horner is quick to point out that she does not mean that most women "want to fail" or have a "motive to approach failure." Possessing a "will to fail" would imply that women actively seek out failure because they anticipate or expect punitive consequences from failure. The presence of a motive to avoid success, on the other hand, signifies that achievement-directed tendencies of women who would otherwise be positively motivated are inhibited by the belief that negative consequences will result from any success they attain.[36]

In her initial study, Horner hypothesized that the motive to avoid success would be significantly more characteristic of women than men, and also more characteristic of high-achievement-oriented−high-ability women who aspire to and/or are capable of achieving success than low-achievement-oriented−low-ability women who neither aspire to nor can presumably achieve success.[37]

She tested this by comparing the responses of ninety female and eighty-eight male freshmen and sophomores to a story whose lead was "After first-term finals Anne finds herself at the top of her medical school class" for the women and "After first-term finals John finds himself at the top of his medical school class" for the males. Horner found that over 90 percent of the males in the study showed strong positive feelings, increased striving, confidence in the future, and a general belief that this success would be instrumental in helping to fulfill other goals. On the other hand, 65 percent of the women were discontented, troubled, or confused by the cue. For them, success was clearly associated with a loss of femininity, social rejection, personal or societal distraction, or combinations of the above. Their responses were basically ones of negative consequences, righteous indignation, and withdrawal rather than enhanced striving.[38] Horner sums up her findings as follows:

> It is clear from all we have said thus far that unfortunately femininity and competitive achievement in American society continue even today to be viewed as two desirable but mutually exclusive ends. As a result, despite the recent emphasis on the new freedom for women, there remains a psychological barrier in many otherwise achievement-motivated and able young women that prevents them from actively seeking success or making obvious their abilities and potential.[39]

Basically, then, otherwise achievement-oriented young women, when faced with a conflict between their feminine image and expressing their competencies or developing their abilities, adjust instead to restrictive sex-role stereotypes.[40]

Since Horner's initial research there have been a number of others which have refined her thesis. Cherry and Deaux claim that their investigations support a cultural explanation for differential responses. In their study, both men and women created fear of success imagery for a woman in a nontraditional career field (such as medicine). Further, both men and women created similar stories entailing negative consequences for a male in a nontraditional career field (for example, nursing). Therefore, Cherry and Deaux hold that there is a tendency for both sexes to express avoidance of nontraditional activities. Men and women manifest avoidance of gender inappropriate activities and anticipate negative consequences for individuals who are seen as violating sex-role norms.[41]

Other studies show that the cue given by Horner may provide evidence about occupational stereotypes as well as sexual stereotypes. For example, Jorda, O'Grady, and Capps found that male students exhibited a high fear of success toward nursing cues, and females toward engineering cues.[42]

Although there is controversy over Horner's interpretation, there is little question that the female experience in school is inhibiting and is different from that of the male.

THE MALE SCHOOL EXPERIENCE

Boys are usually considered to be developmentally behind girls by at least twelve months by age 6 and approximately 18 months by age nine.[43] Yet both sexes are expected to begin school at the same age and progress through the grades at the same rate, although the boy is initially at a distinct disadvantage. When he first begins school, the boy simply is not ready to acquire those skills that are rewarded in the classroom. The young boy is sent to a classroom for which he is developmentally and psychologically unprepared, what he envisions as a "girl's world."[44] School thus becomes an uncomfortable experience for many boys, as they must constantly struggle to make sense of the contradiction between the world they are exposed to at home and that of the school. What finally happens, though, is that the school overcompensates for the boy at the expense of the girl. As they move through high school, the boy's academic achievement improves, and his occupational future becomes brighter than that of his female counterpart.[45] Thus, the schools stack the deck in favor of the male child.

One of the most important opportunities for male success is found outside of the classroom in the area of athletics. Young males are encouraged to engage in competitive sports and are thereby exposed to the socializing impact of this societal norm. By high school, athletic achievement becomes firmly linked to status for boys; indeed, it is often the single most important factor for determining a male adolescent's social standing while he is in high school.[46] Athletic participation provides the male with prestige, and his membership on a team acts as an initiation rite which helps ease the transition from boyhood to manhood.[47] In effect, team sports socialize the male for occupational roles in two primary ways. First, boys incorporate personality traits necessary for success on the athletic field—competitive spirit, achievement orientation, courage, aggressiveness, and endurance. Second, they learn to identify with the team, a form of male bonding.[48] Team spirit thereby develops a boy's ability to cooperate with other males in a competitive framework.[49]

Although it is obvious that the need for physical strength has decreased in our technological society and that many middle-class high schools are tending to deemphasize athletics somewhat, their socialization value remains. Athletics still receive the greatest organizational support within high schools. More money, time allocation, and physical facilities are provided for boys varsity teams than for female competitive events or either sex's acquisition of general overall athletic skills. Schools communicate in numerous ways that girls' sports are not as important in the total educational experience as are boys' sports.[50]

There is, however, indication that this form of discrimination may change with the enforcement of Title IX of the Educational Amendments Act. Passed by Congress in 1972, it forbids sex discrimination in any educational institution receiving federal funds. This prohibition applies to the athletic field as well as the classroom.

THE IMPLICATIONS OF TITLE IX

The language of Title IX is deceptively simple: "No person shall on the basis of sex, be excluded from participation in, be denied the benefits of, or be subjected to discrimination under any educational program or activity receiving federal financial assistance."

The importance of Title IX lies in the fact that it is the first comprehensive antisex discrimination law that covers students, and therefore may potentially revolutionize the American educational experience. Although the majority of attention given to the law since its passage has focused on its impact on the colleges, Title IX should in the long run have the greatest impact on elementary and secondary education, since all school districts in the United States receiving federal funds will have to abide by Title IX regulations if they want to keep receiving these funds.[51] The regulations for high schools went into effect in July 1972 and a number of programs were altered considerably. In Oakridge, Tennessee, for example, HEW threatened the school district with a loss of $750,000 unless the girls' athletic program was upgraded.[52]

The whole area of competitive sports in higher education, however, remains muddled, and the rules governing college and university levels only went into effect in July of 1978. Although it is definitely illegal to restrict participation in noncontact sports to one sex without offering the other sex a chance to participate in that sport, it is still unclear whether this can be accomplished through coed teams or through separate teams for each sport.

HEW, too, has so far chosen to encourage compliance rather than intervene. Although most school districts still have not complied with the regulations, some results can be reported at the univeristy level. For instance, the University of Michigan, which is a perennial powerhouse in mens' athletics and which had in 1973 only informal competition for women, had ten varsity teams for women compared to eleven for men by 1978. And at the urging of HEW, the University of Georgia, which spent approximately $1000 on women's athletics in 1973, spent $120,000 five years later. (This, however, was still considerably less than the $2.5 million spent on men.)[53]

What should be the most far reaching implications of Title IX, though, are the differences in socialization that may come about. As Walum states:

> Only through such an expansion might girls learn to participate successfully in sports as they are now constituted. And only through such a program might the girls develop a movement vocabulary that can express confidence and strength in their daily lives and, consequently, allow them to act with greater freedom from gender-stereotypes.[54]

Due to the newness of this emphasis upon equal opportunity for female athletics, it is difficult to speculate on the final outcome. However, at this time it does seem to represent a step in the right direction. And whatever form these changes take, there can be no doubt that they will have profound implications for American society. Women are challenging the subservient role they have traditionally been called on to play and are beginning to demand equality of treatment in all aspects of life. Perhaps nowhere are the possible ramifications of this challenge to traditional sex-role socialization more obvious or more important than in the realm of economic and occupational achievement.

WOMEN IN THE WORK FORCE

The recent changes in socialization patterns of females have had certain implications in the world of work. For example, the women's share of the labor force in the United States has more than doubled since 1920.[55] Projections by the U.S, Department of Labor predict that by 1990 women will hold 43 percent of all jobs.[56] Most telling is that the number of married women in the labor force increased 337 percent in the twenty-five-year period from 1940 to 1974.[57] This figure indicates that women are gaining a certain measure of economic self-sufficiency, which in turn has produced changes in the division of labor within the American family. Men have increasingly taken a role in what had previously been thought of as women's work in the home, helping with cooking, cleaning, and the socialization of children.[58]

Although the ''cooling off'' of the economy and the subsequent inflation in the 1970s pushed more women into the labor force, married women still have more of a choice than nonmarried women as to whether or not they should work. Therefore, the quality and quantity of women's education and training is extremely important in determining whether or not and at what level they enter the labor force. For example, well-educated women are more likely to seek higher-paying and more challenging jobs, and when they are employed show a much stronger commitment to work.[59]

Women's entrance into the occupational realm is expanding, and women are making some inroads into careers of prestige, power, and monetary reward.[60] However, this does not mean that women are nearing a state of parity with men or that discrimination is ending. Table 11-1 below indicates this.

Women have made substantive gains in such fields as accounting, law, and pharmacy since 1950. However, their achievements in such professions as engineering and medicine are negligible, and there are less women in architecture now than there were in 1950. In short, although the mass media tells us women have come a long way, they still have much catching-up to do.

TABLE 11-1   WOMEN AS A PERCENTAGE OF ALL PERSONS IN SPECIFIC OCCUPATIONS[61]

	1950	1960	1970	1973	1977
Total Workers	28	33	38	38.4	40.5
All professional and technical workers	39	38	40	40	42.6
Accountants	15	17	26	21.6	27.5
Architects	4	2	4	—	3.4
Engineers	1	1	2	—	2.7
Lawyers and judges	4	4	5	—	9.5
Librarians	89	85	82	82.1	83.4
Pharmacists	9	8	12	—	17.4
Physicians	7	7	9	12.2	11.2
Registered nurses	98	98	97	97.8	96.7
Health technicians	57	68	70	71.5	71.4
Social workers	69	63	63	60.8	61.2
Teachers, elementary	—	86	84	84.5	84.2
Teachers, secondary	—	49	49	49.5	51.2
Teachers, college and university	22	24	29	27	31.7
Managers and administrators, salaried	14	14	16	18.4	22.3
Sales workers	34	36	39	41.4	43.3
Clerical and kindred workers	62	68	74	77	79
Operatives	27	29	32	31	40
Service workers	58	62	60	63	62

SUMMARY

In this chapter, we have stressed the view that the differentiation in achievement for males and females in the schools and in society is related to the authority structure in this country. Males are in most positions of power, and often dominate females. Sex-role expectations mirror this hierarchy. This has been historically true in the United States, and we looked at the roots of this phenomenon in the eighteenth and nineteenth centuries.

We then turned back to sex-role discrimination in the modern era, in particular focusing on the subtle and not-so-subtle ways schools discriminate against females in the books they use and in the academic and vocational counseling girls and women receive. Agreeing with Pottker and Fishel that this represents an educational example of "cooling out the mark," we then showed how this relates to what Matina Horner calls "a fear of success" in women.

After this discussion, we looked at the implications of the recent Title IX laws, which may pave the way for reducing discrimination against females both on the athletic field and in the classroom.

Lastly, we looked at the role of women in the work force, concluding that although women have made some gains, their gains were not substantial by any means.

NOTES

1. Nancy Felipe Russo, "Kids Learn Their Lessons Early . . . and Learn Them Well," in Kenneth C. Kammeyer (ed.), *Confronting The Issues*. Boston: Allyn and Bacon, 1975, p. 377.

2. Ann Oakley, *Sex, Gender* and *Society*. New York: Harper Colophon Books, 1972, p. 173.

3. W. W. Hartup and E. A. Zook, "Sex Role Preferences in Three- and Four-year-old Children," *Journal of Consulting Psychology, 24* (1960), pp. 420–426.

4. R. Hartley, "Children's Concepts of Male and Female Roles," *Merrill-Palmer Quarterly, 6* (1960), pp. 83–91.

5. Russo, "Kids Learn Their Lessons Early . . .," p. 377.

6. Margaret Mead, *Sex and Temperament*. New York: Morrow, 1935.

7. This section relies heavily on Eleanor E. Maccoby and Carol N. Jacklin, *The Psychology of Sex Differences*. Stanford, Calif.: Stanford University Press, 1974, which is at present the most comprehensive review of the sex differences literature available.

8. Ibid., p. 367.

9. This section is based on Leatha Scanzoni and John Scanzoni, *Men, Women and Change*. New York: McGraw-Hill, 1972, p. 16.

10. Ibid., p. 20.

11. See in particular Paul Goodman, *New Reformation: Notes of a Neolithic Conservative*. New York: Vintage Books, 1969; and *Compulsory Miseducation and the Community of Scholars*. New York: Vintage Books, 1962.

12. Scanzoni and Scanzoni, *Men, Women and Change*, p. 21.

13. Ibid.

14. Ibid., p. 22.

15. Ibid.

16. Ibid., p. 23.

17. Ibid.

18. Barbara Welter, "The Cult of True Womanhood: 1820–1860," *American Quarterly, 18* (1966), pp. 151–174.

19. Carole Joffe, "As the Twig is Bent," in Judith Stacey, Susan Béreaud, and Joan Daniels (eds.), *And Jill Came Tumbling After: Sexism in American Education.* New York: Dell, 1974, pp. 91–109.

20. Elizabeth Fisher, "Children's Books: The Second Sex, Junior Division," in Stacey et al. (eds.), *And Jill Came Tumbling After,* p. 116.

21. Ibid., p. 120.

22. Women on Words and Images, "Look Jane Look. See Sex Stereotypes," in Stacey et al. (eds.), *And Jill Came Tumbling After,* p. 160.

23. Ibid., pp. 162–176.

24. Ibid., pp. 176–177.

25. Marsha Federbush, "The Sex Problems of School Math Books," in Stacey et al. (eds.), *And Jill Came Tumbling After,* p. 179.

26. Nancy Frazier and Myra Sadker, *Sexism In School and Society.* New York: Harper & Row, 1973, p. 96.

27. James S. Coleman, *The Adolescent Society.* New York: Free Press, 1971, p. 42.

28. Erving Goffman, "On Cooling the Mark Out: Some Aspects of Adaptation to Failure," *Psychiatry: Journal For the Study of Interpersonal Process, 15* (November 1952), pp. 451–463; and Janice Pottker and Andrew Fishel (eds.), "Introduction" in Pottker and Fishel (eds.), *Sex Bias In the Schools.* Rutherford, N. J.: Fairleigh Dickinson University Press, 1976, pp. 13–19.

29. Goffman, "On Cooling the Mark Out."

30. Burton Clark, "The Cooling Out Function in Higher Education," *American Journal of Sociology, 68* (May 1960), pp. 569–576.

31. Pottker and Fishel, "Introduction," in Pottker and Fishel (eds.), *Sex Bias In The Schools,* p. 15.

32. Ibid., pp. 17–18.

33. Matina S. Horner, "Femininity and Successful Achievement: Basic Inconsistency," in J. M. Bardwick, E. Douvan, M. S. Horner, and D. Gutman, (eds.), *Feminine Personality and Conflict.* Belmont, Calif.: Brooks/Cole, 1970, pp. 45–74.

34. See in particular David Ward Tresemer, *Fear of Success.* New York: Plenum, 1978.

35. See especially M. Zuckerman and L. Wheeler, "To Dispel Fantasies about the Fantasy-Based Measure of Fear of Success," *Psychological Bulletin, 82* (1975), pp. 932–946.

36. Matina S. Horner, "Toward an Understanding of Achievement-related Conflicts in Women," in Stacey et al. (eds.), *And Jill Came Tumbling After,* p. 47.

37. Ibid., pp. 48–49.

38. Ibid., pp. 50–51.

39. Ibid., p. 57.

40. Ibid., p. 61.

41. Frances Cherry and Kay Deaux, "Fear of Success versus Fear of Gender-Inappropriate Behavior," *Sex Roles, 1* (February 1978), p. 100.

42. Louis Jorda, Kevin O'Grady, and Charles Capps. "Fear of Success in Males and Females in Sex-Linked Occupations," *Sex Roles, 1* (February 1978), p. 49.

43. Frances Bentzen, "Sex Ratios in Learning and Behavior Disorders." *National Elementary Principal, 46* (1966), pp. 13–17.

44. Jerome Kagan, "The Child's Sex-role Classification of School Objects," *Child Development, 35* (1964), pp. 1051–1056.

45. Laurel Richardson Walum, *The Dynamics of Sex and Gender: A Sociological Perspective.* Chicago: Rand McNally, 1977, p. 61.

46. Coleman, *The Adolescent Society.*

47. Shirley Fiske, "Pigskin Review: An American Initiation," in Mark Hart (ed.), *Sport in the Sociocultural Process.* Dubuque, Iowa: William C. Brown, 1972, pp. 241–258.

48. Jan Felshin, *The American Woman in Sport.* Reading, Mass.: Addison-Wesley, 1974.

49. Walum, *The Dynamics of Sex and Gender,* p. 62.

50. Ibid.

51. Andrew Fishel and Janice Pottker, "Sex Bias in Secondary Schools: The Impact of Title IX," in Pottker and Fishel (eds.), *Sex Bias in the Schools,* pp. 92–104.

52. *Time,* June 26, 1978, p. 58.

53. Ibid., pp. 57–58.

54. Walum, *The Dynamics of Sex and Gender,* p. 66.

55. S. Stencil, "Women's Movement: Achievement and Effects," *Congressional Quarterly* (February 1977), pp. 23–42.

56. U.S. Department of Labor, "Employment and Earnings," *3* (November 1976), pp. 21–22.

57. United States Women's Bureau, *Handbook on Women Workers.* Washington, D.C.: U.S. Department of Labor, 1975, p. 17.

58. See Anthony A. Hickey and JoAnn Hickey, "Working Wives: Social, Economic and Demographic Factors," unpublished paper, George Mason University, Fairfax, Virginia, 1979.

59. See Juanita Kreps, *Sex in the Marketplace: American Women at Work.* Baltimore: The Johns Hopkins University Press, 1971; and John H. Scanzoni, *Sex Roles, Lifestyles and Childbearing: Changing Patterns in Marriage and the Family.* New York: Free Press, 1975.

60. U.S. Women's Bureau, *Handbook on Women Workers.*

61. Composite adapted from Robert J. Havighurst and Bernice L. Neugarten, *Society And Education,* 4th ed. Boston: Allyn and Bacon, 1975, p. 389; U.S. Women's Bureau, *Handbook on Women Workers;* and United States Department of Labor, "Employment and Earnings," (January 1978), pp. 23–24.

12

Higher Education

Just as elementary and secondary education in the United States are best analyzed from a perspective of power and conflict, so is higher education. The history of higher education in this country has been one of constant conflict. At first, this struggle centered around the establishment of stable institutions of learning in a state of what one writer calls "happy anarchy,"[1] where anyone with the necessary funds (whether individuals, private groups, religious bodies, or units of government) could and did establish colleges and universities.

As colleges began to survive and as universities developed, strife broke out between the various factions within the institution. These conflicts, although seemingly reaching their peak in the 1960s, have not disappeared by any means. They have now developed into struggles of justification in reaction to the mounting criticism that postsecondary education has not provided equal opportunity in both education and employment.

In keeping with the general framework of the preceding chapters, we will look at these three major areas of conflict in American higher education.

211

THE HISTORICAL DEVELOPMENT OF THE AMERICAN COLLEGE

Prior to the Civil War, there was no such thing as an American university in the European sense; there were only colleges.[2] During the seventeenth, eighteenth, and most of the nineteenth centuries, America's colleges were essentially appendages of locally established churches, and for the most part resembled secondary schools of today. The typical American college, according to Christopher Jencks and David Riesman:

> did not employ a faculty of scholars. Indeed, only one or two pre-Jacksonian college teachers exercised any significant influence on the intellectual currents of their time. An always upright and usually erudite clergy man served as president. He then hired a few other men (usually young bachelors and often themselves aspiring clergymen) to assist in the teaching. There were only a few professorships in specialized subjects. In most cases everyone taught almost everything, usually at a fairly elementary level.[3]

These colleges, too, were in no sense popular institutions. They were shaped by aristocratic conditions and were founded to serve the aristocratic elements of colonial society.[4] Early American higher education was characterized by a proliferation of colleges, the majority of which were unsuccessful. Enrollment was exceedingly low, and even those colleges which survived remained financially marginal.[5]

The influence of England upon America's colleges was obvious and affected both the curriculum and organization. In order to produce a learned clergy, cultivated gentlemen, and a lettered ruling class—motivations which were paramount in the minds of the founders of America's early colleges—higher learning institutions were based on a liberal arts curriculum grounded in the classics. The emphasis was upon teaching and order rather than scholarship, as was the case in the German universities. The essential ingredient of early American academic life was the residential unit of students and teachers. The curriculum was designed, as it was at Oxford and Cambridge, to mold character and impart an arisocratic life style to the wellborn. Scholarly standards were not high since the life of the mind was not very relevant to the elite.[6]

As long as American colleges were a facsimile of English academic culture, they were of modest intellectual caliber. They considered as their fundamental purpose the preservation and transmission of existing truths rather than any advancement of knowledge.

> The emphasis was quite clearly on teaching. Even as late as 1857, a committee of the Columbia College Board of Trustees attributed the poor quality of the college to the fact that three professors "wrote books."[7]

The English contribution to college life was thus primarily its accent on high culture and the leisurely pursuit of the humanities. The dominant mode of higher learning for almost two and one-half centuries after the founding of Harvard in 1636 was the liberal arts tradition. "Going to college" meant spending four years on an elm-shaded campus and attending classes in ivy-covered buildings, far removed from the temptations of city life.⁸

Those young men (women were systematically excluded) who were interested in scholarship were forced by the lack of a local alternative to leave America's shores and enroll in German universities. It was these men who then returned to America and began to found universities, most notably Johns Hopkins, Clark, the University of Chicago, and Stanford, all based on the Teutonic model.

The Rise of the American University

Johns Hopkins, founded in 1876, was the first graduate university to devote itself to the ideal of research. Frederick Rudolf comments on Johns Hopkins' origins:

> Between 1874 and 1876, when the university opened, the trustees planned and created a new American institution, but they could find no agreement on what a great American university ought to be. Yale, which had awarded the first Ph.D. from an American university in 1861, was slowly moving toward university status by keeping graduate and undergraduate education distinct; Harvard, also moving slowly, chose to tie graduate and undergradute instruction into a scheme of studies that emphasized the unity of learning; Cornell and Michigan were attempting to marry the practical and theoretical, attempting to attract farm boys to their classrooms and scholars to their facilities. The visits of the Hopkins trustees to other universities, their reading, their consultations led them to the conclusion that the time was ripe for the development of a great university on the German model.⁹

With the emphasis upon the discovery of knowledge, the graduate universities also went into the disseminating end of the process. Johns Hopkins became the first university to establish a university press, and was quickly followed by the University of Chicago. In 1877, Johns Hopkins published *The American Journal of Mathematics*. Other journals in chemistry, biology, physiology, psychology, and philology were published shortly afterward. The University of Chicago Press claimed journals in political economy, geology, Hebrew, astrophysics, sociology, theology, and classics.¹⁰

Interestingly enough, the idea of graduate schools devoted to research was not very well received, at first, among the leaders of higher education. In particular, such well-known and influential presidents as Charles William Eliot of Harvard and Andrew D. White of Cornell urged that the radical idea of pure research be subjugated to practical education. Indeed, Eliot publicly held to remarks made at his inaugural in 1869 that "the prime business of American professors in this generation must be regular and assiduous class teaching."¹¹ And up until the beginning of the first decade of the twentieth century, such opinions were not atypical. In 1910, the president and trustees at the University of Minnesota took the position that a chemistry professor's research was "his own private business, much like playing the piano or collecting etchings."[12]

It was the rise of science, though, that changed the minds of higher educational leaders and in the process solidified the structure of the university as we know it today. In the late nineteenth and early twentieth centuries, science came into its own in American higher education. Scientific courses began to proliferate. Other disciplines, seeing the handwriting on the wall, began to imitate the sciences. Social studies became social science, psychology broke with philosophy and began to emphasize the experimental approach; even philosophy began to look toward positivism. As Bernard Berelson has observed:

> The graduate school came into being under the pressures of science . . . and it has lived its life in an increasingly scientific and technological age. . . . In an important way, the institution has from the start been a scientific institution, and it is today.[13]

With the advent of science and the growth of the graduate school came that which most differentiates universities from lower levels of the educational system—the emphasis upon publication and the related concept of professionalism.

One of the first educators to advocate publication was the president of the University of Chicago, William Rainey Harper. In 1892, Harper announced to his board of trustees that henceforth faculty promotion would be dependent upon scholarly research rather than on teaching. In order to set the process in motion, he first introduced the relatively light teaching load, and then stated that although the University would be patient, he expected his faculty to contribute to the world's knowledge. A decade later Yale University encouraged "productive work" for its staff in order to help establish "a national reputation."[14]

Perhaps, though, *the* distinctive characteristic of the American university, was the development of the department, unlike the European emphasis on the "chair." According to Joseph Ben-David:

> The department has been one of the most widely approved features of United States academic organization. There have been attempts at imitating it in practically every country of the European continent, in Japan, and in many other places. Their attempts, however, have not been too successful. The reason it has been so difficult to transplant this relatively simple organizational pattern in other countries is the civil service status of the professors in the majority of the European and the Japanese state universities. This implies that the professor is actually not an employee of the university, but of the state. The state not only pays his salary, but also grants him aid, a customary fixed number of assistants in some cases, and other resources for doing his work. Salaries and other resources are usually fixed, and cannot be manipulated by the individual universities (except in Germany). Thus, each so-called chair is a self-contained unit.

> The university has no authority over this unit, nor in effect has anyone else, because the incumbents of the chairs have tenure, and the resources and facilities for the chairs are rigidly fixed by the statute and administrative rules, or, at least, by time-honored usage.[15]

The professor in the European university is thus truly an "independent practitioner," in the same way an individual was under the medieval social order of the estates and guilds, where members of certain privileged groups, such as clergymen, were entitled to a certain income and way of life guaranteed by the official church, and ultimately by the state.[16]

The European system has tended to produce an aristocratic elitism on the part of those few who ascend to chairs. In the United States, this type of elitism has been supplanted by professionalism.

> The rise of departments tended to emphasize universalistic standards of performance and competence as distinguished from standards congenial to a single patron. It also encouraged the exposure of department members and the graduate students to critical evaluation of their work in a far wider forum: in an intellectual marketplace.[17]

Tied to the concept of professionalism of college and university faculty are the twin concepts of tenure and academic freedom. Since professors are, theoretically, bound to pursue truth wherever it may lead, this can lead to opposition with other segments of the population who do not hold these lofty ideals. Professors who espouse unpopular ideas have to be protected. Although the need for academic freedom and tenure grew out of the controversy over Darwinism and the teaching of principles of evolution, it eventually came to incorporate political ideas. In particular, as academicians sought to assimilate the doctrine of free speech into that of academic freedom, a great deal of friction was generated. Social scientists came into conflict with important business interests in the world outside the university. Frederick Rudolf has catalogued some of the more famous of these conflicts which arose in the late nineteenth century.

> Richard T. Ely, economist at the University of Wisconsin, spoke favorably of strikes and boycotts; for his economic heresy he was tried by a committee of the board of regents in 1894. Edward W. Bemis, economist at the University of Chicago, chose the period of the Pullman strike to make a public attack on the railroads; he was dismissed. James Allen Smith, political scientist at Marietta College, did not like monopolies and he met the same fate as Bemis. President E. Benjamin Andrews of Brown revealed a preference for free trade and bimetalism that made his position at an old eastern college untenable. John R. Commons indulged in a range of economic views so disturbing that he ran into difficulty at both Indiana University and Syracuse. Edward A. Ross, sociologist at Stanford, disapproved of coolie labor, with the consequences that Mrs. Leland Stanford disapproved of him.[18]

Armed with the Ph.D. as a credential which showed the world at large that they were bonafide scholars, professors did not feel that they should be told what to do. They were the experts. In the struggles over who would control higher education, the university professors (as Jencks and Riesman point out) lost most of the publicized battles but eventually won the war.[19] Out of these skirmishes emerged a genuine concern for the principles of academic freedom. Each time someone was dismissed for their unorthodox views, the academic community became more and more aware of its common goals and needs.[20]

In the early decades of the twentieth century the principle of academic tenure became established as a professorial prerogative and evolved into a safeguard for both the professor's freedom of thought and his or her economic security. There are primarily three coordinate elements in a tenure system. First, tenure is interwoven with academic freedom in that it frees a faculty member from restraints and pressures that otherwise might inhibit thought and action. Second, tenure represents a kind of communal acceptance into the professional guild, acceptance by one's peers. Third, tenure is a means for providing job security to promote institutional stability and loyaly as well as to reward individual service and accomplishment.[21] In 1915, the American Association of University Professors (AAUP), a professional society dedicated to the development and protection of standards of academic freedom and tenure, was founded to preserve these standards.

Armed with job security and backed by a professional association, university professors were establishing themselves as a new class of professionals. As a consequence, presidents and boards of trustees were forced to recognize their obligations to the community of free scholars.[22] The birth of the AAUP symbolized the arrival of the academician in the United States, and the concept of tenure solidified the power of the professor.

It must be pointed out, though, that this acceptance of tenure was not easily won at denominational and Catholic schools. Although these schools represent a form of pluralism that is distinctive to the American system of higher education, professors who taught at these schools paid a price when it came to acadenic freedom. The Catholic system of higher education, which is less diversified than the Protestant system, can be taken as representative here.

THE HISTORICAL ROLE OF THE CATHOLIC COLLEGE AND UNIVERSITY[23]

The early Catholic colleges were founded to produce priests, and were therefore not dissimilar to other colleges which educated for the ministry. The first Catholic college in America was Georgetown, established in 1789. St. Mary's College, in Maryland, was founded soon after. All in all, some forty-two Catholic colleges were established in the first half of the nineteenth century. Their basic goals were seminary preparation, missionary activity, and moral development. Catholics were endeavoring to relate their distinct religious and cultural traditions to the changing patterns of the dominant non-Catholic culture.

In the early stages of Catholic higher education, faculties were almost exclusively clerical. There was little conflict between Catholic and secular values since secular values were usually ignored. As the system expanded, however, the layman began slowly to penetrate the faculties of Catholic colleges. The initial influx of the lay faculty member was an exceedingly slow process; refugee scholars from Europe and ex-seminarians constituted the bulk of the lay faculty. In 1850, for example, lay faculty numbered only 26 out of 240 in twenty-five colleges. By 1872, in fifty-five Catholic colleges with a total faculty of 677, only 80 were laymen.[24] As John Donovan points out:

> In American higher education during this post-civil war period, the clear-cut domination of the teaching staff by priests and brothers was a significant point of contrast of the situation in other American colleges. Initially they, too, had been staffed largely by clergymen, but after 1860, despite a continuance of dominational controls the faculty was composed increasingly of lay professors.[25]

The lay faculty were initially relegated to second-class citizenship. It was not until well into the fifth and sixth decades of the twentieth century that they achieved the rights that their secular colleagues took for granted. For example, St. John's University in New York City, at the time the largest Catholic University in the country, did not offer tenure as a contractual right until 1966, when it became the first university in the history of higher education in the United States to be hit with a faculty strike. In the same year, San Diego College for women, a small liberal arts school run by the Sisters of the Sacred Heart of Jesus, fired two assistant professors for criticizing the college's academic standards. The two professors were dismissed by the administration after a closed-door hearing, after which the tapes of the proceedings were burned.[26] It was only when Catholic colleges and universities began to divest themselves of clerical control did their faculties begin to achieve the same guarantees of academic freedom that were available on the secular campus.

The dissension between the professor and the administration, be it religious or secular, was not the only one the professors engaged in. There were also the students to contend with, and the tension between these two groups is as old as the college itself.

FACULTY AND STUDENT CONFLICT[27]

Colleges and universities, like all educational institutions, engage in socialization. Because of the different ages of the two biggest groups in the college, a confrontation between the old and the young becomes inevitable, signifying a ceaseless struggle for power.[28] An acknowledgement of this incompatibility is infinitely more honest than the myths which depict a harmonious relationship on college campuses in the eighteenth and nineteenth centuries, and which subsequently see the conflict that characterized higher education in the 1960s as an aberration.

   The most prominent myth holds that in the good old days when colleges were small, faculty and students had intimate personal contacts on a day-to-day basis. As Jencks and Riesman state:

> The myth has several sources. One is the assumption that because the faculty were not busy with research or consultation they had time and energy for their students. A second reason for the myth is the general American tendency, perhaps the human tendency, to assume that if things are presently bad, they were once better, rather than realizing that they are likely to be considered bad precisely *because* they are getting better.[29]

Yet, whatever its origins, the myth does not coincide with historical reality. Eighteenth- and nineteenth-century colleges, although small enough, were neither harmonious nor intimate. The students were constantly clashing with the faculty, who were almost universally regarded by the young as the enemy. The faculty, in turn, reciprocated primarily by enforcing academic and social rules, most of which were of the most trivial kind.[30]

   The early colleges were essentially quite rigid, and as such tended:

> to resist all compromise with the interests and predilections of the young—and indeed, with the future generally. There could not but be conflict in such institutions. . . . The conflict was intensified by the fact that most colleges also took over from the adult intelligentsia the task of transmitting some version of High Culture to the semi-civilized young. Adult versions of High Culture have never had the same authority in America as in countries like France and Germany, and this is probably true of adult culture in the broad sense as well. Nonetheless, nineteenth-century American educators believed in the value of what they had to teach and sought to impose it on the young, whether the young enjoyed it or not. They seldom succeeded very well, but the mere attempt was often enough to produce continuing guerilla resistance.[31]

   On the whole, though, student opposition tended to focus around essentially small matters rather than on large ones. This is, without doubt, the major distinction between the historical friction between students and faculty and contemporary conflict. Nineteenth-century students seldom if ever challenged the legitimacy of the faculty's authority. Rather, they claimed that it was abusive in particular cases. Theirs was a defiance based upon what the considered to be an injustice of the moment. They developed no theory that something else should replace the authority of their elders. Even when students rioted (and they often did), it was more like a peasant revolt against tyranny than like a revolutionary movement. In the twentieth century, on the other hand, the massing together in high schools and colleges of large numbers of young people of identical ages and backgrounds has produced a separate teenage culture which provides the supportive base upon which an attack on the legitimacy of adult authority has been launched.[32]

Another basic difference is that faculty no longer consider themselves guardians of morality, as they once did when colleges were denominationally affiliated. In most colleges and universities faculty members are scholars, or at least think of themselves as such, and therefore are not interested in the nonacademic aspects of the students' life. Most faculty members could not care less whether students have curfews, live in coed dorms, or are cohabiting. They see themselves concerned with the student only when he or she is in their classrooms.

The additional fact that administrators are uncertain as to how students *ought* to act results in a reluctance to confront students over their extracurricular endeavors. Professors and administrators find it politically expedient to avoid efforts to regulate student behavior. Faculties, though, sometimes use this as an excuse to impose unreasonable expectations on the part of the student's life they are interested in—the student's scholarship. Faculty members expect undergraduates to act like graduate apprentices. Since only a minority of undergraduates have either the motivation or the talent to act like apprentice scholars, many professors disclaim any responsibility for the majority of students. This, in turn, encourages students to create their own lifestyles.[33]

The academic profession thus takes on elitist qualities, which makes it unsuitable as an agency with the responsibility of socialization of the young. Although some students do identify with their professors, the majority cannot afford to, and could not approximate them even if they tried.

Parents, on the other hand, are very much concerned with the nonscholarly side of their children's college life, which may easily bring them into variance with the college or university that their children attend. The ambivalence over the socialization role in higher education, thus, can easily lead to heightened discord on a number of levels. While this dispute over socialization is almost ubiquitous—and therefore exceedingly important if we are to understand the role of higher education in the United States—there is, in our view, another more important kind of strife, that of political dissent. We will now take a close look at this phenomena.

STUDENT PROTEST IN THE UNITED STATES: A HISTORICAL OVERVIEW[34]

One of the major points concerning the political activities of students is that throughout history only a small minority of students in the United States have engaged in any radical activity. This was as true in the heyday of the student riots in the late 1960s as it was in the 1860s. For the most part, American students simply have not been notably radical or very much opposed to the status quo. This makes the

American student movement quite different from that of other countries. As Philip Altbach states:

> American student activism has never constituted an active threat to the stability of the political system—not even during the dramatic protests at the 1968 Democratic Convention or immediately after the events of the Cambodian invasion and the shootings at Kent State in 1970. This contrasts sharply with student movements in other countries, where students have toppled governments or created serious political disorder.[35]

Reasons for this lack of national impact range from the fact that university centers are geographically diverse, to a lack of class consciousness on the part of students, to the complexity of the political infrastructure of America—in particular, its capacity for cooptation.

For the most part, although several currents of student activism can be detected prior to 1900, the foundations of the recent wave of student protests were established about the turn of the century. From 1900 to 1917 two major developments which shaped campus political activism took place. The first, and in the long run most important, was the founding of the Intercollegiate Socialist Society (ISS) in 1905.[36] The ISS later changed its name to the League For Industrial Democracy (LID), the Student League for Industrial Democracy (SLID) and finally in 1962 to Students for a Democratic Society (SDS). The second development was the involvement of students in the settlement house movement of the early 1900s.[37]

We can also divide the student protest movement into three major periods—the first from 1900 to 1930, the second from 1930 to 1970, and the third form 1970 to the present. It was during the first period that the American student movement was formed. The kinds of organizations developed during the first three decades of the twentieth century—political, fraternal, religious, national coordinating groups—were reflected in later organizations. Furthermore, the student movement, especially the ISS, influenced the political views and lives of individuals such as Norman Thomas, A. J. Muste, and Upton Sinclair, who later became important in national political and intellectual life.[38]

Perhaps *the* most important student activism during the early twentieth century revolved around the growth of settlement houses. As Seymour Martin Lipset points out:

> The early twentieth-century demand by many college students for relevance, for the opportunity to apply their values in social betterment, met its greatest fulfillment . . . in settlement work, in direct contact with the poor in urban slums. Thousands of students and young graduates threw themselves into staffing the rapidly growing number of settlement houses. By 1911 there were 413 of them, three-quarters of which had been formed since the turn of the century. They involved twenty-five hundred residents and another ten thousand to fifteen thousand student volunteers.[39]

Student activism, though, seemed to reach its peak in the 1930s. Indeed, more students were involved in political activity in that decade than in the 1960s. For the first time in the history of the United States, student activist groups were successful in making their presence felt on the national political scene. Radical students joined with adult pacifist groups in keeping foreign policy issues before the nation. Nationwide peace studies focused national attention on the antiwar opinion of the time. This, in turn, was followed by student activism in support of the Spanish Republic in its fight against fascism.

The student movement of the thirties, however, failed to maintain its momentum, and by the time World War II ended, a new generation was on the college campuses, the classes of the 1950s, so aptly labeled the "silent generation." This era too, came and went, and a definite change began to take place in the late 1950s and early 1960s. Civil liberties, peace, and civil rights slowly but surely became rallying points for students who desired change in the system. Civil rights became the first focal point, due to its dramatic nature and the small successes of the nonviolent black movement, which had began to develop in the years following the 1954 Supreme Court decision on segregation.

> The emergence of a militant, nonviolent, direct action movement among Southern black students was a powerful impetus to Northern white college students. It provided white activists with important lessons in both tactics and depth of commitment necessary for student activism. It was also a major source of student disillusionment with the government and thus paved the way for the more militant New Left.[40]

The demise of McCarthyism, the establishment of general economic prosperity, and the revived outspokenness of long-silent faculty liberals gave birth to renewed student activism.

It must be noted again, though, that the upsurge in activity, even at its peak in the late 1960s, represented on the whole a small minority of students. The vast majority of students remained essentially apathetic and indifferent to political causes. Most of the activists who carried on the political struggles of the 1960s were veterans of the civil rights movement. As they began to turn their major focus away from civil rights to the peace movement, they came into conflict not only with the government but the faculty of their colleges and universities as well. Although there is evidence that faculties are more liberal than the general public,[41] they are not ultraliberals and dangerous radicals, as some politicians and trustees have characterized them. As Michael Miles points out:

> In reality most faculty are, given time, natural allies of the administration for they are unalterably opposed to direct-action politics in a university setting. In every case of student rebellion the general faculty have condemned direct-action political techniques in unambiguous terms.

In 1964, the Academic Senate of the University of California at Berkeley resolved that "force and violence have no place on this campus."

In 1968, the faculty of Columbia College resolved that "it endorses the right to protest, but strongly condemns both obstructive behavior and physical violence on campus."

In 1969, the faculty of Arts and Sciences of Harvard University resolved to condemn "obstructions of the normal processes and activities essential to the functions of a university community."[42]

Miles goes even further, arguing that faculties are inherently conservative.[43] Here we disagree with him; we feel that the issue is not radical students versus conservative tenured faculty, but rather a difference of opinion (which sometimes becomes extreme) as to the ultimate value of the university to those who have a vested interest in it. Students, being young and having the impatience of the young, want to change immediately what they do not like. Faculty, on the other hand, who see the university as "a community of scholars," a place which preserves their hard-won academic freedom, are not so easily persuaded that change is in their own best interests; or, because they see themselves as professionals servicing society, as in the best interests of that society. Indeed, Barrington Moore, a leading radical sociologist, has defended the university against student attack. According to Moore:

> The general situation does create a dilemma for those of us who find ourselves in passionate opposition to the general drift of American society—a position often reached with uneasy astonishment. As students and teachers we have no objective interest in kicking down the far from sturdy walls that still do protect us. For all their faults and inadequacies the universities . . . do constitute a moat behind which it is still possible to examine and indict the destructive trends in our society. . . . the faculty's overwhelming commitment to free speech in the university community is part of this moat, perhaps its most important part. To attack it heedlessly is irresponsible and self-defeating. This is not merely because we who are so vehemently opposed to many basic trends in American society may broadly need its protection from time to time. The principle is important in its own right.[44]

Although the student upheavals of the sixties passed into history with the coming of the 1970s, the activists had laid the foundation for appreciable change on the college campus. The establishment of minority studies programs and student participation in hiring, firing, and curriculum matters can all be traced to the student protests of the 1960s. As Gerald Grant and David Riesman state:

> Students sought relief in a wide range of popular reforms that gave them a considerably greater degree of autonomy and resulted in dramatic changes in their relationships with teachers. Students were freer than before to pick and choose their way through the curriculum and to move at their own pace without

penalty. The most popular of these reforms—student-designed majors, free-choice curricula, the abolition of fixed requirements—sought not to establish new institutional aims, but to slow the pace and expand the avenues of approach. While these reforms began in the elite academic institutions, they spread to other colleges and universities.[45]

There were divergent reasons for the adoption of these reforms. On the one hand, it was thought that these measures would placate the rebellious students; and on the other, a new generation of faculty, themselves a product of graduate school in the turbulent sixties, sought to significantly alter higher education.

The 1970s, at least the early part, then, were characterized by a spirit of reform and attempted innovation, as numerous experimental colleges opened, and established ones tried to incorporate new ideas into their curriculums. Economic pressures, though, put a swift end to this, as institution after institution found itself in financial trouble resulting from a diminishing population aged 18 to 24 years old, and by movements toward fiscal stringencies on the part of state legislations; in the case of private elitist universities, a shrinking endowment fund was caused by the downtrend in the stock market. Colleges and universities found themselves faced with the prospect of limited or negative growth. Belt-tightening was seen as inevitable, as "retrenchment" became a byword. Experimental education was looked upon as a frill, and became the first casualty of the slowdown of the economy in the second half of the 1970s. A case in point was the James E. Allen Center of the State University of New York at Albany, which, with the help of a $100,000 grant from the Carnegie Foundation, opened in 1972 as a time-shortened interdisciplinary college. In 1976, after graduating its first class, it was disbanded, its faculty let go, and its remaining students absorbed in the main university as New York State found itself in dire financial straits.

The 1970s also witnessed another trend, that of minority and lower-class students who desired entrance to the university as a means to the "good life" they saw themselves historically excluded from. This, then, precipitated another form of conflict, and raised again the question of inequality we looked at in Chapter 9.

MINORITY GROUPS AND INEQUALITY IN HIGHER EDUCATION

Blacks and Higher Education

The higher education of blacks has followed the same pattern as that of their elementary and secondary training. Historically, blacks were excluded from postsecondary education. By the time of the Civil War, perhaps 580 colleges existed and at least as many had failed, yet very few black persons ever attended any of them. (Oberlin College constitued the most prominent exception. Founded in 1833, it began accepting black students two years later. By the 1850s blacks made up approximately 4 to 5 percent of the student body.)[46]

The first black colleges opened in the North before the Civil War, but none granted a B.A. degree until 1865.[47] From the beginning, there were fundamental differences between the black colleges and other colleges which opened around the same time. Black educators played much smaller roles in the founding of colleges than did their white counterparts.

> The private Negro colleges were for the most part financed by white philanthropists, controlled by white boards of trustees, initially administered by white presidents, and largely staffed by white faculty. In due course the administration and faculty usually became predominantly Negro, but by then a psychological and cultural pattern had been established that was hard to break.[48]

At their inception, black colleges did not have sufficient numbers of high school graduates to do college work, and were forced to enroll elementary students as feeders for their secondary departments. As an example, in the academic year 1899–1900, only fifty-eight of the ninety-nine black colleges had any collegiate students.[49]

Black colleges were also predominantly private schools because higher education for blacks was not considered necessary by Southern white governments, and remained so until the beginning of World War I.[50] Southern state governments virtually ignored the various Civil Rights Acts and proceeded to set up white colleges. Even the Morrill Act of 1862, which provided support in each state of at least one college where agriculture and mechanical arts were to be taught, resulted in funds allocated for black colleges in only four southern states.

The North was not much better. In 1900, Yale University, when asked to fill out a questionnaire on black graduates, referred the inquirer to the institution's black janitor. Princeton excluded blacks until after World War II. Although Harvard admitted blacks, in 1915 it established segregated dormitories.[51]

Catholic colleges, too, were exceedingly exclusionary. From 1922 to 1936, Catholic University, despite repeated protests, refused to accept any black students. In the 1920s, the only Catholic colleges which enrolled black students were Fordham University and the University of Detroit. A study in the late 1940s revealed that only seventeen students were enrolled in ten Catholic colleges. Furthermore, over thirty excluded blacks and seven admitted a small number.[52]

Blacks were essentially forced to establish a tradition of private higher education, a system that was exceedingly inadequate. The cumulative result of this was that by 1950 the typical black college was an ill-financed, ill-staffed caricature of white higher education.[53] So poor were black colleges that just a decade ago Jencks and Riseman wrote:

> There are only a handful of Negro colleges where the average freshman scores over 400—approximately the 25th percentile for the white freshman. Most Negro colleges average in the 300's. Some average delow 300—approximately

the 7th percentile for whites taking the test. There are very few white colleges with mean SAT scores below 400, and we know of none with a mean below 300.[54]

And although there has been some improvement in black colleges overall, due to the recent desire of elite white colleges to recruit minority group members, a number of black colleges have seen their entering scores for freshmen plummet, since those blacks who would have been their best students have chosen instead to attend the white schools.

It was only in the 1970s that blacks made any improvement. Richard Freeman, in a study for the Carnegie Commission on Higher Education, has shown that blacks have made substantial progress in income, occupation, and education.[55] The most dramatic gains were made by young college graduates, who, according to Freeman, have achieved full economic equality with their white peers. By 1973, young college graduates aged twenty-five to twenty-nine were earning *more* than the white college graduate in the same age bracket. The same was true of black female graduates.[56] We would advise against too much optimism over these figures, though, since the percentage of black college graduates is still small— approximately 5 percent from 1968–1974.[57] Also, data from the National Longitudinal Study shows that although black high school graduates are now about as likely to enter college as their white counterparts in high school record and family income, their patterns of enrollment are quite different. Forty-eight percent of all black freshmen and 32 percent of those in the highest ability quartile are enrolled in two-year community colleges. The comparable figures for white freshmen are 41 percent and 26 percent.[58] Community colleges, as we will show in a later section of this chapter, are more often than not used to curtail mobility than to overcome inequality.

Women and Higher Education

Higher education for women in the United States lagged sorely behind that of men. American women, however, were a bit better off than those in Europe, perhaps because coeducation was more common in the new world. Even so, it was not until 1837, when Mary Lyon founded the Mount Holyoke Female Seminary for women over sixteen, that we can begin to speak about any real beginnings of female education.[59] And even then, there were tremendous problems since the public high schools of the nineteenth century were not equipped to prepare young women for college.

Still, some women did manage to overcome adverse conditions and attend college. Oberlin had opened as a coeducational college in 1833, and had awarded the first woman's bachelor's degree in 1842.[60] But we would be remiss if we did not point out that coeducation was not esablished at Oberlin for the sake of women, but in order that men at the college might have a more wholesome and realistic view of women than would those at all-male colleges. And as Caroline Bird points out, the women students were expected to wait on dinner tables and remain silent in mixed classes.[61]

The real advance in coeducation was made by the state universities, with some in the West attaching female academics to their branches, which eventually led to coeducational universities.[62] By the decade following the Civil War, the Universities of Iowa, Wisconsin, Michigan, and Maine and Cornell University had admitted women to degree programs. Other state universities followed suit. The old universities of the East resisted this trend, though. As a result, the first exclusively women's colleges providing a real college education arose in this area of the country. Vassar, founded in 1860 in New York State, was the first endowed women's college. Both Wellesley and Smith colleges opened in Massachusetts in 1875, and Bryn Mawr was founded in Pennsylvania in 1885.[63]

Few women college graduates, however, entered professions in the nineteenth century. Legal training, for example, effectively eliminated women because the right to practice was acquired by clerking in the office of a lawyer admitted to the bar, and few male lawyers would take on women clerks. Although a handful of women did manage to graduate from law schools, it was not until 1900 that as many as a hundred women were enrolled in America's law schools; and even then, the elite schools—Harvard, Yale, Columbia, Washington and Lee, University of Virginia—resisted pressures to admit women. (Yale conceded in 1918; Virginia in 1921; Harvard only in 1948.)[64]

Medical education was even worse. Elizabeth Blackwell, English-born but living in the United States, applied to approximately thirty medical schools in the 1840s. Only one accepted her, the Geneva College of Medicine in New York, which did so only after having the students vote on her, with the stipulation that one negative vote would keep her out. The men students thought it would be great fun to have a woman attend and voted her in. But her troubles were far from over. Although she graduated at the head of her class in 1849, she had to fight for the right to take anatomy courses.[65]

After that, medical schools slowly began to admit women, and by 1929 there were 7,219 women doctors in the United States.[66] But, although women have made progress in the medical field, there is a long way to go. As Phyllis Stock points out, America's percentage of women doctors is, except for Spain's, "the worst record of any sizable country in the world."[67]

> Graduate education was a little better than legal and medical education. In 1882 the University of Pennsylvania opened its graduate school to women. Bryn Mawr offered graduate education from its beginnings; by 1900 it had given forty-four master's degrees and eighteen doctorates; Columbia in 1890; Yale in 1891; Brown and Chicago in 1892; and Harvard in 1894 opened graduate education to women. In 1900, 312 men and 31 women received Ph.D. degrees in the United States.[68]

Obviously, women have made great strides in education. Indeed, by

1974—1975, the percentage of women receiving bachelor's degrees had increased to 45.3 percent, master's degrees to 44.8 percent, and doctorates to 21.3 percent.[69] However, we must be careful not to interpret these figures as equivalent to those of the dominant group—men. For example, in 1977, although women totalled 31.7 percent of the total faculty positions in higher education,[70] this figure hides the fact that women fortunate enough to obtain faculty positions frequently meet numerous barriers to their upward mobility. Although 63.3 percent of all male faculty members hold tenure, only 44.4 percent of women faculty do. Women tend to receive temporary and nontenure-track faculty appointments. In 1976, women constituted 50.5 percent of all instructors, yet only 10 percent were full professors. Their average salaries also fall well below their male counterparts, and women tend to cluster at certain types of institutions, comprising 25.6 percent of faculty at community colleges, 22.7 percent at four-year colleges, and 14.8 percent at universities. The representation of women faculty at some elitist schools falls below 10 percent.[71]

Women are also underrepresented in administrative positions in higher education. One recent survey showed that white men held 79 percent of all administrative positions, white women 14 percent, minority men 5 percent, and minority women 2 percent. Furthermore, the presidency was dominated by men. Men held 96 percent of presidencies at both white coeducational and minority institutions, 69 percent at white women's colleges, and 100 percent at white men's colleges.[72]

Other Minorities and Higher Education

The higher education of other minority groups, such as American Indians, Mexican-Americans, and Puerto Ricans have paralleled that of blacks. However, unlike blacks, these groups had no Reconstruction during which—if ever so fleetingly—they exercised genuine political power.[73] Therefore, governmental redress was trifling. According to Meyer Weinberg:

> By failing to fulfill the obligations to supply common schools and by excluding minority children from secondary schools, communities kept the potential supply of minority college students at a negligible level for many years. Blacks were left with segregated higher institutions, but the other three minority groups lacked even these. In time, extremely small numbers were admitted to higher institutions, but on the campuses they suffered much of the exclusion and discrimination familiar in black higher education.[74]

Between 1769 and 1973, Dartmouth College enrolled 187 Indians and graduated 25, or one every eight years. During Dartmouth's first one hundred years, only one American Indian graduated, despite the college's supposed dedication to "the education and Christianizing of Indian Utes and others."[75]

As they did for women and blacks, things have improved a bit for

American Indians today. A 1974 estimate of the undergraduate college enrollement of American Indians by the Office of Civil Rights indicated that 59,394 American Indians were registered in institutions of higher education. This represented 0.6 percent of the total college population. Another survey in the same year indicated that 0.9 percent of all entering freshmen were American Indians.[76]

Again, some caution must be used in the reading of these figures. Whereas at first glance it may be construed that American Indians are slightly overrepresented in higher education based on their percentage in the overall population, the data may be complicated by the fact that many individuals of Hispanic-American ancestry now list their major identity group as Native American, which for census purposes is considered the same as American Indians. Due to the small size of the American Indian population, any addition of Hispanic-Americans would cause a dramatic change in the educational statistics of American Indians.[77] In addition, in 1975, only 3906 or 0.3 percent of all graduate students were Native Americans,[78] which alters once again the educational statistical profile of the Indian. A more realistic interpretation, we believe, is that the larger percentage of enrollment than would be expected for American Indians, given a random distribution, reflects the general overenrollment in community colleges, something which merely gives the illusion of educational progress.

Mexican-Americans fare no better in the higher educational system. Indeed, the collegiate history of Mexican-Americans was virtually nonexistent up until World War I. However, by 1971 Mexican-American students made up 10 percent of the total college enrollment in the five states of the midwest: Arizona, California, Colorado, New Mexico, and Texas.[79] They have a long way to go, though, given their low percentage of high school graduates (only 24.2 percent, as compared to 53.2 percent for the total United States);[80] and, as in the case of blacks and American Indians, those Mexican-Americans who do go on to higher education are overrepresented in community colleges.[81]

Puerto Ricans have an even lower percentage of high school graduates than Mexican-Americans—22.1 percent.[82] Only 3 percent of Puerto Rican youth in this country receive college degrees.[83] It should also come as no surprise now that Puerto Ricans, too, are overrepresented in community colleges. Given this trend toward overrepresentation of minority groups in community colleges, a closer look at this form of higher education is definitely in order.

THE ROLE OF THE COMMUNITY COLLEGE

Community colleges, in our view, are set up to perpetuate inequality. One of the most important techniques used is the "cooling-out process," which we discussed in the last chapter in the context of discouraging women from desiring to achieve. "Cooling-out," as the concept is used, attempts to lower the aspirations of individuals who aspire too high.

These students need to be convinced that they are not capable of undertaking a more extended college education. But since community colleges stand for open access and free choice of curriculum, the students *themselves* must make the decision to adjust their level of aspiration.[84]

Burton Clark has described how this system is kept hidden from the student. He writes:

> The cooling-out function of the junior college is kept hidden . . . as other functions are highlighted. The junior college stresses "the transfer function," "the terminal function," etc., not that of transforming transfer into terminal.[85]

Counselors play a key role in the cooling-out process as they seek to convince the student that he or she is not capable of doing academic work. For example, though 75 percent of community college students state their desire to transfer to a four-year school, only one-fourth to one third ever do so.[86] The usual procedure is for the lower- or working-class student to either switch to a vocational curriculum or drop out, still believing that the system did everything it could for him or her and that whatever difficulties he or she experienced were his or her own fault.[87]

Community colleges thus take students from the lower and working classes (as shown in Tables 12-1 and 12-2 below) and do little if anything to help them rise from their ascribed status. Young people are channeled into the same relative position in the social structure that their parents already occupy. Fewer than 12 percent of community college students ever complete four years of higher education, and less than 5 percent eventually graduate from professional and graduate schools or ever attain an income of over $20,000.[88]

The community college only provides an illusion of upward mobility. The function of the community college is no different from that of the lower levels of public education—the lower classes are kept in their places and come to accept their position as their own lack of ability. There is little difference between the teachers at Midway Elementary School who drill their charges into accepting failure, and the counselors and teachers at the community college who "cool-out"

TABLE 12–1   FATHER'S OCCUPATIONAL CLASSIFICATION BY TYPE OF COLLEGE ENTERED (PERCENTAGES)[89]

Type of college	Skilled, semi-skilled, unskilled	Semi-professional, small business, sales and clerical	Professional and managerial	Total
Public two-year	55	29	16	100
Public four-year	49	32	19	100
Private four-year	38	30	32	100
Public university	32	33	35	100
Private university	20	31	49	100

TABLE 12-2   FATHER'S EDUCATION BY TYPE OF COLLEGE ENTERED (PERCENTAGES)[90]

Type of college	Grammar school or less	Some high school	High school graduate	Some college	College graduate	Post-graduate degree	Total
Public two-year	12.7	21.3	31.7	19.1	11.5	3.8	100
Public four-year	12.1	19.4	34.7	17.9	11.1	4.8	100
Public university	8.0	13.9	29.0	20.3	19.0	9.8	100
Private university	4.6	9.6	21.9	18.9	24.4	20.5	100
Elite	1.2	3.5	10.6	13.1	31.3	40.5	100

those students who still have learned their place in the system. As Jerome Karabel writes:

> The latent ideology of the community college movement thus suggests that everyone should have an opportunity to attain elite status, but that once they have had a chance to prove themselves, an unequal distribution of rewards is acceptable.[91]

A vicious cycle of failure which few can overcome is begun at five years of age[92] and extended by the community college to the age of twenty. The stated purpose of the community college is supposed to be democratic and equalitarian. Its social effect turns out to be the opposite.

> Instead of blunting the pyramid of the American social and economic structure, the community college plays an essential role in maintaining it. It has become just one more barrier between the poor and the disenfranchised and the decent and respectable stake in the social system which they seek.[93]

After looking at the role of higher education in the United States, we are forced to conclude that higher education is not the wideopen means to mobility that is attributed to it. Indeed, an important aspect of it—the community college system—does just the opposite, perpetuating the class structure. To be sure, higher education does provide the opportunity for advancement; the best of the minority groups have used it, and will continue to do so, as a stepping-stone for upward mobility. However, such a tendency is far from the norm, as we have shown. And as for the future, we cannot be optimistic that any great changes will take place. The recent *Bakke* decision is a prime example. The Supreme Court found in favor of Allan Bakke, a white male, who sued to be admitted to the medical school at the University of California at Davis, on the grounds that the school admitted minority students with lower scores and at the same time upheld affirmative action programs which did not specifically use quotas. This case will probably herald a round of judicial sparring, without an end in sight.[94] In its desire to adhere to a middle-of-the-road position (in essence, to find in favor of everyone), the Supreme Court has merely supported the status quo. Left unanswered were such questions as: How many explicit directions does the decision give colleges and universities that want to consider race in order to help increase the number of minority students they admit?

What effect will the *Bakke* decision have on other claims of reverse discrimination? Will the decision ultimately encourage or discourage voluntary affirmative action programs to assist groups that have suffered discrimination?[95] On the whole, black and minority leaders appear discouraged concerning the future implications of affirmative action programs. Given the past history of this nation, we find it difficult to disagree with them.

SUMMARY

In this chapter, we have tried to show that higher education in the United States, like elementary and secondary education, is best analyzed from a perspective of power and conflict. We looked to three major areas of contention. The first concerned the struggle to establish successful colleges out of a large number of attempts. The second area was the friction between various factors within those colleges and universities which managed to survive. The third dispute we discussed was over access to higher education by minority groups, in particular the criticism that post-secondary education has not provided equal educational opportunity.

Concerning the establishment of colleges and universities, we showed how America's early colleges were based on the English model and stressed teaching and a classical liberal arts curriculum. The university, on the other hand, was based on the German university, with the emphasis upon research and science.

Given the stress upon research, American professors began to see themselves as professionals and won for themselves the rights of tenure and academic freedom. This resulted in the intensification of the already existing tension between faculty and students. We then looked at the causes and ramifications of this type of discord, and then went on to analyze what we considered to be the more important issue—student political activism and its effect on the relationship of students with their professors.

Finally, we focused upon minority group access to higher education and the strife generated there. We saw that although blacks and women had progressed tremendously, they still were far from establishing equal footing with white males. Mexican-Americans, American Indians, and Puerto Ricans were seen as making small gains, if any. They, along with blacks, were highly overrepresented in community colleges, which we see as merely providing an illusion of upward mobility for its students.

Finally, we stated that in light of the recent Bakke decision which seemed highly ambivalent, we could not predict any change in the inequality in higher education in the near future. Since this question of changing the educational system strikes us as *the* most important question concerning education, we now turn to the last section, which deals with possibilities and strategies of change.

NOTES

1. Paul Woodring, *The Higher Learning In America: A Reassessment.* New York: McGraw-Hill, 1968, p. 3.

2. Talcott Parsons and Gerald Platt, *The American University*. Cambridge, Mass.: Harvard University Press, 1973, p. 4.

3. Christopher Jencks and David Riesman, *The Academic Revolution*. Garden City, N. Y.; Doubleday, 1968, p. 1.

4. Frederick Rudolf, *The American College and University: A History*. New York: Vintage Books, 1965, p. 18.

5. Jencks and Riesman, *The Academic Revolution*, p. 8.

6. Lionel S. Lewis, *Scaling the Ivory Tower: Merit and Its Limits in Academic Careers*. Baltimore, Md.: The Johns Hopkins University Press, 1975, p. 2.

7. Ibid., p. 3.

8. Woodring, *The Higher Learning In America*, p. 11.

9. Rudolf, *The American College and University*, p. 269.

10. Ibid., p. 405.

11. Quoted in Lewis, *Scaling the Ivory Tower*, p. 5.

12. Quoted in ibid.

13. Bernard Berelson, *Graduate Education in the United States*. New York: McGraw-Hill, 1960, p. 11.

14. Lewis, *Scaling the Ivory Tower*, p. 7.

15. Joseph Ben-David, *Trends in American Higher Education*. Chicago: University of Chicago Press, 1972, pp. 16−17.

16. Ibid., p. 17.

17. Parsons and Platt, *The American University*, p. 111.

18. Rudolf, *The American College and University*, p, 414.

19. Jencks and Riesman, *The Academic Revolution*, p. 15.

20. Rudolf, *The American College and University*, p. 415.

21. William F. McHugh, "Faculty Unionism and Tenure," in Commission on Academic Tenure in Higher Education (eds.), *Faculty Tenure*. San Francisco: Jossey-Bass, 1973, p. 195.

22. Richard Hofstadter and Walter P. Metzger, *The Development of Academic Freedom in the United States*. New York: Columbia University Press, 1955, p. 467.

23. This section is adapted from Joseph A. Scimecca and Roland Damiano, *Crisis At St. John's: Strike and Revolution on the Catholic Campus*. New York: Random House, 1968, pp. 138−186.

24. John D. Donovan, *The Academic Man in the Catholic College*. New York: Sheed and Ward, 1964, p. 23.

25. Ibid., p. 24.

26. "Identity Crisis on the Catholic Campus," *Newsweek*, June 27, 1966, p. 85.

27. This section is based on Jencks and Riesman, *The Academic Revolution*.

28. For a comprehensive effort to treat student−faculty conflict from an historical and comparative framework, see Lewis Feuer, *The Conflict of Generations*. New York: Basic Books, 1969.

29. Jencks and Riesman, *The Academic Revolution*, p. 35.

30. Ibid.

31. Ibid.

32. Ibid., p. 37.

33. Ibid., p. 39.

34. This section relies heavily on Philip G. Altbach, *Student Protest in America: A Historical Analysis*. New York: McGraw-Hill, 1974; and Seymour Martin Lipset and Gerald M. Schaflander, *Passion and Politics: Student Activism in America*. Boston: Little, Brown, 1971, pp. 124−235.

35. Altbach, *Student Protest in America*, p. 4.

36. For a comprehensive history of the Intercollegiate Socialist Society, see Peter Pollak, "The Inter-collegiate Socialist Society and the Consolidation of the American University." Unpublished Ph.D. dissertation, State University of New York at Albany, 1977.

37. Altbach, *Student Protest in America*, p. 21.

38. Ibid., p. 52.

39. Lipset and Schaflander, *Passion and Politics*, p. 152. For an historical account of the rise of

settlement houses, see Judith Ann Troland, *Settlement Houses and the Great Depression.* Detroit, Mich.: Wayne State University Press, 1975.

40. Altbach, *Student Protest in America,* pp. 177—178.

41. See Everett C. Ladd, Jr., and Seymour Martin Lipset, *The Divided Academy: Professors and Politics.* New York: McGraw-Hill, 1975.

42. Michael W. Miles, *The Radical Probe: The Logic of Student Rebellion.* New York: Atheneum, 1971, pp. 31—32.

43. Ibid., p. 31.

44. Quoted in Lipset and Schaflander, *Passion and Politics,* pp. 210—211.

45. Gerald Grant and David Riesman, *The Perpetual Dream: Reform and Experiment in the American College.* Chicago: University of Chicago Press, 1978, p. 16.

46. Weinberg, *A Chance to Learn,* p. 265.

47. Jencks and Riesman, *The Academic Revolution,* p. 417.

48. Ibid., p. 418.

49. Weinberg, *A Chance to Learn,* p. 267.

50. Ibid., p. 268.

51. Ibid., pp. 274—275.

52. Ibid., p. 275.

53. Jencks and Riesman, *The Academic Revolution,* p. 425.

54. Ibid., p. 429.

55. Richard B. Freeman, *Black Elite: The New Market for Highly Educated Black Americans.* New York: McGraw-Hill, 1977.

56. Ibid., pp. 30—34.

57. Frank Brown and Madelon D. Stent, *Minorities in U.S. Institutions of Higher Education.* New York: Praeger, 1977, p. 60.

58. Research Triangle Institute, *National Longitudinal Study of the High School Class of 1972: A Capsule Description of the First Followup Survey Data,* p. 3.

59. Phyllis Stock, *Better Than Rubies: A History of Women's Education,* New York: Putnam, 1978, p. 185.

60. Ibid., p. 190.

61. Caroline Bird, *Born Female.* New York: McKay, 1970, p. 26.

62. Stock, *Better Than Rubies,* p. 190.

63. Ibid., p. 191.

64. Ibid., p. 192.

65. Ibid., p. 204.

66. Ibid., p. 205.

67. Ibid., p. 211.

68. Ibid., p. 193.

69. Judith M. Cappa (ed.), *Improving Equity in Postsecondary Education.* Washington, D. C.: National Institute of Education, December 1977, p. 13.

70. U. S. Department of Labor, "Employment and Earnings," 5 (1978), p. 153.

71. Cappa, *Improving Equity in Postsecondary Education,* p. 15.

72. Ibid.

73. Weinberg, *A Chance To Learn,* p. 337.

74. Ibid.

75. Ibid.

76. Brown and Stent, *Minorities in U.S. Institutions of Higher Education,* p. 26.

77. Ibid., p. 27.

78. Ibid.

79. Weinberg, *A Chance To Learn,* p. 341.

80. Brown and Stent, *Minorities in U.S. Institutions of Higher Education,* p. 54.

81. Weinberg, *A Chance To Learn,* p. 341.

82. Brown and Stent, *Minorities in U.S. Institutions of Higher Education,* p. 54.

83. Cappa, *Improving Equity in Postsecondary Education,* p. 12.

84. L. Steven Zwerling, *Second Best.* New York: McGraw-Hill, 1976, p. 81.

85. Burton Clark, "The 'Cooling Out' Function in Higher Education," *American Journal of Sociology, 68* (May 1960), p. 574.

86. Zwerling, *Second Best,* p. 83.

87. Ibid., p. 82.

88. Ibid., p. xiv.

89. From L.L. Medsker and J.W. Trent, "The influence of different types of public higher institutions on college attendance from varying socioeconomic levels," cited in Jerome Karabel, "Community Colleges and Social Stratification: Submerged Class Conflict in American Higher Education," in Jerome Karabel and A.H. Halsey (eds.), *Power and Ideology in Education.* New York: Oxford University Press, 1977, p. 236.

90. From American Council on Education, cited in Karabel and Halsey (eds.), *Power and Ideology in Education,* p. 237.

91. Karabel, "Community Colleges and Social Stratification," p. 234.

92. See especially Ray C. Rist, "Student Social Class and Teacher Expectations: The Self-fulfilling Prophecy in Ghetto Education," *Harvard Educational Review, 40* (1970), pp. 416–451.

93. Zwerling, *Second Best,* pp. xvi–xvii.

94. For background information on the *Bakke* decision and views on the impact it will have on higher education, see *The Chronicle of Higher Education* (July 10, 1978).

95. Cheryl M. Fields, "In the Wake of Bakke," *The Chronicle of Higher Education* (July 10, 1978), p. 10.

IV

Changing the System

13

Changing the System:
The Revolution in School Finance

Public schools are funded largely by local property taxes.[1] Although homeowners have always grumbled that their taxes are too high, it is only quite recently that the whole system of financing public education has come under attack. This controversy has centered primarily on improving the educational opportunity of children in poor districts, and the courts have been the catalyst for this heightened conflict. In the early 1970s names such as "Serrano" and "Rodriquez," while perhaps not as common as household words, were nevertheless in the consciousness of large numbers of middle- and lower-class individuals who were fighting the educational quality battle on a new front. By the late 1970s, close to half of all states had taken steps to make all school-district spending on pupils more nearly equal. What is the background of the educational finance system and what is its relationship to unequal education? These are historical questions and their answers are found in the past.

THE HISTORICAL DEVELOPMENT OF STATE SUPPORT FOR THE PUBLIC SCHOOLS

Historically, education in the United States has had diverse sources of support. The notion of financing schools at the public expense evolved in a slow and excruciatingly painful manner. The federal Constitution did not mention education, and the Tenth Amendment provided that "the powers not delegated to the United States by the Constitution, nor prohibited by it to the States, are reserved to the States respectively, or to the people." Clearly, the silence of the Constitution, coupled with the Tenth Amendment, placed the burden of public education on the states.

At first, then, there was no precedent for public education in the United States, and the first schools were private ones. Prior to the Civil War, most states largely ignored those children whose parents could not afford sending them to a private school. At best, states maintained pauper schools whose purpose was to provide rudimentary skills for the children of the poor.[2]

In 1874, the famous Kalamazoo, Michigan case brought the problem of state responsibility for education to a head. The decision of the Michigan court upheld the right of school districts in the state to levy and collect taxes, thereby paving the way for a free public school system. Nevertheless, the transition from private to public education was a complicated one. The creation of school districts with power to levy taxes for school support lasted many years, and completely free schools as we know them today came into existence during the first decades of the twentieth century.[3] At this time too, our present conceptual theories of school financing were developed.

THE DEVELOPMENT OF THEORIES OF EDUCATIONAL SUPPORT[4]

The earliest theorists concerned with the financing of public education were college professors. At the turn of the twentieth century, educational financing varied from state to state. Piecemeal legislation had produced conditions that can best be described as chaotic. Wrestling with such questions as: (1) the level of education that should be guaranteed to everyone if the general welfare was to be promoted; (2) the extent to which home rule should be encouraged; and (3) the percentage of school revenue that should come from state support, educators fashioned a basic theory of school finance.

Ellwood P. Cubberly

The development of the theory of state support of public education is usually traced to Ellwood Cubberly. His doctoral dissertation in educational administration at Teachers College, Columbia University, was published in 1905, as a monograph entitled *School Funds and their Apportionment*. In this pioneering work, Cubberly focused on the legal arrangements provided for public education, the effects of the Industrial Revolution on the distribution of wealth, and how this caused the inequalities of educational opportunity among the various school districts in New York State. According to Cubberly:

> The state owes it to itself and to its children, not only to permit the establishment of schools, but also to require them to be established—even more to require that these schools, when established, shall be taught by a qualified teacher for a certain minimum period of time each year, and taught under conditions and according to requirements which the state has, from time to time, seen fit to impose. While leaving the way open for all to go beyond these requirements the state must see that none fall below.[5]

In order to solve the problem of inequality, Cubberly proposed what has come to be known as a flat-grant aid program. Under this plan, the state would distribute aid to school districts according to the number of teachers employed in the given district. It was presumed that every district would receive some funds, thereby benefiting from the aid plan.

> The duty of the state is to secure for all as high a minimum of good instruction as is possible, but not to reduce all of their minimum; to equalize the advantage to all as nearly as can be done with the resources at hand; to place a premium on those local efforts which will enable communities to rise above the legal minimum as far as possible; and to encourage communities to extend their educational energies to new and desirable undertakings.[6]

These basic concepts stated by Cubberly almost three-quarters of a century ago are still applicable and are the basis of the dispute over the best way to finance public education. Because Cubberly's study was the first comprehensive one to be made of state school funding, his views can be used to provide a valuable benchmark for measuring progress (or the lack of it) in school allocations.

George D. Strayer and Robert Murray Haig

George Strayer and Robert Haig, colleagues of Cubberly at Columbia Teachers College, first put forth their theories on school finance in Volume I of the Report of the Educational Finance Inquiry Commission, which was published in 1923.[7] This work zeroed in on the concept of equalization of educational opportunity. They argued that the state should insure equal educational facilities to every child through a system of taxation that is uniform in relation to tax-paying ability. The provision for schools should be proportional to the population desiring education. This minimum foundation plan outlined a conceptual model for planning a state support system which incorporated the principles they had outlined:

(1) A local school tax in support of the satisfactory minimum offering would be levied in each district at a rate which would provide the necessary funds for that purpose in the richest district.

(2) The richest district then might raise all of its school money by means of the local tax, assuming that a satisfactory tax, capable of being locally administered, could be devised.

(3) Every other district could be permitted to levy a local tax at the same rate and apply the proceeds toward the cost of schools, but

(4) since the rate is uniform, this tax would be sufficient to meet the costs only in the richest district and the deficiencies would be made up by state subventions.[8]

Strayer and Haig thus emphasized both the equalization of the tax burden to support schools and the equalization of educational opportunity. They differed from Cubberly in that they attacked the reward for effort or incentive concept in his model. For them it would ''be more rational to seek to achieve local adherence to proper educational standards by methods which do not tend to destroy the very uniformity of effort called for by the doctrine of equality of educational opportunity.''[9]

Paul R. Mort

Paul R. Mort was one of Strayer's students and later became his colleague at Teachers College, Columbia University. Strayer and Haig had referred to a ''satisfactory minimum program'' to equalize education, but offered no suggestions for measuring such a program. Mort took this task upon himself in his doctoral dissertation at Columbia, which was published in 1924 as *The Measurement of Educational Need.*[10] Although Mort accepted almost completely the formulations of Strayer and Haig, he did manage to clarify their theory, advancing some ideas of his own in the process. In particular, Mort introduced the concept of ''weighting'' pupils. Under ''weighting,'' the state makes allowances for pupils enrolled in vocational education, exceptional education, or any form of compensatory education in order to provide for the extra cost of educating them.

Henry C. Morrison

Henry Morrison is sometimes forgotten by students of educational finance. Such an oversight is unfortunate, because Morrison wrote an important book in the field, *School Revenue* (1933).[11] In it, he called attention to the fact that great inequalities of wealth among school districts caused equally great inequalities in educational opportunity. He noted that although according to the United States Constitution education was a state function, many school districts had failed to fulfill that funciton in an equitable manner. Furthermore, attempts to provide equal educational opportunity either by enlarging school districts or offering state equalization funds or subsidies had failed miserably. To rectify this, Morrison proposed a system of state support in which all local school districts would be abolished and the state would take on the administration of schools and become the unit for taxation.[12]

Morrison's ideas on school reform were not well received. The mood of the country was (and still is) to emphasize local home rule. However, in the passing years, little has been done by local districts to offset the conditions that Morrison attacked. If anything, the situation has gotten worse. It is interesting to note, however, that Hawaii has established a state system with no local school districts, similar to the plan advocated by Morrison. And the Federal Elementary and Secondary Education Act of 1965 was enacted by Congress for the express purpose of remedying many of the defects in public education that Morrison recognized over fifty years ago.

TRENDS SINCE 1930

Expenditures for the public schools have greatly increased since 1930. The Great Depression had a profound effect on school financing. In 1930, about 82 percent of school revenue came from local sources, and virtually all local school tax revenue was derived from property taxes. However, during the Depression, property taxes became increasingly onerous as thousands of people found themselves out of work and lost their homes, farms, and businesses. The injustice of being required to pay property taxes when one had no income became a hot political issue. Advocates of state aid plans thus had a receptive audience for their proposals.

World War II also had a notable result on school funding, accelerating the national development of technology even more than had World War I. As Roe Johns states:

> It became apparent to all informed observers, during and immediately after World War II, that an education was a necessity not only for the benefit of the individual but also for the welfare of society. The demands for an improved quality of education became insistent throughout the nation. Furthermore, inflation was causing a rapid increase in prices that far exceeded any increase in the property tax income of the schools. The problem was further complicated by a "baby boom" starting in 1946 and continuing throughout the 1950's.[13]

A number of states began to conduct studies to deal with the rapidly changing situation. There was also a great demand to find sources of revenue other than property taxes for the public schools which would correspond more closely with price changes and school enrollment. Another reason for this need for new money resources was ownership of property was becoming less related to the sources of income of many people.[14]

Briefly, then, the basic problems and issues of state school funding cannot be separated from the problems and issues of federal and local public school financing. What should public education cost? What percent of the gross national product should be allocated to the public schools? These are questions whose answers have fluctuated with the times. In general, though, there has usually been an increase in spending for education. Whereas less than 2 percent of the gross national product was allocated to the public schools at the beginning of the twentieth century, 4.2 percent was allocated in 1970.[15] The total amount for both public and nonpublic education in 1976–1977 was 7.7 percent.[16] Yet, in spite of this tendency towards increased expenditures, no governmental authority at the federal, state, or local level has ever made any conscious decision concerning what percentage should be allocated. Whatever figure is allocated in any given year is merely the summation of the results of thousands of battles for revenue fought in over 15,000 local school districts in the United States, hundred of battles in the fifty state legislatures, and dozens of battles in Congress.[17] In short, the percent of the gross national product that has been allocated to public education since the beginning of the century has been chosen rather arbitrarily and has had no real relationship to educational needs. All of this leads us back to the perplexing question of defining and measuring the results of education and the relationship, if any, this has to educational finance.

TABLE 13–1   GROSS NATIONAL PRODUCT RELATED TO TOTAL EXPENDITURES FOR EDUCATION: UNITED STATES, SELECTED YEARS FROM 1929 to 1977.[18]

Calendar year	Gross National Product (in millions)	School year	Total (in thousands)	Percent of gross national product
1929	$103,095	1929–1930	$3,233,601	3.1
1935	72,247	1935–1936	2,649,914	3.7
1939	90,494	1939–1940	3,199,593	3.5
1945	212,010	1945–1946	4,167,597	2.0
1949	256,484	1949–1950	8,795,635	3.4
1955	397,960	1955–1956	16,811,651	4.2
1959	483,650	1959–1960	24,722,464	5.1
1965	684,884	1965–1966	45,397,713	7.2
1969	930,284	1969–1970	70,077,228	7.5
1976	1,706,461	1976–1977	131,000,000	7.7

FINANCE AND EDUCATIONAL ACHIEVEMENT

The traditional measures of education have been tests of student achievement, even though educators and educational critics rarely agree on exactly what these tests measure. Our position, as stated previously, is that these tests reflect a middle-class bias. The whole question, then, of whether dollars matter is one which must take this prejudice into account. Yet, given the inherent problems in measuring educational returns, we can still reach a general consensus. And this consensus is that the present system of financing public schools is inadequate. It survives, for the most part, because it maintains the allegiance of the middle class and the more affluent members of our society. Suburban schools have traditionally been high quality public institutions due to the socioeconomic status of the community and the willingness of parents to support tax measures which reinforce this position. This support, along with the belief in localism has resulted in the preservation of the status quo, a situation which favors the middle-class child over the lower-class one. There are, however, more and more signs that this system is coming under attack.

Attacking Educational Failure

The first substantive attack against educational failure came on the national level with the passage of Title I of the Federal Elementary and Secondary Education Act in 1965. Ralph Tyler described the general objective of Title I:

> The conditions of life today require the education of everyone who would fully participate in it. At least 15 percent to 20 percent of our children are not now attaining the level of education for employment, for intelligent citizenship, for responsible parenthood or for achieving their own individual potential. These disadvantaged children include those with one or more of various kinds of educational, cultural and emotional conditions. These children are distributed throughout our country, but the particular patterns of handicaps vary widely among the schools. The task for each of us is to study the disadvantaged children in our own school, seeking to understand their handicaps and then to work out a comprehensive program for the school, a program that is calculated to make an effective attack upon the problems these children face and that uses the resources available to the school.[19]

Although the passage of Title I implied a recognition of the need to combat the inadequacies of public education, it began under a severe handicap. Like all compensatory programs, its efforts were misguided. It merely sought to shore up individual weaknesses without addressing the problem of the system which caused the inadequacies and inequality in the first place. As Benson et al. write:

> The problem with Title I was not its theory but its practical execution. Once the Title I philosophy was accepted by most educators, they felt that their only commitment was to inject more dollars into programs for educationally disadvantaged students. Although money per se is a necessary condition for educational progress, it is not the only condition. What was needed and yet lacking was a hard look at the *kind* of educational programs being provided to raise the achievement level of the disadvantaged.[20]

All Title I accomplished was to pour more money into districts having large percentages of disadvantaged students. At the same time, there was no requirement that this money be directed solely to programs that had proved their effectiveness. In short, Title I failed to combat educational failure, and the skepticism that resulted among educators and politicians had a marked effect on other educational reform programs.[21]

State programs were no better, being characterized by inaction. This lethargy, coupled with the failure of traditional reform efforts such as Title I, pushed educational reform into the hands of national and state courts. In particular, the judiciary, after some prodding, began to concentrate on the issue of educational finance as a tool for change.

THE ROLE OF THE COURTS

Arthur Wise was one of the first to call for court intervention in educational finance. In his now-famous work, *Rich Schools, Poor Schools,* he argued that court action to protect an individual's right to vote and to obtain counsel should be extended to insure his or her right to receive an "equal education."[22]

The argument that the right to an education is as fundamental as any of those contained in the Bill of Rights was subsequently laid out in greater detail by John E. Coons, William Clune, and Stephen Sugarman. They claimed that the poor, unlike the rich, do not have the option to choose among a variety of private educational institutions. Indeed, not only are the poor without choice, but they are required by law to keep their children in inferior public schools.[23] Although one might easily assume that Coons et al. prefer state assumption of educational financing, this is not the case. Coons and his colleagues maintain the opposite: if localism in controlling educational resources can be made compatible with fiscal equality, it is to be preferred over a state-operated educational system. They write, "The citizen who is jealous of state prerogatives under the Constitution is likely also to cherish the 'prerogatives' of school district 52 over and against the state. The attitude is not only understandable but, within limits, laudable. It is usually supported upon the rationale [that] local people should support and run their own schools."[24]

As a response to the inequitable distribution of educational resources, Coons et al. lay down the proposition that "the quality of public education may not be a function of wealth other than the wealth of the state as a whole."[25] According to them, this rule is satisfied if, for example, the state establishes a system of "resource equalizing" grants. Such grants would insure that any two school districts choosing to levy the same local tax will have available the same number of dollars per sudent to spend.[26] Such a scheme is called district power equalizing.

The California Supreme Court, on August 30, 1971, accepted Coons' argument that public education represents a "fundamental interest" in the case of *Serrano* v. *Priest.* The interpretation of the California court in this decision called into question the whole system of financing public education, not only in California but in the country at large.

Serrano v. Priest

In *Serrano* v. *Priest,* the California Supreme Court condemned the entire structure of education in the state of California. The plaintiff, represented by attorneys from poverty-law agencies and universities, got a judgment that found the California school-finance system unconstitutional on the grounds that it deprived certain children of "equal educational opportunity," and consequently, of the fundamental right to success and happiness. The court's reasoning in the *Serrano* case focused on the fact that wealth (through property) seemed to play a part in the determination of school aid. Indeed, the relation of wealth to equal educational opportunity was of the utmost concern to John Serrano, Jr., in 1968. Journalist Robert Lindsey offers the following background information:

> "My son was in one of the first Head Start programs in 1964 and he learned to love school there," explains Serrano, who at 40, is now chief of social work for the Eastern Los Angeles Regional Center for the Developmentally Disabled. "When he went into the first grade, the principal called my wife and me in one day and told us they had tested our son. He said, 'If you want your son to get a decent education, you should move out of this area, because we can't give him one.' " Within a few months, the family moved from the Mexican-American barrio of East Los Angeles to the more affluent community of Whittier. The Serranos found a solution to the educational problems of their children without waiting for the educational reform that their suit would bring. As the Serranos climbed the economic ladder, the fight over the school finance issue was just beginning.[27]

In 1968, John Serrano filed suit against Ivy Baker Priest, state treasurer of California. Serrano had gone to a dinner party and met two black lawyers then working with the federally supported Western Center on Law and Poverty, a part of the Office of Economic Opportunity. The center, along with others, had been considering a challenge to the property tax, and Serrano was recruited as a plaintiff.[28]

The Serrano challenge raised fundamental questions such as whether parents should be asked to make the type of personal sacrifice Serrano did in order to obtain a decent education for their children. Should a decent education be a function of the wealth of parents? Should the state be allowed to maintain a school finance system which depends upon a local property tax reflecting the differences in local wealth?[29]

These questions contain the essence of the argument presented to the California Supreme Court. The primary issue was the use of local wealth as a basis for a state school finance structure. In the words of the court:

> Plaintiffs contend that the school financing system classifies on the basis of wealth. We find this proposition irrefutable. . . . Over half of all educational revenue is raised locally by levying taxes on real property in the individual school districts. Above the foundation program minimum, the wealth of a school district . . . is the major determinant of educational expenditures. . . . Districts with small tax bases simply cannot levy taxes at a rate sufficient to produce the revenue that more affluent districts reap with a minimal tax effort. For example, Baldwin Park citizens who paid a school tax of $5.48 per $100 of

assessed valuation, were able to spend less than half as much on education as Beverly Hills residents, who were taxed only $2.38 per $100.[30]

Concluding that the existing system tied the resources reserved for education to each community's wealth, the court promised a new rule of "fiscal neutrality," accepting verbatum Coons, Clune, and Sugarman's basic proposition that the state must not allow the level of spending for public schools to be "a function of wealth other than the wealth of the state as a whole."

The ramifications of this landmark decision were quickly seen. Local school administrators worried about the source of their next dollar. Legislators were confused as to what leadership they might provide for local school districts. And taxpayers, of course, feared the imposition of more and higher taxes.[31]

The issues involved were clearly cut. Not only did school funds depend on the individual community's wealth, but the local districts' tax bases varied widely around the state. In general, the majority of money for education is raised locally by combining the value of real property in a given district with that district's willingness to tax itself. The money which is not raised locally comes to the district via state aid programs. The court found and condemned the wide disparities in both the revenue available to individual districts and in the level of per-pupil expenditure.

The divergence among the districts, however, in and of itself was not sufficient for the court to conclude that pupils failed to receive equal protection under the law. In order to rule that, the court had to be convinced that there was inequality of educational opportunity. By accepting the plaintiff's argument the court did just this. The California Supreme Court established the main legal framework for the reform of educational financing.

A number of similar cases in other states followed *Serrano,* the most important of which were *Rodriquez* v. *San Antonio Independent School District* in Texas, and *Robinson* v. *Cahill* in New Jersey.

San Antonio v. Rodriquez

In the *Rodriquez* case, a three-judge panel of the United States District Court for the Western District of Texas ruled that the method of financing public education in Texas violated the Fourteenth Amendment. They granted state school officials a two-year grace period in which to devise a plan that would reallocate school funds to insure that educational opportunities, as measured by expenditures per student, would no longer be a function of the wealth of the local district (the value of locally taxable property per student).

On March 21, 1973, the United States Supreme Court decided the *Rodriquez* case by overturning the District Court's ruling and supporting the existing Texas school finance system. The Supreme Court did, however, leave open the possibility of opposite findings in other states.

Essentially the majority decision in the *Rodriquez* case is based on a two-part argument:

First the Court sought to determine whether the Texas system of school finance discriminated against a suspect class and whether education is a fundamental interest. A positive finding on either point would require the Court to examine Texas school finance laws under standards of strict judicial scrutiny. In regard to wealth discrimination, the first point, the Court asserted that it could not identify a disadvantaged class. It noted that because low-income people live in both rich and poor school districts, the finance system does not discriminate against a class of people whose incomes are beneath a designated poverty level. Second, the Court noted that there is no group who because of its poverty (in terms of income or property) is *completely* excluded, or absolutely deprived, from enjoying the benefits of public education.[32]

The Supreme Court felt that no fundamental right was at stake and therefore decided it need not apply strict judicial scrutiny to the Texas school finance system. In their opinion, the Texas system showed some rational relationship to legitimate state purposes. The Texas system was similar to those in virtually every other state, and the power to tax local property for educational purposes was a long-standing state prerogative. The Court was satisfied that the state of Texas guaranteed a minimum state-wide educational program while maintaining an appropriate level of local participation and control. In short, the Court held that the finance system in Texas had not purposely discriminated against any group or class. The Court admitted that the Texas system was far from perfect, and that better state systems existed. However, if the Court were to declare the Texas system unconstitutional because other systems could replace it, the Court would be placed in the role of a legislature, a role which it refused to play.[33]

The Court's conservative *Rodriquez* ruling sent the reform advocates back to the state courts, where decisions could be made on educational and equal-protection clauses of individual state constitutions.[34] Along these lines reformers won test cases in New Jersey, Connecticut, and Washington, and lost in Oregon and Idaho. Of these, the New Jersey decision, *Robinson* v. *Cahill* (1973), coming two weeks after *Rodriquez,* is the most important, and contains hope for reform.

Robinson v. *Cahill*[35]

On April 3, 1973, the New Jersey Supreme Court declared the existing system for funding public elementary and secondary education in New Jersey to be unconstitutional, and ordered the state legislature to devise an adequate plan. After three years and over a dozen proposals later, the Court was forced to rule that since no satisfactory plan had been proposed, no public funds could be spent for the operation of any public school in the state after June 30, 1976. Thus, while other states celebrated the nation's bicentennial, New Jersey made history by becoming the only state whose entire school system has been totally shut down.

The events leading up to New Jersey's dubious distinction began in 1970, when a young Jersey City lawyer, Harold Ruvoldt, Jr., filed a complaint which cited students in Jersey City who were not getting an adequate education because the city lacked the tax base to pay the bill. The plaintiff, Kenneth Robinson, was chosen because he came from a family that owned property in Jersey City, he was a student at a local elementary school, and his mother, Ernestine Robinson, like John Serrano, was willing to cooperate. The mayors and boards of education in Jersey City, Plainfield, Paterson, and East Orange and Jersey City's board of school estimate joined Robinson as plaintiffs.

The plaintiffs' arguments were essentially similar to those of school finance reformers in other states. Students in some school districts received an education that cost substantially less than that received by children in other school districts in New Jersey. On behalf of the plaintiffs, Ruvoldt contended that:

> education was a fundamental interest and that delegation of responsibility for education by the state to localities whose property wealth varied widely consti-tuted a classification of students on the basis of wealth, a constitutionally sus-pect distinction among citizens. The Court, he argued, must strictly scrutinize the state's educational finance system to determine if it denied some students equal protection of the laws as guaranteed by the Fourteenth Amendment of the United States Constitution and by the New Jersey Constitution. The quality of a child's education may not be a function of the wealth of the community in which he lives. . . .[36]

The state of New Jersey, it was further charged, provided fewer educational oppor-tunities to black children like Kenneth Robinson than to white children.

One of the more interesting tactics used by the plaintiffs was the calling of ten expert witnesses to testify that the quality of education was related to the amount spent. Ruvoldt then asked defense witnesses if improvements in the quality of inadequate education programs required additional funds. Authorities from the department of education could hardly disagree given that the official position of the commissioner of education was premised on the assumption that increased expendi-tures improved the quality of educational programs.[37]

This argument was then accepted by the state court, and the state legisla-ture was ordered to produce a comprehensive plan which did not tie the quality of a child's education to the wealth of the community in which he or she resided. Finally, after three years of haggling, more litigation, and the closing of the schools, the New Jersey state legislature formulated a comprehensive plan to equalize educa-tion, via the implementation of New Jersey's first state income tax.

The *Robinson* decision was quickly followed by other successes. In late 1976, California's Supreme Court delivered another decision that restricted even further the state's ability to rely on local property taxes to finance schools.[38] In 1977, the Connecticut Supreme Court ruled that the Connecticut system for financ-ing public schools from local property taxes was unconstitutional, charging that children from poor districts were denied the educational opportunities given to children in richer districts.[39] And in 1978, New York State's Supreme Court struck down its property tax system of funding public education.[40] Judge L. Kingsley Smith, in the New York decision, expanded the parameters of the argument, declaring that New York State must come up with a plan that would do more than equalize spending. It must also provide additional help for students in large cities, where special programs for disadvantaged children add immensely to the costs of education.[41] Also, at the time of the New York State decision, litigation in at least fifteen other states—Arkansas, Colorado, Florida, Georgia, Kansas, Louisiana, Maine, Minnesota, Mississippi, Missouri, Ohio, Oklahoma, South Dakota, West Virginia, and Wisconsin—was pending.

Thus, educational reformers, undaunted by failure in the *Rodriquez* decision, have worked toward altering the present systems of educational finance systems which discriminate against the poor and lower classes, and which do not provide equal educational opportunity. How can state systems be modified to do that? Although no all-encompassing plan has yet been devised, some attempts at substantive reform have been formulated and are worth considering.

Full State Assumption (FSA)[42]

The simplest plan to ensure financial equality would entail controlling the amount spent at the state level. The state can spend different amounts on different children in a number of ways: (1) it can stipulate that expenditures must differ at particular grade levels; (2) it may recognize that children, in order to reach their full potential, require costly compensatory and enrichment programs; (3) it can ensure that children with physical, mental, or emotional handicaps receive special programs and services (in spite of the cost); (4) it can make available to children demonstrating special talents specialized courses which would help them develop these talents; and (5) it can mandate that vocational and technical programs be made available to students who desire them.[43]

The basic premise of an FSA plan is that people in similar circumstances will be treated similarly. The distribution of educational resources is thereby based solely on two criteria: (1) learning requirements of individual students; and (2) the prices of educational goods and services (the purchased inputs of the educational process).[44] A second plan is called District Power Equalizing.

District Power Equalizing (DPE)

Under the DPE plan, local districts maintain a degree of control over the level of local spending, but on the whole, revenues available to support educational programs are not based upon local wealth. For example, if the district does not raise enough money to reach the basic expenditure level, the state must make up the difference. But if a district raises more than the guaranteed level, the excess is taken by the state for redistribution to poorer districts.

Comparison of FSA and DPE

Both FSA and DPE preserve the structure of present district lines. DPE, however, unlike FSA, requires some kind of local levy as a measure of effort. In most instances local districts would have to levy a tax on property to raise their share of the costs.

On the other hand, the clear advantage of FSA is the degree of equality achieved. As Benson et al. point out:

> Other plans that permit variations in local district spending open up the possibility that some children will be denied access to educational opportunities. Even if other plans eliminate wealth biases, only FSA eliminates discrimination on the basis of location.[45]

Drawbacks of the FSA plan include the assumption that the state can wisely define a good education and its cost. The problem with such an interpretation is that little is really known about the process of learning. What is the optimal class size for effective learning? What kinds of experiences and background should a teacher have? What books, technologies, and programs should be used? These are questions to which there are no ready answers. Since no one really knows what "effective and efficient education" is, it becomes impossible to determine what it should cost. As Benson and his colleagues so perceptively state the problem: "Any dollar amount established by an FSA plan will be based somewhat on intuition and guesswork but mostly on politics."[46]

The inherent problems in the two plans can be summed up as follows:

> We are led to a choice between two systems—one that emphasizes the rather vague value of subsidiarity and requires some degree of sacrifice on the part of some children (DPE), and another that is unconcerned with subsidiarity and ensures that all children will receive not less than some specified level of educational expenditure (FSA).[47]

In short, although both plans try, there is no guarantee in either that the rights of the poor to an equal education will be insured. The next question is, where does this leave us?

EDUCATIONAL FINANCE REFORM AND THE POOR—WHERE TO?

The importance of public schools is inescapable. As Russell Harrison states: "The pattern of organization, administration and budgeting for public schools have a direct impact on how and where we live, and the way our children will live."[48] The basic problem, then, with the educational finance system, as we see it, is that lower-income families are trapped in the public educational system. Already saddled with a heavy tax burden to support public education, they cannot afford the alternative of private education. Public schooling quite simply has resulted in a disproportionately higher rate of failure for students of lower-status parents.

Unfortunately, as yet no equitable system has been devised. And although there is reason for some elation at the recent state-level decisions which offer hope for alleviating the plight of the children of poor parents, there is as much reason to despair. In particular, the passage of the Jarvis–Gann Initiative (more popularly known as Proposition 13) by the people of California, may eventually prove to be the undoing of the gains won in the courts. Proposition 13, which mandated the rolling back of property taxes to one percent of 1975–1976 assessments, cut California's tax revenue by nearly $7 billion. Although some of this was made up by other taxes and California's $5 billion surplus, the first cutbacks were made in the schools, as California's two largest districts, Los Angeles and San Diego, eliminated summer school programs.[49] While it is easy to talk about "fat cats" and waste in government spending, we see the implication for education of Proposition 13 and measures like it as representing an erosion of the middle class' consensus for paying for schools. If such a withdrawal of support would usher in a revamping of the system, we would applaud it. However, on the basis of past lessons, we believe that a power struggle will emerge over the scarcer educational resources, and the poor, lacking power, will again come out on the short end.

SUMMARY

In this chapter, we were concerned with the system of financing public education (a system based on local property taxes), and the challenges being lodged against it. After looking at how this particular system developed, and at the theories of educational support formulated by such theorists as Ellwood P. Cubberly, George Strayer, Robert Haig, Paul Mort, and Henry C. Morrison, we turned to the role of the courts in the conflict that has arisen over school funding. Specifically, we focused on what are now regarded as landmark decisions in school finance: *Serrano* v. *Priest,* (1971); *Rodriquez* v. *San Antonio* (1973); and *Robinson* v. *Cahill* (1973).

In the first of these decisions, *Serrano* v. *Priest,* the California State Supreme Court held that the level of spending for public schools should not be "a function of wealth other than the wealth of the state as a whole." Before reformers could make headway, though, the United States Supreme Court decided in the *Rodriquez* case that the existing Texas school finance system, which was similar to California's, was not discriminatory against any class of people and therefore did not violate the state and federal constitutions. The Supreme Court did, however, leave open the possibility of opposite findings in other states. Such a finding occurred in New Jersey in the *Robinson* decision, where the state funding system was declared unconstitutional and the state legislature ordered to propose a plan which would ensure equal educational opportunity for all students in New Jersey without favoring those who come from property-rich districts.

We then discussed two plans for revising the educational finance system: Full State Assumption (FSA), and District Power Equalizing (DPE). Both plans were found wanting in that the first (FSA) only ensures a minimum level of expenditure, and the second (DPE) is based on the vague value of subsidiarity as well as the unequal sacrifices required among children.

We concluded by stating that although we are uncertain as to what the eventual impact of Proposition 13 movements will be on state educational finance plans, we are afraid that the poor will be the losers. The so-called "taxpayers revolt" is a middle-class one which will benefit the middle class. If the lower classes are to make headway in the educational system, the impetus must be from another direction. With this in mind, we turn to other strategies which have been offered as possibilities for changing America's system of public education.

NOTES

1. The state of Hawaii is an exception; there, state revenues provide virtually all of the funds for public education.

2. Charles A. Tesconi and Emmanuel Hurwitz, Jr. (eds.), *Education For Whom?* New York: Dodd, Mead, 1974, p. 52.

3. Ibid.

4. This section is based on Roe L. Johns, "State Support for Public Schools," in Roe L. Johns, Kevin Alexander, and Dewey Stollar (eds.), *Status Impact of Educational Finance Project: Vol. 4.* Gainsville, Fla.: National Educational Finance Project, 1971, pp. 1–28; and Russell S. Harrison, *Equality in Public School Finance.* Lexington, Mass.: Lexington Books, 1976.

5. Ellwood P. Cubberly, *School Funds and Their Apportionment.* New York: Teachers College, 1905, p. 16.

6. Ibid., p. 17.

7. George D. Strayer and Robert Murray Haig, *The Financing of Education in the State of New York; Report of the Educational Finance Inquiry Commisison: Vol. I.* New York: Macmillan, 1923, p. 173.

8. Ibid., p. 174.

9. Ibid., p. 175.

10. Paul R. Mort, *The Measurement of Educational Need.* New York: Teachers College, 1924.

11. Henry C. Morrison, *School Revenue.* Chicago: University of Chicago Press, 1933.

12. Ibid.

13. Johns, "State Support For Public Schools," p. 19.

14. Ibid.

15. Ibid.

16. *Digest of Educational Statistics.* Washington, D. C.: U. S. Department of Health, Education and Welfare, 1977–1978, p. 23.

17. Johns, "State Support for Public Schools," p. 21.

18. Modified from *Digest of Educational Statistics, 1977–1978.*

19. Ralph Tyler, "The Task Ahead," in U. S. Office of Education, *National Conference on Education of the Disadvantaged.* Washington, D. C.: U. S. Government Printing Office, 1966, p. 63.

20. Charles S. Benson, Paul M. Goldfinger, E. Gareth Hoachlander, and Jessica S. Pers, *Planning For Educational Reform: Financial and Social Alternatives.* New York: Dodd, Mead, 1974, pp. 29–30.

21. Ibid., p. 30.

22. Arthur E. Wise, *Rich Schools, Poor Schools: The Promise of Equal Educational Opportunity.* Chicago: University of Chicago Press, 1968.

23. John E. Coons, William H. Clune III, and Stephen D. Sugarman, "Educational Opportunity: A Workable Constitutional Test for State Financial Structures," *California Law Review, 57* (April 1969), pp. 387–389.

24. John E. Coons, William H. Clune III, and Stephen D. Sugarman, *Private Wealth and Public Education*. Cambridge, Mass.: Harvard University Press, 1970, p. 15.

25. Coons et al., "Educational Opportunity," p. 311.

26. Benson et al., *Planning For Educational Reform*, p. 39.

27. Robert Lindsey, "New Battles Over School Budgets," *The New York Times Magazine*, September 18, 1977, p. 19.

28. Ibid.

29. Tesconi and Hurwitz, *Education For Whom?*, p. 61.

30. *Serrano* v. *Priest*, California Supreme Court. *California Reporter*, Vol. 96, 1971, p. 608.

31. Tesconi and Hurwitz, *Education For Whom?*, pp. 57−58.

32. Benson et al., *Planning For Educational Reform*, p. 41.

33. *San Antonio Independent School District* v. *Rodriquez*. U. S. Supreme Court, No. 71-1332, March 21, 1973.

34. Lindsey, "New Battles Over School Budgets," p. 64.

35. This section is based on Richard Lehne, *The Quest for Justice: The Politics of School Finance Reform*. New York: Longman, 1978.

36. Ibid., p. 29.

37. Ibid., p. 39.

38. Ibid., p. 196.

39. *The New York Times*, April 19, 1977, p. 1.

40. *The New York Times*, June 25, 1978, pp. 1, 37.

41. Ward Sinclair, "School Financing Undergoes a Revolution," *The Washington Post*, July 10, 1978, p. A3.

42. This section is based on Benson et al., *Planning For Educational Reform*.

43. Ibid., pp. 48−49.

44. Ibid., p. 49.

45. Ibid., p. 54.

46. Ibid., p. 55.

47. Ibid., p. 58.

48. Harrison, *Equality in Public School Finance*, p. 194.

49. Lou Cannon and Joel Kotkin, "Schools Feel Budget Axe in California," *The Washington Post*, June 14, 1978, pp. 8, 13.

14

Changing the System:
Liberal and Radical Strategies

In the preceding chapters, we have tried to show that the middle class has historically dominated public education in the United States. This social class bias has reinforced a pervasive bureaucratic structure which has proven to be extremely resistant to change. Educational inequality is not lessening as apologists for the schools tell us, but is increasing—or at the very least, remaining constant. Even the movement to divorce the quality of education from wealth has not resulted in any real changes in the educational status quo.

One trend, though, does promise some hope for those who seek to alter the educational system. This is the dissatisfaction of large numbers of lower-class parents with the poor quality of the education their children are receiving. No longer are they, and their children, accepting without question that failure in school is the result of individual inadequacies. In short, we are now witnessing a challenge to the legitimizing function of the schools. As Leonard Fein states:

> It is only massive dissatisfaction with performance that permits large numbers of people to rally about the challenge to legitimacy. And the dissatisfaction with

performance is, in effect, a rejection of the experts' claim to expertise. It is, therefore, a fundamental challenge to the working balance between professionalism and participation, for if the professionals do not have special competence, on what basis can they claim exemption from the normal political controls? Why should laymen defer to professionals when professionalism does not lead to effective performance? And, if there is no basis for deference, does not attention quite naturally shift from the dimension of expertise—effectiveness to the dimension of participation—legitimacy?[1]

This "massive dissatisfaction" with the schools has resulted in a number of strategies to change the nature of the schools. We will, in this chapter, present what we consider to be the more important of these strategies, dividing them into liberal ones (which merely try to reform the existing system) and radical ones (which seek to completely overhaul American society and its schools). Though we are in sympathy with the radical strategies, we cannot at this time hope for their fruition, given what we see as their naivete concerning possible implementation. For this reason, we offer a third category, which for want of a better term we will call radical—liberal, and present, under this rubric, a description of the movement toward decentralization—community control; we see this reorganization as the most viable educational strategy for helping the poor and lower class to overcome the failure that has characterized their educational experience.

LIBERAL STRATEGIES FOR CHANGE

The Alternative School Movement

Starting in the mid-1960s, the United States has witnessed the rise of free schools, open schools, minischools, schools-without-walls, schools-within-walls, and dozens of other alternatives to the public school system. Because these different types of schools are so diverse in name as well as in educational goals, for the purpose of parsimony we will refer to them collectively as "alternative schools." If they have a common theme, it is that they are nonsectarian schools which cater to white, middle-class students of average or above average abilities—students, in short, who are capable of succeeding in traditional public schools.[2] As for numbers, they represent less than one percent of elementary and secondary schools in the United States.

For the most part, the emergence of the contemporary alternative school movement has been characterized by an unprecedented degree of parental concern and intervention in their children's education. Not content to merely attend PTA meetings or gripe to the local administrators, some parents have created, staffed, or supported schools of their own.[3] Basically, the alternative school movement entails a dissatisfaction on the part of the middle class with public education—a general awareness that the school which was set up to serve the public has grown unresponsive to them. Bonnie Barrett Stretch has summarized this frustration:

The revolt today is against the institution itself, against the implicit assumption that learning must be imposed on children by adults, that learning is not something one does by and for oneself, but something designated by a teacher. Schools operating on this assumption tend to hold children in a prolonged state of dependency, to keep them from discovering their own capacities for learning, and to encourage a sense of impotence and lack of worth. The search is for alternatives to this kind of initiation.[4]

For the most part, contemporary alternative schools have originated from two major sources. First, they have been influenced by those groups which have traditionally stimulated educational innovation: universities, professors, school administration, corporations, foundations, and the federal government. Secondly, and that which brings a uniqueness to the movement, it has grown out of the disillusionment of parents, students, and teachers.[5] It is because of the latter groups that alternative schools have received so much publicity and that we do not believe it will cause any real change in the present educational system. Started by, catering to, and supported by the middle class, such a movement focuses upon that group least harmed by public schooling in the United States. Indeed, this middle-class interest has insured that alternative schools would be successful. For "in a school that is solidly middle-class it can be expected that any happy, healthy child will eventually learn to read, write, and do basic arithmetic, whether or not he is formally taught."[6] For this reason, although we tend to agree with the criticism of traditional schools raised by alternative school advocates,[7] we see it as being of limited value. The major problem of our nation's public schools is that they support the pervasive inequality in our society. Alternative schools at best make it more pleasant for middle-class children (who would achieve anyway) to succeed. They do not address the power relations of schools and therefore offer no alternative scheme for restructuring the system.

Educational Vouchers[8]

The voucher system is an experiment which would give parents vouchers to pay for the cost of their children's education, redeemable at the school of their choice. Under the plan, an Educational Voucher Agency (EVA) would be established in a community. The EVA would resemble a traditional board of education in that it would be locally controlled and would receive federal, state, and local aid to finance the education of the students within its confines. However, unlike the traditional board, it would not operate any schools of its own. This responsibility would remain with the public and private school boards already in existence. The purpose of the EVA would be to issue vouchers to all parents of schoolchildren in its area. The parents would then take their voucher to the school in which they wanted to enroll their child. They would have the choice of going to any school they desired, public or private. If the school meets the basic eligibility requirements established by the EVA, it would be able to convert the voucher to cash, which would then cover its operating expenses and the amortization of capital costs. The voucher system would enable anyone starting a school to receive public subsidies, so long as they met the basic educational requirements laid down by the EVA and could get enough parents to enroll their children in the school. This program would also give low-income parents the same choice as to where they want to send their children as upper-income parents now have. The voucher system, set up in this manner, seeks to break the monopolistic hold that public schools have over the poor. ''Under a voucher system parents who do not like what a school is doing can simply send their children elsewhere. Schools which attract no applicants go out of business.''[9]

In order to cash in the vouchers, a school would have to offer every student an equal chance of admission. Schools would thus have to announce in advance just how many children they can take in the following year. Parents would then apply and the school would have to take in every student there was space for. In the case of an excess of applicants, the school would be mandated to fill at least half its places by lottery. As high a proportion of minority students as applied would have to be accepted, so that no school could take only the most easily educated students.

It is important that the redemption value of a middle- or upper-income family's voucher approximate the amount that the local public schools would spend on upper-income children. Vouchers for children from low-income families should, therefore, have a somewhat higher redemption value.[10] Participating schools would also be mandated to accept every child's voucher as full payment for his or her education, regardless of its value. Otherwise, those parents who could afford to supplement their children's vouchers would have a better chance of getting their children into higher-cost schools than could lower-income parents who could not spend extra money.

An educational system constituted in this manner could offset the economic and racially exclusive system based on housing patterns now in existence. Under the voucher system, no child could be excluded from a school because his parents could not afford to buy a house near the school. Most families, black and white, would doubtless prefer schools close to home, but at least under the voucher system they would be given a choice of what school they wanted their child to attend. They would not be legally or, as is more often the case, financially required to choose a school they thought educationally inferior. As an additional measure, to insure that every family had access to school, the EVA would pay transportation costs to all schools. Under the voucher system, therefore, lower- and working-class parents would have some say in where they could send their children to school.

A number of criticisms of the voucher system have been raised. One very important objection is that the EVA would have complete control over establishing rules and regulations, perhaps becoming extreme in either direction. State and local regulatory efforts might be uneven or possibly nonexistent. In particular, regulations designed to prevent racial and economic segregation are likely to be watered down or unenforced. While this criticism has merit, advocates answer that the questions raised are just as likely to apply to boards already in existence. Parents and school boards who desire segregated schools have no trouble in finding them and keeping them in operation under the present system.

A second objection is that parents do not have the knowledge (or, as some claim, the "intelligence") to make wise choices among schools. "Giving parents a choice will, according to this argument, simply set in motion an educational equivalent of Gresham's Law, in which hucksterism and mediocre schooling drive out high quality institutions."[11] Such a protest is overtly condescending to lower-class parents and goes against democratic principles.

A third critique is that the voucher system would "destroy the public schools." Since many wealthy parents send their children to public schools they consider to be academically strong, the argument loses much of its potency.

The fourth, and most important, criticism of the voucher system is that it would do little to alter the political structure. EVAs would be controlled by the same political forces that now dominate school boards and would recreate (under the sanction of educational innovation) the same school systems we now have. Although lower- and working-class parents would be given a say as to what schools their children could attend, there is no guarantee that they would have any say over the educational process itself. The voucher system would, therefore, still leave the power to control education (the distinction between "public" and "private" would no longer be important) to the middle class and to professional educators. Given that this coalition has been in control of the schools for at least the past fifty years and has not altered the inequality that permeates education today, there is very little likelihood that the voucher system would provide for any real changes. The voucher system, then, although it goes farther than the usual "individualistic" reforms, still falls far short of actually restructuring the educational system. By failing to provide an alternative to the already existing power relationships, it merely offers cosmetic reforms which, in the long run, would still support the status quo. If the educational system is to change, a redistribution of power is necessary. The voucher system does not provide such a reorganization; therefore, it seems unlikely, even if it were to be instituted on a large scale, that it would alter the disparity in the public schools.[12]

RADICAL STRATEGIES FOR CHANGE

Deschooling[13]

The idea of deschooling originated with Ivan Illich and Evert Reimer,[14] both of whom were concerned with educational development in Latin America. Illich and Reimer first met in Puerto Rico in 1958. Illich, a Catholic priest, was at the time Vice-Chancellor of the Catholic University of Puerto Rico and a member of the Commonwealth Board of Higher Education. Reimer was Executive Secretary of the Committee on Human Resources of the Commonwealth. Reimer, in his capacity as secretary, developed an educational program to meet Puerto Rico's manpower needs, which recommended the reduction of dropouts from all levels of the school system through the lessening of grade standards. The plan was implemented, but it was later found that although students were staying in school longer, they were not learning more.

Reimer joined the Alliance for Progress in 1962 as an advisor and saw that other Latin American countries suffered from the same educational problems as did Puerto Rico. Reimer quickly came to the conclusion that the costs of expanding schooling in Latin America was well beyond the economic resources of the Latin American countries.

Illich, meanwhile, had gone to Mexico in 1961 to train missionaries and volunteers for service in the schools of South America. He quickly became aware that the people he trained were not reaching the poor of Latin America. In fact, he found that they were supporting the power of the upper classes by operating school systems that never reached the masses. Illich's concern for the development of effective social and educational leadership for underdeveloped Latin American nations led him to organize the Center for Intercultural Documentation in Cuernavaca (CIDOC) as an independent institution for Latin American studies. By the late 1960s, Illich and Reimer (who had by then come to CIDOC) began a systematic analysis of schooling and school systems.[15]

The idea of deschooling, therefore, arose out of the inability of underdeveloped and Third World countries to support universal schooling, and the tendency of schooling in Latin America to reinforce the position of the upper classes. Illich, in his book, *Deschooling Society,* advocates the abolition of schools, not their reform. According to him, deschooling represents a social revolution because it means destroying the poor's faith in and acceptance of schooling as a means of achieving success. The trust in an educational equality that does not exist has led to the submissiveness of the poor. The poor accept the myth that they are poor because they did not make it through school. This conviction is predicated on their belief that they were given a fair chance for advancement.

Deschooling implies getting rid of schools and a differentiation and separation of the process of education from the process of schooling. In Illich's words:

> Schools are designed on the assumption that there is a secret to everything in life; that the quality of life depends on knowing that secret; that secrets can be known only in orderly succession; and that only teachers can properly reveal the secrets. An individual with a schooled mind conceives of the world as a pyramid of classified packages accessible only to those who carry the proper tags. New educational institutions would break apart this pyramid. Their purpose must be to facilitate access for the learner: to allow him to look into the windows of the control room or the parliament, if he cannot get in by the door. Moreover, such new institutions should be channels to which the learner would have access without credential or pedigree—public spaces in which peers and elders outside his immediate horizon would become available.[16]

A deschooled society would rest on the basic premise that when an individual wanted to learn something he or she would find some way of learning it. Learning is best accomplished if it is tied to a goal. Illich argues that if someone wants to learn something he or she will seek out someone to teach this skill. Networks of learning would then be established, enabling one to find out who could teach what one wants to know. Illich believes that there are no more than four "channels" or learning exchanges which contain all the resources needed for real learning. He uses the term "opportunity web" to designate specific ways to provide access to each of the four sets of resources. The four opportunity webs are:

1. Reference Services to Educational Objects—which facilitate access to things or processes used for formal learning. Some of these things can be reserved for this purpose, stored in libraries, and showrooms like museums and theatres; others can be in daily use in factories, airports, or on farms, but made available to students as apprentices or on off-hours.
2. Skill Exchanges—which permit persons to list their skills, the conditions under which they are willing to serve as models for others who want to know these skills, and the addresses at which they can be reached.
3. Peer Matching—a communications network which permits persons to describe the learning activity in which they wish to engage, in the hope of finding a partner for the inquiry.
4. Reference Services to Educators-at-Large—who can be listed in a directory of professionals, paraprofessionals, and freelancers, along with conditions of access to their services.[17]

Although Illich's ideas are extremely provocative and get right to the heart of the matter—the structure of society and the schools' relationship to this structure—there is a fundamental problem with his deschooling solution. Society consists of institutions and institutional orders which have existed for a long time and are grounded in very real human needs.[18] And even though the bureaucratic structure is a relatively new phenomenon in the history of mankind, it has become an objective reality, and no amount of argument will wish it away. Deschooling implies deinstitutionalization, and the educational institution will not disappear unless there is a revolution in this country, or indeed, in the world. At present this seems a highly unlikely occurrence. American society will not deinstitutionalize, will not deschool. Secondly, and equally important, even if deschooling theoretically did occur, given the prior socialization of the poor, there is little likelihood that the poor would take advantage of the deschooled society, and improve their lot. They would have to be resocialized to do this, and without institutions this is almost an impossibility. For these two reasons, we feel that it is impractical to expect that deschooling will take place in the near future.[19]

Schooling in Socialist America

As we stated in Chapter 1, we believe that Bowles and Gintis, in their book, *Schooling in Capitalist America,* have offered one of the more perceptive and sophisticated radical critiques of education in the United States. Nonetheless, although we share many of their basic concerns, we do differ with what we consider to be their economic determinism and with their strategies for change, which are tied to their economic views.

Essentially, Bowles and Gintis call for a socialist revolution in the United States. Because they see the major characteristic of the educational system in America as the production of a work force for the capitalist system, they conclude that a liberating school system requires a revolutionary transformation of economic life.[20] Just how this "revolutionary transformation" is to come about, however, is unclear. For example, they skirt the question of violence, stating on the one hand that it seems "almost inconceivable that a socialist revolution in the United States would not involve violence at some stage," and then that violence must be "assigned to a position of secondary importance."[21]

Their plan for ushering in a socialist society (which would then, by their definition, bring with it a democratic, humanitarian educational system) calls for the creation of a working-class consciousness, which would enable working-class groups to embrace as allies others in similar positions of deprivation and exploitation.[22] Workers who seek higher pay would protect consumers' rights; secondary-status jobs and discriminatory hiring would be eliminated. Popular revolutionary groups would coordinate the end product of this new consciousness.[23]

There are two major problems, as we see it, with Bowles and Gintis' proposals for change. The first has been stated succinctly by Diane Ravitch, who writes:

> They [Bowles and Gintis] emphasize whatever supports their thesis and ignore or explain away whatever doesn't. Events of the past are shown either to correspond to capitalist imperatives or to be contradictions generated by capitalism. School reforms that took root were a sham because they bolstered the capitalist system, and school reforms that failed were rejected because they threatened the capitalist system. The argument is not susceptible to disproof: The schools don't promote equality or personal liberation because the capitalist system won't let them, but when they do, it is in order to delude the people and serve capitalism. Both A and not-A are advanced as evidence for the same point.[24]

Second, Bowles and Gintis contradict themselves. On the one hand, their analysis is based on the "correspondence principle"—that the production processes ultimately determine all social institutions and practices in society[25]—and therefore the only way to revolutionize education is to revolutionize society. On the other hand, though, they end their book by offering guidelines toward a socialist strategy for education. These range from pressing for the democratization of the schools by socialist and radical educators to curriculum reforms.[26] Lacking a viable blueprint for change, they fall back on the very same liberal-conservative solutions they initially condemn as counterproductive.

In short, although we would agree with Bowles and Gintis' assertion that the easiest way to change education is to change society, we do not foresee the

United States becoming a socialist nation in the immediate (or for that matter, even the distant) future. That we live in a society dominated by corporate capitalism is undeniable, but to believe that a radical restructuring of the economic process is forthcoming seems naive. Unfortunate though it might be, capitalism has proven flexible enough to incorporate many of the contradictions Marx pointed to—so much so that its resiliency seems undeniable. Rather than wait for contradictions to bring down the system, a more practical strategy is needed. One such strategy, we believe, already exists, one which combines both liberal and radical reforms—that of decentralization–community control.

DECENTRALIZATION–COMMUNITY CONTROL: A RADICAL-LIBERAL STRATEGY FOR CHANGE

The critical question confronting educational reformers is: are schools a viable source of societal change, or vice versa? It can be inferred from the above critique of major liberal and radical strategies for educational change that liberal strategists tend toward the view that by reforming the schools, change in the society will follow; radical theorists take the opposite view, that society must be radically altered if the schools are to make a dent in the pervasive inequality that characterizes America's stratification system.

The position offered here falls between these two views. Rather than posit massive societal change which we do not see as imminent, we instead stress structural change. The bureaucratic nature of public schools must be changed if educational inequality is to be eliminated. Bureaucratically run schools, as Michael Katz points out:

> are imperial institutions designed to civilize the natives; they exist to do something to poor children, especially, now, children who are black or brown. Their main purpose is to make these children orderly, industrious, law-abiding, and respectful of authority. Their literature and their spokesmen proclaim the schools to be symbols of opportunity, but their slitted or windowless walls say clearly what their history would reveal as well: They were designed to reflect and confirm the social structure that erected them.[27]

Bureaucracy inhibits reform, creating a resistance to change which often sabotages innovations. When this fails, bureaucracies fall back on a time-tested strategy—they blame the victim.[28] In this case, the educational system claims that pupils fail because they come to the schools from deprived cultural backgrounds.

Educational bureaucrats refuse to accept what we have argued throughout this work—that education is a political process. The reason for the existing educational system is that one group has historically been able to impose its will and values on another; in order to change the educational system, power relations must be changed. If lower- and working-class children are failing in the schools because their parents do not have the power to offset the advantages of the middle class and those upper-class individuals who send their children to public schools, then the lower and working classes must somehow share in the educational power structure. However, to insure the participation of lower-income parents is, of course, easier said than done. Neither teachers (who have just recently achieved some power) nor superintendents and middle-class school boards (who have had a long tradition of dominance) are suddenly going to see the light and share their authority. It is the lower classes themselves who are going to have to play a part in initiating the changes that would give their children an equal chance in the schools. It is precisely because decentralization—community control can do just this that we see it as a real possibility for producing educational change.

What is Decentralization—Community Control?

Decentralization and community control are two concepts which, although usually linked together, need not be so. Decentralization means only administrative reform, while community control implies political restructuring. Administrative decentralization, then, when used alone, should not be mistaken for community control. It can facilitate community participation by locating decision-making agencies close to the community, but in and of itself it does not guarantee community participation. In fact, in some instances, decentralization, if it lacks sufficient decision-making authority, can thwart community wishes by deflecting them from the real focus of power.[29] Therefore, we will use the two terms together, (decentralization—community control) to describe the alternative education system proposed here, one that involves a sharing of the decision-making.

Origins of Decentralization—Community Control

The recognition of a declining educational climate and a lack of success in achieving integration led to the emergence of the decentralization—community control concept as a new method for achieving real changes in education. This idea was predicated on the realization that the political environment of school decision-making was *the* determinant of the quality of education.[30]

Decentralization—community control as a concept was born among a group of parents and activists at Intermediate School 201 in New York City, who had struggled for years to integrate the school. In the summer of 1966, faced with the realization that they were no nearer to their goal than when they had begun, they asked the New York City Board of Education for a direct voice in the operation of the school. They used the phrase "community control" for the first time. Many of the community activists and parents were trained in the Community Action Programs (CAP) funded by the War on Poverty, and they recognized the futility of nonpolicy-making participatory roles for community people. In essence, they shifted the emphasis from community participation to community control. They were joined by middle-class reformers who called for the decentralization of school systems to make them more responsive to community interests.[31]

The parents did not abandon integration; they merely reestablished a prior claim for quality education. Fantini and Gittell comment on this:

> What they did not fully realize was that both efforts, integration and decentralization—community control, attacked the same institutional core: a status-oriented school system devised to protect middle-class interests. Both reforms tampered with the distribution of power, which concentrated control in the hands of school professionals, who would feel threatened by any change in the structure. It was not an accident that the alignment of forces on both issues tended to be the same. Many who opposed integration generally opposed decentralization, whereas many of those who had long supported integration were in the forefront of the movement for local neighborhood control of schools.[32]

Since New York City's attempts to decentralize its school system were the most massive, well-known, and conflict-ridden, we will describe the problems that manifested themselves in this "experiment."

New York City's central Board of Education had long been seen as a cumbersome and unwieldly educational policy-making agency.[33] Calls for decentralization had begun to develop into concrete suggestions as early as 1967, when the Public Education Association (composed primarily of white parents), the mayor's office, local groups, and even the Board of Education itself suggested various means of achieving decentralization.[34] In April of that year, the New York State Legislature offered increased state aid to New York City conditional on Mayor John Lindsay's presenting a decentralization plan to the New York State Board of Regents (the chief educational agency in the state) by December 1967. Lindsay named a blue-ribbon panel headed by McGeorge Bundy, former Kennedy administrator and then President of the Ford Foundation. Bundy appointed Mario Fantini as executive secretary of what became known as the Bundy panel. The New York City Board of Education, however, seeking to avert any radical reorganization and lessening of its powers, moved to head off the Bundy panel by instituting a trial program of its own. The Board announced that three experimental districts, the IS 201 district in Harlem, Twin Bridges on the Lower East Side, and Ocean Hill—Brownsville in Brooklyn would be created. As one observer phrased it: "The sincerity of the Board is open to question, since local powers were never defined, and every time the local board attempted to exercise either power or initiative, the Board declared that they had never meant the experimental group to do such things."[35] In the fall of 1967, the Bundy plan for school decentralization was issued,[36] and important elements of the plan were written into legislative recommendations by the New York State Board of Regents in the 1968 legislative session.

New York City educators were immediately alarmed by the proposed changes. The President of the Board of Education, Alfred Giardino, the sole dissenting member of the Bundy panel, sharply criticized the plan. The UFT and the Council of Supervisory Associations (CSA) joined forces to lobby against a decentralization bill based on the Bundy strategy introduced in the state legislature.

The legislature failed to confront the issue head on, and instead passed the compromise Marchi Bill, which provided for the expansion of the New York City Board of Education from 13 to 19 members. This made it possible for Mayor Lindsay to appoint new members, creating a majority who favored decentralization. This new Board was to establish an interim decentralization plan until the 1968 state legislative session could come up with one of its own.[37]

While the legislature debated the issue of decentralization for the New York City schools, the Ocean Hill–Brownsville local school board, one of the previously created experimental boards, released thirteen teachers and six supervisory personnel on May 9, 1968, precipitating one of the most bitter confrontations in American educational history. This was a real test of whether or not the local school boards had any power. Although the newspapers subsequently charged that the nineteen had been fired, the district had merely asked for their transfer. C. Herbert Oliver, the chairman of the Ocean Hill–Brownsville local board, commented on this issue. In his own words:

> We knew we could not fire anyone, so we avoided that route. The Board of Education insisted that we bring charges and go the route of firing. We refused to go that route. We decided to use a bylaw of the Board of Education and transfer out people that we felt should be transferred out. We demanded that Donovan [Superintendent of Schools] do so for the sake of our children. Donovan simply refused to transfer them out, and it appears that he would rather transfer the whole community than transfer nineteen people. This is the attitude he had. . . . This is the kind of thing we're faced with—total disregard for parents and our children.[38]

Superintendent Donovan ordered the nineteen back to work. The parents and the local board banded together to prevent their return. The UFT began to talk about a possible strike. On May 15, the central Board of Education closed three of the eight schools in the district. One week later, approximately 350 teachers in Ocean Hill–Brownsville walked out in support of their nineteen colleagues.

At the end of May, the UFT and the local board agreed to nonbinding arbitration, and well-known labor mediator Theodore Kheel was called in. Kheel suggested that all teachers except the nineteen return to work, while the talks continued. The UFT accepted this proposal, but the local board did not. On June 20, Rhody McCoy, the community-appointed district superintendent, sent dismissal notices to all 350 striking teachers. The school year drew to an end, with the expectation that the showdown between the Ocean Hill–Brownsville community and the UFT would begin in September.[39]

The new school year opened in September with over 90 percent of the city's teachers on strike. In the face of this massive show of support, the central Board of Education promised to reinstate the nineteen teachers. Two days later, the teachers returned to the schools, but those who went back to Ocean Hill–Brownsville were greeted by parents who were determined to keep the teachers out. Over the summer, McCoy had recruited young, dedicated (though inexperienced) teachers who professed a belief in decentralization–community control, and who now manned the schools. Open conflict erupted between the UFT teachers and the local community and new teachers. After two days of out-and-out hostility, the UFT called a second strike.

The city's teachers remained on strike for two weeks. Finally, Mayor Lindsay managed to convince the UFT to accept the stationing of policemen in the Ocean Hill–Brownsville schools to protect UFT teachers, and school reopened on September 30. No one informed the local board about the arrangements.[40]

A very shaky truce kept peace for two weeks. Then on October 13, the UFT voted to strike again, and the next day began the third and final walkout, one that lasted until November 19. The strike was only ended when the State Commissioner of Education, James E. Allen, stepped in, suspended Rhody McCoy and the local school board, and literally took over the district. The state trusteeship lasted for four months. until the legislature approved a watered-down decentralized plan which wiped out the Ocean Hill district, and which gave very little power to subsequent locally elected school boards around the city.[41]

Decentralization–community control as a threat to the educational status quo in New York City was virtually stopped, and the state legislature effectively diffused the problems of decentralization with the passage of the 1969 decentralization bill. Fantini and Gitell have provided an analysis of this piece of legislation.

> Local boards, as authorized in this legislation, have no control over personnel, because they are constrained by centrally negotiated contracts and centrally compiled lists of eligible teachers and principals. All budget powers, except control of a fund for local repairs. are retained by the central board. The local districts were established at a large size (20,000 students) which limits possibilities of experimentation and local prerogative. Finally, the first prodecentralization city Board of Education was removed and replaced by a relatively weak, interim Board.
>
> The interim Board of Education controlled the setting of the district boundaries for the 31 school districts. This was an essential determinant in the elections for district school boards held in the spring and summer of 1970. The districts were gerrymandered, so that, in many instances, minority groups were divided between two districts, instead of being incorporated into one, in order to make it impossible for them to control the majority of a local school board.[42]

The New York City decentralization–community control experiment is a perfect example of the importance of conflict as an analytical tool. Parents and local community activists, without any real power base, sought to establish control over the schools in their community. They came up against a system with powerful, entrenched interests favoring a continuation of the status quo. The UFT, for example, one of these factions, had just recently gained the right of collective bargaining, using this to greatly improve the lot of the teacher. As a result, the UFT had no intention of relinquishing any of its newly-won power. They, along with district supervisors, the superintendent, and the central Board (which although composed of laymen, were middle-class laymen), joined forces to fight off the lower-class parents who sought control of local schools. Decentralization—community control was seen by this coalition, and rightly so, as a threat to their authority to run the schools as they saw fit. The obvious result was conflict, and again the lower-class participants lost out.

The decentralization—community control concept, as a means of running an urban school district, underwent its first test in the Ocean Hill—Brownsville dispute with the UFT. The question, though, is whether it received a fair test as an educational innovation. We believe not. Decentralization—community control involves a power struggle. In short, we feel that decentralization—community control was and is an experiment that was never fully tested. Therefore, we must evaluate it on other grounds. We will present the major arguments for and against decentralization in hopes of giving it a fair hearing. The major criticisms of decentralization—community control and its advocates' responses to them are presented below:[43]

1. *Decentralization—community control would Balkanize the city.* The creation of a number of quasiautonomous districts would penalize children who moved from one district to another. Countering this argument is the Bundy Report, which advocated that each district be required to adhere to state educational standards.

2. *Decentralization—community control would deal a blow to integrating efforts.* Interestingly enough, this fear was most often expressed by whites. The Bundy panel, while supporting the desirability of racial integration in the schools, took the position that, in New York City, integration had become a secondary issue. A decade of efforts to reduce racial imbalance had failed due to white resistance, professional indifference, and population shifts. The panel's recommendation, did, however, preserve the right of the central board to mandate integration policies.

3. *Decentralization—community control would produce chaos and turn the schools over to "vigilantes" and "racists."* UFT President Albert Shanker, for example, stated that he feared the plan would open the way for "local vigilantes to constantly harass teachers."[44] In reply, advocates of the plan point out that the panel had written a number of strong safeguards into its plan—particularly the requirement that the community school districts would be subject to the state education law and the administrative powers of the commissioner, just as school districts always have been.

4. *Ghetto parents (if not laymen generally) are incompetent to deal with educational issues.* The argument is that laymen do not have the expertise to make decisions. Proponents of decentralization—community control reply by pointing to the traditional lay control of education. They claim that although members of school boards have the role of reflecting community concerns and needs, they are neither required or supposed to

be versed in educational technology in order to oversee the day-to-day operations of the school. Also, as a black educator states: ''We consider it an insult to be asked to prove whether we can do a better job in order to be granted the necessary resources and support. We should not be forced into answering the question, 'Can you do it better?' to those who have failed miserably in the past despite their control over substantial resources.''[45]

5. *Decentralization−community control would deprive ghetto schools of adequate staffs and would destroy the merit system.* The Bundy report points out that teachers would still be required to meet state standards, and that the present examination system had produced an administrative structure in which initiative and innovation are not rewarded.

6. *Decentralization−community control would weaken the teachers union.* Although the Bundy plan proposed that labor negotiations remain centralized, union leaders argued that the ''breakup'' of the system would make it more difficult to bargain forcefully. Also, the UFT had made inroads into administrative policy and felt that dealing with local boards would counteract their gains. This criticism is a difficult one to answer. Decentralization−community control represents a restructuring of power. Advocates argue that teacher unions must be made to see that the concept implies a sharing of power, not the destruction of teacher unions.

7. *Decentralization−community control is seen as a shrewd effort to foist responsibility for the failure of the schools onto the shoulders of the poor.* Some critics see the plan as a means of shifting blame to the community. There are few facts to refute or support this view. The panel and advocates claim that low-income parents, given the opportunity to participate, would be motivated to seek high-quality alternatives. Furthermore, the panel itself asked, what are the alternatives, given the failure over the years of educational reform?

8. *Decentralization−community control is a distraction from the need for greater comprehensive attacks on all social ills.* This argument represents an enlargement of Number 7. Until a comprehensive plan for housing, jobs, health, and so on, is instituted, every plan to reform the school will fail. Advocates of decentralization−community control fall back on the argument that schools can be major instruments of social mobility and that efforts to reform them cannot be suspended until the other institutions are reformed.

9. *Decentralization−community control deals only with administration; it does not solve financial problems or contain any educational innovations.* The argument that urban school systems are badly under-financed and would remain so under decentralization−community control cannot be refuted. The claim that decentralization would lack educational innovations represents short-sightedness and narrow thinking on the part of its critics.

POSSIBILITIES FOR THE FUTURE

Decentralization—community control offers political innovation. It seeks to break down the bureaucratic form of schooling by changing the nature of its political control.[46] Participation by parents as equal partners, and not through the sufferance of professional educators, can be an educationally potent weapon in the struggle for equality in education. Although decentralization—community control may not offer a radical reconstruction of capitalism, as called for by Marxists, it can provide the beginnings of real structural change, particularly the need to alter the power base of the educational bureaucrats who control public education.

We must be careful here to avoid misinterpretation; we are not advocating giving away control of the schools to parents, lower-class or otherwise. Such a view would ignore the conflict perspective maintained throughout this book. Teachers, for example, have fought long, hard battles to attain a measure of control over their work situation and are not going to give up gains they have recently made. And, more importantly, teachers are not the enemy. As Michael Katz points out:

> Education has not suffered from any freedom granted teachers to run schools as they see fit; it has suffered from the suffocating atmosphere in which teachers have had to work. The popular attitude, and even those of reformers, equates the aims of administrators with those of teachers; it blames teachers for bureaucracy. The important point is that a distinction must be made; teachers do not run the schools. They are, as they will often tell you, harassed by the administration, which if they are any good, continually gets in their way.[47]

Autonomy is a two-way street, and if decentralization—community control is to be given a chance, power must be shared. It must be shared on one level between parents and teachers, and on another level, among educators. In practice, this means community people must democratically elect school boards,[48] and educators must democratically elect their supervisors. Whether the community should appoint a superintendent or whether he or she should also be elected by teachers can be open to negotiation. It is important that power flow away from bureaucratically oriented administrators and toward local communities and teachers.

It is obvious that the system of education we how have, a system based on the unequal distribution of power, has only worked for some. Structural change is needed which can redistribute power in the public schools so that one group cannot dominate another, as the middle class has done to the lower class for so long. Although it is not a panacea, decentralization—community control, if given a fair chance, can alter the unequal distribution of power. In order to change the educational system, the coercive use of power by one group over another must be eliminated; anything else simply perpetuates the status quo. And while it would obviously facilitate change (assuming that such other institutions as the political, economic, and military spheres went through the same process), we cannot wait for this to happen. Education is a weak link in the chain of inequality because it, along with the family, is the only major institution that everyone is exposed to. Structural change in the schools can thereby affect change in the rest of society.

Unfortunately, however, although we would like to state that decentralization−community control is the answer, we cannot, because as we have shown, it is a strategy that has never been fairly tried.[49] All that can be said is that it offers the possibility of change. We live under a system of inequality that has resisted real change for over two centuries; thus any mention of a hope for reform should be greeted with elation. We literally have no other alternatives. Regarding access to upward mobility and genuine equality, education as "rigged" as it may be, is for the poor, still "the only game in town." Even if we cannot change the game, perhaps we can begin to change the rules.

SUMMARY

Although decentralization−community control still remains virtually an untested strategy for restructuring education in the United States, we believe it is a more viable one than the others we looked at in this chapter: alternative schools, voucher systems, deschooling, and socialistic education.

Alternative schools, at best, can make schools a pleasanter place for children to attend. Obviously, although this is a definite plus, in terms of the overall inequality so pervasive in the schools, it offers little hope for any real change. Educational vouchers, too, would not radically alter the essentially unequal nature of America's public schools, leaving the power of control still in the hands of the middle class.

Deschooling, on the other hand, would shift power relations by eliminating the very institutions that preserve the system. Practically speaking, though, it seems exceedingly unlikely that the deinstitutionalization and deschooling that Ivan Illich talks of will ever occur. The same goes for Bowles and Gintis' call for a socialist state and a socialistic system of education. Given the political, economic, and social realities of American society, the Socialist Revolution they call for seems an impossibility.

Decentralization−community control, on the other hand does offer the possibility of structural change—a chance to redress the inequality of America's educational system. Such a chance, we feel, is worth taking, for when we look at the alternatives, we are faced with a choice between impractical visions and the system as it now functions.

NOTES

1. Leonard J. Fein, *The Ecology of Public Schools*. New York: Pegasus, 1971, p. 72.

2. A noted exception to this is the free school started by Jonathan Kozol in the Roxbury section of Boston. For a description of the beginning of this school, whose clientele are mostly black and poor, see Jonathan Kozol, *Free Schools*. Boston: Houghton Mifflin, 1972.

3. Daniel Linden Duke, "The Re-Transformation of the School: Factors Relating to the Emergence of Contemporary Alternative Schools in the United States." Unpublished Ed. D. dissertation, State University of New York at Albany, 1974.

4. Bonnie Barrett Stretch, "The Rise of the Free School," in Martin Carnoy, (ed.), *Schooling in a Corporate Society*. New York: McKay, 1972, p. 211.

5. Duke, "The Re-Transformation of the School," p. 192.

6. Stretch, "The Rise of the Free School," p. 215.

7. See in particular Allen Graubard, *Free the Children: Radical Reform and the Free School Movement*. New York: Pantheon Books, 1973; Kozol, *Free Schools*; and Donald A. Myers and Lilian Myers (eds.), *Open Education Re-Examined*. Lexington, Mass.: Lexington Books, 1973.

8. This section is based on Christopher Jencks, "Educational Vouchers," *The New Republic, 163* (July 4, 1970), pp. 19–21.

9. Ibid., p. 19.

10. Ibid., p. 20.

11. Ibid., p. 21.

12. The voucher system has been tried in certain school districts around the country, the largest of which is San Jose, California. However, it is still to early to judge whether or not the experiment has produced any significant results.

13. This section is based on Ivan Illich, *Deschooling Society*. New York: Harper & Row, 1972; and Joel Spring, "Deschooling as a Form of Social Revolution," in Clarence Karier, Paul Violas, and Joel Spring (eds.), *Roots of Crisis: American Education In The Twentieth Century*. Chicago: Rand McNally, 1973, pp. 138–147.

14. For Reimer's views which are similar to Illich's, see Evert Reimer, *School Is Dead*. Garden City, N.Y.: Doubleday, 1971.

15. Spring, "Deschooling as Social Revolution," p. 139.

16. Illich, *Deschooling Society*, pp. 108–109.

17. Ibid., pp. 112–113.

18. For works which deal with the human need for structure, see Peter Berger and Thomas Luckmann, *The Social Construction of Reality*. Garden City, N.Y.: Doubleday, 1966; and Peter Berger, *The Sacred Canopy*. Garden City, N.Y.: Doubleday, 1967.

19. For a criticism of Illich's notion of deschooling from a socialist perspective, see Herbert Gintis, "Toward a Political Economy of Education: A Radical Critique of Ivan Illich's *Deschooling Society*," *Harvard Educational Review, 42* (February 1972), pp. 70–96.

20. Samuel Bowles and Herbert Gintis, *Schooling in Capitalist America*. New York: Basic Books, 1976, p. 265.

21. Ibid., p. 284.

22. Ibid., p. 285.

23. Ibid.

24. Diane Ravitch, *The Revisionists Revised*. New York: Basic Books, 1978, pp. 146–147.

25. For a concise statement of the "Correspondence Principle," see Michael A. Carter, "Contradiction and Correspondence: Analysis of the Relation of Schooling to Work," in Martin Carnoy and Henry M. Levin (eds.), *The Limits of Educational Reform*. New York: McKay, 1976, pp. 52–82.

26. Bowles and Gintis, *Schooling in Capitalist America*, pp. 277–278.

27. Michael B. Katz, *Class, Bureaucracy and Schools: The Illusion of Educational Change in America*. New York: Praeger, 1975, p. xviii.

28. For an explication and application of the "blaming the victim" ideology in the United States, see William Ryan, *Blaming the Victim*, rev. ed. New York: Pantheon Books, 1976.

29. Mario Fantini, Marilyn Gittell, and Richard Magat, *Community Control and the Urban School*. New York: Praeger, 1972, p. 13.

30. Mario Fantini and Marilyn Gittell, *Decentralization: Achieving Reform*. New York: Praeger, 1973, p. 44.

31. Ibid., p. 46.

32. Ibid.

33. For what still remains the best criticism of a centralized Board of Education, see David Rogers, *110 Livingston Street: Politics and Bureaucracy in the New York City School System.* New York: Random House, 1968.

34. Melvin L. Urofsky, "Reflections on Ocean Hill," in Melvin L. Urofsky, (ed.), *Why Teachers Strike: Teachers' Rights and Community Control.* Garden City, N.Y.: Doubleday, 1970, p. 11.

35. Ibid., p. 12.

36. This has been published as Mayor's Advisory Panel on Decentralization of the New York City Schools, *Reconnections for Learning: A Community School System for New York City.* New York: Praeger, 1969.

37. Fantini and Gittell, *Decentralization,* p. 61.

38. Interview with C. Herbert Oliver, in Urofsky (ed.), *Why Teachers Strike,* p. 216.

39. Urofsky, "Reflections on Ocean Hill," in Urofsky (ed.), *Why Teachers Strike,* p. 15.

40. Ibid., p. 17.

41. Ibid.

42. Fantini and Gittell, *Decentralization,* pp. 62−63.

43. Summarized from Fantini et al., *Community Control and the Urban School,* pp. 127−136.

44. Quoted in ibid., p. 128.

45. Quoted in ibid., p. 130.

46. Katz, *Class, Bureaucracy and Schools,* p. 119−120.

47. Ibid., p. 131.

48. This would mean that, for example, the UFT would not be able to influence local school board elections, as they have done in New York City.

49. That we have to ask for a fair test of a plan that was developed over ten years ago, as an alternative for today, attests to the resistence of bureaucracy to resist anything that might alter the status quo.

Bibliography

Abel, J.F. *Consolidation of Schools and Transportation of Pupils,* Bulletin No. 41. Washington, D.C.: U.S. Department of Interior, 1923.

Abrams, Roger L. "Not One Judge's Opinion: *Morgan v. Hennigen and the Boston Schools.*" *Harvard Educational Review,* Reprint Series No. 11, *School Desegregation: The Continuing Challenge.* Cambridge, Mass.: 1976. pp. 5–16.

Alsworth, Philip L., and Roger R. Woock. "Ocean Hill–Brownsville: Urban Conflict and the Schools." *Urban Education, 4* (1970), pp. 25–40.

Altbach, Philip G. *Student Protest in America: A Historical Analysis.* New York: McGraw-Hill, 1974.

Amster, H., and V. Wiegard. "Developmental Study of Sex Differences in Free Recall." Proceedings, 80th Annual Convention, American Psychological Association, 1972.

Anderson, Barry. "School Bureaucratization and Alienation from High School." *Sociology of Education, 46* (Summer 1973), pp. 315–334.

Anderson, Charles H. *Toward a New Sociology,* rev. ed. Homewood, Ill.: Dorsey Press, 1974.

Armor, David J. "The Double Double Standard! A Reply." *The Public Interest, 30* (Winter 1973), pp. 119−131.

Armor, David J. "The Evidence on Busing." *The Public Interest, 28* (Summer 1972), pp. 90−126.

Backman, M.E. "Patterns of Mental Abilities: Ethnic, Socioeconomic and Sex Differences." *American Educational Research Journal, 9* (1972), pp. 1−21.

Baltzell, E. Digby. *The Protestant Establishment.* New York: Random House, 1964.

Becker, Howard S. *The Outsiders.* New York: Free Press, 1963.

Becker, Howard S. "Social Class Variation in the Teacher−Pupil Relationship." *Journal of Educational Sociology, 25* (April 1952), pp. 451−465.

Ben-David, Joseph. *Trends in American Higher Education.* Chicago: University of Chicago Press, 1972.

Bendiner, Robert. *The Politics of Schools.* New York: Harper & Row, 1969.

Bensman, Joseph, and Arthur J. Vidich. *The New American Society: The Revolution of the Middle Class.* Chicago: Quadrangle Books, 1971.

Benson, Charles S., Paul M. Goldfinger, E. Gareth Hoachlander, and Jessica S. Pers. *Planning for Educational Reform: Financial and Social Alternatives.* New York: Dodd, Mead, 1974.

Bentzen, Frances. "Sex Ratios in Learning and Behavior Disorders." *National Elementary Principal, 46* (1966), pp. 13−17.

Berelson, Bernard. *Graduate Education in the United States.* New York: McGraw-Hill, 1960.

Berger, Peter. *The Sacred Canopy.* Garden City, N.Y.: Doubleday, 1967.

Berger, Peter, and Thomas Luckmann. *The Social Construction of Reality.* Garden City, N.Y.: Doubleday, 1966.

Bernstein, Basil. "Education Cannot Compensate for Society." In D. Rubenstein and C. Stoneman (eds.), *Education for Democracy.* Hammondsworth, England: Penguin Books, 1973, pp. 104−116.

Bernstein, Basil. *Class, Codes and Control,* Vol. I. London: Routledge, 1971.

Bernstein, Basil. "Elaborated and Restricted Code: Their Social Origin and Some Consequences." *American Anthropologist, 66* (December 1966), pp. 55−69.

Bidwell, Charles. "The School as a Formal Organization." In James G. Marsh (ed.), *Handbook of Organizations.* Chicago: Rand McNally, 1965, pp. 972−1022.

Bierstedt, Robert. *The Social Order,* 3d ed. New York: McGraw-Hill, 1970.

Bird, Caroline. *The Case Against College.* New York: McKay, 1975.

Bird, Caroline. *Born Female.* New York: McKay, 1970.

Blau, Peter M. "The Flow of Occupational Supply and Recruitment." *American Sociological Review, 30* (August 1965), pp. 475−490.

Blau, Peter M., and Otis D. Duncan. *The American Occupational Structure.* New York: Wiley, 1967.

Blau, Peter M., and Richard W. Scott. *Formal Organizations*. San Francisco: Chandler, 1962.

Blauch, Lloyd E., and Charles F. Reid. *Public Education in the Territories and Outlying Possessions*. Washington, D.C.: U.S. Government Printing Office, 1939.

Blaustein, Albert P., and Clarence C. Ferguson, Jr. "Desegregation and the Law: The Meaning and Effect of the School Segregation Cases." In Charles A. Tesconi, Jr., and Emanuel Hurwitz (eds.), *Education for Whom?* New York: Dodd, Mead, 1974, pp. 107−124.

Block, N.J., and Gerald Dworkin, eds. *The I.Q. Controversy*. New York: Pantheon, 1976.

Boocock, Sarene. *An Introduction to the Sociology of Learning*. Boston: Houghton Mifflin, 1972.

Borrowman, Merle L., ed. *Teacher Education in America: A Documentary History*. New York: Teachers College, 1965.

Bowles, Samuel, and Herbert Gintis. *Schooling in Capitalist America*. New York: Basic Books, 1976.

Bowles, Samuel, and Herbert Gintis. "I.Q. in the Social Structure." *Social Policy, 3* (1972−1973), pp. 65−96.

Bowles, Samuel, Herbert Gintis, and Peter Meyer. "The Long Shadow of Work: Education, the Family and the Reproduction of the Social Division of Labor." *Insurgent Sociologist, V* (1975), pp. 3−22.

Bowles, Samuel, and Henry M. Levin. "The Determinants of Scholastic Achievement—An Appraisal of Some Recent Evidence." *The Journal of Human Resources, III* (Winter 1968), pp. 3−24.

Boyd, William L. "School Board−Administration Staff Relations." In Peter J. Cistone (ed.), *Understanding School Boards*. Lexington, Mass.: Lexington Books, 1975, pp. 103−129.

Brigham, Charles C. "Intelligence Tests of Immigrant Groups." *Psychological Review, 37* (March 1930), pp. 158−165.

Brigham, Charles C. *A Study of American Intelligence*. Princeton, N.J.: Princeton University Press, 1923.

Brown, Frank, and Madelon D. Stent. *Minorities in U.S. Institutions of Higher Education*. New York: Praeger, 1977.

Browning, R. Stephen, ed. *From Brown to Bradley: School Desegregation— 1954−1974*. Cincinnati: Jefferson Law Book Company, 1975.

Bullock, Henry Allen. *A History of Negro Education in the South: From 1619 to the Present*. Cambridge, Mass.: Harvard University Press, 1967.

Bystzdzienski, Jill M. "The Status of Public School Teachers in America: An Unfulfilled Quest for Professionalism." Unpublished Ph.D. dissertation, State University of New York at Albany, 1979.

Callahan, Raymond E. "The American Board of Education, 1789−1960." In Peter J. Cistone (ed.), *Understanding School Boards*. Lexington, Mass.: Lexington Books, 1975, pp. 19−46.

Callahan, Raymond E. *Education and the Cult of Efficiency*. Chicago: University of Chicago Press, 1962.

Campbell, Roald, F., Lavern L. Cunningham, and Roderick F. McPhee. *The Organization and Control of American Schools*. Columbus, O.: Merrill, 1965.

Cannon, Lou, and Joel Kotkin. "Schools Feel Budget Axe in California." *The Washington Post,* June 14, 1978, pp. 8, 13.

Carlson, Richard O. *School Superintendents: Careers and Performance*. Columbus, O.: Merrill, 1972.

Carnoy, Martin, and Henry M. Levin. *The Limits of Educational Reform*. New York: McKay, 1976.

Carter, Michael A. "Contradiction and Correspondence: Analysis of the Relation of Schooling to Work." In Martin Carnoy and Henry M. Levin (eds.), *The Limits of Educational Reform*. New York: McKay, 1976, pp. 52–82.

Carter, Thomas P. *Mexican-Americans in School*. New York: College Entrance Examination Board, 1970.

Cervantes, L.F. "The Isolated Nuclear Family and the Drop-out." *Sociological Quarterly, 6* (1965), pp. 103–118.

Chambliss, William J., ed. *Sociological Readings in the Conflict Perspective*. Reading, Mass.: Addison-Wesley, 1973.

Charnofsky, Stanley. *Educating the Powerless*. Belmont, Calif.: Wadsworth, 1971.

Cherry, Frances, and Kay Deaux. "Fear of Success versus Fear of Gender in Appropriate Behavior." *Sex Roles, 1* (February 1978), pp. 97–101.

Childers, Laurence Murrell. "Education in California under Spain and Mexico and under American Rule to 1851." Unpublished master's thesis, University of California at Berkeley, 1930.

Chiswick, Barry R. *Income Inequality*. New York: National Bureau of Research, 1974.

Chomsky, Noam. "IQ Tests: Building Blocks for the New Class System." In Clarence Karier (ed.), *Shaping the American Educational State: 1900 to the Present*. New York: Free Press, 1975, pp. 393–406.

Chronicle of Higher Education. July 10, 1978.

Church, Robert L., and Michael W. Sedlak. *Education in the United States: An Interpretive History*. New York: Free Press, 1976.

Cicourel, Aaron, and John Kitsuse. *The Educational Decision-Makers*. Indianapolis: Bobbs-Merrill, 1963.

Cistone, Peter J. "The Recruitment of School Board Members." In Peter J. Cistone (ed.), *Understanding School Boards*. Lexington. Mass.: Lexington Books, 1975, pp. 47–61.

Clark, Burton. "The Cooling Out Function in Higher Education." *American Journal of Sociology, 65* (May 1960), pp. 569–576.

Clark, Kenneth B. "Social Policy, Power, and Social Science Research." In *Harvard Educational Review* Editors (eds.), *Perspectives on Inequality,* Reprint No. 8. Cambridge, Mass.: Harvard Educational Review, 1973, pp. 77–85.

Clark, Kenneth B. "Clash of Cultures in the Classroom." In Meyer Weinberg (ed.), *Integrated Education—Learning Together*. Chicago: Integrated Education Association, 1964, pp. 15−25.

Clement, Dorothy C., Margaret Eisenhart, and John R. Wood. "School Desegregation and Educational Inequality: Trends in the Literature, 1960−1975." In *The Desegregation Literature: A Critical Appraisal*. Washington, D.C.: U.S. Department of Health, Education and Welfare, 1976, pp. 1−77.

Cole, Stephen. *The Unionization of Teachers*. New York: Praeger, 1969.

Coleman, James S., ed. *Education and Political Development*. Princeton, N.J.: Princeton University Press, 1965.

Coleman, James S. *The Adolescent Society*. New York: Free Press, 1961.

Coleman, James S., Sara P. Kelly, and John A. Moore. "Recent Trends in School Integration." Paper presented at the Annual Meetings of the American Educational Research Association, Washington, D.C., April 2, 1975.

Coleman, James S., Ernest Q. Campbell, Carol J. Hobson, James McPartland, Alexander M. Mood, Frederick D. Weinfield, and Robert L. York. *Equality of Educational Opportunity*, 2 vols. Washington, D.C.: U.S. Government Printing Office, 1966.

Collins, Randall. *Conflict Sociology*. New York: Academic Press, 1975.

Collins, Thomas W., and George W. Noblitt. "The Process of Interracial Schooling: An Assessment of Conceptual Frameworks and Methodological Orientations." In National Institute of Education, *The Desegregation Literature: A Critical Appraisal*. Washington, D.C.: U.S. Department of Health, Education and Welfare, 1976, pp. 79−110.

Committee on Labor and Public Welfare, Special Subcommittee on Indian Education Report. *Indian Education: A National Challenge*. Washington, D.C.: U.S. Government Printing Office, 1969.

Comte, Auguste. *The Positive Philosophy of Auguste Comte*, translated and edited by Harriet Martineau. London: J. Chapman, 1853.

Conant, James B. *The Education of American Teachers*. New York: McGraw-Hill, 1963.

Connell, R.W. "Political Socialization and The American Family: The Evidence Re-examined." *Public Opinion Quarterly*, 36 (1972), pp. 323−333.

Connolly, William, ed. *The Bias of Pluralism*. New York: Atherton Press, 1969.

Cooke, W. Henry. "The Segregation of Mexican-American Children in Southern California." In Wayne Moquin and Charles Van Doren (eds.), *A Documentary History of the Mexican Americans*. New York: Praeger, pp. 324−326.

Coons, John E., William H. Clune III, and Stephen A. Sugarman. *Private Wealth and Public Education*. Cambridge, Mass.: Harvard University Press, 1970.

Coons, John E., William H. Clune III, and Stephen A. Sugarman. "Educational Opportunity: A Workable Constitutional Test for State Financial Structures." *California Law Review*, 57 (April 1969), pp. 321−348.

Corwin, Ronald G. *Education in Crisis: A Sociological Analysis of Schools in Transition*. New York: Wiley, 1974.

Corwin, Ronald G. *Militant Professionalism: A Study of Organizational Conflict in High Schools*. New York: Appleton, 1970.

Counts, George. *The Social Composition of School Boards*. New York: Arno Press, 1969.

Cronin, Joseph M. *The Control of Urban Schools*. New York: Free Press, 1973.

Cuban, Larry. *Urban School Chiefs Under Fire*. Chicago: University of Chicago Press, 1976.

Cubberly, Ellwood P. *Public School Administration*. Boston: Houghton Mifflin, 1916.

Cubberly, Ellwood P. *Changing Conceptions of Education*. Boston: Houghton Mifflin, 1909.

Cubberly, Ellwood P. *School Funds and Their Apportionment*. New York: Teachers College, 1905.

Dahl, Robert. *Who Governs?* New Haven: Yale University Press, 1962.

Davis, Nanette J. "Labeling Theory in Deviance Research: A Critique." *Sociological Quarterly, 13* (1972), pp. 447−474.

Dawson, Richard E., Kenneth Prewitt, and Karen S. Dawson. *Political Socialization,* 2d ed. Boston: Little, Brown, 1977.

Dewey, John. "The Relation of Theory to Practice." In Merle E. Borrowman (ed.), *Teacher Education in America: A Documentary History*. New York: Teachers College, 1965, pp. 140−171.

Dewey, John. *Toward the New Education*. New York: Teachers Union, 1918.

Digest of Educational Statistics. Washington, D.C.: U.S. Department of Health, Education and Welfare, 1977−1978.

Dillon, S.V., and J. A. Grout. "Schools and Alienation." *The Elementary School Journal, 76* (May 1976), pp. 481−490.

Donley, Marshall O., Jr. *Power to the Teacher*. Bloomington, Ind.: Indiana University Press, 1976.

Donovan, John D. *The Academic Man in the Catholic College*. New York: Sheed and Ward, 1964.

Dreeben, Robert. *The Nature of Teaching*. Glenview, Ill.: Scott, Foresman, 1970.

Duke, Daniel Linden. "The Re-Transformation of the School: Factors Relating to the Emergence of Contemporary Alternative Schools in the United States," Unpublished Ed. D. dissertation, State University of New York at Albany, 1974.

Duke, James. *Power and Conflict in Social Life*. Provo, Utah: Brigham Young University Press, 1976.

Easton, David. "The Function of Formal Education in a Political System." *The School Review, 65* (1957), pp. 304−316.

Easton, Robert, and Jack Dennis. *Children in the Political System: Origin of Political Legitimacy*. New York: McGraw-Hill, 1969.

Edwards, Richard. "Normal Schools in the United States." In Merle L. Borrowman (ed.), *Teacher Education in America: A Documentary History*. New York: Teachers College, 1965, pp. 74−83.

Elder, Glen H. "Family Structure and Educational Attainment." *American Sociological Review, 30* (1965), pp. 81−96.

Eliot, T.H. "Toward an Understanding of Local School Politics." *American Political Science Review, 52* (1959), pp. 1037–1051.

Entwisle, Doris R., and Murray Webster, Jr. "Expectation in Mixed Racial Groups." *Sociology of Education, 47* (1974), pp. 301–318.

Etzioni, Amitai, ed. *The Semi-Professions and Their Organization*. New York: Free Press, 1969.

Etzioni, Amitai. *Modern Organizations*. Englewood Cliffs, N.J.: Prentice-Hall, 1964.

Fantini, Mario, and Marilyn Gittell. *Decentralization: Achieving Reform*. New York: Praeger, 1973.

Fantini, Mario, Marilyn Gittell, and Richard Magat. *Community Control and the Urban School*. New York: Praeger, 1972.

Federbush, Marsha. "The Sex Problems of School Math Books." In Judith Stacey, Susan Béreaud, and Joan Daniels (eds.), *And Jill Came Tumbling After*. New York: Dell, 1974, pp. 178–184.

Fein, Leonard J. *The Ecology of Public Schools*. New York: Pegasus, 1971.

Felshin, Jan. *The American Woman in Sport*. Reading, Mass.: Addison-Wesley, 1974.

Felzen, E., and M. Anisfeld. "Semantic and Phonetic Relations in the False Recognition of Words by Third and Sixth Grade Children." *Developmental Psychology, 3* (1970), pp. 163–168.

Feurer, Lewis. *The Conflict of Generations*. New York: Basic Books, 1969.

Fields, Cheryl M. "In the Wake of Bakke." *The Chronicle of Higher Education*, July 10, 1978, pp. 10–12.

Fischer, Louis, and David Schimmel. *The Civil Rights of Teachers*. New York: Harper & Row, 1973.

Fishel, Andrew, and Janice Pottker, "Sex Bias in Secondary Schools: The Impact of Title IX." In Janice Pottker and Andrew Fishel (eds.), *Sex Bias in the Schools*. Rutherford, N.J.: Fairleigh Dickinson University Press, 1977, pp. 92–104.

Fisher, Elizabeth. "Children's Books: The Second Sex, Junior Division." In Judith Stacey, Susan Béreaud, and Joan Daniels (eds.), *And Jill Came Tumbling After*. New York: Dell, 1974, pp. 116–122.

Fiske, Shirley. "Pigskin Review: An American Institution." In Mark Hart (ed.), *Sport in the Sociocultural Process*. Dubuque, Iowa: William C. Brown, 1972, pp. 241–258.

Flacks, Richard E. "The Liberated Generation: An Exploration of the Roots of Student Protest." *Journal of Social Issues, 23* (July 1967), pp. 52–57.

Frazier, Nancy, and Myra Sadker. *Sexism in School and Society*. New York: Harper & Row, 1973.

Freeman, Bonnie Cook. "Female Education in Patriarchial Power Systems." In Philip G. Altbach and Gail P. Kelly (eds.), *Education and Colonialism*. New York: Longman, 1978, pp. 207–242.

Freeman, Richard B. *Black Elite: The New Market for Highly Educated Black Americans*. New York: McGraw-Hill, 1977.

Freeman, Richard B. *The Over-Educated American*. New York: Academic Press, 1976.

Freire, Paulo. *Pedagogy of the Oppressed*. New York: Herder and Herder, 1970.

Friedman, Leon, ed. *Argument: The Oral Argument before the Supreme Court in Brown v. Board of Education of Topeka, 1952–1955*. New York: Chelsea House, 1969.

Friedson, Eliot. *The Professions and Their Prospects*. Beverly Hills, Calif.: Sage, 1973.

Fuchs, Estelle, and Robert J. Havighurst. *To Live on This Earth*. Garden City, N.Y.: Doubleday, 1972.

Funicello, Thomas. "Role Strain Among School Superintendents." Unpublished Ed.D. dissertation, State University of New York at Albany, 1976.

Gappa, Judith, ed. *Improving Equity in Postsecondary Education*. Washington, D.C.: National Institute of Education, December 1977.

Gerace, T.A., and W.E. Caldwell. "Perceptual Distortion as a Function of Stimulus Objects, Sex, Naivete, and Trials using a Portable Model of the Ames Distorted Room." *Genetic Psychology Monographs, 84* (1971), pp. 3–33.

Gerth, Hans H., and C. Wright Mills. *Character and Social Structure*. New York: Harcourt, 1953/Harbinger Books, 1964.

Gilland, Thomas M. *The Origin and Development of the Powers and Duties of the City School Superintendent*. Chicago: University of Chicago Press, 1935.

Gintis, Herbert. "Toward a Political Economy of Education: A Radical Critique of Ivan Illich's *Deschooling Society*." *Harvard Educational Review, 42* (February 1972), pp. 70–96.

Goffman, Erving. "On Cooling the Mark Out: Some Aspects of Adoption to Failure." *Psychiatry: Journal for the Study of Interpersonal Process, 15* (November 1952), pp. 451–463.

Goldhammer, Keith. *The School Board*. New York: The Center for Applied Research in Education, 1964.

Goldschmidt, M.L. "Democratic Theory and Contemporary Political Science." *Western Political Scientific Quarterly, 19* (September 1966 Supplement), pp. 5–12.

Goode, William. "The Librarian: From Occupation to Profession." *Literary Quarterly, 31* (October 1961), pp. 306–320.

Goodman, Paul. *New Reformation: Notes of a Neolithic Conservative*. New York: Vintage Books, 1969.

Goodman, Paul. *Compulsory Miseducation and the Community of Scholars*. New York: Vintage Books, 1962.

Gordon, Leonard V. *The Measurement of Interpersonal Values*. Chicago: Science Research Associates, 1975.

Goslin, David. *The School in Contemporary Society*. Glenview, Ill.: Scott, Foresman, 1965.

Gouldner, Alvin W. "Cosmopolitans and Locals: Towards an Analysis of Latent

Social Roles—II." *Administrative Science Quarterly, 2* (March 1958), pp. 441–480.

Gouldner, Alvin W. "Cosmopolitans and Locals: Toward an Analysis of Latent Social Roles—I." *Administrative Science Quarterly, 2* (December 1957), pp. 281–306.

Gouldner, Alvin W. "Metaphysical Pathos and the Theory of Bureaucracy." *American Political Science Review, 49* (1955), pp. 496–507.

Gracey, Harry L. *Curriculum or Craftsmanship.* Chicago: University of Chicago Press, 1972.

Gramsci, Antonio. *Selections from the Prison Notebooks,* edited and translated by Quintin Hoare and Geoffrey Nowell Smith. New York: International Publishers, 1971.

Grant, Gerald, and David Riesman. *The Perpetual Dream: Reform and Experiment in the American College.* Chicago: University of Chicago Press, 1978.

Graubard, Allen. *Free the Children: Radical Reform and the Free School Movement.* New York: Pantheon, 1973.

Greeley, Andrew M. *Ethnicity in the United States.* New York: Wiley, 1974.

Greer, Colin. *The Great School Legend.* New York: Viking, 1971.

Griffiths, Daniel E. "Intellectualism and Professionalism." *New York University Education Quarterly, V* (Fall 1973).

Gross, Neal, and Robert E. Herriott. *Staff Leadership in Public Schools.* New York: Wiley, 1965.

Guirard, Pierre. *Le Français Populaire.* Paris: Presses Universitaires de France, 1965.

Gunnell, John G. "Social Science and Political Reality: The Problem of Explanation." *Social Research, 35* (1968), pp. 159–201.

Habermas, Jurgen. "Toward a Theory of Human Communicative Competence." In Hans P. Dreitzel (ed.), *Recent Sociology No. 2.* New York: Macmillan, 1972, pp. 115–148.

Hargreaves, David H., Stephen K. Hestor, and Frank J. Mellor. *Deviance in Classrooms.* London: Routledge, 1975.

Harper, Charles A. *A Century of Public Teacher Education.* Washington, D.C.: National Education Association, 1939.

Harrison, Russell. *Equality in Public School Finance.* Lexington, Mass.: Lexington Books, 1976.

Hartley, R. "Children's Concepts of Male and Female Roles." *Merrill-Palmer Quarterly, 6* (1960), pp. 83–91.

Hartup, W.W., and E.A. Zook. "Sex Role Preferences in Three- and Four-Year-Old Children." *Journal of Consulting Psychology, 24* (1970), pp. 420–426.

Havighurst, Robert J., and Bernice L. Neugarten. *Society and Education,* 4th ed. Boston: Allyn and Bacon, 1975.

Heller, Celia S., ed. *Structural Social Inequality.* New York: Macmillan, 1969.

Herndon, James. *The Way It Spozed to Be.* New York: Simon and Schuster, 1968.

Herrnstein, Richard J. *IQ in the Meritocracy*. Boston: Little, Brown, 1973.

Hess, Robert D., and Judith V. Torney. *The Development of Political Attitudes in Children*. Garden City, N.Y.: Anchor Books, 1968.

Heyns, Barbara. "Social Selection and Stratification Within Schools." *American Journal of Sociology, 79* (May 1974), pp. 1434–1451.

Hickcox, E.S., and R.J. Snow. "Profile of Superintendents of Schools." In Lee Deighton (ed.), *The Encyclopedia of Education, 8* (1971), pp. 545–555.

Hickerson, Nathaniel. *Education for Alienation*. Englewood Cliffs, N.J.: Prentice-Hall, 1966.

Hickey, Anthony A., and JoAnn Hickey. "Working Wives: Social, Economic and Demographic Factors." Unpublished paper, George Mason University, Fairfax, Virginia, 1979.

Hofstadter, Richard. "The Pseudo-Conservative Revolt Revisited: A Postscript." In Daniel Bell (ed.), *The Radical Right*. Garden City, N.Y.: Doubleday/Anchor Books, 1964, pp. 97–104.

Hofstadter, Richard, and Walter P. Metzger. *The Development of Academic Freedom in the United States*. New York: Columbia University Press, 1955.

Hollingshead, August B. *Elmstown's Youth: The Impact of Social Classes on Adolescents*. New York: Wiley, 1949.

Horner, Matina S. "Toward an Understanding of Achievement Related Conflicts in Women." In Judith Stacey and Béreaud Joan Daniels (eds.), *And Jill Came Tumbling After*. New York: Dell, 1974, pp. 43–63.

Horner, Matina S. "Femininity and Successful Achievement: Basic Inconsistency." In J.M. Bardwick, E. Douvan, M.S. Horner, and P. Gutman (eds.), *Feminine Personality and Conflict*. Belmont, Calif.: Brooks/Cole, 1970, pp. 45–74.

Hughes, Evert C. "Professions." *Daedalus, 92* (Fall 1963), pp. 655–668.

Huntington, Samuel P. "The Founding Fathers and the Division of Power." In Arthur Maas (ed.), *Area and Power*. New York: Free Press, 1959, pp. 150–205.

Hurn, Christopher J. *The Limits and Possibilities of Education*. Boston: Allyn and Bacon, 1978.

Hyman, Herbert H. "The Value Systems of Different Classes: A Social Psychological Contribution to the Analysis of Stratification." In R. Bendix and S.M. Lipset (eds.), *Class, Status and Power*. New York: Free Press, 1953.

Iannaccone, Laurence. *Politics in Education*. New York: The Center for Applied Research in Education, 1967.

"Identity Crisis on the Catholic Campus." *Newsweek,* June 27, 1966. p. 85.

Illich, Ivan. *Deschooling Society*. New York: Harper & Row, 1972.

Itzkoff, Seymour W. *A New Public Education*. New York: McKay, 1975.

Iverson, Katherine. "Civlization and Assimilation in the Colonized Schooling of Native Americans." In Philip G. Altbach and Gail P. Kelly (eds.), *Education and Colonialism*. New York: Longman, 1978, pp. 149–180.

Jackson, Philip. *Life in Classrooms*. New York: Holt, Rinehart and Winston, 1968.

Jencks, Christopher. "Educational Vouchers." *The New Republic, 163* (July 4, 1970), pp. 19–21.

Jencks, Christopher, Marshall Smith, Henry Acland, Mary Jo Bane, David Cohen, Herbert Gintis, Barbara Heyns, and Stephen Michelson. *Inequality: A Reassessment of the Effect of Family and Schooling in America*. New York: Basic Books, 1972.

Jencks, Christopher, and David Riesman. *The Academic Revolution*. Garden City, N.Y.: Doubleday, 1968.

Jennings, M. Kent, and L. Harmon Zeigler. *The Governing of School Districts*. Eugene, Ore.: Center for the Advanced Study of Educational Administration, 1969.

Jensen, Arthur R. "How Much Can We Boost IQ and Scholastic Achievement?" *Harvard Educational Review, 39* (Winter 1969), pp. 1–123.

Joffe, Carol. "As the Twig Is Bent." In Judith Stacey, Susan Béreaud, and Joan Daniels (eds.), *And Jill Came Tumbling After*. New York: Dell, 1974, pp. 91–109.

Johns, Roe L. "State Support for Public Schools." In Roe L. Johns, Kevin Alexander, and Dewey Stollar (eds.), *Status Impact of Educational Finance Project*, Vol. 4. Gainsville, Fla.: National Educational Finance Project, 1971, pp. 1–28.

Johnson, T. *Professionalism and Power*. London: Macmillan, 1972.

Jorda, Louis, Kevin O'Grady, and Charles Capps. "Fear of Success in Males and Females in Sex-Linked Occupations." *Sex Roles, 1* (February 1978), pp. 43–50.

Kaestle, Carl F. *The Evolution of an Urban School System: New York City, 1750–1850*. Cambridge, Mass.: Harvard University Press, 1973.

Kagan, Jerome. "The Child's Sex Role Classifications of School Objects." *Child Development, 35* (1964), pp. 1051–1056.

Kahl, Joseph A. *The American Class Structure*. New York: Holt, Rinehart and Winston, 1967.

Kahl, Joseph A. "Educational and Occupational Aspiration of 'Common Man' Boys." *Harvard Educational Review, 23* (1953), pp. 186–203.

Kamin, Leon J. "Heridity, Politics, and Psychology." In Clarence Karier (ed.), *Shaping the American Educational State: 1900 to the Present*. New York: Free Press, 1975, pp. 367–393.

Kamin, Leon J. *The Science and Politics of IQ*. New York: Wiley, 1974.

Kanter, Rosabeth Moss. *Men and Women of the Corporation*. New York: Basic Books, 1977.

Karabel, Jerome. "Community Colleges and Social Stratification: Submerged Class Conflict in American Higher Education." In Jerome Karabel and A.H. Halsey (eds.), *Power and Ideology in Education*. New York: Oxford University Press, 1977, pp. 232–254.

Karier, Clarence, ed. *Shaping the American Educational State: 1900 to the Present*. New York: Free Press, 1975.

Karier, Clarence. "Testing For Order and Control in the Corporate Liberal State." *Educational Theory, 22* (Spring 1972), pp. 159−180.

Katz, Michael B. *Class, Bureaucracy and Schools: The Illusion of Educational Change in America.* New York: Praeger, 1975.

Kenniston, Kenneth. *Young Radicals.* New York: Harcourt, 1968.

Kerr, N.O. "The School Board as an Agency of Legitimation." *Sociology of Education, 38,* (1964), pp. 34−59.

Kinney, L.B. *Certification in Education.* Englewood Cliffs, N.J.: Prentice-Hall, 1969.

Kitano, Harry. *Japanese-Americans: The Evolution of a Subculture.* Englewood Cliffs, N.J.: Prentice-Hall, 1969.

Klingberg, Frank J. *The Appraisal of the Negro in Colonial South Carolina: A Study in Americanization.* Washington, D.C.: Associated Publishers, 1941.

Knight, Athelia. "Teacher Attitudes on Blacks Sparked Va. Dispute." *The Washington Post,* May 9, 1978, p. C-1.

Knight, Michael. "Scholars in New Rift over 'White Flight'." *The New York Times,* June 1, 1978, p. 27.

Koerner, James D. *Who Controls American Education?* Boston: Beacon Press, 1968.

Kohl, Herbert. *36 Children.* New York: American Library, 1967.

Kohn, Melvin L. *Class and Conformity.* Homewood, Ill.: Dorsey Press, 1969.

Kohn, Melvin L. "Social Class and Parent−Child Relationships: An Interpretation." *American Journal of Sociology, 68* (1963), pp. 471−480.

Kornacher, Mildred. *How Urban High School Teachers View Their Jobs.* Washington, D.C.: U.S. Office of Educational Cooperative Research Project No. 5-8144, 1966.

Kozol, Jonathan. *Free Schools.* Boston: Houghton Mifflin, 1972.

Kozol, Jonathan. *Death at an Early Age: The Destruction of the Hearts and Minds of Negro Children in the Boston Public Schools.* New York: Bantam Books, 1968.

Kreps, Juanita. *Sex in the Marketplace: American Women at Work.* Baltimore: The Johns Hopkins University Press, 1971.

Krug, Edward. *The Shaping of the American High School.* New York: Harper & Row, 1964.

Ladd, Everett C., Jr., and Seymour Martin Lipset. *Professors and Politics.* New York: McGraw-Hill, 1975.

Langston, Kenneth P. *Political Socialization.* New York: Oxford University Press, 1971.

Laska, John A. *Schooling and Education: Basic Concepts and Problems.* New York: Van Nostrand, 1976.

Lauter, Paul, and Florence Howe. "How the School System is Rigged for Failure." In Robert Lejeune (ed.), *Class and Class Conflict in American Society.* Chicago: Markham, 1972, pp. 197−216.

Lehne, Richard. *The Quest for Justice: The Politics of School Finance Reform*. New York: Longman, 1978.

Lemert, Edwin. *Human Deviance, Social Problems and Social Control*. Englewood Cliffs, N.J.: Prentice-Hall, 1967.

Lessinger, Leon M. *Every Kid a Winner: Accountability in Education*. Palo Alto, Calif.: Science Research Associates, 1970.

Levitt, Martin. "The Ideology of Accountability in Schooling." *Educational Studies, III* (Fall 1972), pp. 133–140.

Levy, Gerald. *Ghetto School*. New York: Pegasus Press, 1970.

Lewis, Lionel. *Scaling the Ivory Tower: Merit and Its Limits in Academic Careers*. Baltimore, Md.: The Johns Hopkins University Press, 1975.

Lieberman, Myron. *Education as a Profession*. Englewood Cliffs, N.J.: Prentice-Hall, 1956.

Lindsey, Robert. "New Battles over School Budgets." *The New York Times Magazine,* September 18, 1977, pp. 17–19, 62–71.

Lipset, Seymour Martin. "The Sources of the Radical Right." In Daniel Bell (ed.), *The Radical Right*. Garden City, N.Y.: Doubleday/Anchor Books, 1964, pp. 307–372.

Lipset, Seymour Martin, and Gerald M. Schaflander. *Passion and Politics: Student Activism in America*. Boston: Little, Brown, 1971.

Litt, Edgar. "Civic Education, Norms and Political Indoctrination." *American Sociological Review, 28* (February 1963), pp. 69–75.

Lopreato, Joseph. *Italian Americans*. New York: Random House, 1970.

Lortie, Dan. *School-Teacher*. Chicago: University of Chicago Press, 1976.

Lortie, Dan. "The Balance of Control and Autonomy in Elementary School Teaching." In Amitai Etzioni (ed.), *The Semi-Professions and Their Organization*. New York: Free Press, 1969, pp. 1–53.

Lowe, William T. "Who Joins Teachers Groups?" *Teachers College Record, 5* (April 1965), pp. 614–619.

Lutz, Frank W., Lou Kleinman, and Sy Evans. *Grievances and Their Resolution: Problems in School Personnel Administration*. Danville, Ill.: Interstate, 1967.

Lyman, Stanford M. *Chinese Americans*. New York: Random House, 1974.

Lyman, Stanford M. "Contrasts in the Community Organization of Chinese and Japanese Americans." In Norman R. Yetman and C. Hoy Steele (eds.), *Majority and Minority: The Dynamics of Racial and Ethnic Relations,* 2d ed. Boston: Allyn and Bacon, 1975.

Maccoby, Eleanor E., and Carol N. Jacklin. *The Psychology of Sex Differences*. Stanford, Calif.: Stanford University Press, 1974.

Malinowski, Bronislaw. *A Scientific Theory of Culture*. New York: Oxford University Press, 1960.

Margolis, Richard J. *The Losers: A Report on Puerto Ricans and the Public Schools*. New York: Aspira, 1968.

Marks, Russell. "Race and Immigration: The Politics of Intelligence Testing." In

Clarence Karier (ed.), *Shaping the American Educational State: 1900 to the Present*. New York: Free Press, 1975, pp. 316–342.

Marks, Russell. "Testing, Trackers and Trustees: The Ideology of the Intelligence Testing Movement in America, 1900–1954." Unpublished Ph.D. Dissertation, University of Illinois, 1972.

Martin, Don T., George E. Overholt, and Wayne J. Urban. *Accountability in American Education: A Critique*. Princeton, N.J.: Princeton Book Company, 1976.

Mason, W.S. *The Beginning Teacher*. Washington, D.C.: U.S. Department of Health, Education and Welfare, Office of Education, 1961.

Matson, Floyd. *The Broken Image: Men, Science and Society*. Garden City, N.Y.: Doubleday/Anchor Books, 1966.

Mayor's Advisory Panel on Decentralization of the New York City Schools, *Reconnections for Learning: A Community School System for New York City*. New York: Praeger, 1969.

McHugh, William F. "Faculty Unionism and Tenure." In Commission on Academic Tenure in Higher Education (eds.), *Faculty Tenure*. San Francisco: Jossey-Bass, 1973, pp. 194–214.

McLachlan, James. *American Boarding Schools: An Historical Study*. New York: Scribner, 1970.

McLellan, David. *Karl Marx: His Life and Thought*. New York: Harper Colophon Books, 1973.

Mead, Margaret. *Sex and Temperment*. New York: Morrow, 1935.

Mercer, Jane R. *Labelling the Mentally Retarded*. Berkeley, Calif.: University of California Press, 1973.

Merton, Robert. *Social Theory and Social Structure*. New York: Free Press, 1963.

Miles, Michael C. *The Radical Probe: The Logic of Student Rebellion*. New York: Atheneum, 1971.

Mills, C. Wright. *Power, Politics and People: The Collected Essays of C. Wright Mills,* edited by Irving Louis Horowitz. New York: Ballantine Books, 1964.

Mills, C. Wright. *The Sociological Imagination*. New York: Oxford University Press, 1959.

Mills, C. Wright. *The Power Elite*. New York: Oxford University Press, 1956.

Mills, Nicolas, ed. *The Great School Bus Controversy*. New York: Teachers College, 1973.

Minar, David. "Community Characteristics, Conflict and Power Structures." In Robert S. Cahill and Stephen P. Hensley (eds.), *The Politics of Education in the Local Community*. Danville, Ill.: Interstate, 1964, pp. 125–143.

Mincer, Jacob. *Schooling, Experience and Earnings*. New York: National Bureau of Economic Research, 1974.

Morgan v. *Hennigan,* 379 F. Suppl. 410 (D. Mass, 1974).

Morrison, Henry C. *School Revenue*. Chicago: University of Chicago Press, 1933.

Mort, Paul R. *The Measurement of Educational Need*. New York: Teachers College, 1924.

Mosteller, Frederick, and Daniel P. Moynihan, eds. *On Equality of Educational Opportunity*. New York: Vintage Books, 1972.

Moynihan, Daniel P. "Sources of Resistance to the Coleman Report." *Harvard Educational Review, 38,* (Winter 1968), pp. 22–36.

Mueller, Claus. *The Politics of Communication*. New York: Oxford University Press, 1973.

Mueller, Claus. "On Distorted Communication." In Hans P. Dreitzel (ed.), *Recent Sociology, No. 2*. New York: Macmillan, 1972, pp. 101–114.

Myers, Donald A. *Teacher Power—Professionalization and Collective Bargaining*. Lexington, Mass.: Lexington Books, 1973.

Myers, Donald, and Lilian Meyers, eds. *Open Education Re-examined*. Lexington, Mass.: Lexington Books, 1973.

National Education Association Research Division. *Status of the American Public School Teacher, 1975–1976*. Washington, D.C.: National Education Association, 1977.

National Education Association Research Division. *Status of the American Public School Teacher, 1970–1971*. Washington, D.C.: National Education Association, 1972.

National Education Association, Research Division. *Professional Negotiation with School Boards, A Legal Analysis and Review: School Law Series, Research Report, 1965, R-3*. Washington. D.C.: National Education Association.

National Institute of Education. *Violent Schools—Safe Schools: The Safe School Study Report to Congress*, Vol. I. Washington. D.C.: U.S. Department of Health, Education and Welfare, 1978.

National Institute of Education. *Compensatory Education Study: Final Report to Congress*. Washington, D.C.: National Institute of Education, U.S. Department of Health, Education and Welfare, September 1978.

National Institute of Education. *Compensatory Education Study*. Washington, D.C.: National Institute of Education, U.S. Department of Health, Education and Welfare, 1977.

National School Boards Association. *Women on School Boards*. Evanston, Ill.: The Association, 1974.

National Teachers Association. *Proceedings, 1857–1895*. Washington, D.C.: National Education Association.

Nearing, Scott. "Who's Who on Our Boards of Education." *School and Society* (January 20, 1917), pp. 89–90.

Newlon, Jesse. *Education as Social Policy*. New York: Scribner, 1934.

Nisbet, Robert. *The Sociological Tradition*. New York: Basic Books, 1966.

Nolte, Chester M. *Status and Scope of Collective Bargaining in Education*. Eugene, Ore.: Eric Clearinghouse on Educational Administration, University of Oregon, 1970.

Nunn, Clyde Z. "Support of Civil Liberties among College Students." *Social Problems, 20* (Winter 1973), pp. 303–310.

Oakley, Ann. *Sex, Gender and Society*. New York: Harper Colophon Books, 1972.

Orfield, Gary. "Congress, the President, and Anti-Busing Legislation, 1966–1974." In R. Stephen Browning (ed.), *From Brown to Bradley: School Desegregation, 1954–1974*. Cincinnati: Jefferson Law Book Company, 1975, pp. 81–139.

Parenti, Michael J. *Democracy for the Few*, rev. ed. New York: St. Martin's, 1977.

Parsons, Talcott. "The School Class as a Social System." *Harvard Educational Review, 29*(4) (Fall 1959), pp. 297–318.

Parsons, Talcott, *The Social System*. New York: Free Press, 1951.

Parsons, Talcott, and Gerald Platt. *The American University*. Cambridge, Mass.: Harvard University Press, 1973.

Pedersen, F.A., and R.Q. Bell. "Sex Differences in Preschool Children Without Histories of Complications in Pregnancy and Delivery." *Developmental Psychology, 3* (1970), pp. 10–15.

Persell, Caroline Hodges. *Education and Inequality*. New York: Free Press, 1977.

Peterson-Hardt, Sandra. "The Relationship between Self-Esteem and Achievement Behavior among Low Income Youth." Unpublished Ph.D. dissertation, Syracuse University, 1976.

Pettigrew, Thomas F., and Robert L. Green. "School Desegregation in Large Cities: A Critique of the Coleman 'White Flight' Thesis." *Harvard Educational Review Report Series No. 11. School Desegregation: The Continuing Challenge*. Cambridge, Mass.: 1976, pp. 17–69.

Pettigrew, Thomas F., Elizabeth L. Useem, Clarence Normand, and Marshall Smith. "Busing: A Review of 'The Evidence'." *The Public Interest, 30* (Winter 1973), pp. 88–118.

Pfeiffer, John. *New Look at Education: Systems Analysis in Our Schools and Colleges*. Indianapolis: Odyssey, 1968.

Pierce, Paul R. *The Origin and Development of the Public School Principalship*. Chicago: University of Chicago Press, 1935.

Pollak, Peter, "The Intercollegiate Socialist Society and the Consolidation of the American University." Unpublished Ph.D. dissertation, State University of New York at Albany, 1977.

Pottker, Janice, and Andrew Fishel, eds. *Sex Bias in the Schools*. Rutherford, N.J.: Fairleigh Dickinson University, 1977.

Pratte, Richard. *Ideology and Education*. New York: McKay, 1977.

Ravitch, Diane. *The Revisionists Revised*. New York: Basic Books, 1978.

Ravitch, Diane. "The 'White Flight' Controversy." *The Public Interest, 51* (Spring 1978), pp. 135–149.

Reimer, Evert. *School Is Dead*. Garden City, N.Y.: Doubleday, 1971.

Reinhold, Robert. "Coleman Concedes Views Exceeded New Racial Data." *The New York Times*, July 11, 1975, p. 7.

Reller, Theodore L. *The Development of the City Superintendency of Schools in the United States*. Philadelphia: Published by the author, 1935.

Rensberger, Boyce. "Briton's Classic IQ Data Now Viewed as Fraudulent. *The New York Times*, November 28, 1976, p. 26.

Research Triangle Institute. *National Longitudinal Study of the High School Class of 1972: A Capsule Description of First Follow-up Survey Data.* Washington. D.C.: U.S. Government Printing Office, 1976.

Rhyberg, Richard A., and Evelyn R. Rosenthal. *Class and Merit in the American High School.* New York: Longman, 1978.

Rice, Lawrence D. *The Negro in Texas, 1874–1900.* Baton Rouge: Louisiana State University Press, 1971.

Rickover, Hyman G. *Education and Freedom.* New York: Dutton, 1959.

Rist, Ray C. "The Milieu of a Ghetto School as a Precipitator of Educational Failure." *Phylon, 33* (1972), pp. 348–360.

Rist, Ray C. "Student Social Class and Teacher Expectations: The Self-Fulfilling Prophecy in Ghetto Education." *Harvard Educational Review,* 40 (1970), pp. 416–451.

Ritzer, George. *Sociology: A Multi-paradigm Science.* Boston: Allyn and Bacon, 1975.

Roe, William H., and Thelbert L. Drake. *The Principalship.* New York: Macmillan, 1974.

Rogers, David. *110 Livingston Street: Politics and Bureaucracy in the New York City School System.* New York: Random House, 1968.

Rosen, Bernard C. "The Achievement Syndrome: A Psycho-cultural Dimension of Social Stratification." *American Sociological Review, 21* (1956), pp. 203–211.

Rosen, Bernard S., and R. D'Andrade. "The Psycho-social Origin of Achievement Motivation." *Sociometry, 22* (1959), pp. 185–217.

Rosenbaum, James. *Making Inequality: The Hidden Curriculum of High School Tracking.* New York: Wiley, 1976.

Rosenfeld, Gerry. *Shut Those Thick Lips: A Study of Slum School Failure.* New York: Holt, Rinehart and Winston, 1971.

Rosenthal, Robert, and Lenore Jacobsen. *Pygmalion in the Classroom: Teacher Expectations and Pupils' Intellectual Development.* New York: Holt, Rinehart and Winston, 1968.

Rossell, Christine. "School Desegregation and White Flight." *Political Science Quarterly, 90* (Winter 1975–1976), pp. 675–695.

Rudolf, Frederick. *The American College and University: A History.* New York: Vintage Books, 1965.

Russo, Nancy Felipe. "Kids Learn Their Lessons Early . . . and Learn Them Well." In Kenneth C. Kammeyer (ed.), *Confronting the Issues.* Boston: Allyn and Bacon, 1975, pp. 377–387.

San Antonio Independent School District v. *Rodriquez.* U.S. Supreme Court, No. 71–1332, 1973.

Sarason, I.G., and J. Minard. "Text Anxiety, Experimental Instructions and the Wechsler Adult Intelligence Scale." *Educational Psychology, 53,* (1962), pp. 299–302.

Scanzoni, John H. *Sex Roles, Lifestyles and Childbearing: Changing Patterns in Marriage and the Family.* New York: Free Press, 1975.

Scanzoni, Leatha, and John H. Scanzoni. *Men, Women and Change.* New York: McGraw-Hill, 1972.

Schafer, Walter E., and Carol Olexa. *Tracking and Opportunity: The Locking Out Process and Beyond.* Scranton, Pa.: Chandler, 1971.

Schultz, Stanley K. *The Culture Factory: Boston Public Schools, 1789–1860.* New York: Oxford University Press, 1973.

Schwartz, Audrey James. *The Schools and Socialization.* New York: Harper & Row, 1975.

Schwartz, Audrey James. "A Comparative Study of Values and Achievement: Mexican American and Anglo Youth." *Sociology of Education, 48* (Fall 1971), pp. 438–442.

Scimecca, Joseph A., and Francis X. Femminella, "Italian-Americans and Radical Politics." In Francis X. Femminella (ed.), *Power and Class: The Italian American Experience Today.* New York: American-Italian Historical Association, 1973, pp. 12–19.

Scimecca, Joseph A., and Roland Damiano, *Crisis at St. John's: Strike and Revolution on the Catholic Campus.* New York: Random House, 1968.

Sennett, Richard, and Jonathan Cobb. *The Hidden Injuries of Class.* New York: Vintage Books, 1973.

Serbin, L.A., K.D. O'Leary, R.N. Kent, and J.A. Tonick. "A Comparison of Teacher Response to the Pre-academic and Problem Behavior of Boys and Girls." *Child Development, 44* (1973), pp. 796–804.

Serrano v. *Priest.* California Supreme Court. *California Reporter,* Vol. 96, 1971, pp. 601–626.

Sexton, Patricia. *Women in Education.* Bloomington, Ind.: Phi Delta Kappa Educational Foundation, 1976.

Shanker, Albert. "The Big Lie About the Public Schools." *The New York Times,* May 9, 1971, U.F.T. Column.

Sinclair, Ward. "School Financing Undergoes a Revolution." *The Washington Post,* July 10, 1978, p. A3.

Sitkes, E.G., and C.E. Meyers. "Comparative Structure of Intellect in Middle- and Lower-Class Four-Year-Olds of Two Ethnic Groups." *Developmental Psychology, 1* (1969), pp. 592–604.

Sklare, Marshall. *America's Jews.* New York: Random House, 1971.

Smith, P.K., and K. Connolly. "Patterns of Play and Social Interaction in Preschool Children." In N.B. Jones (ed.), *Ethological Studies of Child Behavior.* London: Cambridge University Press, 1972, pp. 65–95.

Spady, William L. "Educational Mobility and Access: Growth and Paradoxes." *American Journal of Sociology, 73* (November 1967), pp. 273–286.

Spring, Joel. *The Sorting Machine.* New York: McKay, 1976.

Spring, Joel. "Deschooling as a Form of Social Revolution." In Clarence Karier, Paul Violas, and Joe Spring (eds.), *Roots of Crisis: American Education in the Twentieth Century.* Chicago: Rand McNally, 1973, pp. 138–147.

Spring, Joel. *Education and the Rise of the Corporate State*. Boston: Beacon Press, 1972.

Stencil, S. "Women's Movement: Achievement and Effects." *Congressional Quarterly* (February 1977), pp. 23–42.

Stephens, Jerone. "The Logic of Functional and Systems Analysis in Political Science." *Midwest Journal of Political Science, 13* (1969), pp. 367–394.

Steward, Julian H. *The People of Puerto Rico*. Urbana, Ill.: University of Illinois Press, 1956.

St. John, Nancy H. *School Desegregation Outcomes for Children*. New York: Wiley, 1975.

Stock, Phyllis. *Better Than Rubies: A History of Women's Education*. New York: Putnam, 1978.

Stone, Thomas B. "The Elementary School Principalship—Toward the Twenty-first Century." In Department of Elementary School Principals (eds.), *Selected Articles for Elementary School Principals*. Washington, D.C.: National Education Association, 1968.

Strauss, Anselm, and Lenore Schatzman. "Social Class and Modes of Communication." *American Journal of Sociology, 60* (January 1955), pp. 329–338.

Strayer, George D. *The Structure and Administration of Education in American Democracy*. Washington, D.C.: National Education Association, 1938.

Strayer, George D., and Robert Murray Haig. *The Financing of Education in the State of New York: Report of the Educational Finance Inquiry Commission*, Vol. I. New York: Macmillan, 1923.

Stretch, Bonnie Barrett. "The Rise of the Free School." In Martin Carnoy (ed.), *Schooling in a Corporate Society*. New York: McKay, 1972, pp. 211–223.

Strodtbeck, Fred L. "Family Interaction, Values and Achievement." In David C. McClelland et al. (eds.), *Talent and Society*. New York: Van Nostrand, 1958, pp. 135–194.

Struble, George. "A Study of School Board Personnel." *The American School Board Journal, XV* (October 1922), pp. 48–49, 137–138.

Swann v. *Charlotte-Mecklenburg Board of Education* (402 U.S.1, 15, 1971).

Swift, David W. *Ideology and Change in the Public Schools: Latent Functions of Progressive Education*. Columbus, Ohio: Merrill, 1971.

Szasz, Margaret. *Education and the American Indians*. Albuquerque, N.M.: University of New Mexico Press, 1974.

Taft, Phillip. *United They Teach: The Story of the United Federation of Teachers*. Los Angeles: Nash, 1974.

Tannenbaum, Frank. *Crime and Community*. Boston: Ginn, 1938.

Tesconi, Charles A., and Emmanuel Hurwitz, Jr., eds. *Education for Whom?* New York: Dodd, Mead, 1974.

Time. June 26, 1978, pp. 54–59.

Tresemer, David. *Fear of Success*. New York: Plenum, 1978.

Trolander, Judith Ann. *Settlement Houses and the Great Depression*. Detroit: Wayne State University Press, 1975.

Turner, Ralph H. *The Social Context of Ambition*. San Francisco: Chandler, 1964.

Tyack, David B. *The One Best System: A History of American Urban Education.* Cambridge, Mass.: Harvard University Press, 1974.

Tyack, David B. *Turning Points in Educational History.* Waltham, Mass.: Blaisdell, 1967.

Tyler, Ralph. "The Task Ahead." In U.S. Office of Education (eds.), *National Conference on Education of the Disadvantaged.* Washington, D.C.: U.S. Government Printing Office, 1966.

United States Department of Labor. "Employment and Earnings." Washington, D.C.: U.S. Department of Labor (January 1978).

United States Department of Labor. "Employment and Earnings." Washington, D.C.: U.S. Department of Labor (November 1976).

United States Bureau of the Census, Current Population Reports, Series P-60, No. 101. "Money Income in 1974 of Families and Persons in the United States." Washington, D.C.: U.S. Government Printing Office, 1976.

United States Women's Bureau. *Handbook on Women Workers.* Washington, D.C.: U.S. Department of Labor, 1975.

Urofsky, Melvin L., ed. *Why Teachers Strike: Teachers' Rights and Community Control.* Garden City, N.Y.: Doubleday, 1970.

Very, P.S. "Differential Factor Structures in Mathematical Abilities." *Genetic Psychology Monographs, 75* (1967), pp. 169–207.

Violas, Paul C. *The Training of the Urban Working Class.* Chicago: Rand McNally, 1978.

Waller, Willard. *The Sociology of Teaching.* New York: Wiley, 1965.

Walum, Laurel Richardson. *The Dynamics of Sex and Gender: A Sociological Perspective.* Chicago: Rand McNally, 1977.

Weber, Max. *The Theory of Social and Economic Organization,* edited and translated by Talcott Parsons. New York: Free Press, 1964.

Weber, Max. *From Max Weber: Essay in Sociology,* edited and translated by Hans H. Gerth and C. Wright Mills. New York: Oxford University Press, 1958.

Weinberg, Meyer. *A Chance to Learn: The History of Race and Education in the United States.* New York: Cambridge University Press, 1977.

Welter, Barbara. "The Cult of True Womanhood: 1820–1860." *American Quarterly, 18* (1966), pp. 151–174.

Wesley, Edgar B. *NEA: The First Hundred Years.* New York: Harper & Row, 1957.

Wharton, Vernon L. *The Negro in Mississippi, 1865–1890.* New York: Harper Torchbooks, 1965.

White, Alpheus L. *Local School Boards: Organizations and Politics,* Office of Education Bulletin No. 8. Washington, D.C.: U.S. Government Printing Office, 1962.

Wilson, Alan B. "Sociological Perspectives on the Development of Academic Competencies in Urban Areas." In A. Harry Passow (ed.), *Urban Education in the 1970s: Reflections and a Look Ahead.* New York: Teachers College, 1971, pp. 120–140.

Wirt, Frederick M., ed. *The Polity of the Schools.* Lexington, Mass.: Heath, 1975.

Wirt, Frederick M., and Michael W. Kirst. *Political and Social Foundations of Education,* rev. ed. Berkeley, Calif.: McCutcheon, 1975.

Wise, Arthur E. *Rich Schools, Poor Schools: The Promise of Equal Educational Opportunity*. Chicago: University of Chicago Press, 1968.

Wittke, Carl. *The Irish in America*. Baton Rouge: Louisiana State University Press, 1956.

Women on Words and Images. "Look Jane Look. See Sex Stereotypes." In Judith Stacey, Susan Béreaud, and Joan Daniels (eds.), *And Jill Came Tumbling After*. New York: Dell, 1974, pp. 159–177.

Woodring, Paul. *The Higher Learning in America: A Reassessment*. New York: McGraw-Hill, 1968.

Woodson, Carter G. *The Education of the Negro Prior to 1861*. Washington. D.C.: Associated Publishers, 1919.

Wylie, Laurence. *Village in the Vaucluse*. Cambridge, Mass.: Harvard University Press, 1957.

Zeigler, Harmon. *The Political Life of American Teachers*. Englewood Cliffs, N.J.: Prentice-Hall, 1967.

Zeigler, L. Harmon, and M. Kent Jennings. *Governing American Schools: Political Interaction in Local School Districts*. North Scituate, Mass.: Duxbury Press, 1974.

Zeitlin, Irving M. *Rethinking Sociology: A Critique of Contemporary Theory*. Englewood Cliffs, N.J.: Prentice-Hall, 1973.

Zuckerman, M., and L. Wheeler. "To Dispel Fantasies about the Fantasy Based Measure of Fear of Success." *Psychological Bulletin, 82* (1975), pp. 932–946.

Zwerling, L. Steven. *Second Best*. New York: McGraw-Hill, 1976.

Index